741.597
Ric   Ricca, Brad.
              Super Boys

FEB 1 5 2014	
	PRINTED IN U.S.A.

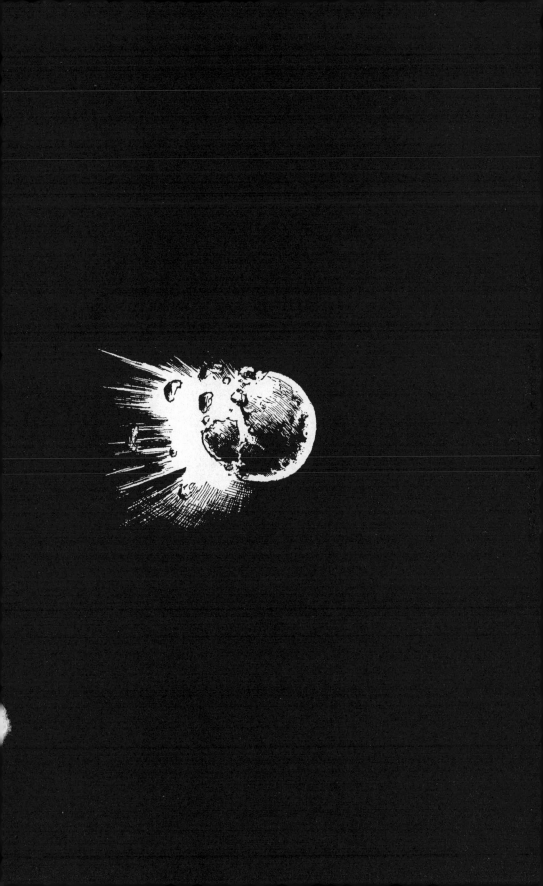

THE **AMAZING ADVENTURES** OF
JERRY SIEGEL AND **JOE SHUSTER**

THE CREATORS OF SUPERMAN

SUPER BOYS

BRAD RICCA

ST. MARTIN'S PRESS Ⅿ NEW YORK

South Sioux City Public Library
2121 Dakota Avenue
South Sioux City, NE 68776

SUPER BOYS. Copyright © 2013 by Brad Ricca. All rights reserved. Printed in the United States of America. For information, address St. Martin's Press, 175 Fifth Avenue, New York, N.Y. 10010.

www.stmartins.com

Library of Congress Cataloging-in-Publication Data

Ricca, Brad.
    Super boys : the amazing adventures of Jerry Siegel and Joe Shuster—the creators of Superman/Brad Ricca.—First edition.
        pages cm
    ISBN 978-0-312-64380-5 (hardcover)
    ISBN 978-1-250-03167-9 (e-book)
    1. Siegel, Jerry, 1914–1996.   2. Shuster, Joe.   3. Cartoonists—United States—Biography.
4. Superman (Fictitious character)   5. Comic books, strips, etc.—United States—History and
criticism.   I. Title.
    PN6727.S515487Z84 2013
    741.5'973—dc23
    [B]

                                                                                              2013004046

St. Martin's Press books may be purchased for educational, business, or promotional use. For information on bulk purchases, please contact Macmillan Corporate and Premium Sales Department at 1-800-221-7945 extension 5442 or write specialmarkets@macmillan.com.

10 9 8 7 6 5 4 3 2

For my dad

Contents

Acknowledgments

I wrote this book myself. None of it was done without important levels of help.

I worked on the project while teaching at Case Western Reserve University, first in the Department of English and then in the SAGES program. Thanks particularly to Bill Siebenschuh and Mary Grimm for their departmental support and personal encouragement. Thanks to Peter Whiting for his professional respect and for taking a chance on a class about comics. And thanks to Carrie Kurutz, Janet Alder, Alegra Martin, Sharmon Sollitto, Latricia Allen, Susan Grimm, and Julie Amon for too many things to mention. And thanks to my friend Freddy Ward. I am grateful to Gary Lee Stonum for his presence in my thinking and for encouraging me in previous work to do this kind of stuff. Thanks also to Judy Oster, Beverly Saylor, Clover Beal, Katherine Kickel, Kristine Kelly, Kimberly Emmons, Bill Claspy, Kurt Koenigsberger, Susanne Vees-Gulani, Arthur Evenchik, Narcisz Fejes, Bernard Jim, Amy Absher, Nora Morrison, Athena Vrettos, Linda Ehrlich, Jay Mann, College Scholars, John Orlock and Maggie Anderson with the Baker-Nord Center for the Humanities, Mano Singham, Molly Berger, Peter McCall, Case Senior Scholars, Mayo Bulloch, Jeffrey Wolcowitz, Tim Fogarty, Patricia Princehouse, the Popular Culture Working Group with Barbara Burgess-Van Aken and Katherine Clark, all graduate students past and present, all my fellow adjunct professional teachers who inspire with their amazing work, and everyone else for their encouragement at weird times and places that I did not forget. I am grateful to Susan Griffith for always believing that I have things to say. And thanks to President Barbara Snyder for her welcome letter of encouragement. Thanks as well to Joyce Kessler and the Cleveland Institute of Art. And thanks to every student, especially the one who pointed out that the man on the cover of *Action #1* is really an adult scared of a kid.

And special thanks to Tim Beal who, one morning at Edison's, told me how this would all work out.

In the wonderful world of comics, I want to thank Matthew J. Smith for his friendship and opportunities, Randy Duncan, John A. Lent, Jason Tondro, Jim Halperin, Phil Yeh, Jacque Nodell, The Collector's Society, Jeff Trexler, Alan Light, Murray Bishoff, Robert Beerbohm, Daniel Best, Patrick McLaughlin, Mark Waid, Roy Thomas, Arlen Schumer, and friends Craig Yoe and Clizia Gussoni, for all of their professional and personal encouragement. I am also greatly indebted to Gerard Jones, who opened Pandora's box and inspired this book in so many ways, both in content and his unassailable style. Thanks to Marc Tyler Nobleman, for his friendship and enthusiasm, and for pushing us all always to look for more. Great thanks as well to Thomas Andrae, who truly changed how so many of us think of a fictional character in tights. I am also grateful to Jim Steranko, for my very favorite book about comics.

This is an unauthorized biography, meaning that it has not been approved by the families of the men I write about. It is my great desire, as both a fan and a scholar, that both families do eventually tell their own remarkable stories. This is my interpretation of the facts, not necessarily theirs. That being said, I am unbelievably grateful to all the family members I met and should have stayed objectively distant from, but instead became friends with, especially Jean Shuster Peavy for her overwhelming friendship and generosity. Jean has done more to heal this story than anyone else; in so many ways, she is the soul of this book. I am also thankful to her daughter Dawn and son Warren for their own strong sense of family; I have tried my absolute best to give Joe the focus he deserves here.

I am also grateful to Joanne and Laura Siegel for being so very nice to me, in ways far more important and more real than a book whose time will come and go. To all of the people who warned me about the Siegel family—you were all very, very wrong.

Thanks to my friend Nate Brightman for his wonderful memories and radio stories, to Patricia Hassard for her friendship and photos, to Arnold Miller for showing up and sharing, to Nicky Brown for her endless laughter and Southern comfort, and to my friend Lauren Agostino for her unique, always welcome perspective on the circus of Superman (and for somehow always stealing the bill). And to my friend Sid Couchey, the greatest Cleveland Indians fan I have ever had the great pleasure of knowing. Maybe next year, pal.

I am also very grateful to the family members who responded to phone calls or e-mails from a stranger, including Eugene Baily, Craig Corrigan, Thad Kulik, the great Jerry Fine, and so many others. You are all a part of this story. And thanks to Joanie Sikela, whom I met too late for this book, but somehow just at the right time.

I could not have done anything without all the professional institutions that helped me, especially the libraries. I am greatly indebted to the Cleveland Public Library, where I spent years of Saturdays. Special thanks to the wonderful staff in their Microfilm Room who delved deep into basements for strange dusty boxes and helped to fix cranky printers when needed. Over the years, I didn't get all of your names as you came and went, but I cannot thank you enough. Thanks also to Kelvin Smith Library at Case Western Reserve University, especially to Susie Hanson, Nora Blackman, and Andy Kaplan who set up (and valiantly protected) the first Siegel and Shuster library collection in the world. Thanks also to Jared Bendis, Tom Hayes, and Mace Mentch, for their work with the Freedman Fellowship. Thanks also to the Ohio State University Billy Ireland Cartoon Library & Museum for not judging me. The New York Public Library helped me find a strange, bizarre article. Thanks as well to Lynda Bender at the Maltz Museum of Jewish Heritage, Miami University in Hamilton, the Avon Public Library, the Popular Culture Association, the San Diego Comic-Con, the New York Comic-Con, and the Chicago Comic-Con for inviting me to speak about portions of this book.

To everyone who played the film that led to this book, including the Las Vegas, San Francisco, Buffalo-Niagara, San Diego, Dark River, Akron, Ingenuity, Rio, and Toronto Jewish film festivals. Special film thanks to Rob Lucas, Ellie Skrow, and Marisa Furtado. And thanks to the amazing people at the Roxie for moving me to the big theater.

Thanks as well to everyone who contributed in more secret ways: George Bettinger, The Great Kreskin, Mike Burkey, Shawn Kelly, Peter Smith, Stephen Lipson, Mel Higgins, David Buchmueller, Mike Domenick, Dean Valore, Scott Dean, Dan Rowell, Rob Huge, Nino Frostino, Sean Mulder, Chris Rose, Brian Deckert, Elaine Arvan Andrews, Laura Lauth, Michael and Mark Pace, Neal Adams, Harvey Pekar for the best advice, Glenn Goggin for his generosity, and Kevin Harrison for his absolutely indispensable resource. Great thanks to David Stern and Joshua Maurer for not only really getting the story but for applying their amazing telescopic vision to it. And thanks to Black Lawrence Press for my secret identity. And to all my teachers, every last one, especially the English ones.

Many journalists and comics writers helped me along the way in getting parts of this story out: Heidi MacDonald at www.comicsbeat.com, Steve Younis, Jamie Coville, Tor Kinlok, Erick Trickey, Jared Bond, Joy Benedict, Annette Lawless, Dee Perry and Dave DeOreo, John Hitch, Tom Spurgeon, and Gloria Goodale, among many others. Thanks also to David Kracijek and Luis Torres for the big breaks. I am also grateful, as I worked all day and night to finish, for Cleveland radio, especially WCPN, local WKNR and WTAM, and the syndicated *Coast-to-Coast,* which was weirdly reassuring. And thanks to everyone who sells and loves books, especially all my old pals at Borders Westlake, where I learned so much about everything.

I am also in debt, in more ways than one, to Drug Mart, Convenient, and Baluk's, who started this part of my life. And communal thanks to Bill Vuk, Mike Misencik, Tom and Chris Kelley, and everyone else in the neighborhood who talked and traded comics at the intersection of Gershwin and Mozart in the summer. Thanks also to Kevin and Tara Kerwin, Dave Kerwin, Joe Stojkov, Duke Schork, Joe Sampson, Scott Holton, Chris Lambert, Mark Bassett, Joe Kickel, Liz Mason, Ed and Rose Menger, and to everyone else who came out to see a story. And to Chris Claremont and Brent Eric Anderson, who first showed me that comics can tell real stories.

In Cleveland, we should all thank Jefferson and Hattie Gray and their family, who not only safeguard the Siegel house but generously welcome in any fan sitting outside in their car. There is no better place to spend a summer afternoon than their front porch. Thanks to James Levin and the Ingenuity Festival for taking a chance on an amateur. I am grateful to all the comic stores out there, particularly Scott Rudge, Ed Benci, and Matt Hess from Comics are Go! Thanks also to Carol and John's, North Coast Nostalgia, Comic Heaven, Reality Recess, and Davey's. Thanks and respect to those who came before in Cleveland: Gus DiCorpo, Dave Dooley, Gary Engle, Irwin L. Horowitz, Tim Gorman, Chris Lambert, and Tony Isabella. I am grateful to the Cleveland Police Department, particularly Pat Sanney, who first heard my idea, and Police Chief Michael McGrath.

Glenville High School was very helpful to me, especially librarian Sara

Banks, who made me feel like I was in my school library again, which was wonderful. She protected this legacy more than anyone, in a role now handled just as admirably by librarian Kimberly Smith. Thanks also to Principal Jacqueline Bell for her graciousness and to the nice student who helped me find the front door.

In New York, my home away from here, thanks to Jim Hanley's, Midtown, Forbidden Planet, and the Strand, for shelter from the storm. Thanks to the new friends I've made there over many research trips, including Elise Branca, Jennifer Congo, Dana Robertson, and Karen Schatz. And in Riverhead, thanks to Theresa, Richard, Bobby, Alexa Markel, and their wonderful family, for everything.

I am so lucky to have talked to the third-grade class of Thomas Jefferson School in Cleveland. Especially to James Ball Jr. for his wise, hushed words that completely surprised me—but were ones I immediately, completely agreed with. And always will.

Thanks as well to my cousin, Dan Hoecker, for all the fantastic Superman artwork over the years that hung on my walls and inspired me to keep going.

I am very lucky to be able to count on the Siegel and Shuster Society for their love, support, and incredible hard work as a nonprofit organization: to Norma Wolkov and Rita Hubar for their unconditional dedication to all of us, to Dick Pace for his ability to make seemingly impossible things happen with a smile, and to Mike Olszewski for his leadership and infectious love of Cleveland history, especially when it comes to Superman. Jamie Reigle of www.supercollectibles.com has been involved with this story before any of us, and his support, as well as that of his family, Dawn, Kalel, and Lex, has been tenacious. Thanks also to Jeanne McMaster for her warmth and ability to keep us all in line. Matthew Rizzuto has also been a constant source of help, and is the greatest Superman fan in the world. I also want to thank Tracey Kirksey for the joy she brings to her city, Mayor Beryl Rothschild for her ongoing commitment to civic pride, Leigh Goldie for her passion in representing her family, the Shusters, and to Steve Presser for his absolutely astounding imagination. And last, but not least, thanks to Irving Fine, who doesn't work for praise. Irv has, I think, figured out life in a way we could all hope to do. We are the Justice League.

Brad Meltzer provided advice and guidance that helped me in many subtle, but important ways. I can't thank him enough; not only for his help and for his own writing and work but also for Dr. Impossible. The first time I met Brad, he was dressed in a black blazer, sunk into a chair, looking down at a long table. He said, in a very small voice, "Superman is really Clark Kent," and everything changed for me.

I am especially grateful to Dr. Peter Coogan, for calling me up to the big panel table in San Diego one afternoon in July. Pete not only showed me how to think about superheroes but in many secret, generous ways, he helped make this unimaginable thing happen, as any good mentor (and friend) does.

I would not have gotten very far without the friendship and help of Mike Sangiacomo, who provided the early realization to me on Saturdays in the newspaper that comics could be written about in smart ways in important places. Mike's devotion to this story, to comics, to truth, and to his adopted hometown is nothing short of heroic. He is Clark Kent.

I give ongoing thanks to my editor, Michael Homler, not only for his initial interest and belief in this story and my ability to tell it but for his patience, guidance, and assurances at exactly the right moments throughout this long process. Michael fought hard for this book and the room it needed; he gave me space to explore all of its corners. On every possible alternate earth, he is always the editor of this book. I am also grateful to the fantastic people at St. Martin's Press, including Sarah Jae-Jones, John Morrone, Elizabeth Catalano, Hector DeJean, and especially Sona Vogel for her focused eye for detail. To all at St. Martin's who spent time on this: thank you very much.

Scott Mendel has changed my life in some pretty fundamental ways. I always wanted to do this, to write like this, but Scott is the one who somehow believed it more than I did, and pushed me to make it happen. Scott's championing of this book all over the world and his ability to parse out the very core of my questions and words is extraordinary in every sense of the word. His is a mighty gift, to make dreams come true.

And thank you to my family, last only because you are by far the most important thing in my life. I can write about most stuff, but words fail me here, especially now. The good stuff will always outweigh the bad. In that, we are, all of us, together. I could not have done any of this without your ongoing love, support, and echoing laughter. Starting with Mom and Dad, Chris and Stephanie, and Caroline—but then reaching out to every corner, in every branch, large and small, old and new, over here and over there; always everywhere.

And to Caroline, for being the light at the end of the stairs.

It was dead!

Stiletto Vance discerned that at once.

"Confronting us," he informed me, "is evidently an insoluble mystery. Who murdered this man? Why?"

I shook my head, puzzled, and confessed my perplexity.

"There is a solution!—must be one—and I shall find it!" he declared confidently.

—Jerry Siegel, *The Glenville Torch*
March 12, 1931

Introduction

I am at Cleveland City Hall waiting for a copy of a birth certificate that is not mine. The final typed draft of this book—marked-up, messy, and almost done—lies in an immense pile on my desk at home. But there is one more fact to check, so I am downtown, on a gray October day. Numbers and dates and spelling: these things are important. These are places to start from.

This book is not only a story but it is about one. The story we all somehow absorb of a child rocketed to Earth from a dying planet. The orphan grows up with incredible powers and is embraced by an Earth he is sworn to protect. He likes a girl who doesn't give him a second glance. He wears a red, flowing cape, but also hides in plain sight. It is a silly story sometimes; silly in the face of what the world sometimes shows to us, yet it has given hope and solace to generations. That is important, too.

I am still waiting for the birth certificate and am now worried about how much time is left on my parking meter. To my right, on the black benches, two employees are trying to help an elderly woman get a death certificate for her late husband. The woman doesn't understand why the insurance company is making her do this. She came here on the bus. She is crying. At the snack stand, which sells candy, pop, and cheeseburgers, the clerk closes his eyes. On the small TV mounted over the wrought-iron cashier's cage, local junior high flag football is being played. A kid catches a bomb and sails into the end zone.

When my dad would tell me that Superman was created here in Cleveland, I never really believed him. We took excursions downtown from the suburbs and explored it like it was some once-great civilization, with huge parts of it empty and exploded away. There were secrets and stories here, of a past that might once have been golden. As I grew up, I began to see why he might be right. At the time I am writing this, our football team has not won a game in eleven months. Our baseball team has not won a championship since 1948. The newspapers are filled with bad things. The air is getting cold and the skies will be overcast for the next six months. When we see a patch of blue, we look up and stare.

Superman is not real.

But here, at some point, he somehow was.

This story is not like the others. This story is not just about Superman but is about two men and their work, both in public and in secret, over a significant portion of the twentieth century. This is about what they really did, not what we wanted them to. That is important, too.

I never knew Jerry Siegel and Joe Shuster. I am not even remotely related to them. But their story—creating the impossible Superman as teenagers during the Great Depression—is one that somehow resounds through all of us with a soundtrack we can almost always just hear. In the comics, Superman is always looking for secrets to his heritage. That is no coincidence. We all want to know where we come from. The same goes for our dreams and fictions. Why have these characters lasted? What can they tell us? Most people may claim to like Batman better, but it is Superman who measures the best of us. We want to know why.

But how? Not only through dusty facts and forgotten artifacts but through the very actions that stole their hours. The truth is, Jerry and Joe told us their own secrets in the comics and stories they puzzled over for decades. We have been distracted by half-remembered tales when the answer has been right in front of us the whole time. The work: that is their secret identity.

Superman is not real. But the facts I discovered are just as unbelievable: a mystical cult, a bald, power-mad millionaire, a bulletproof strongman, the real Lois Lane, and a writer's unlikely, secret service to his country. I found out that the first Superman story was stolen. I not only learned the true cause of Jerry's father's death but who the culprits could be. How? I live in Cleveland; I went to all the places and read all the comics. It took a long time. I read Jerry's last, unpublished story and my spine, as the comics always promised, actually tingled. And I discovered someone real who, by all accounts, is supposed to be a lie. And somewhere in this book is who I think Superman really is. But that's my interpretation; you have to find yours.

They call my name and I pay $25 for a birth certificate of someone I did once meet, but am not related to. I open it and pause. It is a new date and a new spelling, one that sounds suspiciously like a famous Superman character. This is how it starts: how truth can become imagination, and thus, a window into a hopeful world right next to our own. But creation has a cost.

Superman isn't real. But sometimes we wish he could be.

This is the story of that wish coming true.

Part One:
Distant Planet

Prologue

I N THE BACK OF THE STORE, the white-haired man was reading the late edition of the city newspaper. He pressed it flat, like a map, over the long cutting table. The sheets of ink reflected nothing of the lights above. Outside, a fat, black lake of a thunderstorm was brewing over the flickering streets of Cleveland, Ohio. The clothing store, small and narrow, was on the corner of Central Avenue and East Thirty-first Street. Because of the weather, it was almost empty, as were most of the stores that night. But there was money to be made, the owner thought, so his lights were lit, still hopeful for some customers. It was June 2, 1932.

Inside, clothes and hats filled every corner and table. A slight wisp of smoke curled below the overhead lamp. This was not the glass-counter fantasy world of Higbee's or Taylor's, the massive downtown department stores with their endless displays of merchandise. There were no men in vests working the elevators or pretty girls spritzing strong perfume. There was only this dark building with a white, roughly painted sign that read, "2nd Hand Clothing." The place was exactly what it claimed to be. The rain began to fall.

The store had a smell like any father's closet: dark blazers, thick wool pants, and brushed-cotton shirts all hung from golden hooks. They all had stories, these suits and slacks, ties and bracers, sliding up and down the wooden dowels. But most of their stories were sad ones, because these clothes were sometimes sold to pay for things like rent or birthday presents. Many were even sold off the backs of the dead.

The white-haired man reading the paper was the owner, a sturdy man with a frowning mouth. In a corner near the front, a thin black man shuffled through some loose shirts and ties. The clock read eight o'clock. The owner hoped the man would buy something so he could close the store and go home.

The handle of the front door began to turn, and then it stopped. The white-haired man in the back raised his head slightly. The doorknob turned again, and three men entered the store, their scuffed shoes dragging, their eyes toward the floor. The white-haired man asked in a thickly accented voice if they needed any help. The new customers looked at him from underneath their hats as if he were speaking another language. One of them smiled.

Across town, in the tree-lined neighborhood of Glenville, seventeen-year-old Jerry Siegel was reading. Short, with bushy hair and glasses, he plomped onto his bed. The house was quiet and close. His mother was downstairs doing something. It was so warm that Jerry left his window open, even though rain was starting to come in. Jerry didn't care about his bed, but he made swift motions to move the important stuff out of the way of any possible drops.

Library books were scattered here and there, but they were outnumbered in favor of the floppy magazines from the thick pile under his bed. They had strange names that baffled his parents: *Weird Tales, Astounding Stories, Argosy,* and *Detective Monthly.* As the sky cracked and lit up the room, bald scientists and massive, hulking robots stared out from the bright covers. Jerry even had an issue of *Weird Tales* with a woman on the cover who was almost completely naked. He kept that one on the bottom of the pile. Jerry loved this stuff—especially how writers with names like Walter B. Gibson or Dr. David Keller could make you scared or believe in made-up things like four-armed Martians with ray guns. These pulp magazines, named after the cheap wood paper they were printed on, were churned out monthly by publishers such as Street & Smith, Munsey, and Gernsback. They arrived at drugstores and newsstands in huge, colorful stacks for ten to twenty cents each. They had thick, painted covers from artists like Margaret Brundage, Jerome Rozen, or Frank Paul, who was his friend Joe's favorite. Jerry turned the pages again and again until it seemed they might tear. There were columns and columns of small, smudgy text preceded by giant black-and-white illustrations. Jerry even knew the ads by heart—the ones that sold home detective courses, forbidden secrets of magic, and strength-training manuals. He read these magazines over and over. These names, these situations, these *things*: This was why he wanted to be a writer more than anything else in the world. He glanced at the black typewriter on his desk and its big, heavy letters: *Underwood*. Words gave things weight.

Jerry thought of his father, working down at the clothing store he owned on Central Avenue. "The store," as it was known around the dinner table, always filled Jerry with a sense of dread. Though the business had given the family their nice house (as his father so often reminded him), it was also a constant point of contention. *Stop that writing and come down to the store!* Jerry's father would yell at him from the bottom of the stairs. Friends and classmates would recall this command as a frequent one.[1] But try as Jerry might to fight this battle, his father's words had a sense of tightening inevitability. As both he and his father were getting older, it was looking more and more as though Jerry were going to have to work at the store full-time after his graduation from high school.

Jerry sighed and took a look at the cover of *Astounding Stories*. On it, a spongy alien with a curved orange beak and green tentacles threatened a silver-clad space hero with a jaw like an anvil. Jerry thought the monster looked a bit like his father. Especially the eyebrows. The storm made the branches outside his window look like long fingers. His father wouldn't be home for a while. With all that lightning and rain, Jerry was trying to come up with a good story himself. Maybe the best ever written. It had to be if he was going to get out of this. He looked at the notebooks on his bed and his typewriter on the desk. He had been sending stories to some of the magazines, but none of them had been published. Not yet. A few of his letters had been printed, though, which he still found incredible. He turned to the back of one of the magazines, the one with a yellow flying saucer on it (a *saucer?*), and read, again, his very own words, which still looked strange in their set, blocked type:

> *Dear Editor . . . I have bought all the pamphlets that have appeared in the Science Fiction Library, and am immediately awaiting the appearance of some more. I read all the stories immediately upon their arrival and it wasn't long before I had finished them and had nothing to read. So hurry up with some more. . . .* [2]

This was how Jerry always felt: *Hurry up*. He wanted to do everything he could in that very same second, even if others told him to slow down. It wasn't that he hated his shared, little brown room in the back of the house, now hot as blazes. He just wanted more. Jerry knew the next part by heart but was still struck by its audacity:

> *Jerome Siegel,*
> *10622 Kimberley Avenue Cleveland, O.*[3]

This was his introduction. He was a writer, after all. And Thursday, June 2, 1932, whether he knew it yet or not, was a good night to write.

Back at the store, unbeknownst to Jerry, the men who walked in the front door were like slow chess pieces moving toward an uncertain conclusion. The black man in the front eyed the three men suspiciously. Something was wrong. They all congregated at the front of the store as Siegel's father came out to help them. One of the three had picked out a suit and had it draped over one arm. His hand smoothed the dark fabric. The others started to move in closely. The man with the suit paused, then went for the door. Or they took the suit after the owner gave it to them. It didn't matter; they were going, either way. Or they were still there. People were moving. The white-haired Michel Siegel, in his early sixties—who throughout his life was known as Michel (pronounced "Mitchell"), Michael, and Mike—shouted, fumbled, and made his way toward the door as fast as he could. But then something hit him, hard. It felt as if the strongest fist he could ever imagine had punched him square in the chest. This was too much. This is too much. He is sweating. He is closing his eyes.

Over at the house on Kimberley, the phone rang, and Jerry's eyes shuddered open. He wasn't sure if he was even awake. He heard his mother cry out. Then he heard another call being made. Then his mother's voice, calling out: *Jerome! Jerome!* His room, his magazines, were in his peripheral vision as he ran downstairs.

Later, at the hospital, the reporter talked to his mother, who for all her usual imperiousness now looked small and alone. She kept grabbing at her purse as if it were going to fall into the exact center of the earth. She steadied herself, looked away, and gave a small answer. The reporter wrote it down in a little notebook in fast, light script. He used the word *murder*. He couldn't stop writing. Jerry's father was dead. He couldn't stop writing. His father was dead. His father from Russia who had brought over his bride and children to save them from evil was dead. A tall, dark cop was comforting him. The rain was falling. His father was dead. Is dead.

The next day, *The Plain Dealer,* the city's biggest newspaper, ran no mention of the crime whatsoever.[4]

And it rained and thunder cracked all night, like the end of the world.

Chapter 1
The Eyes

JOE SHUSTER BLINKED at the back of his art teacher. She was bent over a student who clearly needed help portraying the simple bowl of fruit at the front of the room. Joe had finished his sketch a good ten minutes ago and was looking for something else to draw. With his left hand, he brought his pencil down at a forty-five-degree angle over the paper. It hovered there for a moment, floating over the page. His books wobbled in a pile under his desk. He tried to shift his dangling feet so no one could see they weren't hitting the floor. Joe was short and skinny, parted his dark hair carefully on the side, and wore glasses that were incredibly thick. When it seemed that no one was looking, Joe put his face close—so close—down to the page, about two or three inches away, so he could finally see it.

Joe looked down at his drawing. He really wanted to draw something coming out of the apple—maybe an arrow or a smiling worm with funny eyebrows and a big cigar—but he didn't want to get into trouble. He liked his teacher too much. Someday he would be a famous artist and he would come back to this classroom and she would be impressed. *Class,* she would say, *this is a former student of mine who is a very successful artist, and his name is Joe Shuster.* Or maybe *Joseph Shuster.* There would be clapping and she would smile and look very pleased. Joe looked at her and in his mind started drawing beams radiating from her head. But she straightened up and caught him staring even though he wasn't really. Turning red, he went back to his sketch, brushing thick lines all going one way in the background. He hoped he could bring this one home to show his mother, he thought. He drew more lines.

At home, Joe's mother, Ida, moved between the laundry and the stove. She knew she had only an hour or so before her boys, Joe and Frank, would be home from school. Their little sister, Jeanetta, was already staring out the window in anticipation of her two favorite, patient brothers. Ida's husband, Julius, was working downtown at the Richman Brothers clothing store factory. Ida stopped for a moment, looked around her small apartment, and blinked. It looked small, but it was still an empire, so far from home.

Ida was born to Shemon Katharske and his wife, Chesie, around 1890 in a small town in the central region of Russia.[1] Like many of the towns in the region, it was known by several names, depending upon where, whom, and when you asked.[2] Here, in the town of many names, protected by a weak and crumbling fortress, Ida lived in a world of farms and hills. The area had enjoyed some peace, but there was always the promise of dreadful violence, especially against her people, the Jews, who were uneasy neighbors to the Russians. On April 27, 1881, a fight at a neighborhood bar resulted in the midnight destruction of several Jewish homes and businesses as police looked on. This went on for two days without any interest by the military authorities. The news spread fast through the towns and cities.[3]

Another wave of anti-Semitic violence was reported by *The New York Times* on December 13, 1905:

RUSSIAN CITY BURNING, JEWS BEING MASSACRED
ODESSA IS PANIC-STRICKEN
Reports received here through refugees are to the effect that
since Sunday the town of Elizabethgrad, Russia, has been
burning and that a mob has been killing and plundering in
the Jewish quarter.[4]

The looting was done by torchlight. The streets were covered with glass and feathers. The mob got larger as government officials looked on. Fires raged down the little streets. The midnight reports were terrifying. As the government internally debated the legality of the "action," news spread that a Jew had been killed. Ida, whose name in Hebrew meant "life," had heard enough of this word *pogrom* and its simple meaning, "destroy." In a short, sad range of years, thousands of Jews were killed or financially ruined. Some of them organized into renegade militias, but they were no match for the Russian army, who marched with bright medals and silver swords. The army were not all soldiers, not all blood-thirsty, but they all had their orders.[5]

Ida never imagined she would have a child who would one day end up going to an American school in a place called Cleveland and sketch a simple bowl of fruit for her. America was not a place for her to think of. But she did anyway. When she saw the men marching up the streets, she knew there had to be a better place. Not in specific details, but more as a vague idea, like an exotic photograph of Paris or Rome. This imaginary escape had at least the possibility of being real in the most extravagant way imaginable. America *ganef,* they said. The future of the place where she lived would see people beaten, bloodied, and stiff. These were old, inscrutable grudges. If these ways would not change, the place must. Imagination had to become real.

When Ida and her sister, Bessie, were finally old enough to leave, they did.[6] They packed up their belongings and escaped down the long north road. There were tense moments, but once they reached Rotterdam they were relieved. They were going to find a ship.

Rotterdam was a completely different world to the sisters. There, white buildings all crowded together, and the scent of the sea seemed to change everything. In Rotterdam, there was a substantial advertising campaign to encourage immigration to Canada. Colorful playbills had giant fingers pointing, to photos of Manitoba's rippling rivers and promised free prairie land. Clifford Sifton, Canada's minister of the interior, had organized hundreds of agents in Holland to give talks extolling the virtues of Canada. Sifton even worked with ship lines to get reduced rates for immigrants. In dark stage rooms all across Rotterdam, magic lanterns lit up scenes of a Canada free from screaming and fire.[7]

The invisible force behind some of the increasing violence, and the push toward the Americas, was the steep economic fall in Europe following World War I. Frustration was so high that all options had become viable. So many people were coming over that eventually the U.S. Immigration Act of 1924 would limit immigrants from any one country to 2 percent. The rationale was to "maintain the racial preponderance of the basic strain on our people and thereby to stabilize the ethnic composition of the population."[8] The act would refer to these immigrants as "aliens."[9]

Ida and Bessie finally booked their passage to Canada but had to wait a week before ship-off.[10] So they found a second-floor room in a hotel right by the river that was for emigrants waiting to leave. The hotel at Wijnbrugstraat 8 was a little more expensive than they wanted, but the man in charge winked at them and may have taken a little off for their troubles. His name was Jacob Shusterowich and he was a Jew, so it would be fine. They would spend a week in Rotterdam with him, his wife, Roza, and their family, including two of his sons, Julius and Jack.

Something happened during that week, in the hotel near the sea. Maybe it was when Julius helped Ida carry her trunk up the stairs, or when he saw her for the first time at the dinner table, or when he convinced himself from an upper window that she would want to talk to him in the first place, but something completely unexpected happened during that week: Ida and Julius fell in love. Part of it was probably the shortness of the time before her departure, but every waking moment between Julius and Ida was soon filled with glances, touches, and eventually eager promises. This turn of events was of equal surprise to Julius, but he embraced it, as he did everything, wholeheartedly. He no longer wanted to stay at home. He wanted to protect this girl, this *her*. When the week finally ended, quickly, and they left, the boys made quick plans to follow them. When their ship was ready to sail, Julius Shusterowitz, son of Jacob, dramatically announced his intentions to follow Ida to Canada, where he would marry her. He was that kind of person, given to dining room pronouncements. His father scoffed, *Why would you do this?* But Julius remained undeterred. And to make matters more interesting, Julius's brother Jack had fallen for Ida's sister, Bessie—and was also going to leave.[11]

Their father's heart was broken. Julius was thin and upright, with dark hair and a lean face that always seemed ready to laugh. But he was young, and his father knew he was beat. Still, he had one last gambit. Their father retorted that if Julius and Jack were going to Canada, they would have to pay for it themselves. Surely the prospect of an endless ocean would end this nonsense. He knew Julius had some money, but not enough to best the gray Atlantic. He was wrong. Pleading with the shipmaster, Julius and his brother secured jobs as deckhands on the boat.[12] And soon, slowly, to the accompaniment of deep droning horns and swaying decks, they set sail for North America, streaming toward an imagined horizon.[13] His father watched Julius disappear on a ship named the *Uranium*.[14] Julius had $20 on him.[15] They were off to the future.

Julius and Jack finally landed on September 2, 1912, in Halifax on

Nova Scotia.[16] He married Ida a year later on September 14, 1913.[17] They lived in a few different places, including a shared house on 455 Richman Street.[18] Julius kept smiling and got a job as a tailor. He and Ida smiled at each other and held hands. They wondered sometimes at what they had done, but *this was destiny,* Julius said. *This was fate.*

The alien couple Ida and Julius had three children in Canada, and "Shusterowitz," in the slip of a pen became "Schusterowitz" and, then, "Schuster." The eldest, named after Julius, was born on July 14, 1914, ten months from the day they were married.[19] He would be followed by Frank four years later and little sister Jeanetta in six. Throughout the course of his life, Julius Jr. would never once use his given name in public; few, if any, knew of its secret existence. He would always be known by his middle name: Joe.[20]

The Schusters lived all over Toronto: on Bathurst, Borden, and Oxford streets.[21] Joe attended public school at Lansdowne and Ryerson. Canada's Depression preceded America's, and the family moved around a lot to make rent. At one point, they lived in a house with Bessie and Jack: Joe lived downstairs, while his cousin Frank lived up. Growing up in these small apartments, Joe watched as his mother busied herself with his baby brother. Joe loved the newspaper *The Toronto Star,* and though he could not yet read, he was astounded by the comics page. He didn't know how to tell time either, but he knew when his father came home, so he would stand in the middle of the room with the paper and wait for him. And when he heard his steps at the door, he would grip the paper in his hands even tighter. Julius would rush in, hoist Joe on his knee, and read him the comics. Joe knew them all by image rather than names: *The Katzenjammer Kids, Boob McNutt, Happy Hooligan,* and *Barney Google.* And on weekends, when the comics were printed in glorious color, minutes turned to an hour. As his father read the balloons of words, Joe's eyes widened at the pictures. On Sundays, *Little Nemo in Slumberland* made him freeze with awe.[22] Winsor McCay depicted nightmares and dreamscapes that included massive futuristic cities that were incredibly detailed. The paper became a window into an almost impossible world. And Joe, enchanted, would try to draw his own elaborate scenes on his bedroom wall—at the age of four. Joe never remembered doing this, but his father would often remind him.[23]

Toronto was such a cartoon-crazy town that it would even include comic characters as part of its annual Santa Claus parade. Large, jangly, out-of-joint, exaggerated wooden puppets of fairy-tale characters clacked down Bloor Street for smiling kids and their workaday parents. But the final participant of the parade was always the same: a fellow who commanded the respect of the entire crowd as a force for good. Santa Claus was a character who was larger than life; his positive nature was overwhelming among the buildings and streets, as he centered himself within a mass of cheering people. He had powers beyond those of mortal men. At the end of the parade, everyone swarmed his sleigh and he stood up triumphantly, cloaked in red.[24]

Joe said he worked as a young newsboy, slinging copies of *The Toronto Star*.[25] His best pal was his cousin Frank, who would grow up to be half of the famous Canadian comedy team Wayne and Shuster, starring on countless albums, radio shows, and television programs.[26] But in Toronto, as kids, they just saw movies together, watching the silent pictures at the theater where Jack worked as a projectionist.

Back in Rotterdam, Jacob Schusterowitz died in 1915 at age sixty-one, having never seen his grandchildren. In 1912, he and a partner had opened their own moviehouse, the Imperial Bioscope. Jacob left the money he had made to all of his children. Julius opened a tailor shop, and Jacob opened his own movie theater. Julius was a good tailor, having learned the trade back home. But as his relatives would say, he was a bad businessman and didn't charge people what he should have. When customers were short of cash or friends came in, he had a tendency to smile and wave them off.[27]

With business drying up, Julius got word from a friend that Richman Brothers had just opened a huge clothing manufacturing company in Cleveland, across Lake Erie, in America. It had always been the plan to go to the States, so even though they liked Toronto, they were again tempted by the thought of better times and moved south to Cleveland in August 1924 by train, crossing the border at Niagara Falls.[28]

Joe was ten years old.

CLEVELAND

The Shusters lost the "c" in their name on the way to Cleveland and found themselves in a place smaller in both size and scope, but it was a city of iron and steel. Third in population behind New York and Chicago, Cleveland was the railroad link between the two, making it an important shipping, stop-off, and settling point. The city had opportunities even then, coming off the lake. There was a big public library, plans for a giant sports stadium, and the beginning plans for a single, soaring skyscraper.[29] The city had a modern architectural feel to it that was almost surreal against the constantly gray skies. *Science and Invention* spotlighted the city in an August 1930 article titled "Cleveland—a Scientific Glimpse."[30] The article, complete with sharp photos, showcases the Cleveland Electric Illuminating Company and its three turbogenerators designed to power the tough midwestern city. The article also mentions the Ohio Bell building, which it calls a "fine modern structure" reliant on a "slotted effect" to "emit maximum light."[31] This was Cleveland: the modern world creeping into the old in bold, shocking strokes. Yet the economy was terrible and the police force had holes in it big enough to drive through. The newspapers welcomed the nice Canadian family with stories of crime and ruin.

Once they arrived in Cleveland, the Shusters lived at 3401 East 143rd Street, just southeast of downtown.[32] At fourteen Joe enrolled at Alexander Hamilton Junior High School, a stone fortress in the neighborhood of Woodland at the corner of East 130th and Kinsman on the city's east side. Hamilton, with its tall windows and wide wooden stairs, was nearly brand-new, having opened in September 1928. It had a gym on the second floor with a planked floor and an empty trophy case. And because the school had just opened, its library was still waiting for its books.

Joe, who was impatiently awaiting a growth spurt, moved hurriedly through the Hamilton halls. He jumped up the stairs to the third floor, turned left, and went all the way down the hall to the last door on the right. Walking through it, he could smell paints and paper and see the sun: this was the art room. His mother wanted him to be a doctor, but this was all Joe wanted: a pencil, some paper, and someplace to work.[33] Everywhere he looked he could see extensions of the real world and what might happen if he could change things—like if he suddenly grew wings or slipped on a banana peel. Drawing was nothing more than imagination. And nothing less.

Hamilton quickly started up a student newspaper named *The Federalist*. The paper filled its columns mainly with sports coverage, but it also had articles on class projects and clubs and boasted an unbroken line of elected female editors. *The Federalist* also had cartoons. Joe started contributing some of his own, modeled after what he was seeing in the newspapers.

Joe taught himself to draw by tracing the funnies in the paper. So his figures were elongated and goofy-looking with smiley grins. Meaning was exaggeration: the speaker is being pelted by his classmates—and the teacher doesn't care. Joe signed it with the only constant to his art—a long tail with a circle at the end of it, a flourish he stole from one of his idols, Chester Gould, who wrote and drew the great *Dick Tracy* in the newspapers every day. This tail at the end of his signature would turn out to be Joe's one unmistakable identity, his tell, throughout the various art jobs he would do during his life.

Joe was handed his copy of *The Federalist* and could not believe his cartoon was in it. *Got any more in you, kid?* He had plenty. So he sat down at home and screwed his eyes shut and thought about what the other kids wanted to see. What did he want to see? He heard a bird outside near the window and realized there was only one thought on anyone's mind now: summer vacation. In this four-panel cartoon, Joe looks forward to summer and shows a command of his audience apparent from the first panel.

The panels are grand in scope and include an ocean liner and a horse race—and a kid content to cool off in a tub with a fan and a case of ice-cold Cokes. Maybe Joe makes a Depression-era statement about the nature of treasure and riches—who could even afford a trip across the sea or a visit to Churchill Downs? But more important, who would want to? The last panel is the most telling: a towering column of students in sad lockstep make their way to summer school, all looking dreamily at the happy kids swimming in a cool pool. Above, the sun beams and laughs at them. Early on, Joe shows his love of big, crazy scenes that speak directly to his young audience.

Another early strip Joe worked on at Hamilton was called *Jerry the Journalist,* about a tall, easygoing *Federalist* reporter named Jerry Fine and his misadventures getting news stories for the paper. Hamilton kids loved it. At the end of the year, though, Joe found out his family was moving to another neighborhood and he would be attending Glenville High School. Fine suggested Joe look up his cousin Jerry, who was also at Glenville: *You'd have a lot in common,* he said. His cousin's name was Jerry, too.[34]

Jerry Siegel.

Chapter 2

The Dreamer

AFEW MILES TO THE NORTH, at a different school, Jerry Siegel stared at a different blackboard and had a very different problem: He couldn't concentrate on *anything*. There were words and numbers in front of him, but he imagined spaceships and bug-eyed monsters instead. And when that got boring, he imagined even crazier things. He wondered what it would be like to have the power to stop time for everyone but himself. Then he could wander around the school, finish his messy homework, and maybe kiss the girl with the plaid skirt and white sweater sitting in the front row. The teacher moved toward the board again, swiftly tapping the chalk across the board as more numbers appeared out of nowhere. Jerry's socks were itching again and he shifted in his desk chair. He did not like school.

The room with windows and wooden floors closed him in; it was early in the day and students were still half-asleep. Something was wrong, and it wasn't just the math. Jerry couldn't quite get a handle on what it was. He looked around the room. Everyone seemed to be looking at him. Then he heard it, that most innocuous but terrible of sounds for a young male student to hear: a girl's giggle. The sound turned his spine to stone because it was followed by another word: *Look*. The word came from across the room. He craned his neck, and sure enough, a short, smiling teenage girl was pointing at Jerry, specifically to his shoe. *His shoe? Had he stepped in . . . ? Oh no.* Looking down to his feet, Jerry saw a swatch of striped cotton fabric protruding from his bottom pant leg. In his rush to get ready that morning, he had left his pajamas on under his suit. This is a true story.[1]

Jerry hastily tried to push his pajamas back under his pants with his other shoe. But his face was already red. He smiled and tried to fold his one leg under the other, halfheartedly, in defeat. Maybe the girls would find this whole thing cute and disarming. They did not. Jerry at this time in his life was very visibly a teenager. He was not tall or muscular. His hair was thick and wiry and was pushed every morning (coerced was more like it) to one side. He wore small round glasses, and his voice was thin and high and sometimes unbearably nasal. He dressed normally, in wool suits and ties, but it was not his priority. His open face always seemed to wear an unconscious half-smirk, no matter the occasion, that made some people angry. He had a ton of energy that the photos don't always show—he could burst through doors and fly up stairs, but only if there was something on the other end to get to. He was a young adult who acted sometimes like an older man with ideas bigger and more serious than he was. Yet he always wanted to be that young man who did the right things, got the pretty girl, and was talked about by others. He had the last one down, but not in the way he wanted.

Even before his father's death in 1932, Jerome Siegel, born on October 17, 1914, in Cleveland, always saw himself as somewhat of a lone individual.[2] He was the last of six children, after all, and was the youngest, last son to Michel and Sarah, two Lithuanian immigrants from a shadowy world far beyond his understanding or care. But he felt this lineage every day as a kind of isolation: all of his sisters and brothers, most of whom were married or had a career by the time he was a teenager, were notches of height he could never quite catch up to.[3]

When Jerry was born, the Siegels lived at 1949 East Seventy-ninth Street in Cleveland as part of a large home that had been converted to apartments.[4] It had maple woodwork and small hallways and was a perfect arena for the young Jerry, with his brothers and sisters still around, to grow up and compete for attention. His father worked as a tailor and opened up a clothing shop. His mother cooked and sewed and helped at the store.

In the Siegel house, the newspaper was a daily gift from the outside universe. It was big and made lots of noise and you had to wipe your hands off after you read it. As much as Jerry loved the paper and always wanted to read it, he had to wait for his father to finish looking at it, as he sat in his chair, hidden by the tall, off-white sheets with their ragged edge. He would go over the paper as if it were homework. In Cleveland, "the paper" could mean one of three major dailies—*The Cleveland Press, The Plain Dealer,* or *The Cleveland News*—in addition to several smaller periodicals. Some catered to ethnicity and religion, others to race. They all had stories to tell about the real world, but they were also sources of hope and escape.

Jerry wanted escape. One of the sections he liked best was produced specifically for children: the *Seckatary Hawkins* page, a big, kids-only playground of letters, stories, and pictures. The eponymous character was George "Seckatary" Hawkins, a portly boy with a bad cowlick who was the "seckatary" of a club of boys who operated out of a clubhouse on the banks of a midwestern river. Seck and his gang would be called on by adults to solve mysteries. Seck would tap his pen, get in his canoe, and consult his Bible for advice. He even had a best friend, Lincoln "Link" Lambert ("the Skinny Guy"), who was Seck's "old side partner." And Seck always stood up for his father: "A boy wants his daddy by his side all the time he can. . . . What a boy wants is to make his daddy his pal."[5]

Jerry liked the stories so much, he decided to write in. His first published work appears on the *Seckatary Hawkins* page in the *Plain Dealer Sunday Magazine* section on September 12, 1926.

> *Dear Sec.:*
> *My name is Jerome Siegel and I wish some member would correspond with me.*
>
> *I have a tube set but sorry to say I don't think I can tune in on WLW.*
> > *Yours fair and square,*
> > > *JEROME SIEGEL*
> ★ ★ ★
> > *1949 E. 79th Street.*
> > *Cleveland, O.*[6]

Jerry enjoyed reading about Seck in the paper, but he also wanted real friends, just like in the stories. Jerry couldn't hear the voices on the radio; all he heard were wavy sounds and static. All he had were the words and how they sounded in his head. He was twelve years old.

Jerry, like all of the young writers, is urged to "keep trying."[7] In fact, the writer of the column gives advice to all of its readers:

Now, don't wait, but sit down at once and write your letter. If
you have tried in the previous contest and have not won a
prize, do not be discouraged. Remember, the old motto. "Try,
try again." Is a very good one to follow. If you keep at a thing
long enough, you are bound to succeed in time.[8]

A quitter never wins; a winner never quits. This was the Seck Hawkins
motto.

CLICK-CLACK

In 1928, the Siegels moved to Glenville, a more well-off Jewish neighborhood to the northeast. Michel and Sarah bought their dream home at
10622 Kimberley Avenue, a three-story wooden house on a quiet street
off East 105th Street, the main thoroughfare of Glenville.[9] The house was
big but was easily filled with the last of the Siegel children and Sarah's
mother and father. Living near the bustle of East 105th was a completely
new experience for Jerry. As he got to know the area that summer, he
became aware of a bigger world that was now open to him. An essay in
the Glenville yearbook by a high school senior describes life on East
105th:

> You should never take a street car if you want to travel on East
> 105th Street. If you do, you miss its atmosphere. The best time
> to take your stroll is between eight and nine o'clock in a Satur-
> day night . . . [Newsboys] are shouting to let you know that
> gangland warfare has broken out anew and the body of a noto-
> rious gangster has been found shot to death. . . . You lift your
> chin up . . . and on your left you see something that makes you
> slow down. There is a large, long, low church with beautifully
> colored pictures in its window panes.
>
> You find yourself in the midst of the Jewish section of the
> street. You see old women gathered at street corners. . . . They
> are prattling away in some foreign tongue you cannot under-
> stand.
>
> Little, dirty, ragged urchins chasing each other into the
> streets, playing tag or hide-and-go-seek. Running helter-skelter

on the sidewalks, bumping into people, tripping over themselves, lurching from left to right, running off the sidewalks and
narrowly escaping injury from passing automobiles.

You pass butcher shops with curious Hebrew hieroglyphics
on the windows.

You pass on and find yourself in the gambling section. Small
cigar stores, smoke shops and barber shops, where, in the back
room, behind the thin partitions which veil the player from the
passer-by, many a dollar is lost and won.

When you notice a delightful odor in the air which makes
your very blood tingle and you turn around to find that it
comes from a store which has the sign "Delicatessen" in it, then
you know you are in the "corned beef belt." Do not walk in to
buy if you have just eaten, because you must be hungry to appreciate the delightful aroma and the taste of these corned beef
sandwiches.[10]

Charles Redlick, the writer of the essay, offers a telling coda, with
which the young Jerry Siegel would have no doubt agreed: "This is a
street of romance and adventure."[11]

Jerry's father's clothing store had been doing well, even in the dour
economic climate, so the new house was roomy and comfortable. After
walking up onto the covered wooden porch and into the house, you entered a narrow front room. In later years, the first thing anyone would
notice was the Tiffany lamp on the table. To the right of the front door
was the radio, and a chair and lamp reserved for Jerry's father.

The straight hallway opened into a kitchen where you could see the
small, green backyard. The kitchen had an adjoining pantry on the right.
On the other side of the staircase was the dining room, where everyone
had their meals on Friday. When Jerry was growing up, there were two
refrigerators in the kitchen, one devoted entirely to his brother Harry, a
mailman, who was paying his own rent and living in a barricaded room
free from Jerry's snooping. Jerry's sister Rose worked as a bookkeeper.
Minnie was a stenographer at a department store. Ida worked in an office.
Leo was the most successful: he became a dentist. Jerry worked at his
father's store once in a while, but mostly he read his magazines.[12]

Up the narrow stairs, the first hard left on the second floor was Jerry and Leo's shared bedroom. Jerry had a desk in a little alcove on his left, directly above the downstairs pantry. His black typewriter stood on the desk, its white alphabet making a sort of weird, squarish smile.

On the third floor was the attic, with a triangular roof and a window looking out on the street. Jerry sat here, but only once in a while. The attic was used for storage and was much too hot in the summer and too cold in the winter to do anything, much less write, in. There was also, at one point, a full-sized dentist chair on the third floor, courtesy of Leo. From the attic window, Jerry could see the tops of some of the trees on Kimberley—white, green, or orange—depending on the time of year. Fall was the only time the attic was bearable.

In this house, in 1929, Jerry would still be writing his letters, only by this time on his black typewriter. At fifteen, he was no longer interested in noble Seck Hawkins and his pals; he was reading about arks in space and extradimensional beings. The word *nerd* would not come into popular use until Dr. Seuss's *If I Ran the Zoo* in 1950, so Jerry was just a "science fiction reading teenager."[13] But that might have been enough. These fantastic stories were based in reality, but the connection was tenuous at best. Jerry tried imagining his own stories about planets and spacemen, so he toyed with the keys, the silver heavy circles with each letter in white type on a black, circular dial. His fingers fit those circles perfectly on the up and down, over the slight resistance. The question mark was a funny little squiggle, fat like an "S." The space bar was worn, the ribbon sometimes stuck, but the return was liquid, and the bar still shined. His first attempts involved staring at a lot of white paper. During the day, he sometimes typed on his mother's sewing machine table.[14]

But when inspiration struck at midnight and Jerry got up to write, he had a major obstacle: his sleeping brother Leo. When this happened, Jerry hoisted up the old black hulk of a typewriter and padded down the stairs, careful not to wake his parents. He could hear his father snoring—which would be soft, then louder, then farther away. Jerry slid all the way to the basement, which was cold and damp but secluded enough that he could tap out his stories and not wake anyone.[15]

So he went into the basement at night, where it looked the way he felt. In the basement there was a furnace and coal and lots of empty jars. The floor was cold, and the walls were dark.

Antares was a cruel and unyielding world to any soul unfortunate to land there. He saw a shadow in the corner. A spider.

The sleek craft sped through the cosmos.

There was a better there than here.

So when he finally rose, yawning, he would place the typewriter back on its rubber feet and put the papers away. Some days, confused and late from staying up all night in the basement, he threw on his clothes over anything else he had on and ran off to school.

SPIRIT OF RADIO

When Jerry couldn't write, or was sick of school, or Leo, or his father, he would end up at the local drugstore, looking at the magazines. He knew when the new ones came out (Wednesdays) and saved his money accordingly. Jerry didn't buy baseball cards. And though he bought adventure, police, and even horror mags, he always liked the science fiction ones the best. These kinds of magazines were fairly new in the late 1920s and early 1930s, at least as a popular genre. In the magazines, these types of stories actually began in the backs of real science magazines—specifically, a New York title named *Science and Invention.*

Hugo Gernsback was the hands-on editor of *Science and Invention* who had his own radio station, the legendary WRNY. Gernsback was exactly the type of man the Depression celebrated for being a self-proclaimed master of many modern disciplines. In the backs of his magazines, hidden between the circuit board plans and scientific demonstrations, Gernsback slowly began to run stories of "scientification," early tales of science fiction by writers such as Percival Lowell, an astronomer who was obsessed with finding Planet X and thought the canals on Mars were indicative of a mysterious civilization. Amid economic despair, there was plenty of room for this type of mad dreaming.[16]

Response to this new type of fiction was so positive that Gernsback began a second magazine in 1926 with a title, *Amazing Stories,* that would become legendary to generations of readers. The title was built around Gernsback's notion that a perfect science fiction story was "75 percent literature interwoven with 25 percent science."[17] *Amazing* also differed from its peers by publishing not only letters from readers but their addresses as well, thus encouraging fans to write one another and discuss the magazine on their own time. *Amazing* was an interactive, collective experience and soon became referred to by readers as "our" magazine.[18] The decision to include readers was important because the state of the magazine industry was so volatile. Readers liked the disposable entertainment—there were magazines covering everything from screen romances to western ranch life. The magazines were cheap and thick and had lushly painted covers that were hard to resist at the newsstand. On its surface, the magazine publishing business flourished.

But behind the scenes, the magazines came and went. They were traded and folded by their owners like so many cards at a poker game. Magazine tycoons had to deal with paper companies, distribution systems, and other shadowy conglomerates that could finish them at the drop of a bill. What was profitable one month might not be the next, so there were constant bankruptcies as owners changed, went broke, or had their companies stolen outright through unsavory business practices.

Gernsback, who had cultivated a fatherly, Edison-like public persona in his magazines, had a reputation for being ruthless with his editors and writers. Upset authors nicknamed him "the Rat" because he sometimes paid them too little too late. These editorial practices—shady accounting, poor payment to contributors, and genuine unethical behavior—became the stuff of New York publishing legend. But just as other publishers feared him, they learned as well: Gernsback was constantly adapting to the evolving market, something he did to great success. In 1929, Gernsback lost ownership of his first magazines after a bankruptcy lawsuit. After losing control of *Amazing Stories,* Gernsback founded two new science fiction magazines, *Science Wonder Stories* and *Air Wonder Stories.* A year later, the two merged into *Wonder Stories,* which remained the name until 1936, when it was renamed *Thrilling Wonder Stories.*[19] It was all the same thing under new names and barely disguised identities.

Jerry also knew Gernsback as an author. He eagerly read Gernsback's first novel, *Ralph 124C 41+,* when it was reprinted in *Amazing Stories Quarterly*'s winter 1929 issue. *Ralph* was one of the first science fiction novels, and by the time Jerry got to it as a teenager, it was already infamous among the letter-writing community. The punning title suggests the futurist tone of the story, which takes place in 2660 and is essentially a collection of bizarre inventions Gernsback thought would someday be real, including videophones, radar, and tape recorders, among many others.[20]

Inspired by his Seck Hawkins fame and Gernsback's embrace of his readers, Jerry wrote into these magazines, careful to adopt a voice and tone that wouldn't give him away as a lowly Cleveland teenager. His second letter appeared in the "Discussion" section of Gernsback's August 1929 *Amazing Stories*.

> *I'm starting my letter off with a request which I am sure will be seconded by a large host of AMAZING STORIES readers. What I wish you would do is reprint A. Merritt's story, "Through the Dragon Glass," which appeared in the* All-Story *magazine years ago.*
>
> *I'm for reprints, but I do not mean the ones that were written so long ago that their forecasts had already come true.*
>
> *By the way, will your readers please stop casting slurs at "Weird Tales" magazine? I buy every issue of "Argosy," "Weird Tales," and "Our" magazine as they appear, for all have the same authors or most of them. . . . So you see when you criticize that type of fiction appearing in these magazines, you are in turn throwing dirt at your own.*
>
> *And Editor, give us another cover (story) contest. I have written many science stories, amateurishly, and can hardly hold myself in restraint, when I know that some of my friends who have also written science stories galore, chiefly among them, John Reibel, author of "Voice from the Moon," also of "Emperor of Ten Worlds," both Sunday Times, and Bernard Kantor, author of "Invisible World" and "Beyond This Finite World," are also waiting for a chance to number as contributor to "our" magazine.*
>
> *Jerome Siegel*
> *10622 Kimberly Avenue, Cleveland, Ohio*[21]

At fifteen years of age, Jerry Siegel was not just into science fiction, he was a full-blown fanatic for it. During the height of the Depression, he was buying at least three magazines a month and had so well versed himself in the writers he liked that he could rattle them off like favorite players on a baseball roster. He was staying inside to read more and more, and his parents were getting worried. But Jerry was gaining a much-needed confidence. *Amazing* was the most popular national magazine of its type, and Jerry, the kid writing in his basement, was having his letters published in it. The stories may not have been real, but something in the magazine was.

In the November 1929 issue of *Science Wonder Stories,* Jerry has another letter in "The Reader Speaks":

Mr. Gernsback, will you please answer this question (I notice that when you answer some letters you leave some of the most important questions unanswered), ARE YOU GOING TO HAVE A COVER CONTEST? I've been longing to have some science story magazine come along with one; as we readers would have a chance to number as contributors to the magazine we enjoy reading.

I have bought all the pamphlets that have thus appeared in the Science Fiction Library, and am impatiently awaiting the appearance of some more. I read all the stories immediately upon their arrival and it wasn't long before I had finished them and had nothing to read. So hurry up with some more, and this time put in a story by Ed Earl Repp.

Jerome Siegel,
10622 Kimberley Ave., Cleveland, O.[22]

Gernsback himself responds in the postscript:

Mr. Siegel will undoubtedly be glad to note that the present issue contains a cover contest. We are quick to respond to our readers' desires; sometimes before the desires are expressed. We confidently expect that this contest will reveal a great amount of new talent.
—Editor).[23]

Jerry read this and rushed to his typewriter. Hours later, he hit return, guided the roll bar back, and pulled out the page. He entered the heck out of that cover contest, probably under multiple names. He waited by the mailbox for months for the issue to come out. But he didn't win. He knew he had to get better.

Chapter 3

The Education of
Jerry Siegel

JERRY STOOD AT THE BOTTOM of the wooden stairs and stared at the giant double doors above him. All around him was towering brick overlaid with climbing ivy. Boys and girls his own age and older brushed by and over him like a scrubbed, knock-kneed wave. Students were already climbing in, with bags, with milk, and with hair as shiny as their shoes. The girls wore dresses and had short hairstyles that curled around their ears; some were even blond. Jerry adjusted his glasses. They had pretty sweaters. The stone arch above them did not move. He saw some football players with a big block letter *G* sewn into their red sweaters. The football team, the Tarblooders, known for the chant "Tar-Blood! Whack-Thud!,"[1] once drove all the way out to Vermilion, Ohio, in a pickup truck to stop a fire at the South West Fisheries. Jerry couldn't believe how big these people were. They had ties and jewelry and nicknames like Dewey and Chic. He sighed and pushed forward. He felt completely invisible.[2] Above the doors, letters spelled out his fate in stone: *Glenville High School.*

Located on the corner of Parkwood and Everton about four blocks from Jerry's house, Glenville High School was built in 1919 and claimed an entire city block. The halls were wide, and a huge American flag was draped over the ceiling inside the main entrance. Sunlight from the windows above the front doors filtered through the billowing white-and-red fabric. Their colors were red and black. Glenville students had good test scores, and some even went on to college. But for many of its students, of a population 90 percent Jewish, Glenville would be the last stop in their education, so they made it count.

Jerry was determined to make this walk across the threshold a fresh start. School for him had always been treacherous—he would later remember the tripping, shoving, and bullying he had gone through in primary school. These were the things he had learned more than any other combination of numbers or letters. They would stick with him for a long time.[3]

But Glenville High was different. It was filled with impossible hallways, rooms without numbers, a mysterious attic, and a principal who was ready to confiscate any valuable you owned. The faculty was tough but respected by the student body, which harbored a strong allegiance to their school. In addition to a full slate of classes, students were expected to join clubs as part of their daily schedule. Jerry knew them all from his siblings' yearbooks, filled with black-and-white photos of the Sports Club, Camera Club, Friendship Club, and others. The Chorus Club was so good that they traveled to Chicago and sang live on a local radio station. Their picture was in the paper, and it was full of smiling girls. Jerry would join it a year later. There were less traditional clubs as well, including a group that played Hollywood movies during lunchtime and the Esperanto Club, devoted to the strange new language. The Film Club even procured a motion picture camera to make a movie about Glenville. It was "shown to ninth graders," and its purpose was "to show them what a really swell school Glenville is."[4]

Glenville, for all its academic formality, also had a well-known tradition of humor. In 1930, when a power failure turned the school dark, *The Plain Dealer* reported that in the silent, alarmingly dark cafeteria, the first thing anyone heard was, "Get your finger out of my soup!"[5] This was humor as response to a darkening world. And at Glenville, it was particularly infectious.

There was one group in particular that Jerry had his eye on since before his first day at school. He would walk by room 114 just to steal a glance inside and hear the clicking of well-oiled typewriter keys. He stole glances at boys and girls with pencils behind their ears and engaging in ad hoc meetings around desks: it looked real, sounded important, and smelled like ink. This was where he wanted to be—the office of the school's weekly newspaper, *The Glenville Torch*.[6]

The Torch had been around as long as the school had and was a long-form, four-page folded newspaper that came out every Thursday. Students could even get subscriptions. *The Torch* won numerous state awards and was so respected that the Cleveland Public Library was a subscriber. *The Torch* even had its own *Style Guide,* a pocket-sized book that had to be studied by each incoming writer and editor. In addition to the usual rules of grammar and active voice, the style guide warns reporters of "errors of fact" and shouts at them to "BE ACCURATE."[7] But writers are also told to "get life and action into your story."[8]

As it happened, 1929 was a tumultuous year for *The Torch*—after losing its steady editor in chief, Lois Donaldson, and copyreader Maxine Kent, a *Torch* mainstay with her brunette bob and dark-lined mouth, *The Torch* got a little less formal, so much so that it was uniformly banned from study hall.[9] This just meant it was getting more popular. *The Torch* had a masthead of more than a dozen boys and girls and covered student events, class activities, and visiting speakers. The paper also continued to cover its embarrassing sports teams (Glenville at one point lost in basketball to Cathedral Latin with a blistering final score of 22–19). Jerry read every issue and started thinking about how he could get onto its pages. His classes were boring, his grades were not good, and girls didn't notice him. *The Torch* made personalities. It could make him.

But working his way up the ladder would take a lot of time, so Jerry focused on a quick and easy route, just like the one he was demanding of Hugo Gernsback in the pulps. He wanted a contest. He found it in the *Torch*'s literary annual, which shipped with the paper at the end of the year. Titled "The Reflector," this supplement was filled with stories and poems that students had submitted for prizes. Jerry brushed off a pulp story he had been working on and sneaked it into the *Torch* drop box. He walked away slowly, his heart pounding in his ears. The next days and weeks felt like glue. When "The Reflector" came out on May 29, 1930, at the end of a long first year at school, Jerry opened the paper and saw his name. He stopped in his tracks and read it again. He hadn't won a prize, but his story, "In the Happy Days to Come," was staring at him from a thin column on the right side of page two. He stood there in the hallway and read it.[10]

Jerry's story is set in the future; in it, a character named John Jones wakes up and summons Bojo, his robot butler, to give him a Synthetic Food-Pill, which substitutes all of his meals for the day. The story is not completely original. Elements such as the Food-Pill are taken directly from Gernsback's *Ralph 124C 41+*. The idolatry that science fiction inspired in its growing number of fans was resulting in a widespread appropriation of plots, images, and even names.

But Jerry boils it down to a dating game, which makes it much funnier. Jones asks Bojo if there has been "a phone call from Miss Miriam." Bojo responds: "She will not accept your proposal," to which Jones responds, "Hm—too bad! Any more calls?" "Yes, from Miss Selma. She too, will not accept your proposal." Jones, undeterred, presses the subject: "Did you tell her I love her?" He tells Bojo to visit her again and profess his love in earnest. Meanwhile, Jones has still not even gotten out of bed. Jones thinks to himself: "If Selma refuses, I've still got Alice, and if Alice refuses, I've still Betty, but if Betty refuses—I believe I'll have to order a female from the Robot Factory . . . a Robot is the only woman that will obey a man's wishes." "Exhausted," Jones "slipped the vibratory-quilt over him" and "was soon asleep and in a land inhabited by female Robots alone." It is signed, "—Jerome Siegel, 10B."[11]

So though Jerry has taken elements of Gernsback's story, he is laughing at it, too. John Jones has all of these amenities, but they result in him being lazy in bed and without any real companionship: girls, robot, or otherwise. Generations of steel-eyed fans of science fiction will say that science fiction is not funny, but when you look at some of the contraptions the pulps were depicting on their colorful covers, it's possible they were received with a humor that is lost to us. So though Jerry's story is teenage fantasy (he is going to "order" a girl from the legions he is allegedly on speaking terms with from the Robot Factory), Jones falls asleep utterly alone—girls are too smart to take him seriously. This was the self-deprecation that made Jerry's story accessible, even though it was obnoxious. This was, even at the very beginning, the mix of the meek with the amazing.

The *Torch* itself had always been a place to let off teenage steam. The second page was filled with inside jokes, gags, and terrible puns. This was never more apparent than in Jerry's time. And since the majority of the masthead was male, most of these jokes were all about girls and the apparent absence of them from most of the *Torch* staff's lives. Much of Jerry's early *Torch* writing is along the same lines: trying to impress girls, understand them, and eventually communicate with them, as if they were space aliens. But these aren't completely imaginary transmissions, though they are still somewhat desperate: the "Miriam" in the story was a real-life student.[12] Jerry's main focus was always the pulps, but since he kept encountering resistance there, he began adapting some of his stories for *The Torch,* often in satirical ways that expressed his frustration at not winning Gernsback's contests. The result was that he got a good writer's workout on how to write short, grabby stories. The pulps taught him to open his imagination, but *The Torch* was where he learned how to write.

NEXT STEP

In the next term, on October 12, 1930, *The Torch* once again found its way into the hands of Glenville students—some read it right away and others just shoved it into their bags. But Jerry got his issue and was careful not to bend or tear it. He slowly opened it and found two stories of his on the second page. He looked around the halls to see if others had noticed this incredible occurrence and were pointing at him with whispering grins. A few people were reading the paper, but they obviously had not made the connection yet.

The first story, about a detective named Stiletto Vance, is called "Foreign Ambassador Receives Loan from Gullible Detective," and it ends when Stiletto, "the great detective," lends a man a dime. Consequently, "Stiletto has never seen the ambassador since." On the same page is a fictional letter written by Jerry to someone named "Bernard J. Kenton," the editor of a fictional magazine called *Fantastic Fiction Magazine.* In this "letter," Jerry attempts to employ fuzzy math in order to trick editor Kenton into publishing his story. He pleads with the editor, "If you accept the enclosed story, one thousand words in length, I shall pay you twenty dollars." Jerry explains:

> *This is to the advantage of both of us,*
> *My advantage*
> *I have a story published and acquire a number of readers.*
> *Your advantage*
> *(a) I pay you $20 to publish my tale.*
> *(b) You save $20 by not paying for it.*
> *(c) You make $250 in proportion to the readers who peruse it.*
> *$20—I pay you.*
> *$20—You save.*
> *$150—You make.*
> *$190—Sum.*

So you see it will be in your interest to accept the enclosed story and
check.
I hope to hear from you soon.

Sincerely,
Jerome Siegel[13]

The name "Kenton" sounds very much like the mysterious writer
Jerry mentions in the earlier letter to *Amazing Stories,* where he claims
that a "Bernard Kantor" has lots of good stories to send in. The name is
usually agreed to be an alias of Siegel himself, which was a popular practice of pulp writers of the time.[14] Jerry just could not understand: if his
story would help them sell issues (which he knew it would), then why
wouldn't they just buy and publish it? *The Torch* probably ran the piece
because of its semi-clever math puzzle, but Jerry was really working out
his ongoing writing frustrations.

A week later, a skinny column on page two entitled "Professor Sights
Stupefying Vision" tells the story of a Professor I. M. Blank and his four
assistants who look into a long telescope trained on faraway Mars.[15] The
Professor looks into the viewfinder and jumps, saying, "I saw a man!"
Somehow, the tiny man at the end of the telescope begins speaking to the
Professor—and it turns out his name is Sam and he is from New York.
The Professor finally realizes that Sam is actually working *inside* the tele-
scope to fix it and is not on Mars at all. It is a funny twist but has a grim
ending: "A half an hour later the news came to the world that the dead
bodies of two men had been found floating down the Hudson . . . Samuel
Brown and Eugene Iden, assistant to Professor Blank." The story is
signed, "Jerome Siegel."[16]

For a school with such a large Jewish population, *The Torch* made a
big deal of Christmas. Part of this was the general culture of the time.
During the Depression, Christmas became more popular than ever; people didn't have money, but there was free hope and cheer to spare. Nowhere was this more evident than Cleveland, where the annual Christmas
Charity Drive was always successful, though many of its contributors
could probably have used some charity themselves. At Glenville High,
Christmas also signaled the welcome prospect of winter break. The last
issue before the vacation had a big picture of some elvish squires being
towed on a log with a script, "Greetings from Ye *Torch.*" This issue, only
a week before Christmas, also revealed on the front page: FOUR STUDENTS

WIN MENTION IN CONTEST. Aaron Pailes won this holiday story contest for "A Question of Ethics," followed by honorable mentions to "Sacrifice" by Edward Diamant, "Brothers" by Estelle Krauss, and "The Yuletide Spirit" by Jerome Siegel. Jerry's story was not published, and though he was proud to be mentioned (and frustrated not to have won), he may have hid the news from his Orthodox Jewish parents when he went home that night.[17] For Jerry, writing and school were rapidly becoming two different lives.

STILETTO VANCE, P.I.

The Siegels moved to Glenville not only because of the lure of the quiet suburbs but because of the increase in crime in downtown Cleveland. Even a quick glance at the newspapers in Cleveland at the time reveals that every day had some kind of front-page account of a storekeeper being held up or murdered. Socialite deaths, mysterious disappearances, and automobile accidents—unintentional and not—were splashed all over the papers like ink-black blood.

Crime stories were weirdly popular in Cleveland, just as they were across the country. Maybe it was the fascination with people who were getting rich by being bad, but people wanted to read about crime in newspapers and in fiction and to see it on the movie screen, in glorious shoot-'em-ups such as *The Racket* (1928), *Public Enemy* (1931), and *Little Caesar* (1931).[18] For as much as crime tragically touched the lives of many citizens in the form of escalating murder rates and robberies, people still seemed to almost revel in this strange, dramatic underworld of evil. People may have felt a need to understand it, solve it, or just romanticize it to take away its sting. Jerry was no exception and fiercely read about crime and detection in magazines such as *Black Mask, Detective Fiction Weekly, Detective Story Magazine,* and *The Phantom Detective.* The covers often had blue cops, dark detectives, and women in bright red dresses with impossible legs. There was poison and gunfire and madmen from the Orient on every page. Jerry liked the detective stories because they offered a special kind of challenge compared to the space opera of science fiction. Detective stories offered a different level of interaction, as they gave you a chance to actually solve a mystery before the main character did. Jerry enjoyed the thought of matching wits with these famous authors.

At home, Jerry would pretend his room was his office and that prospective clients would walk in, eager for him to take their cases. So even though it was just his mom gathering laundry or Leo taking back a stolen shirt, Jerry could imagine other possibilities. He even considered placing an ad in the paper offering his services as a private eye, but he thought about what his mother might say. So he just bought more magazines instead.

Sitting in his room, with few friends, Jerry desperately wanted a new identity. So he slowly wrote himself one. He justified it by imagining that a pen name would help him get more stories accepted in *The Torch*. Pulp writers used false names, so Jerry did, too. His fictional detective in *The Torch,* Stiletto Vance, was the first secret identity he used with abandon. Stiletto was named after Philo Vance, the foppish detective star in a series of books (and a later newspaper comic strip) by S. S. Van Dine, which was a pseudonym of Willard Huntington Wright.[19] In early *Torch* references, Vance is given the first name "Phyla" or "Phulla" so the readers know he is indeed "full of" it. The origin of "Stiletto" is harder to pin down but is probably just an indication of the character's sharp and skewering satirical nature. Van Dine himself remains known among would-be writers for his infamous "twenty rules" of detective fiction, which appeared in print in 1928, where he instructs: "The detective story is a kind of intellectual game. It is more—it is a sporting event. And for the writing of detective stories there are very definite laws—unwritten, perhaps, but none the less binding; and every respectable and self-respecting concocter of literary mysteries lives up to them."[20]

Van Dine's rules are similar in tone to Seck's rules of fair play: Readers must have "equal opportunity" to solve the mystery, the author can use no "willful tricks or deceptions," and, unfortunately, there must "be no love interest"—the mystery itself always takes precedence. Scientific means toward a solution are permissible, but as Van Dine notes, "Once an author soars into the realm of fantasy, in the Jules Verne manner, he is outside the bounds of detective fiction, cavorting in the uncharted reaches of adventure."[21]

Stiletto would appear, on and off, for the rest of Jerry's *Torch* career. On December 11, 1930, another Stiletto yarn made it into *The Torch,* with the outlandishly alliterative title "Renowned Defective Detective Deducts Deductions," underneath which the solution (in direct opposition to Van Dine's rules) is given away: "Stiletto Vance Solves Baffling Crime Not Yet Committed by Shooting to Kill."[22] He appears again on March 5, 1931, when Stiletto makes up his mind between practicing detective work and writing poetry in "Vance Deserts Crime for Literary Contests."

This longer story is mostly dialogue between Vance and his Watsonesque narrator, who this time is explicitly named "Jerry." In the story, Vance finds a sheet of paper and tosses it over to Jerry. "Read it," he says.

> *Miriam, Miriam,*
> *As you circle mile after mile,*
> *Stopping not to even smile,*
> *You drive me to delirium,*
> *As you swim by in your aquarium.*[23]

"Jerry" retorts cluelessly: "'I returned it to Stiletto.' 'What does it mean?' 'If I could answer that,' he replied, 'I'd win forty cents!'" His response: "Mere mention of that fabulous sum left me cold."[24]

"Miriam," who also appeared in the early story about robot wives, was clearly the name of a girl who had caught Jerry's eye at school. Vance and "Jerry" analyze the poem:

> Miriam neither smiles at the writer nor stops to talk to him. The second last line: This, too, can be taken as it is. Miriam provokes the writer into unheard of emotions. Bewilders him. Tortures him. And now for the last line: Miriam is not a fish, as you might suppose at first thought. No. She is different— outstanding. She is alone in her glory. None can compare with her. She is continually passing through the writer's mind.[25]

It is the oldest high school story in the universe.

The Vance stories continued to roll out with regularity—*The Torch* had never, like it or not, seen so much of a recurring character. Stiletto was becoming a serial adventurer, like Dick Tracy. But having abandoned fair play in using his writing to try to get a girl to notice him, Jerry had to turn to other sources for story ideas. On March 12, 1931, the story "Vance's Breath-o-Scope Solves Mystery Puzzle" is given a first honest byline, "By Jerome Siegel," and begins with serious drama: "It was a problem fit for a master mind! On the floor lay the inert body, utterly devoid of life." Stiletto kneels besides the body and explains how he will solve it: "The Breath-o-scope! He explained." The "Breath-o-scope" indeed determines that the person on the floor is not dead at all, but merely passed-out drunk.[26]

"Detective Tries Composing" on April 30, 1931, concerns another poem that Vance and Jerry attempt to decipher. The poem is titled "Recalling" and is about "a little boy, a little girl, some golden locks, a wavy curl," and their idyllic time together as childhood playmates. Jerry moans at the poem's syrupy nature, but then, of course, "A shot rang out!" and poetry turns to action. Vance's detective nose literally sniffs out the gunshot next door. They find "a woman slumped in a chair." They find a note that reads: "I can't stand the unbearable ravings of the poor creature next door any longer. Sincerely, Ruth Kaltenborn."[27] Jerry was building a meek, mild-mannered, helplessly-in-love persona whom women didn't like. But readers did—they couldn't help it.

On November 19, 1931, in "Two *Torch* Sleuths Murdered but Only Dead from Neck Up," Jerry takes the final step:

> Two distinguished sleuths of the *Torch* agency lay smeared upon the floor of Murder Room 114 (pictures on page 5). The extinguished bodies of Phulla Vance and Izzy Murphy. . . . In slithered Jerry Siegel, tripping daintily over rifles, toy cannons, stacks of daggers and such. Izzy Murphy (another *Torch* false detective, named after the movie character) and Vance are dead, but instead of being alarmed, Jerry starts playing solitaire until the ambulance rolls up and the medic shouts "Say aren't those guys dead?" Inspector Siegel turned ponderously, "Sure— from the neck up!"[28]

Jerry finally moves from narrator to becoming the main character; in his story, he had become the hero.

OFFICIAL

As Stiletto Vance continued to appear throughout the year, Jerry was feeling proud of himself. He was placing articles with regularity and was referring to himself (in his head, at least) as a *Torch* man. No longer did he have to slow down as he passed the office to casually steal a glance inside; he could just turn and stroll right in, eager to get going on this week's copy. He attended story meetings, stayed late after school, and even made some friends. School was less scary and he was happier; he felt less invisible. Jerry's importance to *The Torch* became official on February 19, 1931, when his name finally made the masthead.[29] He was overjoyed because he thought the girls read the fine type like a social register to find out who the up-and-coming boys were. They did not.

Still, 1931 was an interesting year at Glenville. On February 26, the whole school was visited by Televox, an honest-to-goodness robot from Pittsburgh whose boxy demeanor wowed the crowd with glowing eyes and an awkwardly moving arm that could turn the lights on and off. Televox, eight feet tall, also had a beating heart.[30] On May 12, the eerie spiritualist Ralph Emerson Powell visited Glenville and tried to pierce the veil between this world and the next through incantations and crystal ball gazing.[31] With the lights turned off, the students at Glenville were clutching the sides of their chairs.

In the beginning of 1931, Jerry placed another published letter outside of *The Torch,* this time in the "Reader's Corner" section of the January 1931 issue of *Astounding Stories of Super-Science:*

> *Dear Editor:*
> *Continue up to your present standard and you'll continue to stand*
> *above all other Science Fiction magazines where stories of super-*
> *science are concerned, now and forever,—Jerome Siegel, 10622*
> *Kimberley Ave, Cleveland, Ohio.*[32]

Jerry wrote now with far more confidence, though he still tended to flatter. He was writing to some of the other letter writers, too. He was becoming more of a professional. He was looking in the mirror and seeing what to change.

On May 28, 1931, Jerry and a couple of his *Torch* pals worked up a satire of the paper called *The Glenville Porch.* Their hope was to get it printed in full, but they had to settle for a portion of page two in the regular weekly issue. The *Porch* featured such stories as "One and a Quarter Seniors Jump into Lake Erie" (the last one only dipped their toenails in). In the left-hand corner, under the headline "Bulumni," the writer (probably Jerry) relates that "having lost his meal-ticket, Bernard Kenton has decided to stow away to Honolulu unless he consumes a dinner by next month." The writer berates his readers: "Come on, Glenvillites! Some of you will have to invite him over to the house. Send your address to me and I'll bring him over. He's cross-eyed, bow-legged, pigeon-toed and wheezes, but he's good company, girls."[33]

On the same day, another poem by Stiletto Vance appears in the "Blow Torch" section:

> *Every day I ask her,*
> *If she'd like to go*
> *Driving in an auto,*
> *Or to a show.*
>
> *Every time she answers,*
> *"You know I wouldn't go,"*
> *That just makes me feel good,*
> *For I haven't any "dough."*
> *—Stiletto Vance*[34]

Monetary issues were clearly on Jerry's mind. But was he really so unhappy that he had to have two alternate personas floating around the *Torch* office at once—Stiletto, the romantic detective poet, and Kenton, the frustrated science fiction writer?

The aliases existed for an important reason. There was more at stake here than publication. On March 5, 1931, yet another poem is printed:

> *Attention "M"*
>
> *He was asked to read his essay*
> *In English, the other day,*
> *And he read it to his lassie,*
> *Who turned her nose away.*
>
> *Now he's gone and burned the essay,*
> *And he often rues the day,*
> *When he read it to his lassie,*
> *Who no longer looks his way.*
> *—Stiletto J. S. Vance*[35]

Whether this sad classroom moment happened or not, the pain felt by the teenage writer is real. Jerry has given enough clues to his readers that we—and she—know by now that "M" is Miriam. But it seems painful enough to be real, so Jerry just gives up and shoehorns his initials into

Stiletto's middle name to finally announce his identity. Not that it mattered.

Jerry was cranking out *Torch* copy as if it were a full-time job. His grades suffered, but he didn't care. He started referring to room 114 as "the office." These were children playing a grown-up game. But they were very, very good at it. The room was filled with boys who would become heavy hitters: Willie Gilbert would write for *The Howdy Doody Show* and would pen the Broadway hit *How to Succeed in Business Without Really Trying*. Seymour Heller would become Liberace's business manager. Charlotte Plimmer would go on to be the editor of *Seventeen*. Hal Leibowitz would cover Cleveland sports for decades.[36]

After the winter holiday dawned on a cold and snowy 1932, Jerry's grades were so bad that he was kicked off the masthead, though he was still allowed to write. At this point, frankly, they couldn't do it without him. At this time, the main *Torch* bigwig was Jerome Schwartz, who wrote the "Spices and Cinnamon" column and would go on to Ohio State University and eventually co-write a string of massive theatrical successes (as Jerome Lawrence), including *Inherit the Wind*. Schwartz scored a *Torch* interview with Milt Gross, the famous cartoonist of *Banana Oil, Pete the Pooch, Count Screwloose from Tooloose, Draw Your Own Conclusion,* and *That's My Pop!* among many, many others. In their interview, Gross says: "Most authors, cartoonists and other prodigies make a mistake by associating with a bunch of old fogies who have set ideas, while it's the younger generation they should be heeding. The kids have new inspirations and far more modern ideas that the genius can very easily put into scribbling."[37]

Jerry hated the newsstand magazines for rejecting him, so he repaid them in a bit of rebellious humor. But he was shy, so he hid behind false, imagined personas that were so flimsy, they were barely a mask. Jerry Siegel had entered high school as a nervous proto-nerd, but within a year, he was writing stories for the paper on almost a weekly basis. The boost to his self-confidence was stratospheric. Then optimistic Jerry Siegel met quiet Joe Shuster. And things began to jump.

Chapter 4

How to Meet Your Best Friend

THE SHUSTERS MOVED TO GLENVILLE IN 1929 when Julius lost his job at the Richman Brothers factory.[1] They first lived in apartment #5 in the Doan building at 10527 Morison Avenue in Glenville.[2] Soon after, they moved to apartment #6 at 10905 Amor Avenue, where they paid $20 a month in rent, which was less.[3] It was a square brick building with pillars right down the middle, splitting it into two fairly equal sides. The building sat right up off the street, separated only by a thin sidewalk on the corner of Amor and Parkwood. Heavy trees obscured the windows in summer and helped to provide much-needed shade. But in the winter, it was shivering cold and looked like a giant block that was holding the street down. The apartment had a burning stove that didn't always have coal, and there was no radio. They did have a Victrola, through which Joe would develop his lifelong love of music. He and his mother listened to orchestras and love songs.[4] But money and rent were always an issue, as they were for many in the neighborhood.

When Julius lost his job in 1929, the family had to take charity for a while before he picked up hours as an elevator operator at Mount Sinai Hospital for $18 a week.[5] He would flash the Shuster smile to everyone, roll the cage, press a button, and soar straight into the air. Joe would come and ride it sometimes, feeling his stomach lift and his feet fall. His father was lucky to have work. Joe watched him come home tired but always happy to be there. And so Joe grew up, if not taller, then more aware. And he kept watching, reading, and drawing.

Once the Shusters moved, Joe was bundled into his wool suits and sent to Glenville High School with wide eyes held in check by his impenetrable glasses and shy personality. He knew he was short, but not by how much until high school.[6] But he wasn't afraid. Like Jerry, he found his own niches within the larger jigsaw puzzle of athletes and brainiacs. Within a year, in *The Torch,* it was announced that Joe Shuster was elected president of the school's new Art Club, which would meet at various members' homes. Joe also played sports, including tumbling and gymnastics.[7] Like Jerry, he was a go-getter, but not in a way that drew attention. Though less verbal, less hyperbolic, Joe was a very hard worker—he would dip his head into whatever he was doing and get it done right.

Jerry Fine's introduction helped break the ice once Joe got to Glenville.[8] Joe Shuster and Jerry Siegel were alphabetized together and saw each other in the same places. They would talk about science fiction, but they were not creating Superman. Not yet. Eventually, Jerry showed him the letters he had published. And Joe showed him his drawings. As Jerry would say many years later, "When Joe and I first met, it was like the right chemicals coming together."[9] Science fiction fans, comic readers, any devotees of a secret medium of imaginary escape, have always been astonished by the fact that there are others like them out there. Each boy saw himself in the other, like looking in a mirror.

The pulps cemented their friendship. For the first time, Jerry didn't have to write letters to a faceless cross-country name to talk about his magazines because Joe was reading them, too. Joe, like Jerry, especially loved the science fiction titles. In the beginning, they would go to Joe's after school and read these magazines in half-silence. Because they were boys, they understood everything in glances. Jerry was the talker, so he would go on about something, moving his arms around, and Joe would nod. Joe's favorite science fiction artist was Frank Paul, an Austrian immigrant whom Hugo Gernsback discovered and put to work, having him do countless pulp covers, most of them for *Amazing Stories* or *Wonder Stories.* Paul specialized in the technology of the massive: big, soaring ships and rockets over stretched-out alien landscapes. Joe would trace and mimic Paul's work as if it were a holy manuscript. One of the earliest drawings Joe kept, from 1931, is of a ship-laden sky in the Paul style featuring all manner of blimps, rocket ships, and buildings. Joe traced some and designed others and, before signing it, titled it all the "World in Future, 1980." Jerry, who was not an artist himself, saw this picture and froze. All the best pulp stories always started with a big black-and-white illustration.

Jerry had the words. And he had just met the pictures.

In the early 1930s, in a scary school, these boys became best friends over recognition of some kind of weird future they were only beginning to imagine.

BACKSTAGE

In the fall of 1931, Jerry received his own column in *The Torch*. This column, "Backstage," appeared weekly in the right-bottom corner of page two and was designed to report on the goings-on of the school's Drama Club. Blessed with a brand-new auditorium, the Drama Club produced plays like *The Bat, The First Dress Suit, The Man Who Died at 12 o'Clock, The Wedding, The Valiant, Decision at Dawn,* and *The Only Way,* among many others. These were mostly contemporary plays: *The Valiant* was about James Dyke, a death row murderer who maintains a secret identity for the good of those around him. *The Bat* was an adaptation of a mystery novel by Mary Roberts Rinehart titled *The Circular Staircase* and was the inspiration for film adaptations in 1926 and 1930. Someone, possibly Joe, created an eerie poster for the production with the main villain's signature image of a bat.[10]

Jerry sat in the back during rehearsals, which occurred every day during fifth period. He sat there with his notebook and his feet on the headrest in front of him, but only if Mr. Davies was looking the other way. Jerry watched student actors block out scenes onstage and sketched notes absentmindedly. At the back of the stage, he saw Joe, white shirtsleeves up, putting a touch of paint on some scenery. The wooden planks on the stage creaked as the actors moved from right to left. The red curtain folded in on itself slowly as people moved through it. Jerry's columns began as expected with facts and pleas to come see shows; apparently even the faculty did not regularly attend. Under Jerry's pen, the column became something like a high school Walter Winchell column, instigating gossip and breaking news of behind-the-scenes hookups that no one really cared about, except Jerry, who made a point to single out the work of the set makers: "You come up against their work every time a play is presented. . . . They are the artists and designers. Joe Shuster, Bernard Schmittke, and George Shoen are their names."[11]

JUNGLE ACTION

Finally home after another long day at school, Jerry rushed through the front door, leaving the key in the door. He clicked on the radio and turned the heavy dial to WTAM 1070. With no musical fanfare or outrageous announcer, a deep baritone voice rolled through the air after an almost painful pause: "Tarzan of the Apes, the character of Edgar Rice Burroughs' famous books." The voice was followed by the roar of a lion that seemed as close as the next room.

Edgar Rice Burroughs was another writer Jerry idolized. Burroughs got his start in the pulp magazine *Argosy,* which Jerry championed in one of his early pulp letters. Jerry was introduced to Tarzan, King of the Jungle, via books, newspaper comics, and movies. By 1932, when Tarzan began appearing on daily fifteen-minute radio shows, Jerry was already hooked. The story of an infant son of an English aristocrat being raised by apes in deepest Africa touched several nerves in America, most notably for Depression audiences—the story of how a man with nothing could rise through his own devices to rule the most primitive, dangerous environment imaginable had a welcome audience. Tarzan was Roosevelt in a loincloth.[12] In the newspaper comics, he jumped from panel to panel and landed like a jungle cat. He crouched, climbed, and pulled. His leopard-skin costume signified his powers but also showcased his jungle muscles. In the third episode of the original radio serial, which first aired on September 14, 1932, the young Tarzan is even described as a "super-man!"[13]

But Jerry's favorite Burroughs story didn't take place in Africa. It took place much farther away but still close enough to see. On clear spring nights, Jerry would look up and search for it as a single flickering dot in the east: Mars. Edgar Rice Burroughs's 1917 novel, *A Princess of Mars,*

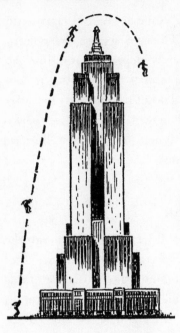

which was first serialized in *The All-Story* starting in February 1912, had a mesmerizing hold over Jerry. In the story, John Carter, a captain in the Virginia Army, is transported through bizarre means to the red planet of Mars. Known to its inhabitants as Barsoom, Carter (and the reader) enters a surreal world of tharks, thoats, calots, banths, and savage white apes. At the center of the narrative is, of course, a girl: Dejah Thoris, the gorgeous princess of Helium, who in true pulp fashion fights most of her adventures naked. Because of the lesser Martian gravity, Carter is able to leap thirty feet into the air, making him an ideal, albeit alien, superpowered hero.[14]

This kind of gravitational fantasy was explored in the early scientific magazines as well.

But it was the weight of the story itself that got Jerry: the planet was in turmoil and Carter was the only one who could save his weird, adopted world. Carter's ongoing adventures, and subsequent parallel books about Venus, were huge favorites in the young-man science fiction community.[15] Jerry adored them.[16]

Jerry was so entranced by romantic Barsoom that he read everything he could about Burroughs himself, who was described in the press as a "super-creature with a brain like Darwin's, a body like Tunney's, and [who] doesn't drink but now and again enjoys a pipe."[17] Burroughs was so successful that he had a sprawling California estate named Tarzana; ten million copies of his books had been published in sixteen different languages.[18] In addition to the thrill of adventure, Jerry saw dollar signs and fame. Burroughs "keeps on working . . . he never lets anything interfere with his daily routine of writing new and more fascinating stories. . . . And the long list of his innumerable friends throughout the world continues to grow."[19] These were the things Jerry desperately wanted.

Jerry's imagined relationship with Miriam through the persona of Stiletto also echoed the Tarzan tales. Though Tarzan is first and foremost an ape-man who successfully woos Jane, the brunette, adventuresome wonder-girl, he also is a secret English aristocrat by birth. It is a three-way love triangle between Jane, the powerful ape-man, and the lost, aristocratic nature of his birth. Tarzan is manners and etiquette versus brute supernatural strength and heroics. Jerry enjoyed these themes and constantly tried to copy them in his own writing.

Jerry's first stab at a Tarzan character was in *The Torch*. On May 7, 1931, Goober the Mighty (named after the 1928 Tarzan film) made his debut. Goober, a Tarzan-like ape-man (the son of a lion named "Oolala"), is massive, strong, but altogether dim. "If I take breathing exercises one hundred times a day for one hundred years," he informs himself, "I'll have the greatest chest in existence!" But Goober is not Tarzan. Like Stiletto, he is a satire. For one, the teenage Jerry tags him with a racist name for whites, emphasizing the giggle factor of his teenage readership. His "mother" then proceeds to bite a piece out of his leg.[20]

Goober, Son of the Lion, flexes his muscles and smiles. "By Jove!" he mutters presciently, "one year from now I'll be the strongest man on earth!" He is right. "He shouted at the top of his voice, as, in a fit of superhuman energy, he snapped a twig between two great hands."

> Except for a dislocated hip, a broken arm, fallen arches, a twisted arm and a missing ear, he was the model of physical perfection.
>
> Suddenly he stopped.
>
> He had seen a girl!
>
> He waltzed up to her. "Ever hear of me, kid?" he asked. "I'm Goober, the apeman! Raised by the lions, I was. I ate up Boop-boop-a-doop, the leader of the lion pack, when I was two months old. That's how I got the scar on my—oh, pardon me."[21]

Goober steps on the girl's foot, but it feels cold . . . because she is a statue, which he proceeds to lift up and break. Girls are not only always cold to him, he has no idea how to handle them.

On October 1, 1931, "Goober, the Mighty, Returns to Page with Breath-Taking Story of Battle in Jungle." In this installment, Goober engages in the requisite Tarzan wildlife battle as he takes on an alligator and ape, named Looneyjack and Izzy. It gets weird(er) when Oolala the lion, Goober's foster-mother, appears. She asks him to "stop playing for a few minutes" and Goober gets mad: "Listen, mama," warned the ape-man.

"You'd better beat it before you stir me up. I've often thought you'd make a good fur-coat. And I feel a growing temptation to skin you, stealing over me. How'd you like to go to a cabaret?"[22] Tarzan never talked to his mother like that. But Jerry, as a teenager, may have wanted to.[23]

Goober was the first Jerry Siegel *Torch* story with a real illustration: a lion chasing an exaggerated black-skinned, white-eyed depiction of an African native. The pedigree of the drawing is really hard to discern; it is signed only with a horizontal line. Maybe the artist knew that even in 1931 the picture might raise a few eyebrows. But the swirling ball at the end of the signature might give away who drew it.

SUMMERTIME

After they collaborated on Goober, Jerry thought he and Joe should do more: the "constant work" that Burroughs advised. He wanted to try comics. Like Joe, Jerry loved the comics page. For one, it was not the tiny, microscopic pasture it is today; *The Plain Dealer* ran a full two pages, six days a week. And on Sundays, the comics page was transformed into a broad wonderland of *Thimble Theatre, Flash Gordon,* and *Buck Rogers.* The section would sometimes take a whole day to savor. All of the adventure comic strips were in full cliff-hanging swing—even *Dick Tracy* and the most dramatic strip going, *Little Orphan Annie,* were eagerly awaited every day by readers of all ages.

What really pushed Jerry in this direction was an article about comics called "The Funny Papers" that he read in *Fortune* magazine. The article begins with the shocking fact that "some twenty comic-strip headliners are paid at least $1,000 a week."[24] The article describes in detail how syndicates such as the Chicago Tribune and even Cleveland's Newspaper

Enterprise Association (NEA) worked *for* writers and artists to put their strips into hundreds of papers. According to the article, this "is how the strips get into Big Money." So much so that "the headliners usually get 50 per cent of the gross income."[25] The article's instructions are adamant: "You had better devote your spare time to devising a characters and a strip of your own. And—perhaps in one year, perhaps in ten—some syndicate may decide to give it a trial."[26] Other articles promised even more: "The 'funnies' you read every day bring $8,000,000 a year to a small group of 200 cartoonists."[27] Jerry's pulse rose as he continued. This was something he could at least do a portion of. As the article promised, it was "practically depression proof." As far as artists go, "In many cases they were not artists at all, but just fellows with a knack for sketching who thought of a good idea or a funny character that 'made a hit' with an editor and eventually with newspaper readers." Jerry's pulp ideas were crumbling as fast as the cheap paper they were printed on. He could feel the space between the change in his pocket. The article promised, "If you've got something unique, the publisher will ask you to make it a daily feature. If it goes over big as a daily feature, it will get abroad that you are producing something worthy of national recognition. . . . This is what is called in the craft as being on 'Easy Street.' You sit in your studio and turn out your copy, send it."[28] Jerry had no money, hated working at a clothing store, and knew he wasn't going to college. He had to think big. Sitting in a studio, writing and sending things off for someone else to do the hard stuff? That sounded good.

The first comic Jerry and Joe started on was very much *Buck Rogers* in taste—they called it *Interplanetary Police,* and it involved gadgets, space, and uniforms.[29] *Buck* began as a pulp story in 1928 in *Amazing Stories* and hit the newspaper comics section in 1929.[30] The story by Phillip Frances Nowlan was about a World War I vet who walks into a coal mine and falls into suspended animation until 2419. He wakes in the middle of a science fiction war with jet packs and meets a rebel woman in a sleek helmet and form-fitting bodysuit. What really sent them over about *Buck* was the mention of their hometown, Cleveland, which was marked by the Mongol enemies for attack in the first few weeks of the strip. Jerry and Joe liked that sense of reality because it gave them a feeling of doom.

But not much was accomplished, not yet. Joe went to Canada to visit with his cousin Frank for most of the summer. Jerry had to go to summer school, which was awful.[31] But otherwise, he was mostly alone. He saw movies and took trips to the library. He went to the Fox and Freeze on 105th as well as Mike's Magazines, Novelties, and School Supplies. There was also the Uptown Drug Store on the corner of 105th and St. Clair. He bought and read everything he could afford and worked on his weird stories.

As the summer began to close, Jerry placed his second letter of the year in *Astounding Stories,* in August 1931. He again mentions Bernard J. Kenton.

> *Dear Editor:*
> *The month's issue, May, has the best collection of letters you've ever published. All it lacked was a letter from Bernard J. Kenton, that master of epistles and super-science stories. One of your readers would like to have "The Reader's Corner" omitted. For heaven's sake, don't take it out! I recognize it as one of the best features of our mag, and whenever I open the covers, turn to it directly after having glimpsed the table of contents and the announcement of the stories to appear in the forthcoming issue. I'm glad to see that Starzl is coming back with the next issue. More from him, please. And Hamilton and Williamson should appear more frequently, too.[32] A question Mr. Cummings. . . . —why must you always have a deformed character in your stories? Do they appeal to your dramatic sense?*
>
> *The news that we're going to have a story from Francis Flagg brings raptures of delight to my homely face. If it's a dimensional story, I'll cheer twice. When it comes to writing that kind of a story, Flagg's the king of them all. For sheer interest and originality, he's got his contemporaries in that field outdistanced with a distance that can only be counted by light-years. All our magazine needs is a story about time crusaders, or a planet of mechanical men.*
>
> *The best story you ever published? Who am I to answer? Why not put it up to the Readers for popular vote?—Jerome Siegel, 10600 Kimberly Ave., Cleveland, Ohio.[33]*

Jerry was smart; he was cannily placing his name alongside the big names of science fiction in an effort to associate himself with them. It was half dreaming and half self-promotion.

But school started again, and the routine of classes, dreaming of girls, and trying to write made the months fly. Once fall came, it was Joe who would make the real news. On November 25, 1931, in *The Torch:*

NOTED SENIOR ARTIST WINS CARTOON CONTEST

Displaying once again his proficiency in the field of art, Joe Shuster, homeroom 215, has received the honor of having his Thanksgiving cartoon appear in *The Torch*. Joe assisted in the designing of the stage settings used in the play "Once in a Life-time." Also, in collaboration with Jerome Siegel, room 221, Joe is trying to have a cartoon nationally syndicated. Both of the aforementioned students are seniors.

Jerry may have written the piece (and thus wedged his own name in), but this was Joe's show, free from any sort of alias or secret identity. Joe's winning cartoon is a depiction of that most perfect of days: the Wednesday before Thanksgiving. Not only is there a meal to look forward to, but there is the warm promise of the nearby holidays and time off from the classroom. Joe's cartoon is simple and direct: it shows a hungry kid with silverware at the ready, watching an Oliver Hardy look-alike strut in with a perfect turkey bursting off the page. The lines are simple, but in exact cooperation with one another. People saw it and knew exactly what it felt like, even though many of them wouldn't have a turkey that big for their own holidays, if they had one at all.

Annual Turkey Feast Arrives

TURNING POINT

As the calendar flipped over, the group of boys running the paper became a bunch of Hollywood watchers. On March 10, 1932, the editors revealed their "Ideal High School Faculty" as consisting of "Four Marx Bros, Walter Winchell, Philo Vance, Fu Manchu, Andy Volstead and Emmie Schmaltz."[34] Jerry knew he had an opportunity to submit something good.

His other columns and stories were getting a little old. On May 26, 1932, Jerry imploded the whole point of a news column about the Drama Club by interviewing himself: "Is this the last Backstage?" he typed. "Yes." "Why did you decide to write this column?" "Because I could mention myself favorably since no one else cared to." "Did you have any trouble securing material?" "No, but I did have some trouble getting it printed." "What was your greatest pleasure?" "Writing Backstage." "Your greatest hate?" "Writing Backstage."[35]

Jerry did appear in other people's stories, but not enough for him. In the April 21, 1932, column "Impossible to See," the author lists "Jerry Siegel and Adolf Hitler engaging in a wild game of pinochle."[36] This coincided with Hitler's shockingly high showing in the German presidential election; though he lost, it felt like the beginning of something bad. In the same issue is the announcement "Eighteen-year-old former Glenvillite, Bernard J. Kenton, has sold a novelette, 'Miracles on Antares,' to *Amazing Stories,* popular pseudo–scientific fiction magazine."[37] Did Jerry, using his favorite pseudonym, finally sell a story to his beloved *Amazing*? And if he did, why didn't he take credit for it?

Jerry was getting tired of Stiletto's antics and wanted to write a real detective story. On January 14, 1932, he got his most ambitious story published during his time at Glenville. With the macabre title "Five Men and a Corpse," this was a true pulp detective story, complete with a single black-and-white illustration. It ran in the end-of-year "Reflector" supplement. The drawing, by Bernie Schmittke, shows a man facedown on a table as the other men at the table look on in alarm.[38]

Bernie was a little older than Jerry and Joe, and because he won almost every art prize at Glenville, he was a great source of inspiration for Joe.

"MEN" HE SAID SLOWLY, "HE IS--DEAD!"

Bernie won a statewide contest sponsored by Ohio State University and *The Sun Dial,* the school's humor mag. In World War II, he would go on to draw logos on the flanks of the 322nd Bomber Squadron planes that pounded Germany. He would also create the famous profile caricature of Jerry Lewis that would be used as his official logo for decades—though Lewis only once gave Bernie credit for it.[39]

Jerry's plot for "Five Men" is sparked to life by a magnificent, Poe-like first sentence: "For the last half hour the conviction that one of the learned men seated around the table was insane had been steadily growing upon me." The narrator, Wheeler the astronomer, is determined to find out who the madman is: is it Lewisson the chemist, Brandon the physicist, or Gardner the botanist? The men speak of manly, pulpy things:

> "Tell me, what do you think about all this bosh concerning a supposed message from the planet Mars? I actually believe it is not a fraud, in fact"—Suddenly I stopped speaking and stared forward, horrified. Considine, who sat directly before me, had gasped convulsively, then slumped forward on the table. "What's wrong? Come out of it!" Vincent protested. "Certainly you don't believe that one of us—why this is outrageous! What could one possibly gain by killing poor Considine?"[40]

Jerry presents a classic locked-room mystery: everything the reader needs to solve the mystery is present within the room (and story) before them. Everyone accuses each other, and it turns out that several of the men hold grudges against Considine. Others owe him money, and even the narrator is asked if his hands were on the table: "I suppose I killed him by mind power, I said sarcastically." But then Lewisson starts screaming and points at Considine: "Sitting upright and watching us with an amused smile was—Considine."

> I called you all here to give a demonstration of suspended animation with the use of my specially prepared pills. I was apparently dead for half an hour. I heard every word you gentlemen uttered. Your speech was quite interesting, psychologically speaking; yes, it was quite interesting.
>
> —Jerome Siegel, 11A[41]

Considine was a real Glenvillite who would go on to be the head of the Student Council. But there are other forces at play here. As Jerry was dropped and then re-signed to the *Torch* masthead, he may have been wondering what people were saying about him at meetings. Being "dead" was like a secret identity. The mystery here is cheap, as it is solved by "specially prepared pills," but it is the beginning of something. Far away on an imaginary planet, rumbles and cracks began to form on the surface of an alien world.[42]

Meanwhile, Joe was doing work for the Art Club and was drawing all the time. He kept his work to himself under a roof made of hunched shoulders and scrawny elbows. "I don't recall showing my work to anybody," he would later say; "I used to doodle a lot and sketch a lot in class. People would peek over my shoulder to look at my work but that was all. I never went around showing my work."[43]

But it was 1932, and the spring was giving way once again to another glorious end of school. Things were moving toward a summer that would change everything. A small, anonymous little story appears on March 10, 1932, called "Reader Sights" that is almost certainly Jerry's:

> It was twelve midnight and I was reading the latest edition of "Weird Tales." Outside my window the wind moaned dismally. I was reading the story "The Vampire at the Window," and had just reached the paragraph, "The Dead-Alive begin chanting and tapping on the window," when I stopped abruptly. To my ears had come the sound of claws drawn across glass. And above the whimpering wind had come the wail of a rising chant. The magazine dropped from my nervous fingers. I stared wide-eyed at the window. Glaring in at me were five dreadful faces.
>
> The shock killed me.[44]

Many of the stories Jerry read in his magazines involved mental powers like telepathy and clairvoyance, the ability to see the future. Later, Jerry would remember this story and wonder if he had unknowingly used that same, eerie power.

FRACTURE

On the last day of school, Jerry watched the clock on the wall and had the next forty-five seconds completely mapped out in his mind: the bell would ring, he would sweep his books into his bag—which he had been inching closer to the edge of his desk with his foot—and then he would break awkwardly for the door. He had no reason to linger, no eye to catch. Jerry would miss the *Torch* office most of all, but he needed a break, he thought. When the school year ended, Jerry walked home that last day ecstatic that he would have all summer—all those endless days—to write and write. Everything was turning green. Sure, he'd have to work, but that gave him money to buy more magazines and books.

But the summer, though it stretched out in front of him like all good possibilities, had a dark hole in the center of it, in early June, that changed everything.

Joe went off to Canada to stay with his cousin Frank again.

Jerry got home and stared at the white page.

Then it was June and Jerry's father died.

And no one said a thing.

Michel Siegel was buried in Mt. Olive Cemetery, which was far away from Glenville. But Jerry didn't need to visit to understand what had happened. His father wasn't at the store or at the kitchen table or in his chair in the front room. He wasn't anywhere. He wasn't yelling at Jerry to grow up and go down to work at the store. He didn't have that accent that embarrassed him. He wasn't yelling anything.

But he still was.

Jerry's mother was transformed into a small, black figure. Jerry felt numb.

Everything was different, but it was still somehow the same. He couldn't put it into words. So he didn't. Not yet. There were only whispers and stories.

The page was still white.

Chapter 5

Cosmic

THREE MONTHS LATER, Jerry held an envelope up to the bright lamplight and squinted. But even he, in his endless optimism at his own abilities, already knew what it said. He sighed. Jerry was getting new rejections from the pulps that, once treasured because of their official letterhead, now stung his hands when he opened them. This particular return address was from *Weird Tales;* Jerry had (for the most part) stopped writing reader letters and was just sending full-blown stories now. He wanted the editors to take him seriously as a fiction writer, not think of him as just a letter hack. He ripped open the envelope, and it said the same thing: *unfortunately, but,* or some other qualifier. *Keep us in mind for next time.*

In the wake of Jerry's father's death, the store was for sale. They would keep the house. Jerry still didn't talk about his father's death, not even to Joe, who was finally back home after a long summer. When they went outside to walk around, they just avoided the topic. Like most of those close to Jerry, Joe had heard that Jerry's father had been killed.

Jerry sat in his room, and his mother and aunts would hear him start to click-clack away on his typewriter as they busied themselves in the kitchen, cooking and simmering. When Jerry thought he should be quieter, he pulled up his fingers and the typing sounded like little footsteps. Sometimes, when he really got into the swing of it, he would pound the keys fast and ruthlessly. He imagined wet, messy faces. Once the sun started to set, the typing got more hurried.

The future had a sharper edge now. Jerry still dreamed that writing would lead to impractical riches and the luxury of not having to get a real job after high school. As much as he disliked working at the store, it had always been the unspoken fallback that would be there if everything else failed. But even that option wasn't there anymore. For Jerry, this was both liberating and daunting. The important thing was that he now had to do it *himself.*

Jerry's solution, hatched in his warming room in the summer, as he was looking out the window and clacking the keys absentmindedly, was a bold but practical one: If the magazines weren't taking his stories (which he *knew* were good), then he would eliminate the middleman and publish his own. The key he was pressing stopped, frozen above the black roll. Jerry was sure that he could get famous writers to contribute stories. Maybe he could use some of his own. He was soon projecting subscription rates in his head. What drove him to this idea was not only raw, almost desperate, determination, but a sense of honest-to-goodness teenage hubris. In the wake of his father's death, as the last son in the house, Jerry became the only thing he had left to be: a professional.

PROTOPLASM

Early science fiction fandom was an invisible social network held together with folded letters and wet stamps. Their meeting places were the letter columns of the pulps and, later, the fan-produced, original "magazines" that they all agreed to subscribe to. So when Jerry began to put the call out that he was going to create his own publication, all his years of getting letters printed paid off—people (some of them, at least) recognized his name and signed up.

The list of these first fanboys reads like a mob of make-believe characters, but they would become the giants behind science fiction's great success in America. Even in the 1930s their names set them apart: Forrest J. Ackerman, Julius Schwartz, Otto Binder, and Mort Weisinger. Forry Ackerman was the person who knew everything. His name was in every letter column, on the masthead of most of the fan magazines, and even in some stories. He lived in California, foreshadowing the later move of the genre from the steel file cabinets of New York to the silver screens of Hollywood.[1]

Mort Weisinger was part of the group of New York kids who would shape science fiction in terms of content, politics, and profit. As kids, Mort and his pen pal Julie Schwartz trudged across the boroughs to meet and conspire about aliens and experimental science. They formed a fan club, the Sciencers, which would ultimately generate one of the first fan magazines—*The Time Traveller*—that inspired Jerry to do the same.[2] A few years later, in 1934, using their vast network of contacts, Mort and Julie would form the Solar Sales Service, an agency for young science fiction writers such as Ray Bradbury. They didn't really know what they were doing, but they did it anyway.

Jerry tried to do the exact same things. A year or so earlier, he had attempted a self-published magazine named *Cosmic Stories,* though no copies seem to remain.[3] To publish something himself, Jerry had to overcome a major hurdle: how to physically produce it. According to Jerry, *Cosmic Stories* was hectographic, meaning the manuscript was made after creating a master copy coated in glycerine, which could then be transferred—somewhat messily—onto blank sheets of paper.

The second hurdle was finding contributors. Jerry knew that as much as he wanted to fill up the pages himself, he would need real names to get other subscribers to climb aboard. So he wrote to some of the writers and acquaintances he had made from the back pages of the pulps, some of them local. As a result, the alleged list of contributors to *Cosmic Stories* was impressive, including Clare Winger Harris, who lived in nearby Lakewood, Ohio, a western suburb of Cleveland. Harris, one of the first female genre writers, never used a pseudonym and was well-known for her advice to new writers. In the August 1931 issue of *Wonder Stories,* she lists sixteen common science fiction themes, including "Interplanetary space travel," "Adventures on other worlds," "The creation of super-machines," and "Super intelligence."[4] Even though *Cosmic Stories* failed (or suffered from a very small print run), Jerry might have remembered Harris's advice from one of his favorite magazines. But *Cosmic Stories,* like another possible forerunner called *Cosmic Quarterly,* was just an experiment. Jerry needed a bigger laboratory.

SCIENCE FICTION

When working, Jerry would sometimes imagine that his typewriter was one of Gernsback's futuristic televisor screens and that he could see and communicate with whomever he was thinking about. Sometimes it was a writer he admired, such as Jack Williamson or Edmond Hamilton from nearby Youngstown, Ohio. But mostly he imagined that it was Joe over on Parkwood: *Joe, we have evidence of intelligent plant life from Venus at the house next door—can you help?* Or, later in the evening: *John Carter, this is Jerry Siegel from Earth. I come to you under the direst of emergencies. PLEASE RESPOND. THIS IS URGENT.* Jerry took notes and wrote in longhand, but when he was up against it, he always, always typed.

Frustrated by his attempts with *Cosmic Stories,* Jerry decided he needed to think bigger. For one, hectography was just awful; he needed an alternative process that was easier and less expensive. The Morantz brothers next door sprang to mind—their father owned a printing business. They would split the profits. Jerry got some money together and they ran ads—not in *The Plain Dealer,* but in real national trade magazines, including *The Author and Journalist.* Jerry wanted to appear professional—not like a little kid—so people would take him seriously.

This advertisement was important, so he had to make it count. To make things look kosher, he named a managing editor, again summoning up "Bernard J. Kenton." Jerry and the brothers had been thinking about this for a while; the first ad ran as early as 1931:

> *SCIENCE FICTION,* a new addition to the pseudo-scientific fiction group, is published by the Marontz Publishing Company, 10707 Kimberley Avenue, Cleveland, Ohio. Its Editor-in-chief is Jerome Siegel and the Managing Editor is Bernard J. Kenton. Mr. Kenton writes: "Stories between 8,000 and 15,000 words are in dire need at present." Rates: one-quarter cent to three cents per word, on publication. Stories more fantastic than the usual science fiction type are desired.[5]

Although Gernsback used the term *science fiction* in the first issue of *Science Wonder Stories* in 1929, this ad was among the first times it was used as a title. Editor Kenton goes into even more detail about what they want:

> More boodle for science fiction writers . . . No fairy tales with a 10000-word introduction involving the construction of a space-machine, or the technical potentialities of seven different kinds of *water-glass as a function* of the temperature in expectation of determining the heat or activation of the colloidal coagulation of silici acid, are desired.[6]

The same sarcasm that drove Stiletto Vance is apparent here toward those types of sci-fi tales that concerned themselves only with the silly "colloidal coagulation of silici acid"—Jerry was not interested in being a slavish fan to these types of jargon-driven stories; he was actively trying to make something that was a new response to the genre.

The fact that Jerry was taking out ads in professional magazines shows how serious—or how naïve—he really was. Unfortunately, a few months later, in the same magazine: "Science Fiction, announced as a new magazine at 10707 Kimberley Avenue, Cleveland, Ohio, has indefinitely postponed its plans for publication."[7] The problem was undoubtedly money and submissions—and maybe the Morantzes getting into trouble because of all the things Jerry wanted them to do. Jerry would grudgingly take the operation back, minus the brothers.[8]

The *Science Fiction* that Jerry imagined in those early ads was one of words on a page, with little regard for extensive drawings or illustrations. He kept trying to get a magazine of stories published, but it just wouldn't take. He was missing something. As time passed and Jerry saw how Joe's work was garnering attention at school, he decided to revisit his old idea for a magazine, but this time with illustrations. So in 1932 he brought in some artists, including Joe and Bernie Schmittke. Bernie turned out to be too busy but still managed to do a few illustrations for him.[9] Once he left, it was settled: this was going to be Joe's show.

At his dining room table, Joe felt Jerry hovering over his shoulder, so he drew a slow, perfect circle with the sharp edge of a stylus. School had provided them with a solution to their printing problem: a mimeograph machine. Joe used a stylus to draw dry on mimeo paper, and then Jerry could type right over it. The result was an off-white, blue-black image with vector horizon lines like sunsets. But they had to fill up these pages. At the other end of the table lay all the stories they were thinking of, including those in *Science Fiction*. Jerry walked over and looked at them as if they were plates of food on a table. He had the ones he really wanted to include, so he put those in the front. Joe's mom always invited Jerry to stay for dinner, especially lately, and looked at him for a long time with a sad face when he turned his back. Jeanetta would try to stick her nose in but quickly got bored by all the smudgy words. When Julius came home, he would clap them on the back. *Great job, fellas.*

Because they had to plan the page layout fairly meticulously, Jerry and Joe had to work in tandem. Joe drew the pages first, leaving boxes (or panels) that Jerry could line up in his typewriter. Jerry saw the drawings and was blown away by the futurist imagery. The title page for the first issue begins with Jerry:

WEIRD! FANTASTIC! FUTURISTIC!
Science must serve Civilization; SCIENCE FICTION shall serve Science! . . . Covering the entire field of fantastic WON-DER fiction, whether the stories deal with other planets or the marvels of futuristic chemistry, SCIENCE FICTION swerves from precedent in that it possesses a dynamic personality en-compassed by no other magazine! Theories run rampant with their amazing plausibility in SCIENCE FICTION![10]

Jerry looked it over and smiled. This was it. This was *Science Fiction*.

TABLE OF CONTENTS

In Cleveland, autumn meant that the green trees exploded in a burst of deep reds and coral oranges—and then began to shed, leaving behind nothing but black branches. October was the time of the new beginning of Rosh Hashanah, the atonement of Yom Kippur, and the harvest festi-val of Sukkot. The feast meant gathering as a family in a single space to make the symbolic sounds of assembly, march, and battle. All of this was in the shadow of the death of Jerry's father. Trying to get things done before Sukkot, when no work would be allowed—though there were ways around this—Jerry and Joe brought home the finished copies of *Science Fiction* #1 and laid them carefully on the table. The issues were twelve by nine inches in size and were stapled three times. They would mail them tomorrow to the handful of people who had subscribed and the larger list of people from Jerry's files. As October neared its end, there was also the tingling sense of Halloween: dressing up, begging for candy, and assuming scary new personas.

Jerry got up extra early the next day. His mother blinked when he bounded down the stairs, looking for a breakfast that she had only just begun to make. *Jerome,* she said. There was still a catch in her voice. They sat at the table in a silence that seemed to echo. Jerry still didn't want to talk about it. As he left the house to meet Joe, a little too early, he saw the sunlight arcing over the tops of the houses in front of him as he started toward Glenville High. Today was going to be big. Earlier in the week, he had finally convinced his editor at *The Torch* (mostly as a well-deserved thanks for all the articles he was doing, *thankyouverymuch*) to run a piece about *Science Fiction*. The article was probably written by Jerry himself and appeared, of course, on the front page.

Senior B Student Publishes Science Fiction Magazine

If you were to walk into the office of SCIENCE FICTION you would find its sole occupant terrifically busy. For Jerome Siegel, who that isolated figure is none other than, fills the capacity of owner, editor, secretary, treasurer, and office-boy.

SCIENCE FICTION, The Advance Guard of Future Civilization, is a new magazine which to a great extent uses the work of Glenville students. The stories deal mostly with action-adventure stories upon this and other worlds. Joe Shuster and Bernard Schmittke are among the illustrators. And though it's supposed to be a secret we'll let you know that several prominent Glenvillites appear in its pages, using psuedonyms. The magazine's outstanding features, though, are stories by authors who are already well-known in the popular newstand periodicals.

Until a large enough circulation has been reached to warrant printing, the magazine will remain mimeographed. Meanwhile, a great deal of capital is being used for advertising which is expected to bring staggering results. An ad has already appeared in AMAZING STORIES and others will appear in practically every pulp-paper magazine on the newsstands. Altogether, his advertising will reach in the vicinity of five million magazine readers. A few thousand subscriptions are hoped to be secured from this resort.

We offer our best wishes to this venture and feel sure that Glenville will get behind it and give it a boost toward success. How about it?

When they got to school, Jerry smirked all morning. Joe hunched his shoulders as if he had muscles. This was victory in high school. They wanted the announcement of *Science Fiction* to change everything in an instant. They knew better, but it was a good day nonetheless. The first two issues ran about twenty pages each. When they were sent through the mail to an unknown number of subscribers, Jerry folded them once at the middle and just put the stamps on the back. No one knows how many of each issue were printed, but given that it was the school's machine, paper, and time, the number must have been small.

The issues themselves differed in design: Joe would go from having block text on the cover with a dizzying perspective to a faceless modernist man raising his hand to the sky as the personification of the "Advance Guard of Future Civilization." Joe even worked up a logo of a man's head, in a winged helmet, like Mercury, that looked very much like the official logo for the Cleveland National Air Races, which were held every summer on the lakefront. The contents page had detailed ships and

Joe's favorite high-level bridges, which looked like the Detroit-Superior Bridge that connected downtown to the near west side.[11] There were rough spots, but Joe's blend of cartoony futurism was impressive, especially to its mostly teenage audience.

Meanwhile, Jerry continued to write for *The Torch* and was getting bolder. A "Serialette" shows up on October 13, 1932, where he discusses his lack of writing success in a thinly veiled way:

> Lester Bieburp was determined. He would write trash! For years he had been turning out literary masterpieces. But none had ever been accepted. So Lester had decided to pander his ability for the common rabble. The reason: even an author must eat. . . . It took Lester three days to turn out his effort. He called it "Biscuit Men of Frankfort." Every word disgusted him. When he concluded the drivel, it took all his will-power to keep him from destroying it . . . he mailed the manuscript to Miracle Stories Magazine. That night when he turned in he could not sleep.[12]

The story ends with "To be continued," but like all the ironically named "Serialettes," it never was. "Miracle Stories" was just another way to say *Amazing* (or *Astounding*) *Stories,* both of which rejected Siegel stories. Jerry just wanted to show that he was still trying, even as *The Torch* on November 17, 1932, announced that one of his classmates, Emil Khen, just received a copyright on a book he wrote.[13] Jerry smiled and congratulated him through gritted teeth. At this point in his *Torch* career, Jerry was writing three regular columns: "Dramatics," "Serialettes," and even "Burlesquing the News," "composed weekly by Jerry (Goober the Mighty) Siegel and Wilson Hirschfeld of Student Council (Phooey!) fame." Hirschfeld would go on to *The Plain Dealer,* where as managing editor he slicked back his hair and wore round-rimmed glasses.[14]

By November, the ground was cold and hard and the air clouded up in the morning when you breathed. Everything was flat, and buildings turned dark at five o'clock in the afternoon. There was the hope of holidays mixed with the threat of snow. But through it all, to celebrate this odd hard season, was the midwestern fire of football. The pro teams in and around Cleveland had seen better days, but high school football was thriving. One of the local heroes was Benny Friedman, the Glenville quarterback in the mid-1920s who would play for the University of Michigan in college and the Cleveland Bulldogs as a pro. In 1928, Friedman led scoring categories in extra points, rushing, and passing, which he revolutionized. The football itself was a fat, melonlike blob, forcing Friedman to do forearm exercises to be able to sling the ball all over the field. When he wore the "G" at Glenville, he also wore duo-colored tights. His signature look was a curly lock of black hair, and his smile was all over the papers. He was beloved by the Jewish community, though this resulted in his being called names at away games and the "Son of Palestine" in some papers. After he left, Glenville football started a downward spiral, but it still commanded hysterical levels of loyalty.[15]

The most important game of the high school season was the annual Charity Game, a Thanksgiving weekend contest between the top two teams in the city. In 1932, it was going to be held downtown at the massive new Cleveland Municipal Stadium. Seated on the lake, this vast cavern of steps and seats was, and would continue to be for decades, a mecca for Cleveland football. Part of its excitement was its daring insistence on being located right next to the Lake Erie tundra. To increase attendance at the stadium for the charity game, *The Plain Dealer* ran its annual poster contest:

CHARITY FOOTBALL POSTER IS SOUGHT

Prizes will be awarded on poster merit, that is, for theme value, eye-catching quality, color, execution and originality. Use "half-card" size, 22 by 28 inches. Color it for two impressions in the printing, that is, color and black, or two primary colors. The poster should be the contestant's design, but it may adapt from any source available. Contestants should keep in mind that credit is given for originality. All posters must be in Room 505, Plain Dealer Building by 5 pm Monday, Nov 14.

All over the city, students immediately pulled out paper, pencils, and crayons. Kids painted, sketched, and copied in a mad rush to meet the deadline. Glenville had a history of luck in this contest; Bernie Schmittke had placed the year before. This year, though, Glenville would do even better. In *The Plain Dealer*:

GLENVILLE BOY IS WINNER ON POSTER

Joseph Shuster, 18, of 10905 Amor Avenue NE yesterday was declared winner in the poster contest.... The judges were Alfred Mewett, registrar of the Cleveland School of Art, E. R. Van Bergen, vice president of the Artcraft Printing Co. and Glenn M. Shawn, instructor at the School of Art. Five thousand copies of the winning poster are to be printed to be distributed over Cuyahoga County.[16]

The column goes on to say:

> The judges worked for over three hours yesterday going over the entries. The first prize winner, they said, had produced a poster of excellent quality with attention value and complete legibility. "It's going to be an elegant game," said Sports Writer [Alex] Zirin. "It's going to be a honey." The game is going to cause a lot of happiness on Dec. 25 for the proceeds will be turned over to the Plain Dealer Give-A-Christmas fund and will be translated into baskets for the poor.[17]

The poster itself is reproduced in big ads for the game that appear in the paper. Joe's design is in black and red and depicts a single kicker punting a ball. The face is angular and strong. Hints were given in *The Plain Dealer* on what made a winning design. Glenn M. Shawn at the Cleveland School of Art even referenced a cartoon of Hitler being a good example because it "emphasized one man, Hitler, as standing for a whole school of political thought."[18]

Joe bounded in and showed his mom the paper. She clapped her hand to her mouth. When his father came home, they celebrated. *I'm going to need extras,* he said. They knew there was no money involved, but this

might be a stepping-stone for Joe. And he needed it. On Thursday, November 24, 1932, *The Torch* announced:

PUPIL WINS FIRST PRIZE IN CONTEST
The poster which . . . Won for him a pair of box seats, opposite the fifty-yard line. The poster, in black, red, and gray, shows a player punting, with the words "Charity Football," this carries out the idea of the slogan "Kick That Goal For Charity."[19]

Interviewed by *The Torch*, "Joseph" said, "I'm very glad to win this award. This is the first contest I have ever won. Miss Bernstein helped me with my poster. I'm planning to take my brother, Frank, with me."[20]

Joe's winning poster would get a print run of five thousand lithographs and be plastered all over the city. Not in the art room, not in *The Torch*, but all over Cleveland. Even at the game, his breath frosty and Frank cheering and looking at girls, Joe couldn't believe this was happening to him. The first two issues of *Science Fiction* had only done okay or maybe not even good at all. But as Jerry watched Joe smile and blush and drink in the accolades for this big award, he might have realized that he had been underestimating his friend. Jerry knew that their third issue would have to be big. So he decided to give Joe something bigger to think about.

Chapter 6

Reign

A S WINTER BREAK CAME and the snow started filling the streets, Joe began work on Jerry's big story for *Science Fiction* #3. The house was cold, but it was a welcome change to stay in all day and not have to make the long, stinging walk to school. Joe sat at the dining room table and peeked outside: the snow had turned the world quiet and white. As the temperature dropped, Joe put on cotton gloves because there was no coal. Joe adapted: he had to wear a bunch of sweaters and the gloves made it hard to get a fine line, but he didn't complain.[1] He didn't have a drawing table, so he used his mother's breadboard, which was a wide, nearly flat surface with little side rails that offered something to prop up and push against. The only downside was that his mother needed the board back every Friday night to make the challah bread. When he got the board back, it was warm and smelled good. He did good work then, his mother watching over him.[2]

Joe already had Jerry's new typewritten story, so he didn't expect him to come over and supervise. Not in this weather. Joe laid out his paper on the board and started seeing the pictures in his head. He had thought about it last night. He had been working with the story for a while; it was just a matter of seeing how to do it. Here, on the dining room table in a little apartment, the smell of bread in the air and a mother close by in the kitchen, Joe put his face very close and sketched in a slow and meticulous manner. Sometimes he used real paper. Sometimes he used the brown butcher's paper his mother would bring him from the store. And at one point, he actually grabbed some wallpaper from someone's garbage to draw on the back.[3] Joe was ecstatic when he made that find. As far as supplies went, Joe had few.

Joe could sometimes hear the radio from the Brightmans' apartment at the front of the building. The younger son, Nate, would sometimes sit in his closet with his radio set: a metal coil wound around a cereal box and a small galena crystal. He would move a small wire called a "cat's whisker" over the surface of the tiny mineral, hoping for a spark of distant, unintelligible language.[4] Joe had a similar work ethic based around discovery: draw, destroy, think, draw, repeat. He was enormously hard on himself. He knew he could always be better. And like Jerry, he was feeling the ticks of time. He wanted to go to art school when he was done at Glenville, but the unspoken sense in the Shuster home was that they just could not afford it. Joe's family truly supported him, but love and support couldn't always make a mint.[5]

The story that Joe was working from was planned by Jerry to appeal to a reader just like himself. He was a salesman. Jerry advocated substance over style. He had to. But against the colorfully covered pulps, it was a tough sale. So his prefaces sound like sermons:

> *Science Fiction*
> "Science Must Serve Civilization";
> SCIENCE FICTION Shall Serve Science!
> A PROPHECY
> A printed magazine!
> Price will remain the same!
> Many more pages!
> Fine illustrations by two coming artists whose work will set
> every science fiction fan raving with admiration!
> Scientific fiction cartoon strips!
> Scientific fiction illustrated departments!
> A wonderful picture on the cover!
> Long novel by popular writers such as Repp, Sloan, and Palmer.
> Occasionally, scientific fiction story reprints from the ARGOSY
> or other publications.
> —and a host of other brilliant features
> and surprises we have in store!
> You may not like our physical features at present but you'll be
> enthralled by our fiction. . . . We are carrying on an expensive
> advertising campaign from which we expect great results. And
> we make the following promise to our readers. As soon as our

circulation nears 1000 we shall adopt the features mentioned above in the Prophecy. We make the following plea: STICK WITH US!!![6]

As editor, Jerry felt like a one-man *Torch:* he got to decide everything. But they didn't have that many submissions, and more important, they had no real money to pay for stories. This was a double-edged sword. Jerry could easily run a bunch of his stories, but then people would think it wasn't a legitimate magazine. He worried over this possibility. But they had to fill this issue first so they could get more important people to contribute later. Or at least that's what Jerry might have told himself. In the end he selected one of his stories and gave it to Joe. Now it was time to draw it.

PROCESS

Joe always started with some sketches before actually beginning to draw on the mimeo paper. This time he imagined the picture splashing across two pages to create a greater sense of doom. He would leave room for Jerry's story to start, but the picture, the image, had to set the tone. Joe began with the title across the top third of the sky. In the top right, he placed a full moon to balance out the title. Then he placed a small border in the left corner for Jerry to put his name in; he wasn't sure which name Jerry was going to use, so he left a lot of room.

His sister would show up now and again to watch, her chin on the table, her eyes rolling between Joe and the paper. He cut it all with some searchlights. He was creating a sense of something. Joe drew a box under the word *Man* that reached almost all the way to the bottom—that should give him enough room. He put another text box, much smaller, at the bottom of the first page and taped it off. He took a step back and looked. He had stalled long enough; it was time to get to it.

He inhaled—and began drawing a large head floating menacingly between the title and the lower text box. The nose spread out and the beady eyes were accented by some truly sinister eyebrows. Jeanetta saw this and ran away. The key, though, was the mouth—Joe made it huge, with tense, gritting teeth. The head was terrifying. He followed with a pair of ghost-like hands curled into near claws. He looked sort of like Fu Manchu.[7]

Joe built up the buildings from the line of the ground. Rising on the right side of the page is a densely packed cluster of buildings that stretch all the way to the moon. As with everything, the architectural physics are exaggerated; the tallest building looks like the Terminal Tower, only with a thousand extra floors. The buildings are done in a three-quarter perspective. On the left page is Joe's signature bridgework, connecting the city proper to the poorer places across the river.

Joe erased the very bottom on the right and started drawing tiny outlines of people, marching all one way, toward the bridge and the apparent doom above it. The three-dimensional effect of the villain (for he clearly was one) reaching out of the miasma of shadow of the city's skyline was something even the pulps didn't do with their generally two-dimensional title page illustrations. Here, Joe's sinister head even covered a portion of Jerry's title. This was not comics, not really—but it was getting close.

On the next set of pages, Joe drew two figures that both stretched the length of the page. On the left, a man is strapped in a scientific chair equipped with all manner of coils and tubes.

His hands are tensed, as if something painful is happening to him. On the right, a man in a white frock is using the chair to administer his terrible treatments. The man in the chair looks just like a statue that he and Jerry always walked by when they went to the Cleveland Museum of Art.

Joe exhaled. He did some last apparatus boxes and flourishes. He was ready to give it to Jerry.

Once Jerry took over the page, he started with the smallest possible portion of the picture: the anonymous line of people in the corner. He always moved from the small to the big. Jerry typed carefully—so carefully—so that his words could fit within Joe's layered boxes. This part made Joe nervous, so Jerry did it at his own house—the typewriter couldn't really move around much, anyway. Jerry read from his script. He began his story in the real world: "The bread-line! Its row of downcast, disillusioned men; unlucky creatures who have found that life holds nothing but bitterness for them. The bread-line! Last resort of the starving vagrant!" Regardless of Joe's elaborate technological drawing, this is a tale of the here and now, of the Depression, where men without jobs wait for free food. This was bleaker than any imagined outer space apocalypse because it was real. Jerry then introduced Professor Ernest Smalley, the rich genius, chemist by specialty, who visits this hard-luck place and looks upon these men with a "contemptuous sneer." To him, a man of education and money, these poor men are like mice or rabbits: "To him, who had come of rich parents and had never been forced to face the rigors of life, the miserableness of these men seemed deserved. It appeared to him that if they had the slightest ambition at all they could easily lift themselves from their terrible rut." Jerry looked down at his typewriter and thought about the two things a desperate man wants most. His family was not as poor as Joe's, but there was the real fear of it now after the loss of his father. Jerry felt as if he were in a professional breadline as well—subsisting on mere letters being published when he wanted to see his actual stories. He clicked and clacked himself into Smalley's head as he approaches a weary man with a rumbling stomach.

> "How would you like to have a real meal and a new suit?" he inquired.
>
> The resentment in the vagrant's face died as he saw that Smalley wore costly apparel. "I'd like nothing better, mister." Then, suddenly suspicious—"What do you want me to do for you? Nothing crooked, I hope?"[8]

It is no coincidence that Smalley offers the man "a real meal and a new suit," which is more or less what Michel Siegel died for a few months earlier in June. But instead of having it stolen from him, Smalley offers it as payment for something else: revenge.

Jerry typed away in his brown room, with white ice crystallizing outside on the windowpane. The radio was on downstairs. Smalley assures the poor man that he is in good hands and drives him off. The down-and-outer is named "Bill Dunn, gentleman of the road, at your service!" Many of the members of Cleveland's poor population were similar "gentlemen" hoboes living in the shantytown down by Lake Erie as they paused between New York and Chicago. They slept on mats but wore ties and fedoras. The poortown was thought of as a hideout for criminals and would be burned to the ground later in 1938 when Cleveland safety director Eliot Ness tried to flush out a mass murderer dubbed the Torso Killer.[9] Its own little world, the shantytown had its own barter system, with clothes (especially suits) being of particularly high value. Jerry paused for a moment, then continued.

Once Dunn puts the suit on, Smalley is exuberant: "What a great transformation! It seems impossible that you are the same man!" As the page turns, Smalley's purpose for Dunn finally transforms the story from Depression-era morality tale into full-fledged science fiction. Smalley feeds Dunn (secretly, through his coffee) a serum derived from "what he suspected to be a new element" that he distills from a "fragment of a meteor." This element "exerted a strange influence" that sounds radioactive. After taking the serum, Dunn escapes, "babbles incoherently and starts dashing along the streets at full speed."[10] Jerry paused and thought of a dark street.

Dunn starts hearing the thoughts of others, which is overwhelming. Jerry portrayed this with a lot of random underlined dialogue: "I gotta have that dough , Ma . . . I wonder what she thinks I am; a sap for her to wipe her dirty shoes on? . . . So I tells the umpchay I'm not that kind ova dame . . . and so on. He evens "overhears" a newspaper editor: "Look here, punk. You may be the star reporter on this rag but unless you turn in your copy by three o'clock you'll be out in the street peddling shoelaces." Dunn then hears Smalley's thoughts and realizes what is going on: the serum he had been fed has given him these strange mental powers. His eyesight is also enhanced: he looks into the sky and focuses on Mars, seeing two thirty-foot alien monsters battle each other. Dunn passes out from the exertion. When he wakes, he realizes that he can use his powers to live "the life of a Prince." "I must remedy my financial situation," Dunn says. And it is then, only then, that Jerry names him as "a grin of superiority crossed the Superman's face."[11]

The Superman absorbs all the knowledge of the universe and then goes to the public library, where he reads "Einstein's book on 'The Expanding Universe' "—in German. As he reads, "An elderly gentleman entered the room and sat down beside the Superman. . . . He slipped a small magazine from his pocket and began to read. The Superman read the following two words upon its cover: SCIENCE FICTION." Reading his thoughts, the Superman knows the man is going to quiz him about the "Fitzgerald Equation," which the Superman answers correctly.[12] The man is astonished.

The Superman then robs a drugstore by mentally convincing the clerk that he owes him money. He also gets an illegal bottle of booze. The Superman then looks into the future (a new power) and sees that betting on a horse, "the Blue Angel," and investing in "Colorado Fruits" will make him rich. The Superman muses, "Time is simply duration, and duration is an illusion of the mind." Smalley, furious at hearing accounts of Dunn's exploits in the news, tries to re-create the formula in order to gain his own powers. Smalley is filled with greed for power. The Superman shows up and they finally confront each other. Smalley promises cooperation once he takes the drug, but the Superman hears his murderous thoughts.[13]

Meanwhile, across the globe, the "International Conciliatory Council" with chairman Warren Mansfield is called to session. Anthony Ferroti, Italy's ambassador of peace, starts talking against Balvania, causing an international incident—this is being caused by the Superman. Forrest Ackerman is a reporter who goes to Smalley's and can't find him, though he does find blood. Ackerman leaves confused but is guided telepathically to an address in his head by the Superman. Forrest sits down, and "bars of metal sprang about him from the chair's side, grasping his arms, chest, and legs, in an unbreakable grip."[14]

Dunn admits that "I am about to send the armies of the world to total annihilation against each other." Forrest notes that he has a "twisted face" as "the Superman was broadcasting thoughts of hate which would plunge the Earth into a living hell." In this moment of dread and terror, the reporter sends up a silent prayer to the Creator of the threatened world. He beseeches the Omnipotent One "to blot out this blaspheming devil." Just then, the Superman's face falls as he sees, a day into the future, that he is once again a vagrant, sleeping in the park: "I can't duplicate the drug unless I can reach the Dark Planet where lies the needed element." Instead there now stood a drooping, disillusioned man.[15]

Dunn raises his head and regards the mute reporter. "I see, now, how wrong I was. If I had worked for the good of humanity, my name would have gone down in history with a blessing—instead of a curse."[16] The story ends, and though Dunn can no longer see into the future, it seems that Jerry, whether he knew it or not, somehow could. This story, juvenile as it may be, contains not just a name, but every single element of the superhero character that was beginning to wake.

In the same issue as "Reign of the Super-man," Jerry penned a variety of shorter tales. The "Vandals of Pluto" by Bernard J. Kenton is listed in the table of contents but does not actually appear in the issue. "The Dream Dimension" has a character named "Bart Williamson"[17] and is an occult science fiction story with an eerie "Keeper of the Altar" and "the Seven Fiends," including the evil Malat, which in Hebrew means "to escape or deliver." There is also a "Queerosities" page of science "facts," featuring Joe's drawings of a dinosaur and a machine in the future that will bring dead men back to life.[18]

The letters pages are also surprisingly full:

> *Just received the second issue of S-F and thought I'd write a few words on how the issue impresses me. Of course, I intend to stick with you . . . I hope you decided to print this letter, for if anyone reads this who is willing to sell the first issue of S-F, I would like to hear from him. Sincerely yours,*
> *Julius Schwartz*[19]

Jerry responds: "Thank you for your kind wishes, Mr. Schwartz. . . . We had intended more numerous and radical changes but last-minute figuring and economy, forced us not to. —Ed." Fan praise aside, those issues were really kind of a mess. But Jerry and Joe kept trying to get to what it looked like in their heads—and it showed:

> *Editor, S-F:*
> *My admiration for the staff of S-F increases. I had expected improvements, but not so soon as the second issue. The cover is good. I*

suggest you use it as an emblem for S-F. That stalwart figure really
typifies "the advance guard." . . . All together, I counted at least
eight improvements. . . . I wish to congratulate Shuster on his
excellent drawings. Please have more of them next month. Sincerely,
Daniel McPhail

(We are glad that you like the work of our Art Editor. He is rapidly
gaining an enthusiastic following. He and the Editor have collaborated
on a cartoon-strip INTERPLANETARY POLICE which
received the approval of a newspaper syndicate and is now in the
process of being revised. We are always happy to receive your letters
of constructive criticism. —Ed.)[20]

The loudest fan letters were from contributing writers and fellow fanzine editors who had one thing in common: they liked Joe's art.[21] Jerry
singles out Joe several times: "If you'll observe the drawings of Shuster
carefully, you'll get a good idea of how the artist himself looks. Like
many others, Joe Shuster has the habit of drawing a likeness of himself in
all his characters." Jerry is genuinely happy for his friend, but he is also
quick to hitch his wagon to the star: "And still drolling on Shuster, here's
another bit of interest. The editor of this magazine and our Art Editor are
collaborating on a long novelette. This will be the first time in the history of science fiction that an author will illustrate his own story. Watch
for this take! Report has it that it's a humdinger!"

Hearing these words held within faded type, one would think that
Joe was working on what the future would term an original graphic
novel. But this later issue never came. Jerry was using his barker voice to
sell something before it even existed, something he was good at his whole
life. Part of it was the liar's voice that every writer needs, but part of it
was just gauging his audience. When your life is all ideas, you have to
test them out; to say them is to make them real: "Have you heard Buck
Rogers over the radio? . . . Then hold your breath until you hear THE
INTERPLANETARY POLICE . . . the cartoon-strip has been written
up into radio-play form." He closes with a tease for next month's issue:
"Ray Palmer next month then David H. Keller's CITIES OF GLASS
will run, after which'll come a novel length serial called (?) which is
written by (?) and (?). Well, what the—!!! Darned if the ed. didn't go and
cut the title and the names of the authors of the last mentioned yarn. The

old meanie!" As he sat in his snowbound house, Joe's stomach sounded like thunder.[22]

But that story too never came. *Science Fiction* had a hard time selling subscriptions. And it wasn't alone.

> *Dear Mr. Siegel:-*
> *Your stories look much better than would have have thought possible under the circumstances>>>????—and my congratulations go to you.*
> *Please do not make your magazine too good however, for it would be unpleasant for me to have to join the ranks of the unemployed! Sincerely yours, Harry Bates, Editor ASTOUNDING STORIES*
> *P.S. Well, it's just happened. I've just been instructed to discontinue ASTOUNDING STORES with the Jan. issue. Good luck to you in your venture.*[23]

Whether the letter really was from Harry Bates is not entirely certain, but that it was *Astounding,* the same magazine "Kenton" had allegedly sold "Miracles on Antares" to, made it hurt all the more. The dream of writing for the pulps died right before Jerry's blinking eyes in his own magazine: "When we finished reading the above letter we were all sunk in gloom. Of all the mags on the market why did it have to be AS-TOUNDING that went?"[24] The mags, the authors, their stories, and the readers—this was a world within a world, a hidden earth bustling and pulsing beneath the surface. And for thinking boys from Cleveland or New York, it was a universe of acceptance. And it was crumbling down around them.

Hours later, Jerry breathed a sigh of relief—the Underwood had successfully navigated Joe's maze of pictures on the mimeographed page.[25] The story looked very good. To his left were his script and some notes. He had done it. But on his right was something else. In the darkening light next to him a magazine opened about halfway to a story with a picture of a man on it. In the title, a name that echoed what Jerry had just written in his story. The word was visible in black, block letters: "Superman."

THE SOURCE

The magazine that was open next to Jerry that night when he wrote "Reign of the Super-man" was the November 11, 1931, issue of *Wonder Stories,* which featured a story by Francis Flagg, a writer Jerry praised repeat-

The Superman of Dr. Jukes
By FRANCIS FLAGG

(Illustration by Paul)

edly in his published letters to the pulps. Flagg was a pseudonym for George Henry Weiss, a Canadian-born author and poet who wrote for all of the magazines and corresponded with H. P. Lovecraft, the pale horror writer from Providence, Rhode Island. Flagg's story begins in the underworld of Chicago and concerns a man of "slim and of medium height" with "cold gray eyes." This character is a Mob hit man named "Killer Mike" who angers a Mafia boss named Frazzini, who is nicknamed "Big Shot." On the run, Mike flees all the

way to Arizona, where he ends up destitute. An elderly man approaches the distraught Mike and asks, "You need employment, I presume?" "In the worst way," he responds. This man, Doctor Jukes, explains that he is "interested in certain experiments for which I need a human subject. Nothing dangerous, you understand. 40 dollars a week."[26]

In typical pulp fashion, things happen fast as readers are pulled along in wild, careening sentences toward an uncertain conclusion. Whisked away to Jukes's compound, the Killer is given a series of untested injections. Over time, "his wits seemed to clarify [and his] sight became keener." The Killer remarks to himself, "Lord I feel strong." The formula he is given is one of Jukes's own design based on glandular extractions. Jukes meets with the U.S. secretary of war (a man named Asbury) to sell the serum and orders Mike destroyed as part of covering their tracks. But instead, Mike is accidentally given a pure dose of the serum. He becomes even more powerful and kills an attendant. "Every atom was rioting in Killer Mike's body."[27]

Mike returns to Chicago to have his revenge on Frazzini. But it is not going to be an easy task, as "his Chicago home was a fortress. It stood on the top of a skyscraper." But Mike easily gets in and toys with the powerful gangster:

> I can read your mind, Frazzini. You are thinking how clever you are! But not as clever as me, Frazzini! Not as clever "as the Man-plus."[28]

Frazzini's men open fire, but Mike sidesteps "the loafing bullets."

> Yes, I am speeded up; I can even hear your thoughts. Compared to me, ordinary men are as snails. I can out-move, out-think, out-fight.[29]

He has speed and strength, and he can read minds and stride "through the night like a wraith" as a naked, seven-foot giant, somewhat like Joe's figure on the cover of *Science Fiction*.[30]

But the glandular extracts (seemingly from a jungle cat or panther) begin to take their terrible toll. Madness takes the Killer:

> Or was it clarity of vision as his eyes glow and he sees a vision of a heavenly city. He sees a new world, walks, then stops . . . was it real or madness?[31]

He disappears, overwhelmed by what is happening to him. They later find his "blank eyes gone mad."[32]

When Jerry first read this story, he couldn't even sleep. *This* was a story. When he reread it, trying to get inspired for *Science Fiction,* he may have forgotten that the man's name was Mike, a name shared with his father, for a character who was fighting back and getting revenge on organized crime. Jerry really liked the title of Flagg's story, too: "The Superman of Dr. Jukes."[33]

The idea of a "superman" having these sorts of powers stretches back even further. The July 1929 *Popular Science* claims that "the man of the future is lean. . . . Mentally he will be a superman, [but] Heart trouble and cancer will threaten him." The only solution: "Dr. Oscar Riddle, of the Carnegie Institution . . . has recently made the prediction that through gland extracts and laboratory methods of control, science may be able eventually to produce mental or physical supermen at will."[34] But a year later, in May, the magazine is still looking: "The world awaits the superman. Man's mind will not only improve, but will develop new organs of thought. If this theory is sound, the age is approaching when men will comprehend Einstein as readily as they now understand simple arithmetic."[35] These stories, all of them, are describing Flagg's Superman.

Jerry brought the completed *Science Fiction #3* into school and showed it to his English teacher. When she asked him to stay after class, he was sure it was to shower him with praise. It was not. Alone in the wooden Glenville classroom, she pleaded with him: *Why do you write this type of material when there are so many wonderful things you can write about?* Jerry was shocked, but he answered quickly, *That's what I like.* She sighed and shook her head in painful dismissal. She and some other teachers saw the enormous potential in Jerry. But they felt it was going unfulfilled.[36] It wasn't the writer, it was the genre. Science fiction was as lowbrow as things could be in an already lowbrow time.[37]

In addition to working on *Science Fiction,* Jerry and Joe put out a reprint in booklet form of Edmond Hamilton's *The Metal Giants,* originally a short story first published in the December 1926 *Weird Tales.* The pulps were always advertising reprint series of everything from Jules Verne to their own contemporary authors.[38] Jerry retyped the story, mimeographed the book, and contacted Swanson, a North Dakota bookseller who was also trying to launch his own science fiction magazine called *Galaxy.* In a March 21, 1932, letter to Clark Ashton Smith, H. P. Lovecraft noted that Swanson "can't make typographical arrangements, & the subscriptions haven't come in as he expected—so that's that! However, if granted permission he will hold onto contributor's mss. For a little while—in the hope that he may be able to swing a mimeographed magazine or series of booklets. Getting down close to the amateur class!"[39] *The Metal Giants* is one of these booklets, crudely printed with a hand-lettered cover. It is labeled *Science Fiction Reprints No. 1,* indicating that there may have been a longer series in mind.[40] There are several surviving copies of *The Metal Giants* but none known of the alleged second volume *Guests of the Earth* by Hugh Langley, another Jerry Siegel pseudonym.[41] This underdog world or, as Lovecraft puts it, the "amateur class" was where Jerry Siegel was breeding his ideas.

Unfortunately, Lovecraft's words had prescience, as *Science Fiction*'s days were numbered. In an effort to get more subscriptions, they tried hard to make it feel like a sprawling, national magazine. In issue #4, they covered the upcoming 1933 World's Fair in Chicago, which was being talked about in the magazines and newspapers. For science fiction enthusiasts, the World's Fair was important because it screened the very first film based on a comics character—an odd short of Buck Rogers in which the publisher's son, John Dille Jr., portrays the title character with his girlfriend playing leading lady Wilma Deering. Magician Dr. Harlan Tarbell plays the genius scientist Dr. Huer in a creepy bald cap. But the inclusion of moving spaceships (on strings) was—in 1932—almost faint-inducing.[42]

Joe's depiction of the fair was of gleaming towers and squat spheres, all filled with masses of faceless people being pulled into their orbit. Jerry wrote that the fair was "of immediate interest to the Science Fiction fan," mostly because of the "Yerckes Observatory," which would start a Rube Goldberg–type chain reaction: "From the star Arcturus, forty light years distant from our planet, light will flash through the Yerkes Observatory's forty-inch telescope and be focused upon a photo-electric cell. The electronic impulse thus generated will be sent across the Fair to start the scientific exhibits." Jerry also mentioned other attractions such as a new global map and "visceral" mechanical dinosaurs. They made the fair sound, and look, like a science fiction wonderland.[43]

That issue also displayed one of the biggest illustrations Joe attempted: a depiction of RKO's game-changing monster movie, *King Kong*. The movie would not be released until March 7, 1933, so their review was cannily intended to come out with the film. Joe drew a huge version of the mighty ape roaring over a globelike Manhattan while Jerry filled the bottom of the page with glowing praise for a film he had yet to see:

The greatest science fiction thriller ever filmed, after a year and
a half of the most difficult intricacies of modern photography is

at last ready for release. This story, of a 50-foot giant anthropoid loose upon the city of New York, was conceived by Merian Cooper, who supervised the breath-taking "Most Dangerous Game," and Edgar Wallace, well born writer of popular mystery novels, who passed away suddenly a year ago.[44]

They poured out their enthusiasm over something they could only fantasize about:

> Imagine this colossal ape battling a squadron of planes which is pouring streams of lead into his body while he stands atop the Empire State building. . . . Naturally, there were a great many difficulties to be overcome in order to make possible the filming of this tale. Rival producers laughed at their attempt as an impossible task. But R.K.O. triumphed, using a secret method . . . and in this triumph they have established a shining miracle: this movie shall certainly go down in science fiction history as one of the greatest of its type. Let us hope that, encouraged by its success, movie-land will do more.[45]

Jerry draws very heavily upon a January 22, 1933, *Plain Dealer* article about the upcoming film, especially that it was an "impossible task."[46] And it was for them as well; *Science Fiction*'s next issue was its last. The Superman was done.

For now.

Part Two:
Rocket

Chapter 7
Into the Air

J ERRY KEPT A SMALL STACK of *Science Fiction*s in a neat pile on the corner of his desk, ready to be shipped off at a moment's notice. Just in case. But "in case" never came. He looked at the magazines, thin and dirty, and thought of his physics class: they had a potential energy of *zero*. The first thing he still did when he ran in from school every day was see if there was any mail or any new subscribers.

Jerry sighed. He could still hope.

Jerry couldn't understand why *Science Fiction* wasn't selling. Even with the bleary ink and some of the typos, it was good stuff. But as much as he loved their little magazine, it just wasn't as good as the real pulps. He knew it. They had the right people writing in—Ackerman, Schwartz, Palmer—but it wasn't enough. It didn't have that red-and-yellow color the magazines had. Jerry was frustrated. *Was it really that simple?* He was convinced it wasn't them; and as many times as he was convinced it was Joe, those fears were fading. Joe was doing so well with his drawing, maybe they could play more to his strengths. Maybe they needed some color.

Joe was largely self-taught as an artist but had some instruction at Glenville, including advice from a cartoonist who came in to address his art class. Joe might have also taken courses through the mail. Cleveland had several famous cartoon correspondence schools at the time, including the W. L. Evans School of Cartooning and Caricaturing, whose most famous graduate was E. C. Segar, creator of the incredibly popular *Thimble Theatre* and "Popeye's Pappy."[1] The Evans class in particular would have shown Joe how to build exaggeration into simple drawings for comedic effect.

There was also the Raye Burns School and the Hal H. Cooper School of Art. Joe would later take some night and weekend classes at Huntington Art School and at the prestigious Cleveland School of Art.[2] But most of his art education was in what he read and saw. Joe loved the comics and indeed kept some strips from his youth—cut from the newspapers and carefully folded—in his personal files for his entire life.[3] Besides *Nemo,* Joe really liked Roy Crane, the NEA Cleveland artist of the popular *Wash Tubbs,* about a short, curly-haired kid with glasses who goes on adventures with a square-jawed adventurer named Captain Easy, who would go on to get his own Sunday strip. Joe patterned his own adventure work after Crane: lots of profiles, strong lines, and squinty eyes.[4] There was also the comic strip *Tarzan,* which was about a strongman jumping around fighting people in every panel. Comedy and high adventure was the style Joe Shuster was born to draw. Seeing the reader comments on *Science Fiction* bolstered Jerry to revisit one of their initial projects, *Interplanetary Police.* The project had never really taken off, but maybe, Jerry thought, it was time to try again.

UNPOPULAR COMICS

Exactly when they started making comics is uncertain. There were pictures with words in *Science Fiction,* but that wasn't comics, not really. But given their reading habits, comics were probably something they started on early. So once *Science Fiction* faltered, which in some ways was Jerry's failure, Joe got his chance. Now they did comics as though there were no tomorrow. Within months, Joe's dining room table filled with comics that had replaced all those smudgy *Science Fictions*—and Joe couldn't have been happier. They were working on an anthology comic book to fill up with their own material, like the July 1934 *Famous Funnies* that had just appeared on the stands.

After lots of time at Joe's dining room table, Jerry pacing and Joe pushing his pencil in lines over paper, the boys had a whopping twenty-five original comic pages. It was no longer a separate process: they worked in the same room now, the four corners of the ceiling providing some sort of boundary for their imagination. There was also a large preview panel written by Jerry, proclaiming which of their new cartoon stars would appear in the second issue. *Popular Comics* was really *Science Fiction* 2.0: an independently produced magazine, but this time with comics instead of stories. And it was some stuff.

One of the leads of *Popular Comics* is *Interplanetary Police,* looking not exactly like *Buck* or *Flash,* but more like a surrealist combination of both, with bizarre, highly artistic Craftint shading and an emphasis on X-ray vision, which was rapidly becoming a favorite science fiction trope among teenage boys. In *Interplanetary Police,* X-rays take the form of the "penetrascope," as "Unknown to the world, Steve Walsh, scientific adventurer extraordinary, has invented along with other scientific miracles, the penetrascope, a machine which can peer through all material substances. . . . Together with Ralph Venton, an inseparable comrade, he has determined to discover intrigue and adventure through use of the penetrascope." The narrative—or at least the promise of one—is driven wholly by scientific invention. The manly Walsh is aided by "Venton," another analogue of Jerry's favorite moniker "Kenton."[5]

One of the most polished cartoons in *Popular Comics* is *Snoopy and Smiley,* a Laurel and Hardy–style humor strip. Snoopy and Smiley, two schlubby, suit-wearing "Knights of the Road," are perpetually penniless but are always hatching schemes to change their financial station. In one episode, Smiley retrieves a cigar butt from the middle of the road and is promptly struck by a car. He goes to the hospital but has no money to pay the bill, so he feigns insanity by bouncing up and down on his hospital bed, screaming, "Woopee! I'm a Mexican jumpin' bean!!" Unfortunately, Smiley is promptly thrown into the padded psychiatric ward instead of his comfortable hospital bed.[6] In another episode, Snoopy and Smiley finally scrape together enough money to get a real turkey dinner at a restaurant. As they bask in the hot meal in front of them, a skinny young boy stares at them through the window. They stare back—and in the last panel, the young boy is seated at their table, smiling.[7]

In this panel, Jerry and Joe acknowledge that even though they might be on the verge of personal success (and able finally to pay for a nice meal), it is their lives on the other side that will speak most to an audience. So they bring their own experience as the waif from outside the glass to inside the comic itself, adding emotional reality to the culinary fantasy.

Just as Jerry and Joe were doing, Snoopy and Smiley tried inventing new professions for themselves, even though they weren't even remotely qualified for any of them. When Snoopy and Smiley finally open an office to showcase the latter's apparent new precognitive ability (which, as he doesn't seem to be able to predict, doesn't last), they paint their office door with an ongoing list of possible titles, including Business Consultants, Domestic Advisers, Rumor Confirmers, Publicity Dispensers, Success Surmisers, Tattle-Tales, Forewarners, Procedure Prescribers, Probability Describers, and, finally, Idea Swipers. It's a joke, but not really. Both Jerry and Joe were working: Jerry was writing pulp stories, and they were working on different comics. In addition to working on comics, Jerry and Frank Shuster were launching a mail-order school for humor that would teach subscribers, for a small fee, "How to be Funny."[8]

Goober the Mighty also appears in *Popular Comics,* this time trying to open up a formidable gate to "rescue" a sultry princess who looks like Dejah Thoris. Goober is foiled, though, when he, the muscular ape-man, is stung by a bee and runs away. It is the princess then who must save Goober in a turnaround spoof of the genre. Proving that the swapping of identities could also be used to play jokes on the reader, the Shuster art is signed "Stiletto."[9]

For as fun as the cartoon pieces of *Popular Comics* are, it is in the more dramatic pieces, some of them only a page long, that Joe's art shines and Jerry shows real emotional range. *Jimmy Grant* is a strip about a typical "gosh-maw" Depression-era individualist who is wide-eyed but valiantly bound to do the right thing. His adventure in "Death Rides the Rails" is one of a father in peril. Jimmy learns that his dad was the engineer on a runaway thunderbolt train that explodes: "Dad! Dad! I don't see him! Where is he?" Luckily, Jimmy's dad survives, though laid up in a hospital. Jimmy asks: "How did it ever happen, Dad?" "I don't know. I can't remember what occurred. I'm innocent, son. I swear it!—They say I was drunk." Jimmy rises and says: "I know it's a lie and I'll *prove* it to 'em!" This is how Jerry Siegel was beginning to define a hero: as someone who could shoulder the problems of the generation before.[10]

There was also a version of *Jerry the Journalist,* which Joe initially drew for his junior high paper at Alexander Hamilton with Jerry Fine. This version, with a new script by Jerry, offers a much more romanticized role of the press. At this time, Jerry also by his own admission wrote a one-act play called *The Fighting Journalist,* where an individual reporter goes after political corruption. It was never published, but the ideas were close by.[11]

Popular Comics also pokes fun at Glenville High. In *Public Pests,* Joe draws

"'Beerbelly' Windbag, school teacher by vocation—sadist by avocation—homework fiend; notebook addict; delights in driving useless dates into deadened domes; viper; flunks so many students he has been nicknamed 'The D-Man.'" The big man is a villain and is dictatorial, evil, and bald. There are also lots of similar quick, one-page glimpses of gags, characters, and throwaways. There is *Louisville Lil,* about a sassy entertainer who exclaims to her audience: "Believe me! When you're in show business you've gotta show 'em!" There is a football adventure strip for "Speedy," who kicks in a pose exactly like Joe's winning poster image with a big fat "G" on his chest. There are fake self-help ads on "How to Become a Mental Marvel." There is even *The Pinkbaums,* a strip that pokes fun at a Jewish family. Seated around a small table, a young boy is about to have some soup as his older mother and father look on with concern. "Ouch! This soup is hot!" the boy exclaims. "Blow on it, Dummy!" the man growls. The boy does, and the soup ends up all over the man's face. Luckily for the boy, his mother intervenes as the voice of reason: "Meyer, Meyer! Remember your high-blood pressure!" They look like Jerry's parents.[12]

The one-page *Cornelius* is about a rich man in the Depression done in a slight, almost nouveau style by Joe. The reader watches as Cornelius, with top hat and suspenders, wakes up alone in his mansion, where he is attended to by his many manservants without words. The reader marvels at his rich lifestyle until Cornelius finally asks, "My car, Jason." His servants comply by sticking out their thumbs to hitchhike for him.

Jerry and Joe looked at the finished version, and Jerry couldn't believe his eyes. *Science Fiction* looked okay if you squinted; *Popular Comics* looked like something you might actually pay for. The range, the volume, and even the jokes weren't bad. This was the moment they learned one of the most important lessons of growing up: what they were good at doing.

SOLD

Writing funny was easy. But selling comics, funny or otherwise, was not. One of their odd jobs at this time was delivering copies of *The Cleveland Shopping News,* which was basically a tabloid-sized coupon book that was filled with dozens of small ads, discount tabs, and sale announcements for stores all over Cleveland. The paper was an absolute maze, usually with a midsized black-and-white photograph or line drawing on the front. It was made for big silver magnifying glasses that wives kept on a corner stand somewhere. *The Shopping News* also, especially in the early 1930s, began to have cartoons seep in at the sides—these were still part of ads or promotions, but they began to take a marginal hold.

Jerry and Joe took *Popular Comics* to their boss, Mr. Strong, at *The Cleveland Shopping News* and convinced him that a full-color comics newspaper would be a good investment. *The Shopping News* had its own color printing press at 5309 Hamilton Avenue (which was a big part of its success); this allowed Jerry to look Strong in the eye, act as if he were twenty years older than he was, and convince him that comics would work in this format. There was a long pause and a nod. They couldn't believe it. Jerry walked out of Strong's office at about triple speed. *Popular Comics* was going to be published.[13]

They celebrated with a double feature at the movies. Their agreement with Strong was all they could think about. Jerry would remember years later: "A contract! Signed! Fame, success and big money was just around the corner! See, world—see what faith and stick-to-it-iveness can do! Just keep trying and never give up! Luck and happiness are lurking around the corner, right? Just like in all those old Horatio Alger novels."[14]

But Strong changed his mind. Jerry and Joe had all these comics, all of this work, and it would have to sit there, like them, stuck at home. They were back at square one. Jerry would later refer to it as "a low blow."

> Things seemed awfully blue and depressing. The only thing that kept Joe and me from going bonkers was the delicious odor of corned beef wafting seductively from out of Solomon's Delicatessen on Cleveland's East 105th Street. . . . We were too broke to swagger in and buy a round of corned beef sandwiches for everyone . . . or even one sandwich to wolf down between us.[15]

Strong may have balked at the cost of a comics magazine, the audacity of it, or the realization that these were indeed just teenagers. Perhaps feeling sorry for them, he introduced them to his wife, Sophie Taylor, of Taylor's downtown department store. Taylor's actually ran a few different publications of their own: *The Taylorite* for its employees and various advertising tabloids for store promotions that were actually printed by the *Shopping News* presses. Something called *The Taylor Christmas Tabloid* supposedly printed a version of Jerry and Joe's *Interplanetary Police* in 1934.[16] But for the most part, Jerry and Joe were again Snoopy and Smiley. They sent their comics out to more places, *Comics Cuts* and *Funny Wonder* out of Buffalo.[17] They either never heard back or got rejection letters and never saw their material again.[18] So they boxed up *Cornelius, Louisville Lil, Kaye, Jimmy Grant, The Waif, Gloria Glamour* (which featured a playboy named Frank), and *Radio Team* (featuring cousins Rosie and Frank on the radio) and put it all away in the bedroom closet.[19] They *knew* it was good. But nobody wanted it. So it really didn't matter, after all.

Jerry was fed up. All that work and nothing again. He went to buy more magazines and comics but knew it would just make him more upset. They sent out a comics adaptation of the Raymond Palmer story "Whispering Space," which was accepted by *Wonder Stories* but then dropped.[20] The hits kept coming. But this was 1933, a time of rapid change. Just as they had gone from hectograph to photostats, everything was moving into new forms and stages, like rockets. Head down, hands in his pockets, Jerry saw a comic on the stands that was something brand new to him: it was oversize and had an orange-red cardboard cover. It was called *Detective Dan, Secret Operative No. 48.*

The main character, Dan Dunn (Jerry winced at the name, so similar to his own character in "Reign of the Super-man"), was a flat pastiche of cartoon detectives: he had a jaw like Dick Tracy's, a short, pudgy partner like Pat Patton (Dunn's was named Irwin Higgs), and a tendency to behave violently toward those who deserved it. Inspired by the success of hometown Chester Gould's *Dick Tracy,* Chicago-based Humor Publications gambled on putting new material in comic book form and turned to Norman Marsh, who supplied them with *Detective Dan.*[21]

Even in his low mood, Jerry liked what he saw. And as one half of a fledgling comics team, he also saw opportunity. Unfortunately, nothing they had in *Popular Comics* really fit with what Humor Publications was doing—they had funny animals, football players, and sci-fi heroes, but they didn't have any detectives or law enforcers. They did, however, have something floating around the periphery that was new. So Jerry wrote Humor Publications and arranged a meeting; the publisher was coming into Cleveland soon—possibly to attempt a sale of Dan Dunn to the NEA—so the timing was good. Jerry tried to sell him on the new idea.[22] It might even have been part of the *Popular Comics* pile of stuff that was still in development. But it was still different, very different. That "thing" was an older idea recently given a new form and cast. It was called the Superman.

Chapter 8

Morning

JOE EMERGED FROM HIS ROOM, rubbing his eyes. *Jerry's here.* Joe could tell by the way his mother was half smiling at him. She and Joe, who were very close, would joke endearingly about Jerry. He was strange sometimes and frustrating in the way he wanted things, but he was *one of a kind,* as Joe's mother would say. Joe saw his friend in the front room, already dressed and slightly out of breath. Jeanetta was asking him questions about why he was sweating so much. Jerry looked at Joe with wild, flashing eyes. Joe knew something was up. Not wrong. *Up.*

They went into the next room, and his mother held his sister back, saying, *No, no, they are big boys now.* She could sense it, too. Jerry laid out his notes in furious abandon and was talking but making very little sense. Something about two men and time travel. Joe looked at him again— Jerry acted almost as if he didn't even know Joe was there; he was talking to the paper and the scribbled characters before him. Joe grabbed his arm and said, *Slow down.* He took his pencil and told Jerry: *Tell me what it looks like.* Jerry couldn't speak.

By the end of that day, they had sketched out some of what Jerry was referring to as "the Superman." It was the same name as their old *Science Fiction* story, but the character would be different—he would be more like Flash or Buck, a real action hero. Jerry thought it should be a comic. The picture Joe had drawn needed a lot of work; it was basically a guy with no shirt, jumping around. Jerry kept talking about dual identities and babies, but it was all very hazy. It was *some thing,* but not yet *something.*

Jerry was frustrated. He knew it had made more sense to him last night. What was he forgetting? What had he *lost?*

LAST NIGHT

His eyes blink open. It is very late at night, though he has no idea what time it is. He feels something in his mind. He has an idea. Does he get up and write it down or hope he will remember it in the morning? He knows he will later refer to it as the Idea. He sees it as typeset words, though not yet visible. In his head, he starts to move. His body feels nothing.

He gets up and remembers his name is Jerry Siegel and he is hot and he has an idea. No, the Idea. His feet are scraping across the wooden floor, and he feels it in his teeth. His eyes are closing. *No.*

He is at the desk and starts writing it down in longhand, which is strange because he usually types these sorts of things. But he is tired and hot, and there is the Idea pushing at him like a locomotive. He writes some more. He doesn't know if it will make sense in the morning. He writes it down anyway. It is so hot in the room. He almost feels someone there, but he is alone. He looks at the Idea. It is here in the room with the brown walls. It is in his mind and muscles. He thinks he will run over to Joe's in the morning and show him. He thinks *all of this will make a good story someday.*

The atmosphere was perfect for strange creation: "The air was still and heavy. Clouds drifted past the moon. Up there was wind. If only I could fly. If only . . . and SUPERMAN was conceived, not in his entirety, but little by little throughout a long and sleepless night." Jerry remembered basically the same version to whoever would ask:

> I hop right out of bed and write this down, and then I go back
> and think some more for about two hours and get up again and
> write that down. This goes on all night at two-hour intervals,
> until in the morning I have a complete script.[1]

Without stopping for breakfast, as the story goes, Jerry raced through the deserted Glenville dawn to awaken his friend Joe, a few streets over. Breathlessly, he explained the nature of his creation. Without wasting a moment, they began developing the character in comic strip form. Both were seventeen years old. There are several versions of this story, one placing it in 1934, one making it twelve blocks away, and another having Jerry hop out of bed and writing the whole thing down first.[2]

For the dreamer who had been trying so hard to realize his vision of becoming a writer, this is a magical tale about the creative process. And Jerry tells it like the storyteller he was: adjectives like "still" and "heavy" are pulpy and overwrought. He awakens to a perfectly complete script, like something from a dream. After all of the failures, the one idea comes, as if from heaven, and saves him. And it gets repeated as the story of this lone kid writer, his artist pal safe in slumber, secondary, as Jerry works away. "The Story" also makes "the Idea" sound as though it came, like Athena, fully sprung from his forehead.

It was the night of Sunday, June 18, 1933. Sundays for Jerry were generally good days because Shabbat was over and he could actually do things. Not that Jerry was against his parents' religion, but he just didn't see the point to some of it. On Hanukkah, he made fun of always getting an inscribed pen from his father while his friends got more interesting gifts from Santa.[3] On Sundays, though, his mother was usually out at one of her charity meetings somewhere. He could hear the clock ticking and the floors creaking. Jerry looked over at the big chair. His father was gone, but not really. Not really. Sundays were hard. So Jerry sat down, slowly, and opened the paper. It was hot, really hot, as the city was in the middle of an unprecedented heat wave.[4] *The Plain Dealer* that Sunday was full of sections, inserts, coupons, and comics. It was hours caged in print. Still wanting to be a journalist, especially in 1933, Jerry read the paper, just as his dad used to do.

The front page that day was dominated by news from Chicago that Cleveland's East Tech track-and-field superstar Jesse Owens was now, officially, the new "fastest human," posting times of 9.4 seconds in the 100-yard dash, 20.7 seconds in the 220, and "leaping through space" for more than twenty-four feet. He was the miracle of the national meet; "there never has been an individual who approached the performances staged yesterday by Clevelander Jesse Owens" in this, the "greatest display of individual brilliance in the 29-year history of the national interscholastic track and field championships."[5] The paper didn't mince words.

Owens, whose middle name was "Cleveland," was a track-and-field phenomenon who moved to the city when he was nine. At East Tech High School, he competed in every sport on the grass, sand, and mat. After his record-setting performance in Chicago, Owens went to Ohio State University and was nicknamed "the Buckeye Bullet." Owens enjoyed great athletic success but had to live off campus with other black athletes. When he traveled with the team, Owens was restricted to ordering carry-out or eating at "blacks only" restaurants. Owens did not receive a scholarship for his efforts, so he continued to work part-time jobs to pay for school. He set three world records as a collegiate athlete, one that would last twenty-five years. He ran in the infamous 1936 Berlin Olympics and won four gold medals, which very much annoyed Hitler. On the streets of Berlin, everyone wanted Owens's autograph.[6]

But in 1933, Owens, "the Cleveland Phenom," was just beginning his incredible career, and his promise was so attractive to Depression-weary readers that the paper that day ran four stories on him, all of which said essentially the same thing. A few mention his solitary nature, his skills among other "Negro sprinters," but all are aghast at his humility in the face of such overwhelming ability. After the meet, Owens was so besieged by college recruiters that track coach Edgar Weil had him moved from a downtown hotel to the YMCA under an assumed name. Owens, meek, who didn't want a "swelled head," was a superspeedster with a secret identity to hide. The article called him the East Tech "Wonder-Boy."[7]

If Jesse Owens had not been on the front page that day, Jerry might not have read about him. Though Jerry always read deep into the paper, he wasn't much of a sports guy, not like Joe. But one section he would always turn to every day was entertainment and the comics. In the 1930s, that page was the "Men's Magazine and Amusement Section," which was really the radio page, because it listed the schedule of shows. This page also frequently had photos of girls, which added to its allure for boys, who would look at it discreetly while their mothers cooked in the next room. Today's photo featured Harriet Hilliard in a swimsuit and smile, showing readers her backside.[8]

An irregular column on the radio page was written by "Mr. Kilo Cycle," a syndicated expert who would offer editorial commentary on the exciting world of radio from behind the safety of yet another 1930s pen name. Kilo Cycle wrote about radio from a wry, slightly fictionalized way so as to maximize gossip without actually naming names. On that day, June 18, 1933, Kilo Cycle "Tells of an Air Act; Radio Needs to Look into Its Future."[9] To add an air of familiarity, Kilo Cycle's views were often relayed to the reader through a fictional conversation with an equally ambiguously named "Listener." The rhetorical aim was to make readers feel involved. Everyone was pals with everyone else.

The column begins as "Mr. Kilo Cycle clumped heavily into the office.

His frown was one which strikes fear to the heart."[10] The reference is to the terrifying words that would greet listeners of *The Shadow,* the radio show sponsored by Blue Coal. "Who knows what evil lurks in the hearts of men? The Shadow knows"; the chilling voice permeated rooms across the country, prompting kids to steal quick looks toward their fathers, who were smirking behind their newspapers. The Shadow and his alter ego, Lamont Cranston, had nebulous superpowers, but the character was very radio-ambiguous and could change depending on the peril: he could cloud men's minds, toss villains across the room, hide in shadows, and decipher even the most advanced codes.[11]

By 1933, *The Shadow* was on a hiatus of sorts, after being on NBC two times a week at six thirty. "Now what's the matter!" inquires Listener from Kilo's column, a bit perturbed. "Matter enough," storms Mr. Kilo Cycle. "Last night I went to see one of those personal appearance acts by a radio fellow. I had heard him over the air for two years. I had visionalized him as a dashing, fiery sort of hombre with grand determination in his strong chin and the twinkle of love and human kindness in his eye." Mr. Kilo Cycle continues:

> "As I have said . . . I caught my first glimpse of him last night. He was a fat, short, dumpy person. His eyes were a mild blue. His hands were chubby. He was uneasy even in the make-believe surroundings of the theater. And," at this point Mr. Kilo Cycle fixed Listener with a glassy stare, "he had, so help me, a double chin."[12]

Kilo Cycle iterates a common problem with radio: that the people providing the voices of strong, stalwart heroes often did not look the part when revealed in photos in newspapers or celebrity magazines. This is why so few of them made the transition to movies. If Kilo is talking about *The Shadow,* as his preamble suggests, then he is probably referring to Frank Readick, who joined the show in 1931 ("two years") and who originated the show's deeply intoned opening, done through a water glass for effect. In real life, Readick was "short, and gray-haired."[13] When *The Shadow* did end for a time, Readick actually unmasked onstage in September 1931 to reveal himself as the main character. Prior to this dramatic moment, the program's producers had carefully disguised the actor's identity to make the Shadow more mysterious. But once a very un–Shadow-like Readick revealed himself, the suspension of disbelief fizzled.[14]

The Listener doesn't believe Kilo's blasphemy, but when Kilo offers him free tickets to see for himself, he turns them down, not eager to have his radio illusions shattered. What makes this realization hurt is that both Kilo and the Listener are unapologetic admirers of *The Shadow*. As Kilo says: "I had followed his adventures with loyal interest. I had listened in pop-eyed admiration as his solid fists thudded against the chins of any number of villains."[15]

> "He must have been a whizz," Listener mused, impressed.
> "A whizz?" Mr. Kilo Cycle fairly snorted at the phrase. "Say, fellow, he was a super man!"[16]

Hovering over the page, Jerry might have blinked and read that last line again. Whether he knew it then or was just reacquainting himself with the name from his old *Science Fiction* story, Jerry was seeing "super man" in a new light—a heroic one where a man, a "super man," appears different from how (and who) he really is.

Kilo goes on to seriously consider what he calls "radio's future." He believes that the "broadcasters who really have radio's future at heart will keep striving to hold entertainment in first position on the kilocycles. . . . With the passing of the bloody crime cycle, radio would turn next season to romance." He was saying, Jerry thought, that the crime dramas would give way to something completely different: romance. That would have to be part of it. At the bottom of the column is an illustrated advertisement for round, wire-framed glasses.[17]

In this same edition of the newspaper, Jesse Owens was exhibiting near superpowers, and now Jerry was reading about a "super man" who hid behind a secret, awkward identity. And the city was indeed in the middle of a heat wave. Days later, on July 2, CLEVELAND ROASTS AS MERCURY TWICE RISES TO 90-MARK.[18] TEN DEAD AS OHIO IS HEAT WEARY is the headline, accompanied by a photo illustration of a small boy in a tie with a little smile. The heartbreaking story is that the boy, little John Streal, drowned in the old Ohio Canal trying to learn how to swim. He had no one to rescue him.[19]

Back to the June 18 paper, Jerry reads: AUSTRIA OUTLAWS THE NAZI PARTY, as whispers begin about gathering shadows in Europe. In an article about crime titled "Angry Uncle Sam Fights Gangland," a Department of

Justice agent from Oklahoma City is quoted about a horrible shoot-out that kills a federal agent: "I heard a man shouting up, up," as he sees a "shooting red flame" and he ducks "as bullets splintered our car." The rest of the paper is filled with the usual early-1930s fare: crime, politics, and murder, all in sometimes nearly indistinguishable categories. As one article noted, a "Girl, 6," was even "killed at tag." The world needed help and there was no letup in sight. The forecast is for "Warmer for Beginning of Week." And on the front page, Jesse Owens has his hands outstretched with a shieldlike symbol on his tank top–clad chest.[20]

It was time.

Over on the comics page that day, the first offering was *Sappo* by E. C. Segar, with his trademark fat cigar. In the first panel, a reporter questions a grieving, squat Mrs. Sappo if her "husband left the earth in a space ship."

Sappo wonders whether the Professor is "serious about going to Mars." The Professor responds: "he he he." The comic ends with cutout "Play-Money" for "Spinach Soup."[21]

Half a page down, Segar makes us wait for his other strip, the beloved *Thimble Theatre,* which begins with yet another version of J. Wellington Wimpy's always funny attempt at a free lunch: "Listen, come have a hamburger with me on you." The plot is that Popeye has agreed to fight a gigantic man, "Bullo Oxheart, the strongest man in the world." Popeye agrees to the fight because he is told that it "might rake in a lot of jack."

"I'll take him on," the Sailor-Man says as he marks a target on Ox's belly where he is going to hit him. Once Popeye signs the contract, Oxheart tries to scare him with a series of unbelievable physical feats. Ox first lifts five hundred pounds, to which Popeye responds: "Any swab could lift a pe-annie." Ox responds by lifting a giant iron safe onto his back. When that still isn't enough, Ox lifts an outlandish twenty-five-hundred-pound dumbbell. Popeye, smirking, leaves the house, which then starts shaking as Ox falls over, exclaiming, "Wot de heck! Dis house is movin!" In the last panel, Popeye is seen lifting the house from its corner foundation, barely breaking a sweat: "'Sa good thing I been eatin' spinach lately Arf Arf."[22]

Besides *Tim Tyler's Luck* and *Tillie the Toiler* in the comics stack, there is *Little Orphan Annie,* in which Annie reminisces about her adoptive parents and how nice they were to take her in—as the orphan, the other, the alien. On the last page of the comics, Tarzan leaps and jumps around a man in a black robe. Everything in the funny pages was about play money, cutout dresses, and impossible dreams. Money, products, and imagination were going hand in hand. Wimpy asks Popeye and Oxheart in the *Thimble Theatre* strip, "Do either of you gentlemen know where I can get a hundred thousand dollars?" This was the question that everyone, including Jerry, was asking.

Jerry might have been reading so fast that his eyes were burning. Everything was leading to something, like invisible threads through the universe that he could almost just see. Jerry was a thinker, always running that brain over ideas and possibilities to tell and sell. So when he went to bed that night, if he even did, getting out of the chair and shuffling his feet in disbelief or taking the back stairs like a police car, he must have had an overwhelming sense of sudden inevitability. The constant looking for clues and signs, whether they were from girls, stories, or letters from publishers, had given him an ability to absorb things—and then, like the writer he was trying desperately to become, give them back to an audience. These shards of ideas seemed almost to be boxing him in; he was straining and pushing against them. As he slept, wrote, dreamed, his brain was working all of these threads into the beginnings of an image, a costume, a tapestry.

That particular newspaper, on that particular night, showed how many of these topics were available in the air for the dreamer who was looking for them: feats of strength, secret identities, alien worlds, and unbelievable human suffering all across the globe. But what that night really did, whenever it was, was change Jerry's stance on "Reign of the Super-man." He may have taken parts of the story from the earlier Francis Flagg tale, but Jerry was now at the point where he could steal and develop ideas from himself. And all of it was there in "Reign": the one man as two, the powers, the importance of goodness over greed, and the realization, of Dunn and now Jerry, that a hero would be a much better choice than a villain.

So the next morning, Jerry ran to Joe's and told him everything he knew. And they put together a quick—very quick—proposal for the people in Chicago who made *Detective Dan*. Joe copied the lettering, titles, and pricing from *Detective Dan* almost exactly.[23] Joe did his trademark bridges and cross-hatching. On August 23, 1933, Humor Publications wrote to Jerry:

> *We have delayed in replying . . . until we could give the matter of*
> *"The Superman" deliberate consideration . . . should we desire to put*

out another edition of DETECTIVE DAN, if the author and
artists is not agreeable, we then will be glad to take the matter up
with you.[24]

Jerry might actually have been surprised: *Really?* The new Superman
idea was only half-formed at this point and the art was rushed and rough,
which was completely understandable given the short turnaround. Nonetheless, they got his hopes up, even though he had heard this all before.
But *Detective Dan* never got a sec-
ond issue and was canned.[25]

The story goes that Joe was so
mad that he burned the early
proposal in the fire and that Jerry
could rescue only the cover.[26]
But since it was summer and the
Shusters never had any coal anyway, this seems unlikely. It makes
more sense that Joe was mad because Jerry had told him about
going to another artist.[27] A cover
would turn up years later that
showed a man leaping from
above to stop a robber who is
pointing a gun at a tied-up
hostage—who looks like Joe in
glasses and a suit. Done in black
and white, it is titled "The Su-
perman," a "Science Fiction Story in Cartoons." The cityscape is Joe's,
complete with a bridge lifted almost directly from the old *Science Fiction*
contents pages and "Reign of the Super-man." The robber looks like a
cartoon bulldog and is hunched over, oblivious to the avenger leaping on
him from above. The Superman is shirtless and may have a white streak
in his hair. The piece is unsigned by Joe, though at the very bottom left,
in a small text box, it reads: "©1928—Joe Shuster and Jerome Siegel."[28]

This copyright notice is strange. For one, when Jerry and Joe signed
something, it was usually in script and they never put a © on anything.
Also, "1928" is problematic because they probably didn't even know
each other then—Joe had just arrived in Cleveland and was attending

Hamilton.[29] There is also another version dated 1933.[30] The simple answer might be that Jerry and Joe had slyly backdated their work—to make it look as though they had put more work into it than they actually had.[31]

After getting the rejection letter, Jerry went up to his solitary room, silently furious. He knew the idea was perfect and was upset that it all looked rushed. So he pulled out his list of addresses again and started looking—he was going to find a new artist for the Superman. Jerry was convinced, just as he was in those early pulp days, that you had to align yourself with someone famous to be famous yourself. He and Joe were friends, but something had to give. This was the third strike. Over the next year, Jerry contacted several major artists, including Mel Graff,[32] J. Allen St. John, and even Bernie Schmittke, who drew some samples of Superman for him.[33] But no one really wanted to commit. So Jerry sent another letter to Chicago, this time to someone else.

Back in the Shuster apartment, Joe walked around for a while and rubbed his eyes. Sometimes he was overwhelmed by Jerry. He knew he had not done his best work on the Chicago proposal. Joe looked at his glasses; he hated his glasses, and when he drew, he sometimes put his eyes so close to the page that his mother would turn and frown—not out of displeasure at his actions, but at the necessity of them. They took him to doctors, who said he had weak eyesight and prescribed thick glasses that he would shove in his pocket at any opportunity. There was nothing anyone could do. His eyes, his great strength, were also the source of his greatest fear: losing his sight for good. In some very real ways, you could see it in his work. His characters had narrow slits for eyes, and everything was in broad, thick strokes. Joe was capable of great detail, but his figures were always solidly simple: larger than life and clean and confident. He thought working out would help, and he thought sometimes maybe it did. He put his pencil down. He knew Jerry was angry, but it would pass. It always did. He closed his eyes.

MOVING FORWARD

By 1934, the halls of Glenville were no longer full of mystery and promise. Jerry knew every corner, just about every face, and he snickered at the freshmen when they turned around in the halls. Jerry had been here a long time, and most of his friends were gone. This was their last year at

Glenville, and it was time to move on. Jerry had been there longer than Joe but had been held back because of grades, though losing his father was probably part of it. As he prepared to say good-bye, he adopted more of a reflective mood. On April 14, the whole student body was stunned when Samuel Biskind, a *Torch* writer and friend of Jerry's, died. The *Torch* wrote: "He was respected and admired by everyone, and his short, yet full life, should be an inspiration. All who knew him were affected deeply by his death."[34]

On May 17, The *Torch* announced the winners of its annual short-story contest. The winner, Jeannette Lehman, won $2, and her story was printed in that same issue. The article goes on to say that "Jerry Siegel of 216 won second for his story, 'Death of a Parallelogram.' None of the other winning stories will be printed."[35] Even at the end of his high school career, Jerry couldn't win the big contest. He felt ready to move on.

Jerry Siegel and Joe Shuster finally graduated from Glenville High School in June 1934.[36] Jerry left a mountain of articles, poems, jokes, and funny stories in the pages of an already yellowing archive in the school library that would remain relatively undisturbed for decades. The following summer and fall were all work, paid and otherwise. They both had delivery jobs: Joe delivered groceries for $5 a week; Jerry moved papers for a printing plant for a dollar less. Joe also sold ice-cream bars.[37]

Joe opened his eyes and started drawing. But Jerry was doing something secret.

He had found another artist.

EARTH-2

Russell Keaton sat at his drawing table in Chicago with a thin pipe and a bright lamp. He used to be a "ghost" on Dick Calkins's *Buck Rogers* newspaper strip, meaning he would fill in backgrounds, details, and sometimes faces to keep things moving and on schedule—but all without a byline. Keaton was so good that he eventually took over the *Buck Rogers* Sunday page completely from 1930 to 1933 and turned it into a Technicolor explosion of chubby ships and curling alien tentacles.[38] In 1934, though, Keaton was looking for ways to get his own strip again. So when he got a letter from Cleveland out of nowhere, he put down his pipe to read it.

The letter is dated June 12, 1934, and is typed by someone named "Jerry Siegel." In long paragraphs, Jerry proposes an idea that is "a trifle fantastic," concerning a character with "infinite strength" named "Superman." Jerry promises both "humor and adventure" in tales involving the young Clark Kent, before he becomes Superman.

"Early, he will find that his great strength, instead of making friends for him, causes people to fear him. Mothers will not permit their children to associate with him; he will be hated in school sports because he never loses, and so on. We can weave a very human story about him."

Jerry also included a scripted list of panels beginning in the laboratory of a scientist, "the last man on earth," who is working furiously as "giant cataclysms" shake his "reeling planet." The scientist places "his infant babe" not in a rocket ship, but into "a small time-machine." As the earth explodes, the "time-vehicle" sparks back to "the primitive year, 1935 A.D."

A motorist finds Clark, who is then placed in an orphanage. Soon, the babe from the future starts bending the bars of his crib. He finds outlets for his great strength: "At the age of five, when an older boy sought to bully him, Clark sent him flying thru the air."

When he gets even older, the standards are introduced as Jerry notes that Clark could "leap over a ten story building, raise unheard-of weights . . . run as fast as an express train, and that nothing less than a bursting shell could penetrate his tough skin." But Kent is a good kid and decides to serve mankind by becoming "SUPERMAN, champion of the oppressed, the physical marvel who had sworn to devote his existence to helping those in need!" In the closing, Jerry notes that the Bell Syndicate was already interested in the idea. He casually asks Keaton to "let me know if you would care to work with me upon this strip."[39]

Keaton looked at the letter in disbelief. *Who was this guy?* But he had to admit, the idea was not so bad. The script was professional and the story breaks seemed good. And if Bell was interested, could he afford to miss the opportunity? He didn't know why, but something about the way this guy talked was persuasive. *Superman?* He latched on to some paper and drew it up.

The version that Keaton drew is an origin story of a three-year-old Superman who is rocketed to 1935 from the future instead of a faraway planet. The Kents (here named Molly and Sam) come across the rocket and rescue the infant. They place him into an awful orphanage, where the young child—dressed in gladiator boots and with an "O" symbol on his chest—escapes from his steel-barred cage. The Kents return to adopt him and name him "Clark." While the Kents puzzle over his strength, young Clark takes on a neighbor bully and lifts him high into the air.

The Kents then find Clark in the basement, draped over his time-ship, weeping. Sam remarks: "Why—He's crying! Molly, I think he's homesick— for his real parents." Molly responds: "If only we knew from where he came and who his parents are!" This is a Superman more like *Little Or-*

phan Annie in some ways, whose character is still centered on parents and a father who sends his son out all alone.

Jerry tried to sell this version to the syndicates, but no one was interested, so Keaton gave up. Jerry begged him to stay, but Keaton had other plans: he sold his own strip, *Flyin' Jenny,* an adventure serial about a female aviatrix in World War II. He would write and draw this popular cartoon until he died of melanoma at age thirty-five in 1945.[40] Jerry knew he would have to go back to Joe. He hoped there would be no hard feelings. He just didn't know how to do it.

Sometime later, Jerry ended up at the drugstore, as he always did. He knew he would buy something, though he wasn't too excited by what he saw. Then he saw a cover he had not seen before—it was called *New Fun.* And it was filled with comics. But something was different. He thumbed through it quickly—animals, adventure—this was exactly what they had tried to do with their old *Popular Comics.* Jerry bought it and ran it over to Joe, who smiled, looked, and froze. Their stuff from *Popular Comics* was way better than half of this junk. They didn't really say anything else. They just got started—again. They had a new place to send to.

Chapter 9
Major

MAJOR MALCOLM WHEELER-NICHOLSON was called "the Major" for the simple reason that he actually was one. In his service in the U.S. Cavalry from 1917 to 1923, the Major became a decorated military war hero, traveling from the Philippines to Mexico, battling both invaders and natural disasters in a mixture of genuine American heroism and wartime exaggeration. His life read like the biography of a president or a secret agent: he helped hunt down Pancho Villa in 1916 and ended up in Paris, where he became infatuated by a woman named Elsa. He was full of his own amazing stories, but only he knew which ones were true. He spoke out against President Warren G. Harding and may have even been the victim of an assassination attempt. But after all of these adventures, he ran smack-dab into the Depression and back into the true love of his youth: writing. The Major had grown up on Kipling and knew the power of a good sentence, so he began a new career by crafting his own. Drawing on his army experience, he wrote hundreds of stories, poems, and wartime accounts for the adventure pulps of the early twentieth century, before the science fiction and weird stuff became popular. His style was concise but bombastic, romantic but real. His stories—many anonymous, many not—were dust-filled, sun-drenched battle tales full of horses, honor, and boys made men.[1]

The Major cannily knew a larger business opportunity when he saw it—after seeing *Famous Funnies,* he wanted to publish his own comics magazine to capitalize on the new market.[2] So he set up a card table and chair in an eleventh-floor office of the Hathaway building on Fourth

Avenue in New York City and in 1934 formed National Allied Publications.[3] By February 1935, *New Fun* #1 hit the stands. *New Fun* was historical because it contained new material—all of the popular cartoons
had been syndicated already, so the Major actively looked for (and commissioned) new ones. *New Fun* was not only one of the first comic
books, it was the first independent comic book. Because it was a salon
for new talent, it did more than create the comic book, it helped create
the industry.[4]

The Major was reading some new submissions but kept going back to
the ones from Ohio. His mind wandered over the gulf from Manhattan
to Cleveland—who *were* these boys? Because of his days in the army, he
had never underestimated youth. The Major was impressed with their
talent, especially Shuster's heavily masculine art style, so he sent them a
character to work on. When they got the letter, they got right to
work—this was a tryout, they knew it—and submitted two strips to the
Major: *Henri Duval* and *Dr. Occult*. One was drawn on brown paper and
one on the back of wallpaper. They were just sketches, but the Major
liked them enough to give the boys a shot.[5] And just like that, all the
lost promises and phantom second issues were gone: Siegel and Shuster
had broken into the new industry of comics, on the back of torn butcher's paper.

They read the letter from the Major together: "your remuneration . . .
would not be great."[6] He was offering them $10 each, a total of $20, per
page. They split it fifty-fifty. Their first published collaboration was *Henri
Duval,* which ran for only a few episodes beginning in *New Fun Comics*
#6 in October 1935. *Duval* was a Three Musketeers rip-off and was all
about horses, cavaliers, and pretty ladies in pretty dresses wailing to be
rescued. The genre was popular from the movies. Joe drew fast but with
a searing purpose because they knew this was their big opportunity. He
piled on the hair and copied out some nice carriages. Since he was left-
handed, he would switch to his right to letter when he ran out of steam.
When his ink ran low, he would put in a few drops of water. This made
his line lighter but let it go a bit longer.[7] They sent their strips back to the
Major to be colored and published. School was over and things were happening fast. The Major liked what he saw but dropped *Henri Duval* and
gave the boys work that was more in their wheelhouse. He gave them
more of the Doctor.

STRANGE

Sometimes when his mom was busy, Jerry would go up to his room and slowly close the door behind him. He got out the heavy book and held it up with one hand, on the very tips of his fingers. His arm started wobbling, but he stopped himself. He held the book up almost as if it were levitating. Jerry had his pulp books, even the ones that he had to stuff under the bed. But this book he needed to hide away for real. Since his father's death, his mother was less interested in the contents of Jerry's room. So he took it out and looked at words he didn't understand. The book talked of spirits, the *Jah-El,* and the spectre *umbratile.* It was filled with strange, sweeping symbols. Jerry had ordered it from the last page of a dark, beat-up pulp. It was a book of magic.[8]

Jerry's literary tastes were not limited to science fiction. He also had a penchant for the supernatural. Joe's sister would recall that Jerry would often show her books and pamphlets about magic—the kind that didn't involve rabbits.[9] As with similar eager boys of his generation, this fascination was both focused and magnified by one magazine in particular, the mesmerizing *Weird Tales,* the most influential horror fiction magazine ever published. Boasting authors such as Robert Howard and Clark Ashton Smith, *Weird Tales* inspired generations of writers who would read reprints of these uncanny stories for decades to come. Jerry was there for the original. He wrote an early letter to *Weird Tales* that was printed in October 1933, one of the most famous issues of the title's run, mostly for its eerie Margaret Brundage cover of a woman in black leather dressed like a bat.

> Writes Jerome Siegel, of Cleveland, Ohio: "I was pleased to note the change of type in the latest copy of WEIRD TALES. It is soothing to the eye. An intangible change in my attitude toward WEIRD TALES went out with the old type and one much better has come in. I have never written in before, but have decided to do so after reading the unusually fine issue of August. Edmond Hamilton is at his best and he is sure to be acclaimed once more by the readers who had begun to tire of his routine plot. . . . Another good story was our faithful August W. Derleth's. His short tales are masterpieces of realism. . . . Edmond Hamilton's *Pigmy Island* is in my opinion easily the

best story in the issue. The weird sensation of being but a foot
tall and confronted by huge rats was vividly told."[10]

The 1930s had a larger cultural fascination with the occult as well;
though the fascination with spiritualism was dissipating, any magician
worth his salt still included a spirit act as part of his performance. The
golden age of magic with Houdini and Blackstone had passed, so magicians used elaborate schemes of stagecraft to pull off feats like floating
spirits, thrown voices, and self-decapitation, which was the specialty of
Harry Kellar. Howard Thurston threw out cards with mystical lucky
symbols on them. Magicians could miraculously lift cars.[11]

Modern science was pulling all of this nonsense right off the stage.
Even Gernsback had a standing offer that reached to more than $11,000 for
ironclad proof of the spirit world.[12] With the advent of science fiction,
the occult seemed to flicker away, but it still resisted complete annihilation. So
instead of claiming to be "real," magic just became "weird"—meaning it
moved to more fictional, imaginative spaces. Radio and cinema were ha-
vens of this kind of weird horror in the thirties, terrorizing audience
dreams with their lurching, monstrous sounds and images that relied on
physical reality.

Jerry and Joe channeled this interest into a character named Dr. Occult, the Ghost Detective, a trench-coat-wearing hero who fights evil
forces in and around Cleveland. He also debuted in *New Fun Comics* #6
in October 1935.[13] Dr. Occult carried a powerful magical symbol and
was adept in fighting while in astral form. His early adventures pitted him
against vampires, werewolves, and an evil mine owner who had a work-
force of zombie miners. The character itself might have been an echo of
a radio episode of *The Shadow* on the old *Blue Coal Mystery Revue*. On
October 12, 1932, an episode called "The Image"[14] features a professor
who specializes in the occult—and who horribly transforms into a were-
wolf in front of his own eyes.[15] Dr. Occult does the same in *More Fun* #12
as he watches himself change in a mirror.[16] Jerry adds a supporting cast
that includes Occult's police contact, Captain Ellsworth (named for the
Major's editor, Whitney Ellsworth), and Occult's beautiful assistant, Rose
Psychic. *Dr. Occult* would be first signed with the Siegel/Shuster anagram
of Legar and Reuths—mostly because *Henri Duval* was initially appearing
in the same magazine.

In a longer, multi-issue serial appearing in *More Fun Comics* #14–17,

Dr. Occult battles the evil sorcerer Koth across the astral plane as a champion of the Seven, a mystical cabal of great power. The Seven gifts Occult with a magic belt and a short cape. He also wears a familiar triangular power symbol on his chest. He is led by his mentor, Zator (who shares his name with a small town in Poland), who describes Occult's mission as a "superhuman" one.[17] Jerry liberally steals names from biblical history and other pulp stories.[18] Dr. Occult has no superpowers, but Joe puts a fair amount of detail into his mystical symbol—it is not a cross, a star, or a pentagram, but a curiously inverted triangle, very close in design to a rose croix, the symbol of the Rosicrucian Order.[19]

The Rosicrucian Order was an esoteric philosophy centered on an Order of Secret-Keepers, each of whom is a doctor and a confirmed bachelor. Sure enough, there are ads for Rosicrucian literature, specifically the American version—the Ancient and Mystical Order Rosæ Crucis (AMORC)—in the backs of many of the pulps.[20] The order was interested in the psychic body, karma, sacred architecture, and reincarnation, among other extant hopes and ideas. In his adventures as a mystical detective, Occult fights an array of strange enemies that echo some of AMORC's advertised tenets: the Methuselah Killer,[21] who seems to be immortal, and the Lord of Life,[22] who actually kills Occult and then resurrects him so that he may serve him.[23] Jerry may have been drawn to the occult for answers, especially in the wake of his father's death, but the other quality he seeks in this realm of thinking, justice, is more fictional than satisfying.

LEARNING TO WALK

When Jerry dropped down his front steps in the summer and saw the local kids playing in the street, they were not playing cowboys and Indians. Instead, it was always cops and robbers, as they ran around with sticks for tommy guns and faces dirty from whole mornings spent hiding behind hedges with their heartbeats thundering in their ears. The bad guys slicked their hair back with spit and talked in a bad imitation of Edward G. Robinson—*See?* The real heroes of the 1930s held three positions: cops, G-men, and agents. So it is no surprise that Jerry and Joe did comics stories based on all three. The perception (and in some places reality) was that people everywhere were being threatened by crime, both individually and as a nation. Criminals could knock over a fruit stand or a sovereign government with equal ease. The one thing that stood in that narrowing gap between evil and justice was the golden badge of the law. That badge—and the uncorrupted ideal of it—meant something to people in the 1930s. The shield signified justice, protection, and order.

Radio Squad for *New Fun* was a smart play on a subject matter that was already very popular in comics, radio, and film: the new "science" of radio that allowed roaming squad cars to stay in contact with police stations in order to better protect the city. This was tire-scorching police drama that could be narrated over radio. The technology was borderline science fiction to audiences and had already inspired not only a film but a comic strip called *Radio Patrol,* which was started in 1934 by Eddie Sullivan and Charlie Schmidt.[24] In it, Sergeant Pat, Sam, and the go-get-'em boyhood charm of Pinky Pinkerton dispensed Irish police justice around a fictional version of Boston.[25]

Jerry and Joe's *Radio Squad* drew more on the powerful visuals of the car chase. Joe was one of the first to turn these qualities—sound effects, collisions, and the general uncontrollable mayhem of the automobile— into careening, terrifying imagery. Joe liked cars, but they were a menace in Cleveland—the papers frequently ran gory statistics about how many people were being killed per month in pedestrian and auto accidents. Cleveland had one of the highest car fatality rates in the country.[26] Jerry too had a personal stake in automobile safety; as a kid on Kimberley, he was once sideswiped by a car as he engaged in a popular activity—dodging cars on the street.[27]

Radio Squad ran for seven solid years from 1936 to 1943.[28] The main character was Sandy Kean, the dedicated policeman, and his eventual partner, Larry Trent, who drove trusty Car 54 a good twenty years before the television show of the same name.[29] Whereas *Dr. Occult* catered to Jerry's interest in the supernatural, *Radio Squad* is Shuster at his finest, with detailed cars, plunging hats, and alarming moments as Kean and Trent navigated the squealing corners of the city.

Some of the major exploits included chasing down the Purple Tiger Gang in the first adventure, when the feature was actually named *Calling All Cars.*[30] Sandy helps track a kidnapped woman named Doris Bailey; at one point, they use modern radio technology to keep tabs on the ransom money.[31] But the stories are not all action: there is tense courtroom drama, popular songs (Jerry quotes the Johnny Mercer song "Too Marvelous for Words" in one episode),[32] and lots of mystery solving. Once Sandy's partner, Larry Trent, is introduced, there is a strong partner element to the series that suggests how close Jerry and Joe were working at the time. Just as Sandy and Trent shared an apartment in the strip, Jerry was over at Joe's house every day as they worked out scripts and stories. They were working their own partnership over the flat sheets of paper separated into straight squares and panels.

FEDERAL MEN

Even more elevated than the regular cops were the men of the Federal Bureau of Investigation, the grim, stalwart G-men who fought the criminals who broke the laws of the nation. The FBI boys burst out of cars with machine guns at the ready and peppered tires, windows, and overcoats with their government-issued lead. At least that's what the movies showed and therefore was the public perception of these men: the last, biggest hope of eliminating crime. From the real-life, sometimes embellished gangland victories of J. Edgar Hoover to the massive film success of James Cagney in the 1935 movie *G Men,* federal justice was where the big personalities were.

Siegel and Shuster's *Federal Men* began in *New Comics* #2 in 1936 as a direct response to the Cagney film and starred fictional FBI agent Steve Carson. He would later be partnered with Ralph Ventor (another wink to Kenton) on larger, more dangerous cases. In the first episode, "The Manning Baby Kidnapping," Jerry and Joe audaciously attack the most infamous crime of the decade—the kidnapping of the Lindbergh baby—which dominated headlines, radios, and conversations around coffeepots. The kidnapper in the *Federal Men* version is a brunette named Kate Lane, who is short-haired, gorgeous, and good with a gun.[33] But the squad stops her cold. In subsequent episodes, they would portray undercover work, police corruption, and even secret criminal organizations.

Their most ambitious *Federal Men* appears in issues #4–10 and involves a full-scale terrorist invasion of Washington, D.C. Joe renders futuristic tanks and weird helmeted armies that run roughshod over American soil. You can almost see Joe drooling over his depiction of a giant robot stomping on the Capitol.[34] Once Steve tracks down those responsible, the "Invisible Empire," he is followed by girl reporter Jean Dennis of the *Tribune,* who even gets involved in the fighting. The costumes of the Empire armies are red with a logo on their chests. Things were beginning to percolate. Strange costumes return in *Federal Men of Tomorrow* in *New*

Adventure Comics 12 (the comic switched titles three times). This story, a "what if" tale, takes place in the year 3000, where the main character is a space lawman named Jor-L.[35]

Another staple of 1930s serial fiction was the junior fan club, like the old Seck Hawkins Club. So Jerry started one of his own, the Junior G-men Club, which appeared in *New Adventure Comics* #14. The comic advertised: "If young readers would send in a thin dime, they would receive a personal letter from Steve Carson himself!" In the story, youngsters Frank and Lonny (who sells ice cream) see notorious hood "Blackie" kidnap someone, so they use what they learned reading *Federal Men* (of course) to foil the bad guy with no small amount of comedy. The lines between worlds cross, even more because Joe depicts Blackie as a dead ringer (with similar Jerry dialogue) for Edward G. Robinson. Jerry takes things even further in blurring the barrier between the real world, comics, and Hollywood aspiration when he places *himself* in the story in the form of a rascally newsboy named "Jerry." When the hero of the story goes down, it is up to Jerry and his pals (all of them members of the Junior G-men Club) to catch the criminal. Jerry recognizes the merit in allowing his reader to mentally inhabit one of his characters, just as he does as a writer. At the end of his adventure, Jerry is congratulated by his parents—both of them.[36]

Sometimes when he was writing these stories, Jerry's little nieces Norma and Rita would run in and ask him what he was doing, yelling, *Uncle Jeromey!* at the top of their lungs.[37] Jerry would always gather them in, tell them stories, and compliment their dresses. So when he creates a Junior G-girls Club in *New Adventure Comics* #23, he names the main two characters, two precocious little girls, after them. The fictionalized Norma and Rita stop a snooty, high-society shoplifter, and the next day, the Junior Federal Men Club extends an invitation for the girls to join. But the girls, their pigtails in the air, only say they'll "think it over."[38] Jerry never could write good damsels in distress: he was much more interested in feistier women, young and old, who were in direct competition with their male counterparts, foreshadowing Lois and Clark.

SPY

Spy took police work to the highest, international levels of justice. Starring the dashing Bart Regan, *Spy* was the first of the Siegel/Shuster com-

ics to consistently pair a man and a woman in every episode. But Sally
Norris was no trifling sidekick; she ran and fought with Bart on all of his
globe-trotting adventures. They would eventually marry—and go on
even more hair-raising missions.[39] *Spy* was only four pages long for the
most part and had stories dealing with everything from blimp sabotage to
international femmes fatales. Though clearly the most global of the three
law-and-order comics, *Spy* was also the most topical. In "The Hooded
Hordes" in the later *Detective Comics* #17, Jerry and Joe show Bart and
Sally trying to stop a domestic terrorist group who wear tall white hoods.
Called the Hooded Hordes, they are the comics version of the Ku Klux
Klan.[40] The Klan was very active in Ohio at this time, especially in eastern Ohio, where the story itself takes place.[41] Bart and Sally shut them
down—but only Jerry perhaps knew how dangerous it might have been
to publish this story so close to an actual location of Klan activity. It
didn't stop him; adding real-life elements to his writing never did. Jerry
may have been a nebbish in real life, but in his comics he was fearless. In
addition to depicting the Klan, Jerry writes about a sitting senator in
"Saving Senator Barkly" in *Detective Comics* #20. Alben William Barkley
was the senator from Kentucky who gave the keynote at the 1932 Demo-
cratic convention that nominated Franklin Delano Roosevelt. When
Barkley ran for reelection himself, he gave so many speeches that papers
would later dub him "Iron Man."[42] In "The President's Assignment,"
FDR himself appears to send Bart and Sally on a mission of upmost importance.[43]

From 1935 on, Jerry and Joe got paid, for the most part, for producing
these adventures of the triumphs of the law. They had fictional characters
covering local streets, enforcing federal laws, and stopping international
terrorists. They had a good thing going. They still were not satisfied.

Chapter 10

Next

JOE WAS YAWNING A LOT LATELY. His mom and brother noticed, as did Jerry, who was usually too buried in a book or his own words to notice things like that. They all knew why. Joe had been up again the night before, late. Now that school was over, Joe was in some ways even busier. He worked at one of his delivery jobs during the day, came home, wolfed down his supper, and got right to drawing. Joe didn't necessarily like being sleepy, but he really liked drawing. So he would stay up, well into the small hours. Some nights he would be up so late that when he was about done with the face he was working on, he could hear the birds outside his window. Those nights were hardest on his eyes, and sometimes his mother would watch him, unseen, from the silent hallway.

Joe liked the quiet. He came up with his best work at night: no sun, no distractions, no Jerry. The night was more dramatic and real; he could imagine things better without everything else going on. During the day, he would dream and take notes in his head of the things he would draw that night.

They were doing more than comics these days, though where they found the time was anyone's guess. In 1935, Jerry, acting on behalf of his newest venture, the American Artists League, sold two of Joe's cartoons and a logo to a local golf magazine called *Cleveland District Golfer,* published by the Hub Company. They were paid a total of $7.50. Jerry sold pencil layouts done by Joe to the Advertising Production Company in the city for $10, though the work was never used. In September 1935, Jerry sold some comic poetry for use in valentine cards produced by the Consolidated Printing and Publishing Company for a whopping $15. Jerry kept a stiff and exacting ledger; he had learned this from the clothing store.[1] Joe also sold a total of eighteen *Strange Facts* cartoons to "Artists' Pictorial Publ." for $15. In November 1935, Joe also did an advertising drawing for Bernard J. Kenton, which, given the familiar name, might have just been a shady accounting move by Jerry. The biggest payout was $35 for "3 pages and a cartoon for X-comic tab," the infamous Christmas tabloid.[2] They were doing something steady and measured over a long period of time. Somehow, against all odds, they had found themselves careers.

DETECTIVE

In the midst of all this mad production, the Major, their boss, anxiously wrote them a letter dated March 20, 1936:

> *We are now assembling our third magazine of the group, the financial arrangements of which were settled in a conference today. There will be from four to six pages of work in that for you.*[3]

That third magazine would turn out to be *Detective Comics*. In a letter dated May 13, 1936, Nicholson expanded on what he wanted in no uncertain terms:

> *We need some more work from you. We are getting out at least one new magazine in July and possibly two. The first one is definitely in the works. It will contain longer stories and fewer. From you and Shuster we need sixteen pages monthly. We want a detective hero called Slam Bradley. He is to be an amateur, called in by the police to help unravel difficult cases. He should combine both brains and brawn, be able to think quickly and reason cleverly and be able as well to slam bang his way out of a bar room brawl or mob attack. Take every opportunity to show him in a torn shirt with swelling biceps and powerful torso a la Flash Gordon. The pages are to run the same size as NEW COMICS but to contain eight panels a page instead of six. The budget for the new book allows only $6 per page to start until we have at least one or two editions out and some revenue in. We are all pitching in back here to put this over in order to increase our earnings and the artists feel that it is a good chance to raise the monthly pay check and are playing ball with us. If you will pitch in, you can*

depend on us to raise the page rate as quickly as the Lord and the
supply and demand let me, which as I say, should be on the second or
third edition.[4]

The Major roots his economic promises in scripture: if the boys deliver
and the book sells, he will raise their rates "as quickly as the Lord and the
supply and demand let me."[5] Reading this in Cleveland, Jerry and Joe
may have rolled their eyes a little. They loved the Major, but sometimes
he was late on his payments. But a sixteen-page monthly commitment?
They could not turn it down.

Jerry opened up a letter from their editor, Whitney Ellsworth, dated
May 1936 that accepted their agreement to go ahead with *Slam Bradley* as
the "lead story in the magazine" in twelve-page installments.[6] Ellsworth
apologizes that the page count has gone down from sixteen; this meant
less work for Joe, but also less money. What they could not predict was
that it would be the most fun they would have on a comic strip; Joe
would later recall of *Slam:*

> We turned it out with no restrictions, complete freedom to do
> what we wanted. The only problem was we had a deadline. We
> had to work very fast, so Jerry suggested we save time by put-
> ting less than six panels on a page. The kids loved it because it
> was spectacular. I could do so much more. Later on, the editors
> stopped us from doing that. They said the kids were not getting
> their money's worth.[7]

As Jerry would later remember:

> Joe and I got busy; he at the drawing board, me at the type-
> writer. Slam Bradley, à la Victor McLaglen of the movies and
> like other undaunted B-movie heroes, laughed as he zestfully
> battered implacable villains all over the landscape. He was a
> scrappy daredevil. His diminutive partner-pal Shorty Morgan
> was around for laughs. Shorty was always available to be res-
> cued from horrendous perils. Writing and drawing Slam Brad-
> ley was fun. We rarely knew what Slam might do next, we
> made up the cliff-hanging suspense and hairbreadth escapes as
> we went along.[8]

Slam was six-foot something, with arms like a bear's. His favorite punch was the turning uppercut, which was capable of belting a criminal Chinaman halfway across the room—and then out through the window onto the streets below.[9] Slam's eyes always seemed half-closed, and his loop of black hair was always in his face. And he was always smiling. If Slam Bradley was looking for you, you best turn and run.

Slam Bradley would finally be their shot at a real adventure strip, both in subject and in process. They didn't even have a script most times; they just reeled their way, for the next several years, through story after story. The formula was that Slam and Shorty (the short, cartoonlike, comedy relief) assumed a new job or identity in order to catch a crook, punches would fly, and in the end, Slam always—always—kissed the girl in the final panel as Shorty watched in awe. In their adventures, Slam and Shorty posed as actors, boxers, lumberjacks, swimmers, college students, magicians, and women. In "Undercover in Grade School" in *Detective Comics* #5, Slam and Shorty visit their old stomping grounds—a barely disguised "Glendale" High School—where they are asked to solve a mystery. Not only are some of the teachers actual Glenville instructors, including Principal Davies—who looks exactly like her yearbook photo—but Joe himself makes an appearance in class when he aces a question about physical fitness. The fantasy of the story is very much a real one: the return of the successful, triumphant graduate to the school that once scorned him. Slam, posing as a teacher, gets the praise that school-age Jerry had always wanted to hear, making the comics as entertaining as they are autobiographical.

Slam and Shorty solve the mystery (of course), and Slam plants a smooch on "Miss Campbel," the cute young math teacher, named after Glenville's own math teacher, Miss Campbell.[10]

Jerry and Joe even do a future tale for Slam called "In Two Billion A.D." for *Detective Comics* #23–24. In it, Slam and Shorty join a Professor Kenton in his time machine on a perilous journey to the far future, where they encounter bird- and plant-men who sentence Shorty to death.[11] Our heroes escape, of course, but it was a successful foray (their second) into comics with science fiction themes.

By 1936, when the Major approached them about the idea of Slam, Jerry and Joe were already a two-man comics factory. They were still living at home a few blocks from their old high school, and the work was all they did. For both of them, seeing their work in print was astounding. They just kept *seeing* it. When they did get out, it was only to see related things like movies or the Cleveland Great Lakes Exposition on the lakefront. The Expo offered a localized World's Fair experience that included the Billy Rose Aquacade, the Ripley's Believe It Or Not! exhibit, and streamlined cars and boats; Slam Bradley himself even visits the Expo in *Detective Comics* #3. Visitors looked forward to signing the massive Golden Book as a record of their attendance (later, the book would mysteriously disappear).[12] Jerry and Joe were outside of the New York scene, had few demands, and were liked by the readers. In short, they were an editor's dream. The Major and Whit Ellsworth were professional, mostly courteous, and mostly kind. But it was a job to get them to pay up sometimes. As Jerry would later recount:

> The really greatest suspense of all, though, was wondering when and if we would get paid for producing these extravagant cartoon fantasies. Payment checks, it seemed to us, were painfully slow and far-between in coming. Long, long weeks of waiting for money would drag on and on. Joe would draw, I would write. But where were the checks for which we had toiled and strained our imaginations? Had they been mis-sent to China? Had the magazine suspended publication? To temporarily escape from our worries and woes, Joe and I would redeem empty milk bottles, scavenging a few cents to pay for our admissions into B-movies where we would thrill to the kind of feverish stuff we were pouring into our comics pages.[13]

Ellsworth would frequently respond to these concerns, as he does in a letter on August 20, 1936:

> Most publications, as you know, pay on publication. We have made it a point to pay on acceptance and even in these our stringent times we pay before publication, if not exactly on the line. It resolves down to this: the outlook is very encouraging, but it is necessary for all of us to wait short periods for our money. That maintains from the Major (Nicholson) right on down the line. We can, of course, take stuff from our waiting list, the authors of which would be willing to play ball, but we much prefer to keep the organization as much as possible in the hands of those who have worked with us right along, for it is naturally their right to participate in the good times that seem to be about upon us, just as they have played along with us through the tougher time. A long spiel, but the real McCoy.[14]

Jerry later recalled that he would talk to Joe's mother about this strange way of doing business with promises and threats: "After I glowingly described to her the great future that awaited Joe and me when we would hit it big in the comics field, [she would respond,] 'But where is the money?' I had no answer. It was the Depression. You couldn't eat golden dreams."[15]

Even as they were working on the new *Slam* strip, the Major was having a hard time lining up a printer for the new *Detective*. Whit Ellsworth wrote the boys on December 14, 1936: "We haven't yet acquired a printer for DETECTIVE COMICS, but it looks very much as though our same printer would be able to handle it very shortly now."[16] Two days later, Ellsworth wrote, ". . . I believe the Major at this moment is signing up for DETECTIVE COMICS, so that book will be shortly forthcoming."[17] The next contract they signed with *Detective Comics* in 1937 was for two years. It assured them a healthy $10 a page as the exclusive producers of *Slam Bradley* and *Spy*.

In New York, the Major remained optimistic but was beginning to circle his financial wagons. His aggressive approach to (and success with) "all-new" comic books had not gone unnoticed. He could feel enemies creeping along his borders. Short on available cash, he needed help to get *Detective* printed. He would need allies. In walked a smiling man named Harry Donenfeld, the light shining off his forehead, a cigar in his hand.

For all the work it took to bring the landmark *Detective Comics* to American newsstands, it was to be the Major's final comics publication. It wasn't that he couldn't manage money, it was more that running a magazine in the late 1930s depended on a careful cooperation of different entities—talent, printing, and distribution—that were usually separately owned and thus prone to different levels of imparity and corruption. If one person controlled the biggest component, he could own not only a magazine but maybe even the industry. Good business was often conflated with cold, personal greed.

Harry Donenfeld knew how to work these invisible angles better than anyone. He was a pulp magazine publisher and a principal in the Independent News Company with Cleveland-born Paul Sampliner. The Major took Donenfeld on as a partner in order to publish *Detective Comics* through a new alliance they called Detective Comics, Inc., consisting of Harry, the Major, and Jack S. Liebowitz, Donenfeld's ace NYU-educated accountant. It was a last-ditch attempt by the Major to keep his company alive.[18]

Donenfeld was a legend in East Coast paper. It didn't matter whether he was connected to the Mob or not, because he certainly acted like it: his bully tactics were formidable and ruthless.[19] He had been brought up on vice charges in 1934 for printing so-called spicy pulps, semi-erotic fiction magazines such as *La Paree, Gay Parisienne, Spicy Stories,* and *Pep Stories* with gauzy painted covers of wide-eyed debs.[20] Donenfeld almost went to jail for a particularly racy cover, but, as the story goes, he convinced a grunt employee named Herbie Siegel to do the stint for him. Herbie did so and thus had a job with Donenfeld and his successors for the rest of his life.[21]

While all of this squaring off was going on in New York, doing work for the Major had brought the boys closer. Jerry felt awful for ever having doubted Joe; watching him churn out these comics now was nothing short of incredible. On some level, Joe might have been working so hard just to prove to Jerry that he could. But the vague sense of what was happening in New York was making Jerry anxious. They had the experience now, the in, but where could they channel it if their benefactor left? Jerry and Joe did not rest on their success; they had something at the bottom of the pile they were still working on. It was the Superman idea, and by 1936, it had changed considerably.

Chapter 11
Muscle and Power

J OE STARED DOWN the tall glass he was holding. In it, two raw eggs were circling slowly around each other. Joe had planned on drinking this mess, but he was now having substantial second thoughts about the whole experience. The mixture looked cold and was starting to smell. His sister had her hands almost completely in her mouth and looked ready to scream. Joe made his mother leave the room. He took a breath, tipped his head back, and let it all slide easily down his throat; he didn't even taste it, not really. He wiped his mouth and set both hands on the table. His sister's eyes were saucers. This was transformation.

Joe often did his exercises in pants and a plain white tank top, and when it got hotter, the shirt came off. It didn't matter that he was still a string bean; when he looked in the mirror, he could see past the collarbone and ribs and into the thought of the muscles beneath. Steel and iron on a cold mat pushed up into the air equaled results. Just like his drawing, Joe was making something new of himself.

During those years in the mid-1930s when everything was sparking, Joe had another mission. He wanted to be bigger and stronger, because those were the things he equated with success, discipline, and girls. And bigger and stronger were the things he absolutely was not: he was very short, quiet, and shy. He played sports but never hit a second growth spurt and would later secretly order shoe elevators out of the backs of magazines. When they arrived—black and rubber—he would slip them into his shoes and turn red in the bedroom mirror.

Physical fitness, like its hawkers and promises, was big-time during the

1930s. It was an industry that made its way to prosperity through little ads in magazines, mail-order courses, and touring personalities who were almost cartoonlike in their regalia and stage presence. These men, these strongmen, existed both on the national stage and at local circuses all across the country. In the beginning, they were usually European, burly, and mustached, flexing their immigrant success in a time of national want. The people who went to see them needed to be amazed—and wanted to see them break things in messy, satisfying ways.[1]

Part of the reason Joe felt shorter and skimpier (and that these qualities were uninteresting to girls) was that the booming physical fitness industry was vehemently telling him so. But there was hope. In the world of physical fitness, weaklings could be *remade*:

> We need stronger, more capable men; healthier, superior women. Force is supreme—The king of all mankind. . . . Those who desire capacities of this sort must recognize the importance of a strong, enduring physique. . . . If your efforts are to be crowned with the halo of success, they must be spurred on by the pulsating throbbing powers that accompany physical excellence. These truly extraordinary characteristics come without effort to but few of us, but they can be developed, attained and maintained.[2]

These were the words of Bernarr Macfadden, the physical fitness guru and magazine publisher who had a thick mane of hair and a physique that, while not overly muscular by today's standards, was completely without excess. Macfadden was the most important figure in the rise of physical fitness culture in America. Like all strongmen, he had an origin story, which saw him transformed from a shy, sickly child to a marvelous physical specimen while working on a farm under the big sky of Missouri at the turn of the century. The young Macfadden allegedly left for the city and took an office job but quickly watched his muscles dwindle away and his health worsen. So he went back to physical exertion, and after changing his first name to Bernarr (to sound like a lion's roar), he was, literally, in business.[3]

This story, like Macfadden himself, was hidden behind layers of sinew. Macfadden was very good at strength training, and his obsessive drive for perfection resulted in muscles that were their own best advertisement.

But Macfadden was not just about brawn. His genius lay in developing a system that people could order through the mail. Unlike the largely New York–based training studios of the 1920s, which people had to join and pay a fee to access, anyone in the country could clip a Macfadden subscription form, fill it out, send in a check, and be rewarded with some low-end pulleys that could be stretched toward new muscular imaginations.[4]

Macfadden wrote books, too, including the multivolume *Encyclopedia of Physical Culture, Strengthening the Eyes,* and the infamous *Physical Culture for Babies.* The immense success of the mail-order business (which was informed by his fascination with the pulps) led him to form his own magazine, *Physical Culture,* in 1899. Using false names, Macfadden the control freak wrote or supervised most of the copy; he advised against sex, cigarettes, and corsets. His motto was "Weakness Is a Crime! Don't Be a Criminal!" and he published recipes for an early form of granola he named "strengthfude."[5]

Bernarr Macfadden, like Hugo Gernsback, was a cultural personality who stayed interesting through self-generated variety; he was a living serial adventure. He fasted on Mondays, tried milk-only diets, slept on the floor, and cut round holes in his shoes so he could draw upon the healing power of the planet itself. After an experimental utopian community in New Jersey failed, he moved his offices to the Flatiron building in Manhattan. He met one of his four spouses at a contest he sponsored at Madison Square Garden to find "the Most Beautiful Girl in the World." He married the winner. Macfadden's magazine started to sell even better when he asked his readers to send in their own stories about how his system and ideas had changed their lives. This led to a new magazine, *True Story,* which was an immediate hit and flew off the racks every month for a decade.[6]

Physical Culture was one of Joe's favorite magazines. He bought most of his magazines at the secondhand stores, but he didn't mind.[7] On page thirty-three of almost every issue was a photo spread of swimsuit-clad bathing beauties in poses extolling the virtues of the lifestyle. Headlines such as "If Your Views on Sex Are Old-Fashioned, Read These Modern Books!" and "Should Americans Eat More Rye?" spoke to curious readers. It was sex masquerading as sport. It was also well illustrated: diagrams were drawn over photos to detail how to do certain exercises. *Physical Culture* was also a history class—it often ran articles on pioneering strongmen of the past or enlisted current strength personalities to do guest articles about individual feats that readers could (attempt to) imitate. The whole industry was imitation through work. Joe stared for hours.

SHOW

The stage floor creaked as the large man walked onto it with short, measured steps. The crowd didn't dare say a word to interrupt his concentration. He was wearing dark swim trunks with a shiny gold buckle. His feet were wrapped in tight leather boots like those of a Roman gladiator. His short cape lay pooled on the floor. His biceps expanded, as if filling with air. Jaws dropped as he set himself, lowered his legs, and lifted—lifted!—a steel beam above his head. It stood there, in the air, set for a moment in perfect clarity, frozen in time. Only when he brought it down with a more than audible clump did the crowd explode into applause. The man looked out into the wide darkness, seeing only the quick gleams of glasses and watches. He didn't know who was watching. His name was Siegmund Breitbart, and in the Cleveland papers that morning in 1923, he was called "Hercules." And "Superman."[8]

In the 1920s and 1930s, strongmen such as Breitbart toured the country as celebrities. But they were more than that—because their acts were so raw and physical, they became more about entertainment than sport. They wore colorful costumes to show off their muscles and had one-word names like "Appolyon." They came from Europe, most of them, and toured the country and the world on posters and on trains. They pounded in railroad spikes with their hands and bent iron bars into shapes and letters. They were also frequently represented in the fitness manuals as cartoons.[9]

Joe was not even in Cleveland during Breitbart's several-week reign, but he knew the history of the great strongmen by name, pose, and feat. There was Louis Cyr, the Canadian Hercules, who could lift a fully grown horse over his head. There was Sandow, who would wrap his chest in chains—and then break them apart by exhaling.[10] Even Cleveland had its share of strongmen, the most flamboyant being Professor Zebic, a local personality who would appear frequently in the paper for causing various neighborhood disturbances.[11] Zebic once tried to smuggle a mummy in from South America (he imagined he could charge people to see it)[12] and beat up his next-door neighbor after being accused of being a Communist.[13] All of these men wore strange clothing and golden medals and did things that were out of bounds, both physically and socially. All of them were larger than life.[14]

If there was one strongman who probably made an impression on Joe, it was Joseph Greenstein, the so-called Mighty Atom. Like many of his peers, Greenstein was born in the old world, in Poland. The story went that he was so sickly as an infant from tuberculosis that he could barely breathe. But one day the circus came to town and the great strongman Champion Volanko amazed the crowd with his stupendous feats performed in the dust. Little Joseph then supposedly snuck into the circus to see the strongman—but was caught and beaten up. Volanko stopped the fight and was so impressed by the young man that he took him on tour as his apprentice. After almost two years, the circus returned and Joseph Greenstein had changed so much that even his own family didn't recognize him. He married and eventually moved to America. In 1914, in a small store in Galveston, Texas, a man who had eyes for Joseph's wife, Leah, shot Joseph right between the eyes. The single bullet flattened against Greenstein's forehead and dropped to the floor. Greenstein was unharmed. His legend grew.[15]

Adopting a near mystical regimen of mental focus and diet, Greenstein abandoned his business, the Square Deal Junkyard, and began training and touring as a strongman. He could bite through iron, drive a nail through a deck of cards with his hand, and break chains with his chest. Later in his career, he would hold back cars with his hair and even, one afternoon in Buffalo, pull an airplane with his teeth.[16] It was an act beyond belief. In New York, he saw a meeting place for the Nazi Bund party with a sign that said, "No Dogs or Jews Allowed." Greenstein then crossed the street to buy a new baseball bat: "The action which followed was in the best tradition of a Popeye cartoon."[17] His nickname, the Mighty Atom, came from his five-foot-four-inch height, which Joe Shuster could appreciate. Greenstein would spend the remainder of his days on Coney Island, talking up anyone who would listen and hawking his miracle remedies and priceless stories.[18] He was still a hero to Jewish crowds and an unforgettable encounter to anyone who met him.[19] He was also billed as "A Modern Hercules"—which is exactly the same way that Superman, in a later episode of the comics, would be advertised.[20]

Another strongman of influence in the 1930s was Siegmund Klein, the Prussian "Mr. Perfect," who at age one in 1903 moved with his family from Germany to Cleveland. His first public exhibition was in Cleveland at Luna Park. He worked with trainers and coaches until he grew out of Ohio and moved to New York in 1924, where he took over the famous bodybuilding studio of Professor Louis Attila. Cleveland papers followed Klein in 1925 when he was deemed the world's best-built man by the famous French magazine *Culture Physique*.[21]

Joe liked Klein because his whole program was slanted toward boys who were short and underweight. Klein argued that if you trained for health, muscle would follow. He also was a master poser. Macfadden would run some of Klein's famous classical poses in *Physical Culture*. Joe referred to them when he thought of his own strongman. Klein was also illustrated in cartoon form; he was featured in Robert Ripley's syndicated "Believe It or Not!" column more than ten times. Klein's mail-order barbell course was called "Super-Physique."

Lionel Strongfort was yet another practitioner; his course of "Strongfortism" promised that

> when a pupil has completed his preliminary Course and has strengthened his muscles and his nerves sufficiently to process to the next plane of physical and mental perfection, I then advise him to take this Advanced Course now introduced to you. In my estimation you are now physically fit to undertake it and so become what I call a SUPER-MAN.[22]

The hour was late and Joe was reading *Physical Culture* and looking at a Strongfort pose, memorizing its lines, when all of a sudden the picture got blurry and liquid. He closed his eyes and tried again. It was still blurry, and Strongfort, who before had looked as big as two men, now looked like a pale shadow. Joe thought he would just rest his eyes for a moment.

Joe was short and skinny, but he always tried hard to become stronger, especially with his eyes. His glasses were thick and heavy and sat on his head like Buck Rogers's goggles. It was hard sometimes. Joe thought of his eye-strengthening books. *Close. Open. Focus. Blink.* He did the exercises every single day.[23] He never complained.[24]

Chapter 12

Frankenstein's Monster

THE RED CHAIRS GAVE A LITTLE when the wide, dusty beam opened up behind them. They sat perfectly still in the darkness. The screen in front of them spilled over with light and washed across their glasses. They felt goose bumps creep over their arms and shoulders.

Joe sometimes still had salt on his hands from selling ice cream earlier in the afternoon. Jerry had paper cuts and inkblots on his hands. But these imperfections were invisible as they looked forward, their chins up at a perfect angle. There were a good number of movie theaters in the Glenville area, including the Doan at the corner of East 105th and St. Clair, which was decorated to look like an old Aztec temple. There were several more downtown, including the mighty sisters, the State and Ohio. Movie theaters lured in broke audiences with cash drawings (called "bank nights") and other giveaways of flatware and even crystal. Double feature specials were also popular, and there was a game called "Screeno," which let moviegoers play a bingo-type game for prizes and cash.[1] But that was all to get people in the door; once they were seated, it was up to Hollywood.

The newsreels started first. Over the many years the boys went to the movies, they bore witness to a wide range of dramatic events: the USS *Akron,* one of the world's biggest airships, crashed off the shores of New Jersey on April 4, 1933, tragically killing all seventy-three hands.[2] They saw reports of human suffering, not only abroad but at home as well.[3] They saw FDR take office.[4] They watched a nervous French hairdresser win a huge amount of money in the national lottery.[5] They watched streaming torpedoes being tested in the ocean.[6] They watched downtrodden relief workers rise up against corrupt city officials[7] They watched the Lindberghs ready a silver plane.[8] And they saw a man in uniform, in Germany, rally thousands around his outstretched palm.[9] The world was getting smaller, but also more unbelievable.

The cartoons were next, and they helped replace the black-and-white fears. There was Bugs Bunny, Mickey Mouse, Popeye, and Betty Boop, bouncing up and down with lines coming out of their heads when they were surprised or worried. These were the moments of electric magic: these hand-drawn characters moved like liquid black ink over the screen. Joe would just stare in disbelief as Jerry chuckled at the jokes.

The main feature finally began. Their first choice was always an adventure film, usually something with Douglas Fairbanks Jr. leaping around the rigging of a pirate ship with a sword or dancing over rooftops as Zorro. Or even better, a Tarzan, with jungles and elephants spread across the screen as if on a different planet. And, of course, Jane. Joe saw everything in single frames, memorizing the action as flat, still rectangles.

Growing up, Jerry and Joe would see anything, really—they would howl at their favorite comedy actor, Harold Lloyd, the clumsy, dark-eyed Everyman who would adjust his thick eyeglasses and scale a downtown Los Angeles building like a human fly—just to get away from some girl's furious mother. They saw all the Universal monster movies: *Frankenstein, The Mummy,* and *Dracula.* Jerry even saw the English version of *The Golem,* an ethnic slab of clay brought to mighty life to protect the Jewish ghetto with a single word: *emeth,* which Jerry knew meant "truth." The creature had a magical symbol on his chest.[10] Jerry and Joe saw as much as they could afford, and then they would go look for milk bottles to refund so they could go see more.[11] These images, from all over the world, bounced off a white screen and swirled together before being cast into their brains, burning in like a developing photograph.[12]

Afterward, Jerry would skirt along the edge of the sidewalk with an imaginary sword in his hand as Joe pushed his hands into his pockets. They would talk endlessly about what they had seen and re-create what they liked the most. They would pass by Solomon's Delicatessen and smell the corned beef, packed between fresh rye bread. But they could not afford to eat it. They walked by Gordon's Bike Shop and saw the smiling kids.[13] If they stopped going to the movies or stopped getting ink, then they could go to these places *easy*—but those weren't acceptable losses.

Their meals at home, after their trips to the movies, were becoming increasingly similar. The food they were facing was a pastiche of whatever was on hand. At the end of Kimberley was the kosher butcher, who slaughtered the chickens in the back room while you waited. Baking was done from scratch because it was cheaper that way. Money aside, it was hard to get many ingredients. So from Shaker Heights to Woodland, kitchens filled with similar aromas. There was good old potato soup, which consisted of a few simple ingredients:

- 4 or 5 small potatoes
- Very small onion
- 1 cup top milk
- Butter
- Water to cover
- Pinch of salt

Peel potatoes and cut them up into small pieces in a kettle with the onion. . . . Put on just enough water to cover. Add salt to taste. Bring to boil and then turn down heat so as to simmer. . . . Mash potatoes right in the water. Add 1 cup of top milk, and heat. Do not boil.[14]

And the more satisfying—if you could afford the beef—traditional stew, in *The Plain Dealer* titled "Beef Stew Supreme," using leftover beef roast:

Slice beef thin, place in a casserole with one medium sized onion sliced over it, and one small green pepper, sliced. Moisten leftover gravy with water or milk. Cook tender six medium-sized potatoes, place on top of the stew. Bake in a moderate oven from 30 to 40 minutes.[15]

Almost everyone made versions of these recipes. They mixed and baked and stirred and simmered. This was the era of taking what you had—at hand, at cost—and imaginatively trying to make something better for a greater number of people. Jerry and Joe saw movies and cartoons and news and came home to eat hodgepodge meals. This was the era of Frankenstein in all things, including politics, the cinema, and supper. This was the recipe for Superman.

REBORN

As they worked, sipped soup, and dreamed, their idea for a look for their slowly evolving character took on the same qualities that defined their lives: he would have to be a combination of things. The classic Superman costume, with the red cape, blue tights, red shorts, red boots, and insignia on the chest, is iconic in every sense of the word, even though its overall design is initially (and absolutely) strange and offputting.[16] Joe claimed to have designed most of it immediately, but all of its elements were things they had been looking at for years.[17] The features of the original costume are rooted in Flash Gordon and Buck Rogers, who wore full sci-fi space suits with emblems on their chests. The tights are a mixture of the strong-

man's outfit and the attire of wrestlers and boxers, who frequently wore tights with shorts, often differently colored, on the outside.[18] The belt-buckled shorts look like ads for Jantzen swimsuits where a strong, dark-haired man lifts a grateful woman out of the curling surf or relaxes back in the light of the sun.[19] The cape was born of many sources: weightlifters, swashbucklers, and perhaps the cover of the 1929 Glenville yearbook, where it was combined with a single initial.

The lace-up leather boots are lifted directly from strongmen like Breitbart, who would often pose in gladiatorial gear to suggest nostalgia for classical mythology. But why a costume at all? In the beginning, it wasn't a disguise so much as an announcement of who this character was. Comics were not animated like the cartoons they watched—great feats could be shown, but their actual execution had to be imagined by the reader in between the panels. So Joe made it easier by giving the character an exaggerated costume that welcomed disbelief. This was the clothing of the men Joe desperately wanted to be: men of power and respect. So he designed the costume as a half-imaginary spectacle: as Michael Chabon figures it, as "the intersection of a wish and the tip of a pencil."[20]

The overall physical look of Superman himself is from Johnny Weissmuller, whose face Joe swiped from movie magazines and news articles. Johnny's curly hair made the translation perfectly. Joe just squinted the eyes like his idol Roy Crane and added a Dick Tracy smile.[21] Superman had the dark eyes of the Black Uhlan, the hated boxing heavyweight Max Schmeling, who beat up William "Young" Stribling at Cleveland Municipal Stadium on July 3, 1931, for the heavyweight title.[22] There were drawings of their battle in the papers. Since Joe didn't have a portfolio of life drawings from an art school to use as reference, he used his physical fitness manuals as a visual encyclopedia for Superman's physique. In Joe's mind, this made his drawing more realistic, which was important for such a fantastic creation. Joe was always adamant that it needed to seem *real;* this was science fiction, after all. So he used what was close— his secondhand magazines—to solve his problem.[23]

The colors of blue, red, and yellow were patriotic and primary. But since the early Superman was done in black and white, color may not have been a concern at that point. As for the central "S," the boys would later claim it was an inside joke referring to the shared first letter of their last names. For one, the blank chest looked boring and Joe wanted a crest, though it quickly changed from a complicated shield (like a badge) in the early issues to a simpler, triangular design.[24] That fashion statement—a gold-shielded symbol on a shirt—was also seen in sports uniforms from football to the Olympics. It is more of a monogram than anything, as ads in *The Cleveland Shopping News* often advertised for ladies' summer blouses complete with monograms set within inverted triangles.

Jerry and Joe still liked the name from "Reign of the Super-man" and had realized that it was wasted on a villain. The German philosopher Friedrich Nietzsche used the word *Übermensch* in *The Gay Science* in 1882, which some very loosely translate as "Superman." There is a moment in "Reign of the Super-man" when Bill Dunn scoffs at a Germanic text, but it is Einstein, not Nietzsche. Jerry and Joe likely did not, and could not, read Nietzsche in the early to middle 1930s in Cleveland. Though the philosopher's name shows up occasionally in national newspapers at this time, no one was reading him widely, much less quoting his name in popular culture.[25]

What the boys did read were the magazines and papers where "superman" was a common word. Its usage was almost always preceded by "a." Most times the word was used to refer to an athlete or a politician. The person who was most called a superman in the papers was FDR—not for his great physical strength, but for his strong leadership skills, though his dual identity as national symbol and polio-stricken boy would later make this correlation even more poignant. FDR also had a penchant for wearing cloaks; he even appeared in a few of their early comics, including an episode of *Spy*.[26] FDR's opposites were even measured against the word. A *Plain Dealer* article describes Hitler, at age forty-three, addressing twenty thousand followers:

> We shall win through! . . . but to his befuddled followers he promises nothing more substantial than wind and more wind. Instead of the devastating blast of a true Mussolini this make-believe superman fires puerile words from a popgun.[27]

The word did not have the positive and moral register it does now. But it was still there. For all of these various appearances, though, the place where the word appears the most did have a positive slant; nearly all of the physical fitness magazines mention "superman."[28]

The boys' decision to make the character a good guy also made sense because a bad one would have been much harder to do. Movies at the time were feeling heat from the new 1930 Motion Picture Production Code that began to regulate more violent films. It wasn't a very strict code, but after movies like *The Public Enemy* (1931), Catholic and Boy Scout groups rallied to "disinfect" popular culture. The result was a rise in moral, he-man characters hitting films with actors like Clark Gable, the Ohio boy who plowed fields as a youngster before being discovered by golden Hollywood in a highly romanticized origin story.[29] Jerry may have had his name in mind for the actual character.[30] There was also a story in the December 1933 *Amazing Stories* called "Within Sight of Hell" that features a convict named Clark who hides a secret, heroic identity. This was the era of good guys, of Tarzan, the Shadow, and Doc Savage, who in an early pulp ad is advertised as a "superman."[31]

In later years, Jerry was sharp to avoid direct connections between his Superman and any other literary ancestors, probably for fear of a lawsuit. But they were there. Besides the obvious connections to John Carter jumping around Mars (which was also serialized in *The Plain Dealer* at the time of Superman's creation), science fiction aficionados with library cards have always called out Jerry Siegel for ripping off the Philip Wylie novel *Gladiator*.[32] In the novel, Hugo Danner is experimented on by his father and develops powers like invulnerability, incredible jumping, and super speed. Danner wanders the earth looking for a purpose for his powers before being struck dead at the very end. Though *Gladiator* came out in 1930, Jerry claimed early on that he never read it, and there is no way to prove otherwise.[33] But he surely at least read the review, which appeared in the June 1930 issue of *Amazing Stories,* his favorite magazine:

> The Gladiator is a book which starts well, is quite readable and entertaining throughout, but is, after all, disappointing. It is based on the fact that insects, such as ants and grasshoppers are veritable giants of strength, comparing their size to man. . . . [He] opens doors by tearing them to splinters.[34]

Both of these images appear in *Action Comics* #1. Hugo Danner, "as he gets older, is usually afraid of using his gift of super-human strength" and "accidentally kills a boy during a football game."[35] The review states that Danner is invulnerable, can jump forty feet, and "can run with the speed of an express train." The reviewer, a C. A. Brandt, concludes, "In spite of all the obvious shortcomings of this book, it is quite enjoyable and will not be forgotten as quickly as the average 'best seller.'" The novel itself is notoriously unclear as to what Hugo wants, but Brandt here notes of Danner that "as he grows up, his inferiority complex grows with him" and "wants to make more . . . in order to uplift the world in general."[36]

Jerry was always interested in what was outside his own realm of experience, in the unknown beyond his reach. This meant spaceships, distant planets, secret occult mysteries, and even the ins and outs of publishing. And also money and girls. This interest in the unknown extended to religion as well. Jerry was brought up Jewish, but he and Joe tended to distrust the religion of their old world parents, which was fairly common for first-generation Jewish Americans. Still, there are several parallels between Superman's origin and that of Moses in the Old Testament: An infant arrives in a small vessel and is adopted. As a grown man, he finally embraces his true background to save his adopted people.[37] But people during the Depression were not talking about Moses so much in the papers and on radio. They were talking about Jesus.

The figure of Christ in these times was a palpable one. Because of the economic and emotional despair, Jesus began to be portrayed as a modern, practical hope. On April 4, 1926, *The Plain Dealer* even ran a painting, Jean Béraud's *Le Chemin de Croix* (1894), which placed Christ smack-dab in the middle of a very different-looking crowd. Amid a throng of followers and those begging forgiveness in modern dress, Jesus, glowing, shoulders a gigantic wooden cross, double his size, his legs bent to support the weight.[38] The article, titled "Millions All Over World Preparing for Second Coming of Christ," explains:

> From the four corners of the earth, from Jews, Christians, Brahmins and Buddhists, comes simultaneous expression of the belief that the Messiah is at hand. Whether the divine manifestation is referred to as "Avatar," "Messiah," or "Christ," in accordance with the dictates of the various religions, it is believed to be imminent. The scientists find in the reading of the stars a similar promise of a crisis. . . .
>
> He has been called by many names, he has been visualized in many forms. . . . Always, he was invested with the power to end strife and ill will on earth, to bring brotherly love into the lives of humans [to] descend upon earth under the guidance of a great leader, savior, or god. . . . After 20000 years of denial of even the existence of the Savior, many are ready to claim him as "a man, and a Jew, whose teachings are Jewish in content and detail."[39]

Graphic Portrayal of Belief in Messiah's Return

Being the sons of Orthodox Jews, Jerry and Joe were certainly curious about Jesus and his place in the scheme of things. The article concludes, "In all ages and all lands, the belief of a superman who would establish the Kingdom of Heaven, has fascinated the minds of men."[40] Jerry and

Joe might have also read, or been told, something to the effect that Jesus represented

> a great division between Christian and Jewish ethics. The one is ultra-human, based upon metaphysics and theology: the other is realistic, based upon human experience and history.[41]

Superman is something of a compromise of these ideals, all of them, in an attempt to reconcile the supernatural with the discipline of modern science. In a little 1928 book at the Cleveland Public Library called *The Coming Superman* (about the Second Coming of Christ), the author states plainly: "There are scientists who look for The Superman."[42] On December 12, 1937, these scientists find something else: "A new supernova or exploding star was found 6,000,000 light years away."[43] As different as he seemed, Superman made sense because he was grounded, whether we knew it or not, on purpose or not, in multiple layers of reality, both imagined and not.

Jerry was wearing pajamas that day in school because he had been up the night before doing the only thing that mattered to him. He was writing. The act of writing kept Jerry outside of the world, always circling it, trying to find a place to land. He was up late again, in the basement, clicking away on his typewriter. Like most teenagers, or all of them, Jerry felt he had another self inside of him. He felt he could tell no one—and since nobody cared, it was easy to keep the secret. As they started to put Superman together, it became a negotiation between these two worlds: the real and the imagined. In an early drawing by Joe of Superman and Clark on the same page, they regard each other as two separate creatures with an invisible connection.

THE GREATEST

Scattered all over the table and floor were long black-and-white comic strips. Jerry was carefully watching the jar of ink, only five or so inches away from the edge of the table. Joe, seeing Jerry's fidgeting hands, sighed and moved it toward the middle. This mess of papers represented the work of years. For *Superman,* they now had a week of completely inked strips and three more weeks in pencil.[44] It was Joe's best work yet—both Krypton and Superman were incredibly detailed and exciting—Jor-L looked like a movie star, and Lora, as Jerry would say, was *va-va-voom*. Once the dust and eraser shavings settled, the character was now part strongman, part spaceman, and part reporter-detective. And he was part something entirely new. The idea came in a flash, but it took years of hard work to clean away the edges. And it was finally ready. They expected great, immediate success. They did not get it.

Jerry was in charge of submitting their stuff to the newspaper syndicates. He remembered the article he had read in *Fortune:* for a writer or cartoonist hoping to be published in a newspaper, the only real measure of success was being picked up by a syndicate. The first major American newspaper syndicate was McClure, which marketed comics, columns, and so forth to individual newspapers looking for content. The syndicate would buy the artistic work and then would sell printing rights to the newspapers at a much lower rate. If the strip became popular, it was potentially a lucrative arrangement for an artist or writer—though it was difficult to achieve.

Jerry ran off expensive photostats, searched mastheads for addresses, and sent their proposal all over the country. He used his American Artists League letterhead to puff themselves up like suited men. The packet they sent out consisted of a month's worth of strips, a letter, and a paragraph synopsis meant to tease just how good *Superman* could be. Their words read like good door-to-door sales copy:

> The potentialities of the character, SUPERMAN, has barely been scratched. . . . He's *different* and sure to become the idol of young and old. He'll participate in sports and astound the nation; he'll single-handed rescue a town from a flood through his super-strength. Unlike most adventure strips the scene of the story will not be laid in some fantastic, unknown jungle or planet or country, but will be all the more astounding for having its locale on familiar streets. SUPERMAN will operate against a background of America's most well-known cities, buildings, and pleasure-spots.[45]

They submitted and resubmitted for several years. As they were doing their stuff for the Major, they were still always working on *Superman*. They knew it was special and at times held it back. But it was what they believed in the most.

CONTACT

Jerry stared out of the window in his room. He hated the waiting more than anything. He went up to the hot attic, which he usually avoided, and looked out the eastward window. The sky was blue. He imagined the people in the tall buildings in New York City, much higher than him, reading his words and staring at Joe's artwork. It made him shiver. He looked at Leo's silver dentist chair, sticking out here and there like some sharp, alien flower.

Jerry knew it took under a week to get a letter to New York, so why did it take them weeks, sometimes months, to respond? He bit his thumb. Didn't they know how important this was? Like Joe, he was eager to get started. Neither of them could really believe they would get rejected again. Not after all this.

Over the last three years, Jerry had divided the waiting into two parts. The first was the initial two weeks—that was the time when Jerry believed they could send an urgent telegram stating, "We want it—check to follow," and that would be that. But that didn't happen. The first two weeks of waiting were the hardest, especially if there was a holiday, because then Jerry would extend it, in his mind, to three weeks or maybe more. After that, hope began to dwindle, but Jerry would still keep his eye on the mail.

They just kept trying. Years later, Jerry would recount their enthusiasm:

> We thought we had invented a surefire, superaction hit, and that the overjoyed comics industry would turn cartwheels and come rushing to our doorstops, pressing Cadillacs, mansions and oodles of money on us. Ah, those fevered daydreams. How they soared! But reality yawned.[46]

The evolving, miasmic *Superman* proposal needed constant work. It felt like a long-distance race run on bigger mountains. They worked on it, sent it out sporadically, and revised again and again. They realized it needed something else. A girl. But not just any girl.

Lois.

Chapter 13

The Muse

GIRLS WERE ALWAYS THE PART of the equation they could never quite solve. In school, on the movie screens, and in the glossy magazines, girls smiled, snapped their gum, and turned their heads away from Jerry and Joe. This is where Lois was born. Her character, in fact, may be the key ingredient to the success of the Superman idea. Though it was essentially the first superhero, sooner or later someone else would have done it. But the added register of that character having to hide his true identity under a bold lie—*so as to fool a girl*—defined not only the genre, but its readers as well.

Most female comics characters at the time were either femmes fatales (Roy Crane's Dragon Lady), ditzy, funny housewives (Blondie), or damsels in distress (Olive Oyl). Lois was initially a little of all of these—for though she is surely good, her treatment of Clark sometimes borders on the cruel, which rang true to lots of readers. So where did the truth of this character come from? An October 29, 1975, article in *The Washington Star* by John Sherwood claims that

> Lois Lane was named after Lois Amster, a Cleveland girl whom Joe had a crush on. She was not even aware of his existence. "She's a grandmother now in Cleveland," says Joe, "but I don't think she has any idea that she was the inspiration for Lois Lane."[1]

Lois Amster was a Glenville brunette with a round face and big smile. She was the girl next door, except she didn't live near Joe or Jerry and she wanted absolutely nothing to do with them. But they both liked her. Lois was small and smiling, an A-plus student who was involved in almost everything the school did. She was nicknamed "Little Angel," after her initials. Her high school activities in the yearbook included National Honor Society, Choral Club, English Club, Dramatics, Class Honor Roll, and Senior Sponsor. Coincidentally, Jerry was on two of these clubs—Choral and Dramatics—the only two that he could legitimately join. Jerry did not have a crush on her; he was in love with her. Everyone was.[2]

Since he couldn't score any touchdowns for her, Jerry had to use his writing to get her attention. After he sort of gave up on Miriam, he turned his attention to Lois. Her name first appears in a *Torch* "Serialette" titled "The Penthouse Murders," with a byline of "by Lois I. Living." The story is a split between hyperbole and silliness: "Death, cruel and merciless, stalked the roots of the city! A killer, mad, terrible, was at large!" The killer gives this one-off tale a more unsettling quality of realism: "The killer had struck but all the author wants Lois to know is that he is alive." The joke is really the plea from the authors to Lois that they were indeed alive in the first place. But the column—written by "Seagull and Schtank"—is never continued, because "the writers of this column are being sued for plagiarism."[3]

In the May 19, 1932, "Dramatics," Jerry asks: "Why doesn't Lois Amster come out for Drama Club?" and he is really asking, *Why doesn't Lois Amster go out with me?*[4] With high school ending, there would be no reason to see her. That was a terrible and brutal "fact."[5] Yet Jerry had one hand left to play.

The most brazen attempt at romance that Jerry makes in his writing life is a semianonymous poem that appears in *The Torch* on December 1, 1932. It was the year of the death of his father and the attempt at fame with *Science Fiction*. Jerry may have felt emboldened—or that he had nothing left to lose. He tossed and turned before deciding to submit it. He thought for sure—*for sure*—that this would finally tip the scales his way and Lois would walk up to him and say, *Hi there, I'm Lois.* The day it ran, he dressed nicer than usual and made sure that if Lois was within range, he would laugh and joke with his *Torch* buddies as if nothing were out of the ordinary.

There were some elbows here and there, but mostly he was quiet and too horrified even to look up. She didn't say a thing.[6]

Sick with rejection, Jerry tried to pass it off as humor in the next issue through an imagined, self-deprecating conversation between Lois and Stiletto.[7]

*   *   *

LOIS

I think her eyes are wonderful,
I think her lips divine,
She's delicate as the chlorophyl,
Within a clinging vine.
I think her nose is exquisite,
I think her chin sublime,
To think that we have never met,
Ah, what a horrible crime!
She scarcely ever looks at me,
I worship every glance,
If she would only talk to me
I'd do a jubilant dance.
Oh, Lois, which your thoughtful eyes,
Cute nose and glorious lips,
I wonder if you realize
That you are my dream ship.
   —"One Who Regards You With Hopeless Eyes"
(This looks a lot like Stiletto's work, Miss Amster.)

*   *   *

She must have known. She just didn't care.

Jerry disguised nearly all of his emotions under layers of text and humor, even other identities, but they had all failed. He probably even

Burlesquing The News

By Jerry and Wilson
REPARTEE
(O. K. Blow Torch!)

Stiletto: "I think your eyes are wonderful,"
Lois: "I think you're off your nut,"
Stiletto: "I think your presence powerful,"
Lois: "I think you've said enough."
Stiletto: "You're glorious as the chlorophyl,"
Lois: "I say, are you all here?"
Stiletto: "But, ah, your presence seems to chill."
Lois: "Good Lord, he's nerts, I fear!"
            —He Who Regards You With
                           Hopeless Eyes

*   *   *

interviewed her for the Goober piece, but she never remembered it. When interviewed decades later, Lois claimed she didn't even know Jerry. She only remembered that he was the guy who once wore his pajamas to school. She remembered that she wanted to be a reporter someday. Or maybe a detective.[8]

Lois Amster was never a detective, but she came close, though not in a way she ever could have imagined. In the February 1936 issue of *More Fun*, an episode of *Dr. Occult* begins as "A figure materializes out of the night" in a red dress and a blue cloak. The gorgeous blonde runs out of the snow and pipes up: "Please help me!—I've just escaped from the most awful place!" Dr. Occult recognizes her: "Mrs. Amster!" Her husband, Sander, grabs her shoulders: "Thank Heavens Dr. Occult found you!—But are you ill? Somehow you seem different!" She is different (because she is married), but Jerry, as Dr. Occult, waits in the wings to rescue her. Sure enough, a vampire is terrorizing the area. Occult devises a trap to catch the monster, which conveniently involves staying by her bedside at night, just as in *Dracula*.[9] In real life, Lois Amster had married after high school and was gone out of their lives. But they could imagine things differently.

The name "Lois" was floating around elsewhere, as was "Lane." There was Lois Leeds, who wrote for *The Plain Dealer,* and Lois Long, the infamous columnist from New York. Jerry himself would claim, years later in a letter to *Time,* that the inspiration for the name was

> Glenda Farrell, the movie star who portrayed Torchy Blane, a gutsy, beautiful headline-hunting reporter, in a series of exciting motion pictures. Because the name of the actress Lola Lane (who also played *Torchy*) appealed to me, I called my character Lois Lane. Strangely, the characterization of Lois is amazingly like the real-life personality of my lovely wife.[10]

But Lola Lane didn't star in a Torchy Blane film until *Torchy Blane in Panama* in 1938, which was too late to matter, though Jerry certainly knew her as an actress before that particular role.[11]

A much better candidate for the character's name is a weird pulp story from *Astounding Stories* in April 1934: "The Tooth" by Neil Moran. In this bizarre story, a professor named Radley goes to a dentist named Garney to remove a tooth that he believes might be haunted by a voodoo spirit. But it is a trick: Radley really wants to set up Garney with a beautiful young woman they both know. So Radley, who has learned occult magics in India, hypnotizes the couple (during his dental procedure) so that they undergo a trancelike experience in the ancient world. The couple, as per Radley's hopes, fall in love. The woman's name is familiar: Lois Lane.[12]

When asked decades later if he took names and ideas from the world around him, Jerry answered:

Coincidence? Probably. But for many years, while writing Superman stories, I would often conceive the names of characters appearing in various stories—and then to my surprise, later that same day, I would hear those identical names on the radio news, or read it in a newspaper.[13]

Whether or not Jerry Siegel did have psychic powers, or believed he did, or was simply covering his tracks, the ideas were swirling all around him.

YOU

Across town, a girl pins her hair back, looks at her younger sisters and her tired, scrubbing mother, and wonders what her own future will hold. There is not much money, but she goes to the movies and sees a world that somehow seems more real than her own. She writes for her school newspaper and brings the papers home to show her dad, named Mike, who is covered in black from the steel mill. His job will end soon. Her name is Jolan Kovacs, but nobody at school can say "Jolan" (her parents are Hungarian), so she goes by Helen.[14] That too will change.

She lives in Cleveland and times are tight and she has little sisters, so what she does is think as big as she can. Even though she has no experience at this sort of thing, how hard could it be? She's seen the movies and read all the magazines. So she takes out an ad in the local paper and announces that she is a model and wants work. She is really that interested, that desperate, or just that something. When her ad shows up in the paper, she reads it and laughs out loud. She then gets a little scared.

The letters fly in.[15]

She gathers them up and goes to the big public library downtown. She settles in the big room with all the tables and card catalogs. The ceiling is high and the room is filled with people. She may even bump into a short guy as she goes in. She doesn't see his face. She settles in the great rotunda, a gigantic central room. It is quiet. She takes a deep breath, and before she is even done exhaling, her hands are opening the letters.

Most of them are from guys looking for dates. That makes her grimace but also smile just a bit. One is really bad. She eventually gets to one letter that actually sounds genuine. It is from an artist, a cartoonist, who has been published, won contests, and is seeking a model for a cartoon strip. She likes the funnies, especially on Sundays, and thinks that wouldn't be too bad at all. That might be perfect, actually. She is impressed, so she writes him back. His name is Mr. Joseph Shuster. She says it in a whisper: *Shu-ster.* She likes the way it sounds.

A few weeks and letters later, she takes a bus over to Glenville on a Saturday afternoon, makes a switch, and walks down a few blocks. She is on the other side of town and it is freezing cold. She is nervous and considers running home. *No.* She goes up to the apartment door and knocks. It is two o'clock.[16] The door opens a bit and she sees a boy with wide eyes. *I'm the model that Mr. Shuster is expecting,* she says. *Come on in,* he responds, smiling. They talk, and she asks if she can leave her coat on because it is so cold, but she wants to leave it on for other reasons. But this boy turns out to be really nice, so they start talking about the weather and the movies and things like that. Finally she says, *Does Mr. Shuster know that I'm here?* And the boy says, after a pause, *I'm Mr. Shuster.* That is the way she meets the man who makes her more famous in that one second than she could have ever imagined.

So she tries to look as though she knows what she is doing as Joe sets up. His mom comes in and out, just to make sure everything is kosher. The girl is wearing her sister's bathing suit and it is too big in some important places, so she twists and pinches it back and blushes. Joe's mother laughs a little to herself. Joe smiles and tells her, *I'll fill that in later.*[17]

He does. And so they become lifelong friends, more than friends, in an instant. She strikes weird poses as he tells her about their character in their comic. Someone named Superman. *You're going to be famous,* she says. *I can feel it.*

Waiting in the outer room is Joe's partner, Jerry, who is the writer of the outfit. He is a strange boy and is whipping through magazines, thinking hard of what to say, when he meets this girl they hired. He can't believe they actually did it. *A girl in a bathing suit is BEHIND THAT DOOR.* When she finally does walk in, he realizes he could probably marry her right then and there.

She visits this cold apartment a few more times. She looks front, looks back, and at one point Jerry even balances on the couch and acts as though he's flying so she can figure out the right pose to be carried in. He falls and they all laugh. Jerry had an enormous amount of energy, she would later recall. They tell her all about their characters and their adventures and their mighty dreams. *Who are these two?* she wonders. When she leaves, Joe looks at the pictures and thinks about what he did wrong.

She dates Joe for a little while, and it is nice.[18] But after the last modeling session, she tells them both that she is leaving. She has an opportunity out east and she thinks she can actually make a career of this. She can't be famous in Cleveland, Ohio. But she isn't mean: she can't thank them enough. When she finally leaves, Joe closes the front door behind him and pleads with her, tears in his eyes. *Stay,* he says. But she can't, and he watches her leave. But he doesn't give up. He keeps drawing her and writes her letters every week.[19]

The character of Lois came about when Jerry and Joe decided that they wanted to move their Superman away from a cartoony space yarn to a more realistic drama. In reality, though, they may have seen their need for a female character as just an opportunity to get a girl to come over to their house and pose for them: *What would she wear? What would she do?*[20]

The girl they found, by complete luck, was Jolan Kovacs. Her parents, Michael (Mihaly) and Sophia (Zsofia), were born and met in Bakonyszom-bathely, Veszprém, Hungary. They were both Lutheran. They had six children, all of them girls, two of them twins. Jolan was born December 1, 1917, on the dairy farm they owned in Steubenville, Ohio. A year later, her unborn sister died when her pregnant mother tripped and fell in the barn. Another girl, an infant, died of the flu. Neither Sophie or Mike spoke much English, and Mike actually lost the farm over a language misun-derstanding with a buyer.[21]

The family moved to Cleveland, where Mike started work in the steel mills.[22] He would also cut hair, boasting an impressive collection of scis-sors. He was also a very heavy drinker. According to relatives, he drank "a fifth of liquor, a gallon of wine, and a case of beer at home, every week," though there is no way to prove such a thing.[23] His language and accent were his heavy yokes, and some of his neighbors often yelled at him, call-ing him a "dumb D.P.," which was an insult for a displaced person, an immigrant, an alien.[24]

So when Jolan began to think of changing her name and leaving Cleveland, it was more than a mere flight of fancy: forces were pushing her out. She almost had to dare herself to write the ad that prompted Jerry and Joe to answer. But she did. It ran for one day, in *The Plain Dealer,* on January 13, 1935.[25] The boys gave her the confidence that she could do this kind of work. So she made the move and left Cleveland, leaving them all behind.

But Jerry and Joe weren't content to let her go so easily. An old friend returns in a *Slam Bradley* episode of *Detective Comics* #16. "The Broadway

Bandit" begins with a full-page dramatic depiction of a robber entering a small office and brutally shooting a man behind a desk. The caption explains that Slam and Shorty have traveled to New York, to Broadway of all places, only to find yet another case to solve. As the theater manager seeks to foil a holdup, he is shot, but he lives and entrusts Slam and Shorty with finding this bandit who has been terrorizing productions up and down the avenue. He offers a handsome reward, which Slam and Shorty agree to, but only "if you let us do it in our own peculiar way."[26]

So Slam and Shorty go to a tap-dancing studio and pay $60 to learn everything at once. Slam is adamant that it can be done: "Listen Mush-face! You teach us how to out-dance Fred Astaire—I'll give you only five hours—or that pan of yours undergoes a violent transformation!" Unbelievably, they are soon hired as featured dancers in a show called *Love on Ice* and do some shtick ("Was that your wife I saw you with last night?") to uproarious laughter.[27]

Backstage, Shorty's eyes spy something that lets Joe's visual depiction of three gals in their underwear speak for itself: "Chorus girls! This assignment gets better and better by the minute!" But Slam doesn't believe their luck, for good reason. "That girl on the end!" Slam cries. "Why she's . . ." Slam spins her around: "Just as I thought—Joan Carter!"

Slam explains to his partner:

> Shorty, to look at this beautiful gal, you'd never guess she's the most unscrupulous, mercenary, double-crossing private dick who ever jerked a $10,000 fee from right under my nose!

Shorty, and the reader, can't believe it: "Y'mean she actually beats ya out on cases!" Slam admits it: "This particular dame specializes in trailing me while I'm on a big case, then stepping in at the finish and closing it herself. . . . Well, let me tell you something Miss Carter! This is ONE case where you won't crowd me out!" Joan replies coolly: "I seem to have heard that before someplace!—excuse me—it's time for the chorus to go on." Slam is furious at seeing her and orders Shorty to "trail her day and night!" In a very telling panel, "Joan Carter, who has overheard every word, smiles enigmatically to herself!"[28]

At this time, Jolan Kovacs was indeed using the name "Joan Carter" and was working as a model. After she left Cleveland, she went to Chicago, then Boston, and posed for painters and illustrators after a stint as a figure skater.[29] She went to Provincetown and New York, where she even worked with some photographers. But like Joe, she was a little short, so it held her back. They would talk about this in their letters. She was also in California at one point, working at a famous nightclub, and even got married to someone named Joseph; but they were getting some of that secondhand, so they weren't really sure what was true or not.[30] Joe was very quiet that day. But all the while, she wrote to Joe and encouraged him. She would recall later:

> Many times he used to write to me and say that he was about to give up on it; and I'd say, "Keep at it and you'll make it." I had such a feeling about the strip and about them. I told him, "You're going to be very famous some day."[31]

Her new name was so similar to Edgar Rice Burroughs's own John Carter that Jerry himself might have had a hand in its invention.

The rest of the episode is a race between Joan and Shorty to find and apprehend the bandit. At one point, Joan knocks Shorty out with a vicious uppercut and a sarcastic "SORRY!" She is wearing a red suit with blue high shorts. Joan grabs the bandit (who turns out to be the manager), but he has a gun. Slam bursts in and disarms the criminal with a strange tap-dance move and earns the $5,000 reward. This changes Joan's tune immediately, as she pulls Slam into her arms for a kiss, saying, "$5,000!— oh, you attractive man!" Joe's sketches from the initial sittings with Jolan can be seen in the back of the panel, pasted all over the walls. The boys— Joe especially, who (as Shorty) gets punched out by Joan—clearly felt abandoned by her, even sucker-punched. But they were also showing off—they had done well in getting their comics published and wanted to boast, as they always did, through their colorful avatars.[32] She was their new character—and most important, hopeful audience.

Chapter 14
The Works

FOR DECADES, the same story of how *Superman* was finally sold and published in *Action Comics* #1 has been repeated in a high-toned, newsreel voice: *Relegated to a pile on an editor's desk, Jerry and Joe's super-submission languished for months before it was finally rescued by Sheldon Mayer, who convinced his bosses that it was worth taking a chance on for the history-making* Action Comics #1!

The reality is that *Superman* wasn't discovered; everyone on the East Coast already knew about it by 1937. They knew about it plenty; they just didn't like it enough to commit. Humor Publishing, Star-Spangled Comics, and the Major had all expressed varying levels of interest, but none of them went the actual distance. The why is more speculative. For one, the strip was being submitted as a pitch by two kids from Cleveland. If they had been in New York, it would have been easier to meet with them and gauge their talent. Most papers were also already carrying either *Flash Gordon* or *Buck Rogers* and were hesitant about picking up *another* science fiction comic, which is what their *Superman* proposal in its first weeks very visibly was.[1] Part of this was Jerry and Joe's fault; instead of showing Superman stopping urban crime, which might have appealed to Depression audiences, they focused the first panels on an exploding planet and a rocket ship.

The truth to this legend—*it languished for months*—was that there were indeed people who were interested in it at various times, and Jerry and Joe would then be forced to wait their decisions out. Though the Major was interested when he was still in charge, he never seemed to make a straight legal claim to the material even as he wanted it for his comic books. The Major felt that *Superman* would do much better in a comic book format than in the newspapers. In a letter dated October 4, 1935, the Major acknowledges their *Superman* proposal with some advice:

> It is my own idea, based on a lot of experience in selling in the syndicate game, that you would be much better off doing Superman in full page in four colors for one of our publications. We also have pending an order for a 16-page tabloid in four colors in which we could include Superman around the first of the year, if we have it in colors and running. Use your own judgment on this. I think myself that Superman stands a very good chance.[2]

Because Jerry and Joe were holding out for a newspaper strip, they refused the Major's offer, nebulous as it was. They had probably had enough of his inability to pay on time. So they kept on churning out *More Fun* instead, waiting for a newspaper syndicate to say yes. As it turned out, the Major's words were prescient; they just couldn't see it.

Two years later, in 1937, United Feature Syndicate told the boys that they would publish *Superman* in a comics magazine called *Tip Top* in advance of expected syndication. This was clearly a selling ploy of the comics editor, but Jerry and Joe had hope. On February 18, a letter arrived:

> *I am afraid we are not ready to use your pages in it for some time. The trouble with Superman, for example, is that it is still a rather immature piece of work. It is attractive because of its freshness and naiveté, but this is likely to wear off after the feature runs for a while.[3]*

Frustration again abounded in Cleveland. It was *Science Fiction* all over again. On October 29, 1937, another publisher, Trojan, wrote:

> *The only cloud on the horizon is that every time I hear from you I think back to the time that you suggested that we start a comic strip magazine which, had we published it then, would have been the first on the market. . . . The field is very crowded, and I feel the cream has been skimmed off the business.[4]*

They were now somewhere between laughing and crying. They thought about the Major's offer again. They knew that he was also thinking about a new title called *Action Comics.* In fact, Jerry had sent a December 6, 1937, letter to Jack Liebowitz with details on several other new characters for *Action,* including *Bob Hazard,* a "world-wide adventurer," and *The Crimson Horseman,* a "masked, cloaked rider of mystery who metes out grim justice in a lawless cattle country where the law is openly flouted." The most interesting of the submissions is *The Wraith:*

> *A most unusual detective. Due to abnormal glands all of his senses are acute to a hypersensitive degree. . . . He tracks down criminals like a prowling beast—is called "The Wraith" because he comes and goes as mysteriously as a ghost—frightens criminals half out of their wits because they believe him to be not of this world.*[5]

Jerry also pitches *Chesty Crane,* the "Crack(ed) Athlete," who is "boisterous, boastful, but simple and goodhearted" and full of "sport-action." There is also *Streak Marvel,* who is a "scientific genius." Jerry suggests such variety because he envisions that "ACTION COMICS would contain a well-balanced list of features: adventure, western, sport, and science fiction."[6] Jerry sent these submissions under a new letterhead of "Publication Enterprises, Company," with himself as president and an "Arnold G. Leonard" as general manager. The address was still his mom's house on Kimberley. But Whit Ellsworth didn't like Jerry's characters.

Jerry and Joe were very grateful to the Major but were worried about his finances, so they made the difficult decision to continue to wait for something better. That something was Harry Donenfeld. Though the Major's partnership with Donenfeld and his partners, Sampliner and Liebowitz, had allowed *Detective Comics* to be published, the Major was quickly racking up more debt, or so he was told. So in late 1937, Harry, through his company Donny Press, sued the Major's Nicholson Publishing, Inc., for the $5,878 they owed him.[7] Since the Major obviously couldn't pay it, Harry Donenfeld, after a simple but cold court maneuver, bought out his debt and became the primary content partner of Detective Comics, Inc., and Nicholson Publishing.[8]

The Major was out.[9] Indeed, this might have been Harry's plan all along. He was the grinning, hearty salesman, traveling up and down the coast, always meeting with distributors to increase circulation and rack up profit. Meanwhile, Liebowitz stayed in New York and balanced the ledgers and carried the twos. He wore shiny black pinstripes and glasses.

He was bald but looked sharp. They were the second generation of comics publishers; they had learned from mistakes, and they knew what they were doing.

While this shuffling of ownership was going on in the fall of 1937, Jerry and Joe were still submitting *Superman*. Maxwell Charles "M. C." Gaines was working at the McClure Newspaper Syndicate, where they still desperately wanted to place *Superman* as a newspaper strip.[10] Gaines was a "hard-nosed, pain-wracked, loud, aggressive man" who was another candidate for the "father of the American comic book," having put together the ten-cent *Famous Funnies* in 1934 from Dell Publishing.[11] Jerry sent the proposal to McClure several times but had no luck. Gaines wrote back to Jerry and suggested—strongly—that it would be a good idea to allow Detective to look at the very *Superman* proposal they had just sent to him.[12] The usual story is that it was Sheldon Mayer, one of Gaines's youthful editors, who saw the *Superman* proposal in a pile, went crazy for it, and pushed it onto his boss. Mayer had worked for the Major as a gifted cartoonist himself and would later produce the incredibly popular comic *Sugar and Spike.* Jerry and Joe were still uninterested in a comic book format for *Superman,* but they really wanted McClure, so they did what Gaines suggested.

The boys finally got a letter from editor Vin Sullivan on January 10, 1938, explaining the takeover by Donenfeld and Liebowitz, which was a mere ten days old. Sullivan was now at National/Detective, having replaced Whitney Ellsworth, who had left in 1937 for a bit. He wrote to Cleveland:

> *Dear Jerry:—*
> *No doubt you're quite surprised to be hearing from me from the above address. . . . Nicholson Pub. is in the hands of receivers, . . . due to the taking over of the publication by Detective Comics by the firm in which Mr. Liebowitz is business manager, etc.*
>
> *I have on hand now several features you sent to Mr. Liebowitz. . . . The one feature I liked best, and the one that seems to fit into the proposed schedule is that "Superman." With all the work Joe is doing now (and that includes the features he drew for Fun and Adventure) could it be possible for him to still turn out 13 pages of this new feature?*
>
> *Joe, of course, seems to have the proper touch in putting your stories*

on drawing paper. . . . I'd like to have him turn out this "Super-
man" for the new magazine. He is handling 27 pages for the other
three magazines. Adding another 13 to his already filled schedule is
loading him up to the neck. Please let me know <u>immediately</u> whether
or not he can do this extra feature.

Best regards,
Vin Sullivan[13]

In one letter, the boys from Cleveland learned that their patron, the
Major, who gave them their first big break in comics, was now gone and
they were being given an offer, in writing, to publish *Superman*. Somewhere in the time between Gaines asking them to send it to Detective
and the Major being sued for his company, someone had given the okay—
and a quick one—to *Superman*. What was going on?

No records are known to survive that document exactly what went on
behind the scenes on the deal to publish *Superman*. Or they are locked
away or were held only in half-trusted handshakes.[14] The existing letters
state that Gaines encouraged them to take *Superman* over to Detective,
which was where they were working anyway.[15] Everyone focuses on the
publication of *Action* #1, but the only horse Gaines had in the race, besides printing books for National, was newspaper syndication, not comic
books. Was he just being nice to Harry and throwing him some business,
or was it something more? Mayer may have thought that *Superman* would
work in the newspapers, but Gaines didn't, so someone might have suggested a tryout in one of Harry's new, disposable magazines. The other
plus to such a scenario is that the price to pay for a comic book story
would be much less than paying two creators for ongoing newspaper syndication. This might have been their plan. Might.

Donenfeld and Gaines might have had a side deal—or at least the idea
of one—to maximize their own profit on the side while they had the
chance to see how the character did. Given how things would play out,
this is not that difficult a hypothesis to imagine. For one, McClure was
printing Donenfeld's books, so they were creating business for each
other. Even so, by the time *Superman* was purchased by Detective, Jerry
and Joe were already successful creators—kids were writing fan mail to
them, and their names were being used in advertisements. The facts are
that it was Harry who signed them, at Gaines's direction, and when Mc-
Clure sold the *Superman* strip to the newspapers, McClure bought the

rights from Harry, not the boys. It was then Donenfeld who not only now *owned* the property, but received the lion's share of the profits; whatever Jerry and Joe got was parsed out by him. This was done at much less cost and allowed them to try the strip out—and thus advertise it—for a few months to test the waters before the big syndication purchase. Gaines knew that if he went to the newspapers with a known commodity, he could ask for more money. The businessmen here were using shotguns; it was the public who would make the real decisions.

The actual contract for *Action Comics* #1 is relatively simple:

> *Dated March 1*
> *I, the undersigned, am an artist or author and have performed work*
> *for strip entitled SUPERMAN*
> *In consideration of $130.00 agreed to be paid me by you, I hereby*
> *sell and transfer such work and strip, all good will attached thereto and*
> *exclusive right to the use of the characters and story, continuity and*
> *title of strip contained therein, to you and your assigns to have and*
> *hold forever and to be your exclusive property and I agree not to*
> *employ said characters by their names contained therein or under any*
> *other names at any time hereafter to any other person firm or corpora-*
> *tion, or permit the use thereof by said other parties without obtaining*
> *your written consent therefor. The intent hereof is to give you exclu-*
> *sive right to use and acknowledge that you own said characters or story*
> *and the use thereof, exclusively. I have received the above sum of*
> *money.*
> *Sgd. Joe Shuster*
> *Sgd. Jerome Siegel*
> *Returned by mail on March 3, 1938*[16]

Jerry had to convince Joe to sign, but he did so using the same methods that Detective was using on him: *Syndication will follow, syndication will follow.* So they signed it. The check came, with payments on it for some of their other work (possibly in a ploy to get them to sign it). Liebowitz misspelled both of their names on the front of the check, forcing them to sign it, on the back, in names that weren't theirs.[17] They sent it back the next day. Vin Sullivan wrote them on February 4, 1938, with very specific instructions: "Shoot the works, pronto!"[18] Per instruction, they started disarticulating their newspaper strip and pasting it into a tabloid form. Parts and pieces become somewhat whole, though this was not how they had imagined it.[19] But it was still happening. They worked fast, on the floor, into the night. They had three weeks. They worked fast.

Why Donenfeld wanted *Superman* so quickly after gobbling up the Major's comics company is hard to determine, but it might have had something to do with the way Harry saw it, not that he needed something at the last minute. By 1937, Harry had wanted to branch into more acceptable, less racy magazines and had formed a limited partnership with George Washington Trendle, the owner of the Lone Ranger property, to produce the popular *Lone Ranger* magazine. The magazine did very well, partly because of the colorful painted covers by artist H. J. Ward. But Trendle started poaching some of this magazine art for other Lone Ranger materials, and his partnership with Harry dissolved eight months (and issues) later.[20] Trendle's actions had made Harry mad, but part of it was jealousy: Trendle controlled every aspect of the Lone Ranger license, which translated to a lot of money.[21] So when Harry saw Superman, a similar larger-than-life character, right after losing the Lone Ranger, he may have been seeing his second chance flash right before his eyes. If he had kept the Lone Ranger, he might not have given Superman a second glance.

Mickey Mouse probably played a role in this, too. Mickey was the envy of everyone in entertainment because he had moved from a mute, jerkily animated cartoon character to the head of a growing empire of books, toys, and a popular newspaper comic strip. Everyone was trying to get the next Mickey, a character everyone knew about with a seemingly unlimited ceiling for merchandising. Every editor and publisher with any sense whatsoever envied Walt Disney, who owned outright the complete rights to the character. If you even showed Mickey, *you had to pay Walt.* Harry loved that as much as he hated it. In the months leading up to Harry's decision on whether or not to take *Superman,* Mickey was also seen someplace else—the news page. MICKEY MOUSE IS BANNED BY CENSORS IN YUGOSLAVIA appeared as a shocking headline in *The New York Times* on December 2, 1937. The cartoon in question apparently "told the story of how the uncle of a reigning prince became alarmed at the popularity of Mickey."[22] This was all done for laughs, but the Yugoslavian censors viewed it as dangerous dissent. And soon, "Mickey made his abrupt exit from the *Politika*'s pages, only to emerge in headlines in the press of the world" as a patriotic symbol of American nationalism.[23]

Within two years, Superman would be on the covers of comics arm in arm with midshipmen and army men, on the steel plates of tanks, and painted on the sides of planes spiraling toward German factories. Did Harry foresee this? Or did he just see all the press that Walt's "subversive" character was getting and lick his lips? In the wake of the Yugoslavian incident, Herbert Russell in *The New York Times Magazine* calls Mickey "an internationalist" and wonders if "Mickey shall become Emperor of the World? Perhaps Mickey isn't so dumb as he looks. Maybe that is why he is winning the ordinary folk and the great, building his youth movement through clubs, boring from within in Europe, Asia, Africa, India, and the Americas."[24] This was the economic allure of the Mouse. Harry, the former publisher of *Spicy* and *Pep*, must have recognized that if he could no longer sell sex, then he had to sell something else—something nice and wholesome that could also cause a splash. Something like a guy in a strongman outfit who could beat people up. The possibilities stretched like the sky outside Harry's window.

He took a long look and called for Jack.

SCALE

Over the next few months, Jerry and Joe wrote and drew while Harry chomped and smoked in his squeaky chair. It was impossible to know how well a magazine title was selling that early in those days, but Donenfeld was no dummy—he had a network of newsstands all across the city that kept him abreast of what was moving and what was not. Superman was flying.

It is easy to imagine a straw-haired kid, something of a wiseacre and straight out of a Hal Roach short, going up to the newsstand and saying, *Hey, mister, what's that funny-looking one?* But as with most popular culture phenomena—the yo-yo, the hula hoop—no one knows exactly who was first buying *Superman.* A famous anecdote was that Donenfeld was down at the newsstand at the corner, wincing at the sun, when a ragamuffin kid came up and demanded to buy *the one with Superman in it.* Harry didn't need any sales figures after seeing that.[25] Once the numbers came in from National Periodicals (which was still the umbrella name of the company), Jack looked down his nose and allowed himself the barest of smiles.[26] Their tryout had paid off. Before too long, you could start to see them on New York sidewalks on Wednesdays: kids and men looking for the new issue.[27] People were buying it and no one was complaining; they would have to keep it that way.

The reasons people bought Superman are easy to guess. The character, by design, spoke to the fears of the times, but it was really the cover that did it. The story goes that Donenfeld suggested that the cover be a larger version of a panel in the original proposal strip. He was just blown over by the image of a man lifting a car. In the strongman world, muscle men had been trying to lift cars for years; it was the ultimate expression of man resisting the onslaught of modern machinery. But no one could do it, not really, not without pulleys or angles.[28] But here was Superman doing it with a simple leg press. Donenfeld, or someone around him, saw it as a home run. The cover itself is the most famous image in comics, but to 1938 eyes, it was completely outrageous. It registers to the eye as a cartoon, but it is not a buckskin cowboy or a weird-talking sailor man with supernatural forearms; it is just a mean-looking man in tights. Joe constructed his famous pose from a fitness manual to get the realism just right.[29] The focus is not even on Superman, it is on the meticulously rendered 1938 Hudson Terraplane as copied by Joe from an advertisement.[30] The landscape is orange and rocky, like Mars. But what really grabbed the attention, and the dimes, of the curious kids on the streets was the man's face in the bottom left-hand corner—running away from Superman, screaming. Once they read the comic, kids would find that this man was a criminal, but here, on the cover, this man is just a grown-up running away from the visual mayhem that is Superman. Kids saw adults—parents—running away from the center of the action—so they ran directly toward it.[31] Harry knew that controversy always sold, and he had just dropped his age bracket.[32]

Because *Action* #1 is essentially made up of cut-up newspaper strips, the narrative is as much a jigsaw of things as its main character. The first page, in fact, is devoted to what would become a mainstay of superhero comics: the secret origin.[33] Because new readers were ostensibly dropping in all the time on a serial, publishers had to be sure to bring them up to speed. In Superman's case, someone (possibly Gaines) was so turned off by the endless exposition on Superman's slowly exploding home world that constituted the first few weeks of the newspaper strip, things were realigned to get right to the action. *Action* #1, page one, boils down a baby's escape from a planet that was being "destroyed by old age."[34] Landing on Earth, the young baby is put into an orphanage.[35] But the mysterious baby has powers: even in diapers, he is able to lift a chair over his head. The origin then moves to an explanation of his powers as a mature adult, showing readers that he can "hurdle a twenty story building," "raise tremendous weights," "run faster than an express train, and was (more or less) bulletproof."[36] He also has a very Roosevelt-sounding mission: "Early, Clark decided he must turn his titanic strength into channels that would benefit Mankind." "And so was created" (in full costume near the end): "Superman."

The origin, which brought goose bumps to its shocked young readers (*superpowers?*), provides a clear, somewhat rational explanation of his abilities: A carefully illustrated "scientific explanation of Clark Kent's amazing strength" reveals that his powers act similar to the way insects can leap great distances comparative to their small size and weight. Jerry writes as if he is selling something: "Incredible? No! For even today on our world exist creatures with super-strength!" This is a swipe in subject matter from Hugo Gernsback, who ran an article in *Science and Invention* in March 1931 that not only explored the proportional power of insects but also illustrated how they could fight like mighty warriors.[37]

The first actual *Superman* story in *Action* #1 reads like a series of disparate adventures designed to bludgeon readers over the head with the fists of this new character. First, Superman stops the wrongful execution of Evelyn Curry by breaking into the governor's office just before midnight and presenting new evidence, showing very little regard for state and police authority as he smashes doors and guns. A classic strongman feat was crumpling a door, which, of course, Superman does. He then, after getting a tip as *Daily Star*[38] reporter Clark Kent, confronts some lowlife who is beating his wife at 211 Court Avenue; Superman takes care of it—violently—as Superman.[39] Clark then goes dancing with a very reluctant Lois Lane and stops (as Superman) some mobsters who kidnap her.[40] He then basically tortures a corrupt lobbyist in Washington, D.C., by dangling him off a telephone wire. And this is just the first issue.

They weren't calling it *Action Comics* for nothing.

SECOND

Meanwhile, back in Cleveland, Jerry was getting letters from other syndicates who had seen the success of *Action Comics* and were suddenly interested in the strip they had once rejected. A newspaper bidding war began on Superman, but Jerry knew they had nothing to sell—since the *Action Comics* signing, Harry had the rights to any possible newspaper release. Jerry, who was not dumb, finally saw what had been done to him and Joe. This was the grudge they would hold for decades. Jerry drafted a letter to Harry and begged for the rights back. Harry said, *Come to New York and we'll see what we can do.*[41]

Jerry got on the next train. Joe had to stay behind and draw to make the next *Action* deadline. Jerry didn't have enough money for a sleeper car, so he sat in coach until his back hurt and he couldn't fall asleep. The green chair dug against his back as he watched the silent hills pass by. He was furious. He wished he could jump out of the train, fly to New York, and wring Donenfeld's neck. But he had said they would work something out. *Maybe it would all be okay.*

When the train pulled into Grand Central Terminal, Jerry was scared out of his mind. He smirked and was happy at being in New York as a *writer,* but his suit seemed less appropriate with every step and his shoes looked more scuffed the closer he got to downtown. He tried to push his shoulders back and clear his nose. When the doors opened, Harry greeted him from behind the desk as if he were an old pal: *Jerry, siddown!* The doors closed behind them.

In that meeting, Jerry tried his best to stand up for himself, but he was enormously intimidated by the fat man with the suspenders and the cigar and the silent, scary Liebowitz, who spoke with a tiny mouth full of precise, quiet words. These were not bad men, they were worse—they were businessmen. Jerry would remember that.[42] Harry said the deal was already done, that *Superman* was going to be in the newspapers with McClure, and *isn't that what they wanted?* He said that if he and Joe would sign a ten-year deal, they could do the newspaper strips, and they would get some royalties. When Jerry balked, Harry reminded him that National owned *all* of the rights to Superman and, quite frankly, he could get someone else to write and draw it if he wanted to.[43]

It was a slight gamble on Harry's part—he knew readers had become accustomed to Siegel and Shuster's work, and he didn't want to risk upsetting a secret formula that he still didn't completely understand, especially when it was selling so well. He wanted to keep them at least satiated so they wouldn't try some kind of lawsuit. Liebowitz urged caution and reiterated their stance in a September 28, 1938, letter:

Our company has very little to gain in a monetary sense from the syndication of this material. Also bear in mind, that we own the feature "Superman" and that we can at any time replace you in the drawing of that feature and that without our consent this feature would not be syndicated and therefore you would be the loser in the entire transaction. . . . It is entirely up to you and Joe, whether you wish our pleasant relationship to continue and whether you wish the strip "Superman" to be syndicated.[44]

Jack was lying, sort of. Harry eventually gained at least $100,000, personally, in the sale to McClure.[45] Jerry was so terrified of being shut out of Superman that he gave in; he really had no choice. So Jerry responded that we "are anxious and ready to do our best on SUPERMAN so that all parties concerned will profit."[46]

In the end, it was the newspapers that did it. In addition to *Action Comics,* Jerry and Joe's impossible dream had come true: they were to be published every day in that most treasured of places, the daily American newspaper. They would make a lot of money, but not nearly as much as their boss, who didn't draw or write a thing. Jerry and Joe would be paid very well, but they would never be rich. As soon as Donenfeld made the initial fortune, Gaines jumped ship from McClure to head his own comics imprint with Liebowitz, *All-American Comics,* under Donenfeld's symbolic aegis.[47] Was this a good model for market expansion or a carefully plotted thank-you? When the dust settled, Jerry and Joe weren't so much blackmailed or bamboozled; they were bullied. The creators of *Superman* were bullied.

ACTION

Meanwhile, the first year of Superman's adventures were being pulled from real news events in Ohio and abroad. Lois and Clark travel to cover a foreign war in the fictional "San Monte" in *Action* #2. They encounter a war-torn plain filled with heavy artillery, calling to mind the Chaco War, a several-year dispute between Paraguay and Bolivia over a flat patch of land that coincidentally held oil. The Chaco War was filled with bloody, fierce fighting and heavy guns; it was covered almost every day by *The Plain Dealer* from 1932 to 1938 as readers watched in horror at casualties that would end up near a hundred thousand people.[48] Superman points out the futility of such endless conflict by asking the child's question: "Why are your armies battling?" The general responds: "I don't know! Can you tell me?" "No. Can you?" Superman clarified things.

After restoring peace to San Monte, Superman confronts a coal mine disaster in *Action* #3 in nearby Blakely Town, where Thornton Blakely, an unscrupulous mine owner, subjects his workers to very unsafe conditions and they are trapped in the mine. After rescuing them, Superman turns the tables and traps the fat-cat owner and his socialite cronies in the mine as the "new" safety devices fail miserably. But Blakely learns his lesson and makes the mine as safe as possible. Ohio witnessed a real mine tragedy on November 5, 1930, at the Sunday Creek Coal Company mine in Athens, Ohio. The mine executives were underground looking at "new" safety equipment when an explosion killed eighty-two people. Nineteen trapped miners were rescued. The tragedy eventually changed Ohio safety laws and garnered national press attention.[49]

Another recurring topic that the early Superman comes back to—again and again—is automobile safety. In *Action* #4, a drunk driver speeds away from a hit-skip and Superman finds the car on the train tracks—but the driver "has died of a heart attack!"[50] A few issues later, a furious Superman leaps to City Hall and asks the mayor point-blank: "Why has our city one of the worst traffic situations in the country?" The politician answers: "It's really too bad—but—what can anyone do about it?" Superman responds: "I, for one, am going to do *plenty* about it!" Superman goes straight to radio station WVUX and pushes himself on air, educating the people that "more people have been killed needlessly by autos than died during the World War!" He then proceeds to wreck a bunch of dangerous old cars being sold at used-car lots. "I think I'm going to enjoy this private little war," he says.[51] Though his powers include great strength and the ability to leap great distances, *Superman*'s early stories are more about inspirational situations than smackdowns. In the main story of issue #4, Superman impersonates a college football player to stop a Mob fix on the game's outcome and inspires the player, Tommy Burke, to return to the game himself.

By *Action* #6, six months into the experiment, *Superman* was getting so popular that Jerry and Joe decided to do a story about it. Clark meets a man who introduces himself as "Nick Williams, Superman's personal manager." Clark responds knowingly, "That's absurd!" but Williams assures him that "I have a contract from him giving me sole commercial rights to his name!" Clark is then astonished to see a blimp fly by with an ad with Superman on it for "super-gasoline." Williams explains that he has "licensed Superman bathing-suits, costumes, physical development exercisers, and movie rights, to name a few—why, I've even made provisions for him to appear in the comics!" An inquisitive office boy, blond but with a signature bow tie, shows up for the first time with a "Gosh!" And in a nightclub, a sultry singer in slinky green grabs the microphone and sings a torch song:

> *You're a Superman (swing it boys)*
> *You're a Superman!*
> *You can make my heart leap ten thousand feet*
> *You're a Superman!*
> *But I'm the one gal who can, get under your skin*
> *When you crush me in your arms, I must reveal*
> *I'm only flesh and blood and not*
> *Resistless steel!*[52]

The early issues of *Action* have him tackling real problems and situations. But as the year progressed, Superman started eyeing Jerry's and Joe's personal problems. But this time they weren't using their comics to complain about girls; they were starting to feel they got gypped.

On September 26, 1938, Jerry sent a letter to Jack Liebowitz on important-looking stationery from the American Artists League that, like his old story in *The Torch* to Bernard Kenton, is full of hopeful math:

> *Dear Jack*
>
> *I've just finished talking over with Joe the terms as determined in New York.*
>   *In view that SUPERMAN is a great factor in ACTION COMIC's success . . . that it has played first in the Reader Poll . . . that along with other ACTION COMICS strips it is being resold in Latin America and Mexico . . . that reprint syndicate comics receive as high as $25 per page in other comic publications . . . it is our desire that commencing with the SUPERMAN releases we next submit, we receive $15 per page.—Thus, when our reprint matter is out 50%, we will at least receive $7.50 per page. . . . We are certain that*

you will find this rate for the SUPERMAN pass upon which we insist, completely reasonable when you consider SUPERMAN's worth. Awaiting your prompt reply,

*Cordially
Jerry*[53]

When Jerry stamped it and mailed it away to New York, his heart was pounding like a steam engine. He knew they were worth more than they were getting, but he feared he may have just signed their death warrant for ever working on Superman again.

National knew that Superman was lightning in a bottle, and they didn't want an early escape. They didn't think Jerry and Joe would try to rock the boat this early. But then again, they couldn't have predicted Superman would get so popular, either. For the rest of that first miraculous year, Superman saves a circus by performing as a strongman, exposes a decrepit orphanage, builds some modern public housing, and stops a dam from breaking. But he is still, paradoxically, wanted by the law. Police Chief Burke explains to Clark in *Action* #8: "You can tell your readers that we'll spare no effort to apprehend Superman—but off the record . . . I think he did a splendid thing and I'd like to shake his hand!" "You know, Chief, strangely enough, I feel the same way."[54] Superman was an outsider, and it was that bit of subversive rebelliousness—perhaps inspired by their growing distrust of National—that drew kids to him like nails to a magnet.

The best example of the early Superman's status as vigilante occurs in *Action* #9. Since "Superman has wantonly destroyed public property," Police Chief Burke has "imported Captain Reilly . . . the Chicago dick who . . . WOW!"[55] Reilly, the celebrity detective in question, is a stand-in for Eliot Ness, who led the infamous Untouchables in Chicago and finally brought down Al Capone. Ness, the honest-to-goodness crime fighter, was also the basis for Chester Gould's Dick Tracy. Following his success in Chicago, Ness came to Cleveland as safety director in 1935. After posing for pictures, Ness formed a new group of lawmen and began sweeping reforms of a highly corrupt police department. Ness also helped form the local Boystown and won awards for dramatically lowering the traffic fatality rate. He went after liquor and gambling. He was Superman with a badge.[56]

But Ness would eventually leave Cleveland after a scandal-ridden divorce, only to return for a failed run for mayor in 1947. His greatest failure in Cleveland still haunted voters; they could not forget that he had failed to solve the "Torso Murders" that clutched the city around the throat from 1934 to 1938. Having claimed twelve official victims over the city's landscape in various horrible states, the killer seemingly taunted Ness through the mail and took Cleveland to the very edge of panic.[57] Ness as "Reilly" in *Action* is an ironic figure: not only does he not get Superman or the killer but he is symbolic of the police department's failure to save Jerry's father years before. Clark even refers to Reilly as a "conceited windbag." Superman is the law in this town, complete with his own badge and uniform. Superman exposes all of the holes in the armor of law enforcement—and all of the people it failed.[58]

Every issue of *Action* ends with a complete return to its beginning: the bad guy lies defeated and Lois and Clark return to their détente of bickering over bylines. It's the old *Slam Bradley* ending, but with Clark getting professional recognition instead of the girl. Their relationship gets established very early: Lois, who writes the lovelorn column, is constantly trying to get the big story but is always scooped by Clark, often in the last panel. In the first few months of *Action Comics,* Lois is positively acidic toward Clark as he clumsily attempts to ask her out, but over time they develop a friendship rather than the torrid one-issue affairs of *Slam Bradley.* Clark still puts his foot in his mouth and Lois is still somewhat mean, but they start to look out for each other while chasing down their leads. And when Lois shows interest in another man, Clark goes bananas trying to figure out what she wants. This is part of the magic formula of Superman and the maturity of Jerry in writing it: recognizing that good things take time.

Their relationship is also funny. Lois many times gets a tip and then lies about a fake story (such as the birth of septuplets) just to get rid of Clark (she then calls him a "brainless idiot"), but he always—and sometimes literally—sees through it. For as funny as the Lois and Clark scenes are, the ones between Lois and Superman are equally dramatic. Joe draws still scenes of Superman leaping past the full moon, Lois in his arms, completely silent. But as always, Superman must put her down, usually with a melodramatic "Perhaps we'll meet again." So when Clark shows up moments later, disheveled and full of excuses, Lois unloads: "I can hardly bear looking at him, after having been in the arms of a real he-man."[59] Sometimes she is more exacting: "Clark Kent—I DESPISE

YOU!"[60] These were imagined retorts that Superman's readers could re-
late to. *Action Comics* was about the state of being that is the hapless boy,
but Jerry and Joe managed to mythologize it—the nerd is awkward but
also heroic, selfless, and strong in the drama of his own imagination.

Each adventure was largely self-contained, which made it easy for National to soon consider starting a reprint series to capitalize on Superman's success. So in the summer of 1939, they came out with a new book
titled simply *Superman,* a quarterly publication consisting essentially of
reprints. Eventually, it would contain new material. For now, though,
the lead story in the new *Superman* #1 was the same as in *Action* #1, but
with the addition of four new pages to help it make more sense. These
pages appear after the one-page origin, but before Superman swoops
down to the governor's mansion. A new witness is introduced to explain
that not only did Evelyn Curry not kill the suspiciously named "Jack
Kennedy," but someone named "Bea Carroll" did.[61]

Superman #1 also peeks behind the curtain with a full-page biography
of Jerry and Joe, complete with photos and titled "Boys and Girls, Meet
the Creators":

> Here is Jerry Siegel at his typewriter, thinking up his next thrill-
> ing adventure of Superman. Jerry has written many books and
> stories which have appeared in a great many magazines, but he
> likes SUPERMAN best of all, because he really believes in the
> principles.[62]

Jerry wrote only comics, but National paints him as something of a
full-blown literary novelist. Joe is similarly depicted in photo dots at his
art table:

> This is Joe Shuster, Jerry's life-long friend and associate, from
> whose versatile pen and brush are depicted SUPERMAN's
> amazing feats. I hope the boys and girls of America enjoy read-
> ing SUPERMAN as much as Jerry and I enjoy writing and
> drawing it.[63]

The boys also made a temporary move to New York at this time, and
consequently, Superman moves (without explanation in the comics) from
Cleveland to Metropolis.[64] The adventures then became a little more

fictional as the city too becomes more fantastical.[65] National wanted them to work from their own New York offices at 480 Lexington, just to have them closer (for deadline purposes) and to avoid all the mail.[66] The boys gave it a shot—but hated it. So they moved back home and rented their own studio in Cleveland. They had more work to do.

STAR AND PLANET

As Donenfeld promised, *Superman* had also begun syndication in newspapers. The financial intricacies and percentages were very upsetting, but the fact remained that Jerry and Joe's *Superman* was now a McClure comic strip. The newspaper that Jerry had first written to as a kid was now running his comics every day. The enormity of this was not lost on either of them. *Superman* began on January 16, 1939. A separate Sunday edition was added on November 5, 1939. These strips ran continuously until May 1966. By 1941, the McClure Syndicate had placed the strip in hundreds of newspapers. At its peak, the strip was in more than three hundred daily newspapers and ninety Sunday papers, with a readership of over twenty million readers.[67]

All of these adventures made one thing immediately clear from the beginning: Jerry and Joe were going to need help. So when they moved back to Cleveland, the first thing they did was look for a studio space. They rented an upstairs office located in the Colonnade building at 10609 Euclid Avenue, near East 105th, in room 306. It was possibly the smallest office in Cleveland, about twelve-by-twelve, with four drawing desks and a small anterior space, and all at a cost of $30 a month. They tore out the phone and, unlike Snoopy and Smiley, wiped the front window clean. *No distractions,* said Jerry.

Writing and drawing comics took time, and National was giving them more work than they could possibly handle, so they hired help. They advertised in the paper and elsewhere for an "ARTIST to do inking, lettering on adventure strips: bring 2 samples: salary."[68] A number of artists would come and go, paid by Jerry and Joe, to help with the art chores. There was Paul Cassidy, who came aboard for inking in 1939. Leo Nowak came in one year later. There were others such as John Sikela, Ira Yarbrough, Dennis Neville, Ed Dobrotka, Jack Burnley, and Paul J. Lauretta.[69] Stan Kaye came on late as an inker, but it was Fred Ray and Wayne Boring who rose to the most fame, as they would later on become

the next definitive Superman artists.[70] The importance of these artists—
some famous, some forgotten—to the early success of Superman cannot
be overstated. Without their work, Superman might not have saturated
the culture so quickly and completely.

The one constant of the studio, or the Shuster Shop, as it would later
be dubbed by comics writers, was that everything was up for grabs. Joe
held court because Jerry was always in and out, but people basically did
whatever needed to be done. Pages were passed in silence and inked and
brushed by whoever was free. Joe would come over and help—but never
with too much criticism. He just wanted to draw the faces and the eyes.
Sometimes he would do more. Sometimes he would do a lot less. He
would then close his own eyes for a long period of time. But they all
had a good time and usually got paid on time. They started at nine
thirty and worked until five.[71] Sometimes Jerry would fly in, survey
the room, and retire to his desk in the foyer, and as soon as he closed the
door, the artists would bust up laughing, Joe included. He laughed a lot
during those years. The other great thing about the shop was that it was
smack-dab in an area of nightclubs and movie theaters. Almost directly
downstairs was Lyndsay's Sky Bar. With glowing stars on the ceiling and
plush red-orange chairs at the bar, it was the best jazz bar in Cleveland.
Frankie Laine performed with pianist Art Cutlip; and by the 1940s, the
marquee boasted Billie Holiday, Dizzy Gillespie, Johnny Hodges, Oscar
Peterson, and the great Stan Getz. You could hear them through the
floorboards, humming up through the paper, trading notes and riffs.

A photographer from *The Plain Dealer* came to the new Cleveland studio for an article in connection with the premiere of the newspaper strip.
The photographer walked up the steps to the studio, moved a desk around,
and motioned Jerry over. Joe posed himself ready to draw and Jerry settled himself behind him, as if he were looking over his work. Joe took off
his glasses and pushed his hair back with his left hand. Jerry touched his
shoulder, slight and small. This was the moment, and both smiles are
completely genuine. The flash shook the air and everyone saw shimmer-
ing particles of dust. In the back, the other artists narrowed their eyes and
got back to work. Jerry loosened his tie again: this was nice, but he figured it would be a little local-boys-make-good piece buried in the Sunday section. *Back to work, boys,* he said, mostly for the cameraman.

The article, with their big photo, made the front page on January
18, 1940, with the headline "SUPERMAN" IS COMING TO PLAIN DEALER

SUNDAY.[72] The piece "reveals an interesting Cleveland success story," that local boys "Jerry Siegel and Joe Schuster" (Joe bit his lip) are the creators of the popular Superman. The writer then lists their addresses and relates their tale:

> Began producing comic strips while in Glenville High School in 1930. Through four years of high school and four years after graduation they turned out miles and miles of strips, the chief result of which was miles and miles of rejection slips. Their friends advised them to go to work, but they had faith in their own ability in a field where success meant fame and fortune and they did not give up. Today, "Superman" is appearing in 100 big newspapers and the rewards of perseverance are being reaped by Siegel and Shuster. . . . Both boys took an active part in publication of the Torch at Glenville. Shuster, now the artist of the partnership, was scene designer for high school plays and was on the tumbling and track teams. Shuster's interest in gymnastic feats is probably responsible for the vitality of "Superman."[73]

The writer is sure to note that their "Home Is in City" and intimates that the enormous success of *Superman*—the "Superman Club which boasts 60,000 members"—is due to their midwestern roots.

> In Milwaukee, children began to copy Superman's costume, and this resulted in the manufacture of Superman sweaters and emblems. Hollywood and radio versions are in preparation. . . . Siegel and Shuster have opened a studio in Cleveland and two artists have been engaged to assist Shuster. While Shuster will work primarily on Superman, Siegel is writing continuity for five other strips.[74]

A more personally satisfying media victory came on February 29, 1940, in the pages of their old stomping grounds, *The Glenville Torch*. A reporter at *The Torch* had seen *The Plain Dealer* piece and written to Jerry asking for an interview. It was granted immediately.

In the top left column and spilling onto the whole left front page, *The Torch* finally welcomed back two of its own with the headline SIEGEL,

SCHUSTER START STRIP OF SYNDICATED "SUPERMAN." The article talks about their start at Glenville in detail, touching on *Science Fiction,* which "had an inter-Glenville circulation." Interestingly, the writer of the *Torch* piece is interested (and impressed) only by the fact that Superman will be in newspapers. Comic books seem temporary, and the writer (a high schooler) doesn't even have the language to describe them: "Recently, a complete 'Superman Book,' containing only 'Superman' strips, was released."[75]

The article also reveals a few things that were never—before or after—touched on in any other interviews. For one, Joe admits to having used models "from which to develop his chief characters; but they have become unnecessary." This implies that there may have been models not only for Lois, but for Clark and maybe even Superman.[76] But leisurely drawing from life was no longer practical in dealing with an ongoing serial like *Superman:* "Each strip must be completed six weeks ahead of time . . . so with 100 newspapers a month to accommodate the boys are kept quite busy." Jerry and Joe "also thank 'Mr. Jacob Bahner for the interest he showed in their work, which consisted at the time of cartoons that they drew in study hall.' Until six weeks ago, the two 'Supermen' had their offices in New York, where their publisher, the McClure Syndicate, is located, but now have decided to stay in Cleveland indefinitely."[77] With front-page articles in both their hometown newspaper and their alma mater, they were back. There was no other place for Superman.

Chapter 15
New Frontiers

JERRY NEVER HAD A REAL girlfriend until he got famous.[1] As seen in *Dr. Occult,* he was still using comics to magically evoke girls such as Lois Amster, who would not even look at him in high school. Jerry had no problem naming real names in their comics or in *The Torch,* but up close and personal was another story, as he often mumbled or looked for something to crumple up in his hands. Joe was painfully aware of his appearance, though his smile and easy demeanor were far more charismatic. But it was almost as if, with their newfound success and big newspaper photo, they felt they were finally allowed to have girlfriends. Maybe it was the bit of fame or cash, but it gave them both extra confidence. The model for Lois Lane had left town. And high school had ended some time ago. But then something happened, as these things often do. Jerry met Bella.

Bella Lifshitz was not the girl next door, but she was close enough: she lived across the street at 10629 Kimberley. Cooped up in his mother's house coming up with adventures for Superman all day, Jerry would rush all the way to the top-floor window in the afternoons. He had been out of school for years, but he still remembered when it let out. He slowly sneaked a look out the window, looking for the girl he knew was walking home. She was short, had black hair, and walked with a distinctive gait. Once, she looked up from the street and Jerry ducked under the windowsill as if someone were shooting at him. He could imagine her in the house across the street, moving through its rooms. As if he had X-ray vision, he could see her moving in the kitchen, then up the stairs, then into her room. He blinked his eyes. This may have been how it happened.

As Jerry had always been a reader, when he had a problem, he usually tried to read about a solution then apply it to his own life. Luckily, romantic advice was just as big a topic in the newspapers as Martians were in the pulps. Lois Lane herself actually begins as a "sob sister" columnist. In the "Not in the News" section of *The Middletown Times Herald*, Jerry writes a letter to just such a column:

> *It seems there's always someone belittling. There's always someone to say that a glorious sunset is too bright or too red; someone to ruin your enjoyment of a play by remarking the great actor overacted, or someone too cold or too hot on the mildest, brightest, and best day of the year.*
>
> *Seeking to belittle us for our illusions about romance is Jerome Siegel, Cleveland, O., reader, who put a more practical touch to a story which appeared recently in this column.*
>
> *This story told how a Pennsylvania woman, feeling faint while riding on a bus, was befriended by a strange young man, who later, unbeknown to the woman, was picked by her daughter as the man she wanted to marry. We described this meeting of the mother and the young man, and their second meeting, when the daughter brought her fiancé to her home to meet her parents, as purely coincidental, but Mr. Siegel would have it otherwise.*
>
> *"Dear Mr. Worth Cheney," he writes, "In a recent release of your column you relate Mrs. C.L.G. of Pennsylvania's strange experience upon a bus. I think that there is another answer to the incident other than 'unusual experience.'*
>
> *"Could it not have happened that the chivalrous young man had sometime or other seen this woman's daughter and been attracted to her, but gained no introduction? He might have made it his business to learn her name and address from someone else. Then, perhaps, he got into the habit of occasionally wandering past the young lady's home, hoping to catch glimpses of her.*
>
> *"On one of those journeys he might have sighted the girl's mother and guessed her identity. Then, riding upon the bus one day, he saw and recognized Mrs. C.L.G. When she had her fainting spell, he naturally went to her assistance not only from a sense of chivalry, but because knowing who she was even though she didn't know him, he*

felt a one-sided acquaintance with her, and since he admired the
woman's daughter he felt that he was paying some measure of clandes-
tine attention to the daughter through assisting her mother.

"Later, he might finally have contrived to meet the girl for-
mally . . . and proceeded to marry her.

"No, I don't think it was an unusual coincidence. It happens every
day."

Why, Jerome—you old cynic![2]

Is this how it happened with Bella? Did Jerry follow her around and hatch some elaborate plan so that one day she just turned around and said, *What?* More likely, she knew him from the street, and his glances and stops and starts gave way to a moment talking on the sidewalk or up by the movie theaters.

Bella had the brashness of the fictional Lois. She could eat a hot dog in four bites and had an almost perpetual—but endearing—scowl under her short black hair.[3] She had personality galore, which brought Jerry out of his shell. She talked to Jerry, she challenged him, even yelled at him, but she also genuinely supported him. She was one of the first to question his deal with Donenfeld, urging him to fight back for more money. Though other accounts portray her as a quiet girl, shy and retiring, she was noth-ing of the sort. Bella was an eye-glaring Jewish spark plug: she told you how she felt and was confused if you didn't believe her. In short, she was completely different from the Miriams, Loises, and Joans that Jerry con-jured up in his stories. She must have been amused—who was this older boy who suddenly had an interest in her? One night they kissed. And that must have been that.

Bella graduated high school and Jerry presented her with a fur coat and what relatives would later refer to as "a huge rock" for their engagement.[4] His brothers and sisters didn't question the news, but Jerry's mother hated it. Bella was a nice Jewish girl from across the street from a Glenville family. Her father was a plumber. So was it overprotectiveness? Or some-thing else? Perhaps she feared Bella was just going for her son's newly found money? Or that she was too young? Something was going on; per-haps Bella's loud, sometimes abrasive personality was too close for com-fort. Mrs. Siegel and Mrs. Lifshitz both served in the Cleveland Jewish

Club together, planning luncheons and raising money for Palestine.[5] As with any group, it may have been the source of some tensions.

On June 10, 1939, Jerry and Bella walked across the marble floor underneath the Great Rotunda in Cleveland City Hall and got their marriage certificate in the small room in the back. Jerry held her hand tightly as they were asked to sign the documents. Jerry listed his occupation as "Writer." Bella was eighteen.[6] They stood motionless on the red marble floor. They applied for their license on June 3 and were married on June 18 at the synagogue at Parkwood and Olivet by Hugo H. Klein, an influential rabbi in Cleveland who would frequently comment on the Christian life and vigorously help relatives of people trying to flee Europe. The reception was held at the Hotel Sterling; Jerry's brother Leo was his best man.[7]

They couldn't live at home, so Jerry was going to buy a house. They lived briefly at 16215 Cloverside Avenue in a small white house with a postage-stamp yard.[8] Bella wanted bigger, so they kept looking; she liked University Heights, which was several miles to the east and was the new destination Jewish neighborhood in Cleveland. Joe was looking just down the road for a house for his folks, so he would be close by. So Jerry went ahead and bought a white house at 3866 Tyndall Road.[9]

Jerry the new husband walked around his new home and smiled at the fact that there was a radio in every room. No longer would the basement be cold and scary: their new one was covered in wood paneling and even had a ping-pong table. He and Bella played all the time. There was also a drugstore stand-up of Superman, propped up in the corner like an old relative. This was the next step. He would forget Lois and Joan and concentrate on *Superman* and be a family man. He wondered if Joe had told Joan the news. Jerry wanted to grow up, to have a wife and children. This was his dream.

Jerry's married life with Bella was initially uncomplicated and happy. They both got fat and began to look like each other, big and round and full of smiles. They saw a ton of movies, Jerry stuffing candy bars into his pockets so he could consume them blindly during the feature. Sometimes they didn't last even that long. They lunched on clear plastic dishware and colorful drinks in the backyard in the summer. Bella's father took Jerry out for his first real steak. They all drank and laughed and played croquet like rich people. They collapsed into the backyard hammock, kissing and smiling. This was the life. They made sure to film it.[10]

TABOO

Joe rolled up his white sleeves and looked out across the lake. His sister came up behind him and nudged him in the ribs. Joe turned around. Jeanetta was no longer the small kid sister peeking around the corner; she had grown up into a statuesque, dark-haired woman who loved singing and dancing—and teasing her brother. Joe had also made some changes after high school. Instead of the poufed hair and glasses, he slicked his hair back and made sure to take his glasses off every time someone snapped a picture. Or if there were girls around. It was a complete transformation, as he now looked nothing like his high school picture. He always wore a clean white shirt with dark pants.[11]

The girls at the lake wore bathing suits and smiled as they orbited Joe. He hid a half-smile and nodded. There were small hills in the background, and the sun glittered on the surface of the water. Girls start dancing for the camera. Jerry and Joe mustered up the courage to go to a school dance once, and it was Jeanetta who taught them the different steps, the furniture pushed aside in their living room. She loved her brother and wanted him to be happy.[12]

Joe has always been categorized as a loner who never had a steady girlfriend. He loved women—he drew them, imagined them, and worked out to make himself look better to them. But the truth is that not only did he date Jolan Kovacs for a while, but he dated other girls. When he got out of high school, he met a girl named Annette Greenberg, who went to John Hay High School. Joe's brother, Frank, introduced them. They went steady for a while.[13] When Joe later picked up a few evening classes at the John Huntington art school in Cleveland, he met someone who made his jaw drop. He couldn't believe his luck that she actually wanted to talk to him. She was little, like Joe, with dark hair and, in the words of Joe's sister, "adorable."[14] Her name was Francine. It seemed as if Joe's luck had changed completely and all of the stars had suddenly aligned. He could talk to her for hours and she listened. She listened. But there was one major hitch. Francine was Catholic.[15]

Joe and Francine got so serious that the families got together to talk about marriage. Francine's mother insisted that the children be raised Catholic. Joe stayed silent.

Joe's mother, Ida, wouldn't hear of any of this. She said that the children must be raised Jewish or *no religion whatsoever.*[16]

TOP PAIR: Ida and Julius Shuster (Courtesy of Jean Shuster Peavy)

MIDDLE PAIR: Sarah and Michel Siegel, c. 1930

BOTTOM PAIR: Jerry Siegel and Joe Shuster at Glenville High School

The city of Cleveland, c. 1930 (Western Reserve Historical Society)

Glenville High School exterior, 1933

Glenville High School interior, 1933

Comparison of Superman and popular depictions of strongmen in physical fitness manuals (Superman Copyright DC Comics)

Comparison of Superman and Johnny Weissmuller as Tarzan (Superman Copyright DC Comics)

Comparison of Superman proposal image and a photograph of Jesse Owens in 1934 (Superman Copyright DC Comics)

MOLDING A MIGHTY CHEST
By GEORGE F. JOWETT

Comparison of back cover of *Superman* #1 and a mail-order fitness pamphlet

Situation Wanted—Female.

ARTIST MODEL: No experience. Box
25018. Plain Dealer.
BOOKKEEPER-Stenographer: Very good
experience. Box 25017. Plain Dealer.
CARE of children; will assist for room-
board. Box 8818, Plain Dealer.

Joanne's original ad that led to her becoming the model for
Lois Lane, January 13, 1935 (Courtesy of *The Plain Dealer*)

Comparison of early Lois Lane
sketch with details from early
photographs of Joanne

New Spring Blouses

with initials ꞏ or monograms

Ad in *Cleveland Shopping News*, c. 1933

Lois Amster's senior photo while
at Glenville High School

Charlie Gaines, Harry Donenfeld, and Jack Liebowitz, c. 1940

Jerry Siegel, publicity photo, c. 1939
(Author's collection)

Jerry Siegel and Joe Shuster, publicity photo,
c. 1940 (Courtesy of Special Collections
Research Center, Kelvin Smith Library, Case
Western Reserve University)

Joe Shuster, publicity photo, c. 1939
(Courtesy of Jean Shuster Peavy)

Jerry Siegel in Cleveland, c. 1940 (Author's collection)

Bella Siegel, c. 1939 (Author's collection)

Jerry Siegel at the World's Fair, 1940

THIS PAGE: Ray Middleton as Superman at
the World's Fair, 1940 (Author's collection)

Kids at the World's Fair, 1940 (Author's collection)

The first Superman float at the Macy's Thanksgiving Day parade, 1940 (Author's collection)

The relationship was over, and Francine disappeared. Joe was devastated and wouldn't have a serious girlfriend for almost thirty-five years. His mother, who had supported him through everything else in his life, had finally put her foot down on this. Joe loved his mother and would always defer to her. But he wouldn't forget this. Or Francine.[17]

Distraught, Joe started spending his new money in other ways. He got a house for his entire family just around the corner from Jerry at 1645 Ivydale in University Heights.[18] There was a stone crest over the front door that looked a little like the Superman shield. Inside, his family looked around and stared at the big rooms.

Joe's brother, Frank, was tall and lanky, even though he was younger than Joe. Frank really hit it off with Jerry and could draw, too—he was a cartoonist and "humor editor" on *The John Hay Ledger*. He actually lettered many of the first Superman adventures, though he was never formally credited.[19] While at Hay and later at Glenville, Frank inherited and perpetuated the famous nom de plume of *The Torch*: "Stiletto." Frank was a rebel soul; after graduating high school in 1938, he became a hobo by choice at seventeen and rode the trains for a while, wanting to see more of the country around him. He came back, though, and did some clerical work and was never very far from Joe.

1939

Meanwhile, in the pages of the comics, Superman had spent 1938 broadening his mission. The next year, 1939, began with gloomy news: Amelia Earhart, the spirit of American adventure, was officially declared dead after being missing for eighteen months.[20] Nuclear fission was discovered by the German atomic team led by the scarily brilliant Otto Hahn.[21] And on January 24, Chile was decimated by a catastrophic earthquake that killed more than thirty thousand people.[22] Yet all of this was but a hint of what the next few years would bring. Dark clouds in Europe were giving way to bloody storms of violence.

In Cleveland, Jerry wore suits and ties again, looked over the receipts, and kept a ledger. National owed them money again, but they were keeping tabs and Superman was selling very well, so he wasn't too worried about it. *Superman* #1, with its iconic cover of a now smiling hero looking down over the city he protects, was a big success.

In the second year of his adventures, Superman helps save an orphan from Kidstown by helping Warren Kenyon (another Kenton pun) find sunken treasure.[23] He also stops a suicide and helps a down-and-out former boxing champ believe in himself again in the classic tale "The Comeback of Larry Trent."[24] Superman hunts down illegal gambling dens, beats up thugs, and rescues people from more car crashes. *Superman* #4 also contains a two-page text story, "Changer of Destiny," written by Jerry under the name of Hugh Langley. The story is about a person who sets out to make the world a better place by "speeding up his time-rate!" so that one year passes for him while only one second passes for the rest of world. For Jerry, this wasn't a plot, this was personal fantasy.[25] With so much work to do, he often wished he could shut his eyes and make his own time frame stand still.

Why was this the Golden Age of comics? Superman was new, for one; he was an unknown quantity. But the stories were not always shining beacons of optimism. In fact, they were often the exact opposite. Superman, bright and smiling, would find himself in dark, real situations. Gangsters, murderers, corrupt manufacturers, shady orphanages, and loads of wanton destruction peppered the early stories. This was the Golden Age not because it was perfect but because it was so damn exciting—because all of its evils were real.

Then came the cold beginnings of 1940. The sun went down early, and the crust of snow turned everything white and cold. On the last panel of *Action Comics* #21 in February 1940, there was an arresting green figure that was an eerie shadow of things to come.

SPECTRE

For Detective Jim Corrigan, it was the girlfriend first and the job second. Or was it the other way around? It depended on the girlfriend. Corrigan's dark suit hung on his shoulders and his hat was tipped at just the right angle. But then the Mob came and threw him in a barrel, filled it with concrete, and sank him in the drink. He went right in, with a loud splash, into the dark, gray lake. The well-dressed man nodded and smiled. No problems now. *Dirty copper.* The crooks retreated into the small shack on the waterfront lit by a single lamp. As the circles finally stopped rippling on the water's surface, everything went silent. It was over.

Then the water starts to bubble. The air about it becomes cold, but it almost looks like steam. Something is very wrong. Something is coming up. There are no witnesses to see the green-hooded giant who emerges from the water. His skin is a perfect white. His empty eyes look like tiny skulls. Everything is frozen. The world is all afraid.[26]

With the success of Superman, Jerry thought he could capitalize on the moment and write more books. But Joe and his boys were wheezing and sputtering from doing so much Superman that they could do no more. Resurrecting an old character from the 1937 list to Liebowitz for *Action Comics,* Jerry turned to the Wraith—and changed him to become an actual ghost. But editorial did not share his enthusiasm at doing a new feature, much less one so bizarre. At one point, both Donenfeld and Liebowitz came out to Cleveland and "had a hell of an argument with Jerry," according to artist Wayne Boring.

> They were paying him a fee for writing and they said, "Jerry, stop writing all this other crap! All we want you to do is write *Superman,*" and Jerry had grown up poverty-stricken and said, "Look, I'm gonna write it all!" I think they paid him ten dollars a page for writing and they said they'd make up for it by paying him more to do *Superman,* but he said no. He was going to hang on to *Slam Bradley* and the others.[27]

But Jerry was motivated. He needed to show everyone, and himself, that he could do it alone. He also felt that Superman wouldn't last forever. Nothing ever could. So he sent in his list and lobbied his bosses. They agreed to see a new character. They did not expect the Spectre.

The Spectre remains one of the weirdest characters in all of comics, which is a testament not only to Jerry's imagination as a writer but to his willingness to experiment with different formulas, even after the absolute bull's-eye of Superman. In some ways, the two characters are opposite beings: people love Superman, but they fear the Spectre. This was surely by design, as Siegel sought to one-up his own impossible creation. The Spectre was drawn by Bernard Baily, who was born in April 5, 1916, to Harry and Jenny Bilynson. He grew up in the Bronx and went to Columbia College for two years before getting work at the famous Eisner & Iger comics studio, where he specialized in the one-page celebrity biographies that often featured a prominent head shot of a person who had "made it" in Hollywood. In *Action Comics* #1, Baily drew a story about

"Tex Thomson," a blond-haired Texas boy seeking adventure, a far cry from the caped Superman.[28]

Later in life, Baily would shrug his shoulders and tell family members that he didn't really know where the look for the Spectre came from; he just drew it. The character was Jerry's version of Superman in lurid green instead of red and blue. The premise of the character is that when Detective Corrigan is murdered, he is sent back from the afterlife by a nondenominational "Light" who grants him unlimited power to wreak vengeance. The Spectre's costume is a green cowl, green shorts, and green boots; his grisly white pallor is both bright and terrible.[29] If Superman was a mysterious Christ figure, then the Spectre was his Old Testament counterpart, capable of mass destruction and ritual murder to right the injustices of man. The Spectre was Superman without conscience.

When he debuted in *More Fun Comics* #52 in 1940, the Spectre could do *anything*. Jerry's eyes would narrow in perverse glee as he made the character grow to giant size, shrink down to atoms, and turn gangsters into skeletons (still somehow living) with a single, terrible touch. The Spectre represented a force for justice that was not boundless and heroic, but instant and unbelievable. He was the Shadow given the power of magical, merciless death.

Baily excelled in these bizarre scenes of horror and often portrayed the Spectre as a towering, unstoppable being of godlike, surrealist power.[30] In addition to unlimited mystical powers, the Spectre had a secret identity that made him part of a truly impossible love triangle. Once Corrigan dies, he becomes a "tangible" *ghost,* so nobody knows he's dead, least of all his fiancée, Clarice Winston. Once he becomes the Spectre, he breaks off the engagement—he has to—but Clarice won't disappear so easily. When Corrigan ends up "at the Lakeside Hospital receiving repairs," Clarice shows up, furious. He greets her with a "Hi, Toots." She retorts:

> Don't toots me Jim Corrigan. If I wasn't a lady I'd be inclined to knock your ears off.
>
> Why a real lady like you should be interested in me is beyond me but one thing is certain: there's going to be one boss in our family and that's me.[31]

The fact that the Spectre has to break off his engagement is perhaps a different kind of fantasy. But he doesn't really have a choice. The Voice commands him: "Your mission on earth is unfinished . . . you shall remain earthbound battling crime in your world with supernatural powers, until all vestiges of it are gone!" Corrigan answers: "I want eternal peace." Unfortunately, "his protests are unanswered! 'I'm seated at the bottom of the river—and yet I don't drown.'"[32] The Spectre saves Clarice but wonders: "How can I tell her she's wrong . . . that she holds a ghost in her arms? She must never know!"[33] But in a moment of sheer horror, Corrigan notices there is no moisture coming from his mouth: "Good Lord! I don't breathe."[34]

As a character created to right the injustices of crime, Superman could go only so far. He was too good. The Spectre was good, too, but it was a different *kind* of good. There was more to the Spectre than just biblical justice. As weird as the character was, in both story and depiction, some of it came from a real place.

William Corrigan was a Cleveland motorcycle beat cop operating out of the Central Avenue station, right around the corner from Jerry's father's old store. Even as a rookie, Corrigan started developing a reputation. On February 3, 1929, the *Plain Dealer* tells how "Patrolman William Corrigan had pursued Stevens and a companion . . . after a car driven by Stevens had sideswiped another and failed to stop."[35] This was real-life adventure, and it continued to get more dramatic. On June 23, 1930:

> Detective William Corrigan, who was off duty and visiting an acquaintance across the street, ran out in time to see the last two shots fired. When he drew his pistol and grappled with the gun

wielder, his prisoner tried to shoot him. The firing pin clicked on an empty shell.[36]

Corrigan's copy read like a story in *Illustrated Detective Magazine*. On January 21, 1933, "Police believed they had advanced a step nearer to a solution of the Samuel Moss murder. . . . Moss, 52, kosher meat dealer, was shot to death by a youth while he was serving two customers." Corrigan arrested the suspect.[37] On page one of the newspaper:

> A paroled robber, arrested by police acting on a tip, last night confessed he had participated in the holdup Monday in which Fred Raymont, 68-year-old East Side confectionery proprietor, was murdered . . . Detective cruiser D-2, manned by Vargo and Detectives Thomas Osborne and William Corrigan, was dispatched. . . . There was no one in the rooms, but the detectives found several shirts stolen.[38]

In a town starved for justice, Corrigan rapidly became the symbol for good, two-fisted police work in a city gone mad. He was promoted to detective at the Perkins Avenue/East Fifty-fifth Street precinct and started appearing in the paper even more when he became as lucky as he was courageous. Corrigan didn't mess around as he ran down crime at near unbelievable levels. His popularity among citizens made it even sadder when he died, too early, at age forty-eight.[39] He was given a generous newspaper obituary, complete with a full photo that recalled one of his earliest triumphs:

> He had just finished a 12-hour detail at the Airport and was sitting in his car at Lorain Avenue and W. 117 St. when Henry R. Gerlach, a druggist, ran up and said he had been robbed. Mr. Corrigan overtook one of the robbers and seized him. The other youth grabbed Mr. Gerlach and, using him as a shield, opened fire on the officer. Mr. Corrigan drew his gun and engaged in a duel with the armed robber. Next day, the body of Ralph Paul was found behind Grace Church.[40]

So when Jerry designed a hard-boiled detective who rose from the dead to continue his inhuman crusade for justice, it might have made sense not only to name him Corrigan, after Cleveland's best detective, but to give him the name of his orphaned son, James.[41] Jerry knew that role well.

ENEMY PRONOUN

As the Spectre was meting out otherworldly justice, Superman dealt with social issues. The world was giving rise to new problems that were much harder to grasp. Evils were referred to not by country but by single proper names: Mussolini, Hirohito, and Hitler. In *Action Comics* #13, a seemingly innocuous plotline about frustrated Yellow Cab drivers leads Superman to a dark cabin where he finds a bald man in a white scientist frock, confined to a wheelchair. The fiery eyes of the paralyzed cripple burn with terrible hatred and sinister intelligence: "I am known as 'The Ultra-Humanite!' Why? Because a scientific experiment resulted in my possessing the most agile and learned brain on earth!— unfortunately for mankind, I prefer to use this great intellect for crime. My goal? Domination of the world!"[42] Ultra was Superman's first supervillain. His power would grow. In *Action* #17, Superman is called to the raging seas to tug a boat back to shore. It turns out that Ultra is behind it all and wants $5 million delivered, again, to the unlucky 211 Court Avenue to release the crew.[43] In *Action* #19, a deadly plague strikes the city as purple rotting blotches start appearing on the populace. Jerry doesn't mince words: "Daily, the streets are clogged with death—wagons carting away load upon load of putrefying corpses . . . HORROR GRIPS THE CITY!!"[44] Joe draws a wooden cart with arms and legs poking out of it. All of this evil is again Ultra's work— this time as mastermind and not as scientist, elevating him to a more Hitler-like status. But the plague is stopped and Ultra escapes in a Flash Gordon–like airship. The craft crashes, however, and Ultra seemingly dies.[45] In *Action* #20, Clark goes to Hollywood and stops an assassin from killing movie siren Delores Winters (who looks a lot like Lois), who (unlike Lois) flirts with Clark. But the next day she is cold to him: it turns out that Ultra, who survived, has had his brain transplanted into Winters's body. As Superman confronts her, there is an eerie Joe panel of her looking directly at the reader, with no words and a penetrating gaze.[46] Ultra was a formidable, interesting foe for Superman, but the character lapsed into a level of incredulity that began to separate Superman from his urban roots. So they let Ultra stay dead and they tried again—with Luthor.

Lex Luthor may have been introduced in an attempt to reverse a mistake. When Ultra was killed as a woman, Superman was left without an appropriate adversary. So Luthor entered the scene, looking and acting very much like Ultra as a dictatorial superscientist, though much younger and with red hair. The early Luthor is all over the map in terms of villainous acts. He provokes a war between the nations of "Galonia" and "Toran" in *Action* #23. He mentally enslaves world financial leaders. He describes himself as "an ordinary man, but with the brain of a super-genius."[47] Luthor's crimes are massive in scale: he uses an earthquake machine to terrorize the world from his undersea lair of Pacifico, where he unleashes prehistoric monsters against Superman.[48] Luthor sometimes has an atomic disintegrator and can transmit his image onto trees, cave walls, hi-fi equipment, and statues. In the newspaper strip, a possible artistic goof by Leo Nowak renders Luthor bald, though it may have been on purpose. Either way, it stuck. Luthor cuts off the Metropolis water supply and gains the mysterious "Powerstone" in *Action* #47, which gives him the physical means to actually hurt Superman.[49]

Even during high school, Jerry and Joe walked a lot, sometimes to the library. When they could get downtown, they would see the Terminal Tower, Cleveland's only skyscraper, which dominated the skyline. Closer to home, they would also walk up to the Cleveland Museum of Art, where Joe especially would spend a lot of time, both by himself and earlier as a member of the Glenville High Art Club. Near the museum was a great stone statue that always made them stop. It was of a huge bald man slumped in a chair, looking out with a grim countenance as though he were king of the world.[50]

The subject of the statue was Mark Hanna, a politician of the previous century who was as famous in Cleveland as John D. Rockefeller. He was a Cleveland guy with money pulled out of coal mines and melted into iron. National political cartoons often depicted him wearing a suit made of dollar bills. Impossibly rich, Hanna became a political heavyweight with an uncanny knack for organizing political campaigns. The horse he backed was also a local one: William McKinley, who would win the Ohio governor's race in 1892 and was nominated as the Republican presidential candidate in 1896. Hanna raised an election fund for McKinley from wealthy individuals and corporations and orchestrated the most expensive campaign ever seen at that time, undermining opponent William Jennings Bryan's own grassroots effort. After McKinley won the presidency, one of his cabinet appointments created a vacancy in the U.S. Senate, to which Hanna was elected in 1897. Theodore Roosevelt feared that Hanna might oppose him for the Republican presidential nomination in 1904, but Hanna died suddenly in the early part of that year.[51] Hanna wasn't a bad man, but he was rich, and that might have been enough. If there was a resemblance here, it was a visual one that combined the new Luthor with the old Superman: Hanna in his chair looks very much like the illustration of a slumping man in "Reign of the Super-man."

Even after Hanna dies, economists believe that "the superstition still prevailed in Wall Street that there could be a Superman of Finance who was not only omnipotent but infallible and omniscient."[52] More so, Hanna's powers, those "qualities essential to an American boss[,] are those of a primitive but superman."[53] Hanna's biographer writes that "as he sits quietly at his desk, with a certain massive dignity and poise, you feel that you are in the presence of a man of power."[54] Though Luthor really originated from all the bald scientists in all the bad pulps that Jerry read and pored over, the statue and figure of Hanna might have been a part of the puzzle of creating evil as a being in possession of unlimited economic, tactical, and politically minded greed, just like Dunn near the end of "Reign." But the new Superman's nemesis had to be more scientific, more deductive. His name may have come from a detective Jerry liked named Luther Trant, who had a super-mind and a shock of red hair, just as the early Luthor did.[55]

While Superman was battling his new adversaries, a superhero baby boom was going on at National and All-American Comics: characters like Wonder Woman, Dr. Fate, Star-Man, Hawkman, Green Lantern, Air Wave, Johnny Quick, Hour-Man, and the Flash were overloading young retinas with their colorful costumes and splashy actions. Jerry was concerned. He couldn't understand why National would want to flood the market with so many superpeople who could take sales away from Superman. Maybe that was the point, he thought, ever wary of his next paycheck. So Jerry wrote Jack in protest. On March 1, 1940, Liebowitz responded: "I don't agree with you that the Hour Man is a copy of Superman. It would be definitely against our better interest to have an imitation of Superman in our books, in spite of the fact that all competing magazines carry an imitation of Superman."[56] Both sides knew that something was going to happen; as much as National felt they held all the cards, they knew a lawsuit could still come at any time.

Jerry was still proposing other characters, both to get out from under Superman and to shore up his own position. In addition to the Spectre, he did the Star Spangled Kid and Stripesy, two acrobats who fought together against the Nazis.[57] They were interesting because Stripesy, the sidekick, was not a teenager but an adult male, resulting in a kind of parallel to the Jerry-Joe partnership, at least the way Jerry sometimes viewed it. Jerry also created Robotman, the surprising story of a man named Robert Crane whose brain was transferred to the body of a powerful robot. This idea was inspired not only by the pulps but by similar "robots" like Televox that Jerry had seen as a kid at Glenville. There was also Elektro, the Westinghouse robot that Jerry saw smoke and converse at the World's Fair.[58] In Jerry's origin story, Robotman not only attends the funeral of his own body, he then starts to date his own girlfriend. Her name is Joan Carter.[59]

SHADOW OF THE BAT

As much as the boys didn't like the other superheroes, there was one in particular they really disliked: the Batman. The origins of Batman are also cloudy and pulplike, but the fiat that brought him into comics was not: National wanted another Superman.[60] But this time they wanted a character they could create in-house and not have to worry about whiny kids asking for raises. So when Bob Kane, a young New York illustrator who had been doing mostly one-pagers for the Major, walked in and asked how much Jerry and Joe were making on their comics, editor Vin Sullivan allegedly gave Kane a weekend to create a new Superman. Kane cannily swiped and stitched together a collage of things, including images from a pulp story entitled "The Black Bat," some poses from *Flash Gordon,* and the melodramatic illustrations of Henry Vallely, among many others. In some ways, the creation of Batman was similar to that of Superman; he was a conglomeration of various pieces of the cultural atmosphere. But unlike Jerry and Joe, Kane eventually signed a deal in which he would retain some royalty rights, which made him a rich man.[61]

Although Kane was the one who pitched and drew Batman's first appearance in *Detective Comics* #27, the story was scripted anonymously by a young collaborator of his named Bill Finger, who would go on to ghost-write most of Batman's early adventures.[62] Finger would have a hand in creating much of the character's costume, origin, and lasting mythology, though from a lifelong space of near invisibility. While Jerry and Joe were both recognized as the public faces of Superman, Batman had only the grinning Kane. Because of this, many scholars, comics creators, and fans have come to champion Finger as the rightful co-creator of Batman, even though he is not officially acknowledged as such by the company who published his script for the character's debut. But there is another possible source for the Dark Knight that, though never noted by either man, might have been on Jerry's mind when he first saw Kane and Finger's Batman.

In the May 1937 issue of *More Fun,* two years before Batman's first appearance in *Detective Comics* #27, Jerry and Joe's Doctor Occult confronts vampires; and in the last panel, he gives them a new name:

The figure, and spelling, is very similar to Kane's Batman:

Two issues after Siegel and Shuster's "Bat-Man" in *Dr. Occult* was published, Kane himself started contributing to the same magazine, which means he probably saw the issue. Jerry and Joe's editor on *Dr. Occult,* Vin Sullivan, was also the same man who offered Kane the chance at a new Superman. More than that, Jerry always felt that the origin of Batman— his parents killed, a young orphan vowing to do good—was too close for comfort.[63]

Batman's success also helped steer Superman away from mostly social ills toward the real lasting, great contribution of Batman to comics: the terrifying supervillain. Batman was already proving that a menagerie of bad guys—the Joker, Hugo Strange, the Penguin, the Scarecrow, Two-Face—much as with Dick Tracy, could open up a well of adventures to exploit. Jerry had actually begun this trend himself, though on a much smaller scale, introducing the Ultra-Humanite, the Archer, the Light, and Luthor. The Archer, appearing in *Superman* #13, dressed in green and was an expert marksman. The Archer starts out a hero but turns out to be nothing more than an extortionist; he is a Robin Hood who keeps for himself.[64] The Toyman debuted in *Action Comics* #64, and *Superman* #26 introduced readers to the largely forgotten J. Wilbur Wolfingham. There was the Domino, the Dawn Man, the Lightning Master, the Evolution King, Mister Sinister, the Puzzler, Metalo, and even a ginger-haired mermaid named Princess Kuella.[65] In *Action* #53, Jerry also introduced the Night Owl, a villain whose name, costume, and vehicle weirdly prefigure Alan Moore's seminal character, Nite Owl, in 1986's unforgettable *Watchmen.*[66]

One of the most interesting (and annoying) of the new additions during the 1940s was the imp named "Mr. Mxyztplk," who first appeared in February 1944 in the daily newspaper strip.[67] A renegade imp from the Fifth Dimension, Mxy (his name would later change to the not-much-easier-to-pronounce "Mxyzptlk") looked like Elmer Fudd in a miniature bowler hat but acted like Bugs Bunny with a social disorder. Just as Superman strained the physical laws of the universe with his strength and flight, Mxy obliterated these laws altogether; he could do absolutely anything he wanted: create mass, destroy it, or make it dance around with eyes and teeth. In some ways, Mxy was a cartoon-made comic villain; he was the Spectre meets *Slam Bradley's* Shorty.[68] He taunted Superman mercilessly and allowed readers to see the once invulnerable Man of Steel as something of a buffoon.[69] Mxy laughed at Superman. No one had really done that before. And though he was a ridiculous little imp, it was a sign of things to come.

OVER THERE

Once war broke out in Europe, people looked to see what Superman would do. The only real incursion of Superman into the early days of the war was a commissioned, noncontinuity strip that ran in the February 27, 1940, edition of *Look* magazine, where Superman gathers up Hitler, Mussolini, and Hirohito and deposits them unceremoniously at the World Court for judgment. The Germans were not pleased. A rebuttal ran in *Das schwarze Korps* (*The Black Corps*), the official newspaper of the German SS, on April 25, 1940.[70]

> The inventive Israelite named this pleasant guy with an overdeveloped body and underdeveloped mind "Superman." He advertised widely Superman's sense of justice, well-suited for imitation by the American youth. . . . As you can see, there is nothing the Sadducees won't do for money![71]

Jerry had no idea the Nazis were reading *Superman,* and it was both unsettling and strangely wonderful.[72] The article ends by addressing Jerry *by name:*

> Well, we really ought to ignore these fantasies of Jerry Israel Siegel, but there is a catch. The daring deeds of Superman are those of a Colorado beetle. He works in the dark, in incomprehensible ways. He cries "Strength! Courage! Justice!" to the noble yearnings of American children. Instead of using the chance to encourage really useful virtues, he sows hate, suspicion, evil, laziness, and criminality in their young hearts.
>
> Jerry *Siegellack* stinks. Woe to the American youth, who must live in such a poisoned atmosphere and don't even notice the poison they swallow daily.[73]

Jerry Siegel, born in Cleveland, Ohio, was being threatened in a fullpage Berlin newspaper by the Nazi soldier elite that would soon march on Europe in a mass of black and red. This was really happening.

Jerry had to think about his response, and he gives it about a year later. In *Superman* #10, Lois and Clark cover a "Dukalian" sporting exhibition that Lois feels "looks more like an anti-American demonstration." And, indeed, there is the armband-clad Dukalian consul Karl Wolff—drawn to resemble a balding Hitler figure—who harangues the crowd:

> Present here is the flower of Dukalian youth. You have seen them perform physical feats which no other human beings can. Proof, I tell you, that we Dukalians are superior to any other race or nation. Proof that we are entitled to be the masters of America![74]

Clark makes his excuses to Lois, and moments later Superman soars into the stadium to humble the Dukalian athletes, carrying the sprinter around the track at a dizzying speed, and hurling the shot-put champion across the field. Jerry almost certainly got the idea for this scene from Jesse Owens, whose gold medals at the 1936 Berlin Olympics proved a great embarrassment for his grim, Nazi hosts.

Chapter 16
Top of the World

A COUPLE OF MONTHS LATER, summer and the world became somehow brighter. On a hot concrete walkway, men scurried to pull back a curtain. A giant gray platform began to roll, with a man standing on top. The man was raised about ten feet high, so he steadied himself by grabbing on to a thin, near invisible wire tethered to the base. He really hoped the kids couldn't see this. He kept his feet flat and his stance open. He blew a puff of air at his forelock curl, then looked down. This suit was pretty tight. He adjusted his stance over some bumps—they were pulling this pretty damn fast. He was coming into view of the crowd, so he pushed his shoulders back and looked out over the crowd—not at it or under it—but *over* it. He was *Superman,* after all. That's what it said on his shirt. He was used to people gasping and acting strangely when he played Lincoln, but this was something else entirely. The sun broke early, but there was a little bit of weather coming in: clouds and some wind. But it was still hot. It was still summer. And it was still the 1940 World's Fair in Flushing Meadows, New York. Though in its last summer and, in the eyes of many, much depreciated, it was still the top of the world.[1]

Jerry squinted in the sun. Joe had the camera. Bella, in a blue dress, was fussing that he was going to be late. He smiled meekly with a *yesdear* and got on his way. Then he realized he was holding her purse and shuffled back. She said something mean. The parade had started. Harry Donenfeld was actually riding a real live elephant. He was wearing a suit. Jerry laughed but also had to turn away. He had heard the stories that Harry had taken to wearing a Superman T-shirt under his suit to open up and reveal it at a moment's notice.[2] Jerry was still nervous around Harry. Jerry saw Whit, too, who was back at National, out of the corner of his eye. And all these kids with the Superman symbol on their T-shirts and sweatshirts. The Boy Scouts dipped their flags forward and pushed through the heat.

Then, slowly, a gray pillar wheeled around the bend. Standing on top was Superman. Jerry blinked and made sure Joe was getting this. Someone was. *Weird,* he thought, even as the chills reached his fingertips. As he watched the costume pass, he wished it were him in the suit. The guy they had picked was kind of skinny, but the costume was nearly perfect. Jerry wondered who would get the costume when all was said and done.

The kids with their warm moms parted like a sea as Superman braced himself and gazed with a thousand-yard stare. Everyone was acting as if he were real. Joe thought of the parades he used to go to in Toronto with Felix and Santa Claus. It was quite possibly the most surreal moment of his life. Even Jerry's mom had made the trip. She posed in her nice blue dress with a hat and a smile. *Jerome,* she would say, smiling, her eyes framed by her gray hair. There were celebrity judges for a kids contest. The day was perfect. It would be the last one.

The World's Fair opened its doors in 1939 in Flushing Meadows and was the last flash of national light before 1941 and the low humming over the Pacific. But for all of the romanticism of the fair, it was designed, as most things were in the 1930s, to make money. First conceived (at the suggestion of a little girl) as a way of honoring the 150th anniversary of the New York inauguration of George Washington, the fair was modeled after Chicago's, which Jerry and Joe wrote about in *Science Fiction.*[3] Over two years, the fair, built over a mound of swamp and trash, had convinced forty-five million visitors that they needed to experience marvels such as color photography, air-conditioning, the View-Master, and many other gadgets strewn out over pavilions and stages. It was Disneyland, twenty years early.

From the start, the comics companies wanted a presence at the fair, as they imagined the legions of children who would come through the gates every day. Salesmen were dreaming of admission numbers with spinning, dollar-sign eyeballs. So Harry Donenfeld and Jack Liebowitz cooked up *World's Fair Comics,* which was first sold on opening day on April 30, 1939. It cost twenty-five cents and featured a blond Superman with a cardboard cover not unlike the old *Detective Dan.* The main story was a

Superman adventure at the fair, though the issue also included Zatara, the Sandman, and an Everyman named Hanko the Cowhand. The issue also included a new Slam Bradley adventure by Jerry and Joe. The comic was given a new issue the year after, only with far more superheroes and far less fair, though it would be the first time Superman would pair with Batman. The adventures tended to use the fair in peripheral ways (artists would depict the Trylon and Perisphere), while in the last panel Superman would encourage readers to go see it for themselves, but this interaction was mostly window dressing.[4]

The second year of the World's Fair also saw Superman get his own official day: Wednesday, July 3, 1940. This promotion was concocted by National publicist Allen "Duke" Ducovny with the express notion of grandstanding Superman for the young fairgoers on a hopefully busy holiday week. Having a fair day dedicated to a cartoon character was not unprecedented. The same day was actually also Jiggs Day, complete with a public luncheon for comics creator George McManus. These "Days" were all probably extensions of a promotion a year earlier where children were encouraged to come to the World's Fair dressed as their favorite comics character.[5]

The main event of Superman Day was not the noontime parade but an open invitation physical fitness event for children designed to crown a "Super-Boy" and "Super-Girl." Location was important, too: Superman Day was held on the amusement grounds just in front of the American Jubilee, the so-called lowbrow area of the fair. In fact, when organizers of the 1964 version reimagined the layout, they decided to eliminate any traces of this honky-tonk midway. For though the fair as a whole brought in heads of state, masterpieces of art, and futuristic technologies, people tend to forget that there were also midgets, strippers, and sideshows. The fair was high culture (the best of the world) met down with the low (peanuts and popcorn). The parade started at twelve fifteen, was led by the Boy Scouts, and wound from the Theme Center to the Empire State Bridge. Ads claimed that ten thousand balloons would be released, some with coupons for "Superman prizes."[6]

The General Assembly was an area the size of a football field, covered with fairly shaggy grass and flanked by a short set of bleachers. With their mothers corralling them, the kids posed and flexed in their white Superman shirts with red S symbols pinned on with fat safety pins. Some of the richer kids wore the full costumes bought from Macy's; though plastic and thin, their colors were bright and *they had capes*. There were two age classes: juniors (ages eight to eleven) and seniors (twelve to fourteen). Boys ran the fifty-yard dash and did an obstacle race. Girls ran a twenty-five-yard dash and competed in a rope-skipping contest. Medals would be given all the way to fifth place, but the real prize was the title of "Super."[7]

The finals for the athletic events were at two thirty, and the winners were crowned at four thirty. Super-Boy and Super-Girl were selected by a panel of judges including Frank Buck (the Hollywood wildlife wrangler and author of *Bring 'Em Back Alive*), Eleanor Holm (the infamous ex-swimmer who played Jane in *Tarzan's Revenge*), Buster Crabbe (who played Flash Gordon in the movie serials), actor Ray Middleton (who played Superman in the parade), Lucy Monroe (who sang "The Star-Spangled Banner" at every New York Yankees opening day from 1945 to 1960), and the popular fitness personality Charles Atlas. The winners were pictured in the paper the next day holding their trophies: a smiling Maureen Reynolds, eleven, and William Aronis, fifteen.[8]

Middleton was chosen as the first Superman because he was also starring in the World's Fair's megaproduction of patriotism titled *The American Jubilee,* which played in the same area of the fair. Middleton sort of looked like Superman anyway, meaning he had dark hair and was not fat. In the musical, Middleton played, among other historical people, Abraham Lincoln, and his show featured the real carriage that drove the emancipator to the fated Ford's Theatre. The Superman costume, like Lincoln's, was designed to be as close to primary reality as possible. At the same time, the point for the whole day was undisguised: above the famous "S" chevron is stitched the name "Superman"—so no consumer would have any doubts.

Joe couldn't believe it when he met Charles Atlas at the awards ceremony. Though Atlas was a latecomer to the physical fitness wave, Joe was very impressed. Atlas was one of the first to use a cartoon to make his point, and his company's advertisements still use it today. Joe felt sheepish as he gripped Atlas's mighty hand and said something, but he wasn't really sure what. All the girls fawned over Atlas. Joe thought he had been getting much stronger, especially for the fair, but he felt immeasurably small next to Atlas. He looked down at his shoes.

Joe also went to see Johnny Weissmuller at the fair's most popular show, the Billy Rose Aquacade swimming extravaganza. He and Jerry had seen an early version of the show a couple of years ago at the Cleveland Exposition, full of swimming and leaping on the shores of Lake Erie.[9] But the Aquacade was much bigger, grander, with towering white columns and even more beautiful women. Someone whispered to Joe that there was a place in the fair where you could see girls walking around on a farm, supposedly without their shirts on.

As a public relations gimmick, Superman Day worked, but it also did two things to the brand: One, it moved Superman into a real-life context. The planners were smart: they put him on a pedestal and gave him a flag but kept him slightly removed from the general populace; that simple ten feet made all the difference and was the same reason they couldn't put him in the war. The second thing they did was merchandising. Moving the "S" from his costume to the skinny chests of the readers was an enormous success: the paper reported that three thousand people showed up for the festivities, including kids, parents, and everyone in between.[10]

Afterward, Jerry and Bella went to the top of the Empire State Building to sightsee. Jerry dipped his head over the edge and looked out over the tops of all the buildings. He smiled and even acted, for a moment, as if he were going to jump and fly off like Superman. Then he started laughing.

The next day, on July 4, 1940, a homemade bomb exploded at the fair in a field near the national pavilions, killing two New York City detectives, Joseph Lynch and Ferdinand Socha. They had removed the bomb (in a suitcase) to a deserted field before it exploded, saving dozens, perhaps hundreds, of lives—at the cost of their own.[11] New York was on high alert for weeks as other threats were examined in every borough. No one was caught, though signs (and paranoia) pointed to either Irish extremists or, as most thought, the Nazis, who had become every scary shadow.[12] There is no evidence that the bombers meant to target Superman Day or its remnants. But the coincidence still resonated. Only one day after an amazing triumph at the World's Fair, the once powerful Superman now seemed like a skinny actor who had no real power at all. The world had changed. Dressing up in a costume seemed silly and irrelevant. Superman Day at the fair was the last day, literally, of the Golden Age of comics.

Chapter 17

How to Kill a Superman

A S THE TRAIN DREW BACK TO CLEVELAND, Jerry sat there and watched the hills and vineyards blur by. A thought unfurled in his mind that seemed so alien, he couldn't help considering it more carefully. Jerry pressed his finger against the glass. He remembered his early trip to New York about syndication and how they had humiliated him. He imagined Superman running past the train. Then he couldn't see anything.

The truth of it was that Jerry had reached his limit. Watching Donenfeld ride around on that elephant with an ear-to-ear grin was just too much. The World's Fair was great, but he could see the writing on the wall. Jerry knew they were being squeezed out. Or even if they weren't, it wasn't fair that they were doing all the work while Harry was raking in the money. Jerry had created the character, but he was not his master. By the time they got home, Jerry had a plan more nefarious than any Luthor had ever come up with: Jerry was going to kill Superman.

This was a serious problem that editorial actually agreed with: Superman was just too super. Even after only one year, it was clear that there was no bullet, tank, or gas that could harm him. Part of it was the fair bombing and the bloodshed in Europe, but Jerry wasn't sure there was a place for such a character anymore. So he had to invent something physical that would harm him so people could identify with him again. And he took it directly from the newspapers: radiation.[1] In the comics, the element kryptonite is, more or less, an extremely and (supposedly) rare radioactive isotope that is actually a direct by-product of Krypton's destruction. It is also, for some reason, absolutely lethal to Superman. The irony is that Clark's home world, the site of his greatest emotional pain, continues to hurt and cripple him.[2]

In 1940, kryptonite didn't exist. But the idea of it did. Once he got home, Jerry typed in his name and the date of August 7, 1940. He already knew that it would be an element. Imaginary elements were discovered all the time in the false scientific discoveries of the pulps. But where would it come from? On November 20, 1939, an article in *The Plain Dealer* titled "See Flaming Light Race Across Sky" describes an "illumination, cone-shaped, traveling at a high speed eastward." It was documented as "a large flaming light, resembling a meteor, [that] attracted the attention of at least two Greater Cleveland residents early today. . . . It appeared . . . to be almost as large as the moon and was a brilliant red, turning to white."[3] The meteor was seen mostly on the east side of town, in Cleveland Heights, one neighborhood away from Jerry's new house.

The premise of Jerry's story is that a meteor chunk from Krypton passes through Earth's orbit, but instead of bringing riches and answers from his home planet, it brings only misery to Superman. The meteor contains a unique ore, K-metal, which turns out to be the only thing that can harm Superman, as it somehow robs him of his powers. The story is vintage Jerry: a Professor Barnett Winton (which is similar to Bernard Kenton) informs Superman about the meteor, giving him an almost impossible problem to solve.

Jerry wasn't going to kill Superman outright, but he was going to upset the natural order by doing something even more alarming: not only was he introducing an Achilles' heel but he was going to do something even more staggering—let Lois in on the secret. When National wanted to go this very direction years later, Jerry fought it vehemently, which suggests that writing it into his own script might have been an act of sabotage.[4] The crucial elements of Superman had remained steady for over two years: the Clark Kent–Superman–Lois Lane love triangle that kept the narrative moving was running in well-oiled condition. There were some close calls, but as long as each piece stayed functional, the serial narrative would keep chugging along. Jerry knew that if Lois found out the secret, the tension would fizzle. The other factor in the introduction of K-metal was that Jerry was considering legal action at this point. Thus he may have thought that ruining the character might ensure National wouldn't make money off *Superman* after Jerry was gone. These are educated guesses; at heart, this was about taking control.

In the story, Jerry once again chooses a mine as his place of danger. A group of people, including Clark and Lois, are trapped underground, with their air being rapidly depleted. But where Clark would normally find a way out as Superman, the meteor causes him to lose his powers at the worst possible moment: "My lungs . . . straining . . . bursting . . . like the others. . . . A roaring in my ears. . . . Everything turning black . . . black . . ." But the meteor speeds by (a radio announcer conveniently cuts into the narrative to announce this), and Clark realizes that "my gigantic super-strength—completely returned!" This of course reveals the real twist of the story: "What a dilemma! I can save them all from death! But if I do . . . My true identity as Superman will be revealed!" Once Clark sees that Lois has passed out, there is no choice at all. He rips off his suit and dramatically announces to the onlookers, "Look well because you're going to witness something I never thought mortal eyes would witness." Lois, dazed and half-awake, does not believe her eyes: "Clark Kent . . . Superman! I must be imagining things." Superman immediately punches a hole through the blocked door so they can breathe. "There you are! Breathe deeply!" he tells the people. He throws Lois over his shoulder and descends the mountain to stop the bad guys.[5] It was a tense, game-changing story. The script was miraculously approved by Whitney Ellsworth, then penciled by numerous members of the Shuster Shop, inked, and sent off. But it never ran.[6] The why is unknown, though it makes sense that a higher-up realized this would change Superman's status quo too drastically.

Part of Jerry's push with this story might have been his distrust of the new *Superman* radio serial that was now running full steam. Superman on the radio might have been in the back of everyone's mind since *Action #1*. The driving force was again Ducovny, who enlisted a pulp workhorse named Robert Maxwell from *The Shadow* and *The Spider* shows to write up a radio script. Once they came up with the fast opening that included the now familiar "Look! Up in the sky! It's a bird! It's a plane!" they had no problem selling the show to stations across the country. *The Adventures of Superman* hissed to life on February 12, 1940, on New York City's mighty WOR on 710 AM from Times Square, the flagship of the Mutual Broadcasting System.[7] And sure enough, elements of Jerry's K-metal story would later surface on the radio, where it would finally be named "kryptonite."[8] Whitney Ellsworth, who edited the K-metal story, was National's adviser on the radio show. This would not be the first time that elements of a rejected Siegel manuscript would seemingly later be used without permission. National apparently ran from the ongoing premise that everything Jerry turned in was work-for-hire; everything he dreamed of was somehow already theirs. Kryptonite was green as money.

Jerry also watched as Harry would go after other comics companies who were trying to come up with their own supermen. Harry sued these impostors—Wonder Man, Captain Marvel, and others—usually within days of their release.[9] Jerry himself would testify for National, sometimes being summoned by a telegram from Jack that would instruct him to leave tomorrow for New York.[10] Jerry watched the rabid intensity with which Harry held on to the character and wondered if someday it might be directed at him. The radio show seemed to be going gangbusters, but Jerry and Joe were still being assured by Whit and Harry that the show was making no money, certainly not enough for more residuals for its creators.[11] Jerry had to admit that National was doing an excellent job of protecting the character. He just wasn't so sure they were protecting him.

JOINING US

For many, October 9, 1940, a few months later, was remarkable only because it was a Wednesday, which meant it was time for *The Texaco Star Theatre* with your host, Fred Allen. As fathers watched the clocks from the corners of their eyes, Allen was busy in his studio, crossing out lines and writing in substitutions on his script, lighting up when he hit a particularly funny line. Walking up to the microphones was his wife, Portland Hoffa, who would soon transform into a bubble-voiced straight man. Allen looked off to the left and saw this schlubby kid with his hands folded in front of him. The kid looked terrified. Portland kissed Allen on the cheek: *Let's see how the censors like that.* Allen grinned. *Is that the Superman kid? Cripes. And who's that fat guy?* They both let the pause sit there just long enough. *Which one? Hahaha.* They would have to do a little extra tonight—part of the show would go onto some kind of convention record or something. *Oh well,* it meant money in the pocket in the end. The light flashed and Fred Allen stood up straight. He stepped up to the blocky silver microphone and held out his script with one hand, at a perfect forty-five-degree angle.[12]

Jerry Siegel's appearance on Fred Allen's radio show was a big deal. For one, the interview would later be put onto a record that was played at a meeting of the Independent Magazine Wholesalers Association of the South. Clearly someone, maybe Ducovny, thought that Jerry himself could sell Superman. Donenfeld appeared on the recording as well but came off blustery and stilted. The whole bit begins with a Sousa march and a newscaster's voice: *Parents approve of Superman because he makes no use of guns or other weapons.* An earnest-sounding mother adds her two cents: *I should like to thank the publishers of* Action Comics *magazine for including a health page in every issue. Billy has been eating his cereal and drinking his milk regularly since Superman told him to do so.* As much as Jerry was mad at the radio, it was also providing Superman with enormous levels of publicity.

In the interview itself, Fred asks Jerry how he and Joe came up with Superman. Jerry tells the story of how no one wanted it, yet they kept trying. Jerry, in that thin, nasal squawk, sounds a little like a teenager, but he gets the story out here. Fred then asks Jerry how he finds the time to write all the scripts. Jerry says that it is "Mr. Ellsworth, the editor," who gets on him, and "my wife [does] as well." "They do, eh?" says Fred. "Why don't you get Superman after *them?*" There is laughter. But then Fred asks Jerry point-blank: "You are the only man in America who knows what's going to happen." "I don't feel any different, Fred," says Jerry. But Fred is unconvinced: "Oh, you're just being modest, Mr. Sie-gel. After all, you dominate a muscular marvel with a dual personality. When Superman isn't Superman, he's merely disguised as a reporter, isn't he?" "Yes, he's Clark Kent," says Jerry. "A meek little chap with glasses." And that is exactly what he sounded like.[13]

When Donenfeld finally got up to the microphone, he traded quips with Bud Collyer, who played Superman on the radio show. Collyer, who changed octaves to oscillate between Clark and Superman, made his boss sound a little anxious.[14] Still, this was a big day for Jerry. He was mad about the usual things and Harry being Harry, but this was *Fred Allen.* No one was taking that away.

The biggest spectacle, though, occurred on Thanksgiving in New York. Macy's, which had sponsored most of Superman Day at the World's Fair, had also been doing very well selling exclusive Superman merchan-dise in its toy store on West Thirty-fourth Street in New York. So when the holidays came, they dedicated space on their famed Christmas Toy-land just to Superman.[15] To advertise, they commissioned a float for the Man of Steel.[16] Unfortunately, the first Superman float looked more like a spongy rectangle than the muscled Superman the kids were used to in the comics. No one cared, though, as it soared over their frosty breath and blocked out the sun.[17] In Cleveland, Jerry and Joe posed for a smiling photograph in front of the new Superman puppet show at Higbee's department store in the Toy Town Christmas area. The caption refers to Jerry and Joe as "Superman's Two Papas."[18] In the show itself, kids saw Superman kick some bad guys, help Santa, and, of course, save Christmas. The kids broke free of their parents and cheered.

When Jerry walked into his house now, there was always a stack of mail on the table. He would sift through the letters in order of importance. There were plenty of letters from New York, sometimes three or four a day. The money was coming in, more or less, and family and friends were looking at both Joe and him with different eyes, as if they had forgotten who they were. Jerry and Joe had a real product now: they had comics to touch, hold, point to, and read. Jerry in particular had stacks of *Action Comics* #1 stored in his mother's house, especially in the corners of the attic. They were piled everywhere, bright and perfect and flat. Joe invested in some property and some actual art supplies. Jerry bought a car. No one was telling them to get jobs anymore, though Jerry thought he could see it in the corners of his mother's eyes sometimes. Jerry's relatives were amused. Joe's parents beamed.

The bell clinked when Joe walked into the Tasty Shop with a pad of paper under his arm. He would sit in the corner and draw all afternoon, sometimes looking out the window at the men wiping their brows with their handkerchiefs. Sometimes Jerry would come in for a bit and they would stare over the table at each other—Joe with his head down, drawing, and Jerry talking nonstop about what Superman could tackle next: *I think he should punch him in the mouth. No, it would be better if he trips him down the stairs.* When they were together like this, they would smile goofy smiles and laugh goofy laughs. Without Jerry, though, Joe was all business at the soda shop. But as he shaded and drew, he always kept an eye out for who came in next. Stories and sketches from old Cleveland ladies still get called into *The Plain Dealer* about Joe in the soda shop. If even a third of them are true, then Joe had no problem going up to pretty girls and offering them a quick sketch of Superman. They would talk, he would give them a drawing, and sometimes they'd go out on a date, but that would be it. Some Cleveland girls, it seemed, were unfazed by comic book fame.[19]

Jerry loved the fame as well, though it sometimes brought back a sense of absence. On February 9, 1941, he and Joe were the guests of honor at the Temple at Hotel Statler Father-Son Banquet. The program for the event held lyrics to a sing-along for the guests. The last lines read:

That we'll be pals all our days,
Here's to you, my dear dad, here's to you.[20]

Jerry shifted in his chair while it was being sung and tried hard to smile.

1941

Money was a growing issue, especially since Jerry and Joe had to pay their studio artists out of pocket. In a May 26, 1941, letter to Jack Liebowitz, Jerry writes:

> *Awaiting four checks. Three made out to Joe and myself: the*
> *$4515.00 check for magazine SUPERMAN work, the syndicate*
> *check, and the royalty check you promised to send on this month. And*
> *a fourth check made out to myself for $228.00 for my other features.*
> *—In order to meet current payrolls, we need these checks by Wednes-*
> *day so please send them immediately <u>Air Mail Special Delivery.</u>*
> *Regards to everyone,*
> *Sincerely,*
> *Jerry Siegel*[21]

The first time the press notes displeasure on the parts of Jerry and Joe is on June 18, 1941. In *The Plain Dealer:*

SUPERMAN "DADS" LEARN HARD WAY
BY J. A. WADOVICK

For all the fantastic success of their brain child, Superman, Clevelanders Jerry Siegel and Joe Shuster are two sadder and wiser young men. Fame and material rewards are theirs, but what rankles is the knowledge that, had they seen what their Man of Steel had in store for them, they might have saved for themselves a good chunk of the fortune Superman has earned to date.

As it is, the signing of an innocent piece of paper in their struggling-up-the-ladder-of-success period has cost them a fortune.[22]

Wadovick, who probably talked to Jerry, goes on to provide details: "Before payment, Donenfeld's business manager persuaded Siegel and Shuster to sign a copyright release." Wadovick then claims that Donenfeld earns $500,000 a year and that Jerry and Joe will earn a combined $150,000 next year.[23]

> They have discovered, as they admitted in an interview yesterday, that even such a perfect "escape" dream as Superman is no escape from life's irritations—a fickle public, vigilant parent-teacher clubs, irascible editors and periods of creative vacuum. "We have learned there's a lot more to a popular cartoon strip than just an idea," said rotund Jerry Siegel, the "continuity" half of the partnership. "We have to be careful about what Superman says and does. Everything we turn out is gone over and checked and double-checked by an editorial board."

Producing *Superman* was hard work. But no one, not even the reporters, still really believed it—the funnies were the funnies, after all. In addition, anyone making money in the early 1940s (who wasn't in Hollywood) was considered fair game for public ridicule. So Jerry becomes "rotund" and his partner is described as "owlish Joe Shuster, who draws Superman." They are described as coming "from modest homes, with parents struggling hard to give the boys the benefit of higher education," which they seem to have rejected in favor of funny books.[24]

The most influential article written about Jerry and Joe during their creative lives appears in *The Saturday Evening Post* in an article by John Kobler on June 21, 1941, titled "Up, Up and Awa-a-y! The Rise of Superman, Inc." It is the first big national telling of their story and would in many ways chart the course of their public future for decades. Kobler summarizes their rise to fame by noting that in the three years that "Jerry Siegel, the plump youth," and "Joe Shuster, his neighbor, partner and boyhood crony of the same age," have been producing *Superman* comics,

> they have assumed a solemn obligation to instill faith, wherever possible, in the physical reality of Superman. They have done this in the same spirit in which old-fashioned parents encourage

belief in Santa Claus. Indeed, Siegel and Shuster are suspected
by many of their friends of believing in Superman themselves.[25]

Kobler describes Jerry and Joe as "small, shy, nervous, myopic lads"
who are diametric opposites of their red-and-blue miracle man. Kobler
speculates that because of their status "as the puniest kids in school,
picked on and bullied by their huskier classmates," they might have "mo-
ped off into" Freudian "infantile phantasies," resulting in a shared world
where "they became colossi of brute strength, capable of flattening whole
regiments of class bullies by a click of their pinkies."[26]

The story of them being bullied shows up in a few places, but never in
any detail. In fact, it may have started, at least in print, with this article.
Kobler then gives a version of the financial state of Superman. And it
wasn't—at all—about the $130 sale.

Kobler recounts how Harry sold Superman to McClure for $100,000
personally and how Harry could fire Jerry and Joe at any time. The details are directly from Jerry's personal stash of letters, which must have
made Harry blow his stack. Kobler projects the 1940–1941 profit total for
Superman, Inc., at $1.5 million. Kobler reveals that the boys "are now
making thirty-five dollars a page. Meantime, their syndicate profits have
leaped to $600 a week. . . . Next year, with revenues from radio, movies
and licenses coming in, they stand to make $150,000." Clearly, newspa-
per syndication was bringing in the most money, as it was for everyone.
Kobler reports that Donenfeld bragged about making around $500,000.[27]

This was the Superman, Inc., that Kobler alludes to in his title. Early
on, Jack and Harry started a subsidiary company to manage Superman's
expansion into other mediums. Superman, Inc., unlike the previous Detective Comics, Inc., was concerned with merchandising, promotions,
radio, and eventually television. On the one hand, this was good business, as the subsidiary could focus on new, noncomics endeavors. The
subsidiary was probably created to separate results—meaning, to keep
Superman profits separate from the larger company. The advantage of
such a division was that National could show off to potential advertisers
how well Superman was doing as an entity, which is what Harry had
longed for since he'd missed out on the Lone Ranger. But the subsidiary
also created a web of money that would be very difficult to track. By financially separating Superman from National, which had Jerry and Joe under
contract, the new company created greater distance between the character

and its creators.[28] Jerry and Joe never really knew how much Superman was making outside of the comics, and it was maddening.

Beyond the money, Kobler's article established the modern, mutual biography of Jerry and Joe. Kobler pokes fun at Jerry, pointing out that he has a motorized waist-reducing belt in his attic, pumped $15,000 into his house full of "chrome fixtures," can't mix a cocktail, keeps a Superman costume in his front closet to trick young fans, and is prone to "fruity phrases." But the last paragraph really stings: Kobler relates how after receiving a check from New York, Jerry called Liebowitz and demanded a $500 advance. "But we just mailed you a check," exclaimed Liebowitz. "I know," replied Siegel, "but I have nineteen thousand five hundred dollars in my bank account and I want to round it out to an even twenty." He got the advance.

Kobler closes the article with a teasing look toward the future:

> Messrs. Shuster and Siegel are now in the throes of creating another comic strip. It will be called Superboy and will confine itself to Superman's adolescence. . . . "It will be," Siegel explains, "about Superman before he developed a social conscience."[29]

Jerry finished the article and may have put the magazine down very slowly. He might have walked slowly up to his room and buried his head—deeply—in the same pillows pictured in the article.

More than anything else, the *Post* article accomplished two things: It helped mythologize the creation of Superman for the next seventy years, and it portrayed the creators as somewhat incompetent and divorced from a corporation that was getting bigger by the second. Jerry was painted as an eccentric, slightly whiny weirdo, and Joe was nice but, like any artist, kind of ungraspable. It would take a long time for the media to look at them as underdogs again.

Two months later, on August 17, 1941, Jerry's mom, Sarah, put on her favorite blue dress that she wore to the World's Fair and stepped out of the car onto her driveway on Kimberley. She was what the cousins called a "society lady," as she taught all the girls to dress up when going out because *you never knew whom you were going to meet*. She often wore white gloves and a hat.[30] Stepping out of the car, she felt something in her chest that made her stop. Her grandnieces watched her, the rock of the family, fall down before their widening eyes.[31]

On August 18, 1941, *The Plain Dealer* reports that "Mrs. Sarah Siegel, 69, mother of Jerry Siegel, one of the originators of the comic strip, Superman, died yesterday of a heart attack at her home."[32] Jerry's mother was an influential presence in Jewish Cleveland: she was president of the Dykes Mothers Club, was an original member of the Jewish Consumptive Association, and was on the boards of the Orthodox Orphans Home and many other organizations. Her name shows up again and again in the minutes of nearly every Jewish association in Cleveland as a board member, host, secretary, or organizer.

A month later, Jerry was still in a daze over the loss of his mother when Paramount Pictures released the first *Superman* animation short. The shorts had been previewed in the *Post* article with a spectacular, full-color frame. Paramount Pictures thought, as many fans did, that Superman would make for great cartoons. So they went right to the best: the Fleischer brothers, Dave and Max, whose hardworking studio had produced the wildly popular *Popeye* and *Betty Boop*. The brothers at first turned Paramount down because of the huge costs involved in producing a full-color adventure drama that would do justice to the character. When, astoundingly, Paramount met them halfway, they soon started production on some of the most sophisticated animated films ever produced. Using a technique called "rotoscoping," they filmed human actors (or whoever was nearby) doing actions that their artists would trace over. This resulted in a very realistic animated line. While in Miami with his mother, Joe visited the Fleischer Studios and drew out some basic model sheets for Superman, Lois, and Clark.[33] The artists loved his style and made sure it was preserved in the films. But they could add sound effects and big Technicolor action that Joe could only dream of. And they could finally produce the definitive headquarters of *The Daily Planet*.[34] The cartoons were also the first place where Superman would (more or less) fly. When the first short film previewed in Cleveland on October 10, 1941, Jerry and Joe set up shop for several hours at the majestic State Theater downtown. Joe could be seen at his drawing board, with Jerry writing from "2 to 10 p.m. . . . During those hours they will autograph strips of their work printed in *The Plain Dealer* for their youthful admirers."[35] The first short was nominated for an Academy Award.[36]

The cartoons were so popular that Jerry would write a story about them that would appear a year later. In *Superman* #19, in "Our Very First Imaginary Story," Lois and Clark go to the movies—and see "the Superman animated cartoon."[37] Lois "can hardly wait to see it," but Clark is sweating because he is worried that "Lois is liable to see something that will give away my true identity!" Clark wonders to himself: "How they know so much about me is a puzzle, perhaps they're clairvoyant!" Clark proceeds to get a drink of water, drop Lois's pocketbook, and fake a dizzy spell, all to make sure she doesn't see Clark change to Superman on-screen. It is a really strange story that further divides the "real" Clark from a cinematic, corporate Superman. Lois ends up cheering for Super-man on the screen—"Yea, Superman!"—as artist John Sikela basically teleplays most of the first Fleischer episode. Clark succeeds in keeping Lois from the truth, and as the movie ends, he winks at his super alter ego, saying, "Well, pal, our secret is still a secret from Lois."[38] Jerry really liked the films. But back in 1941, when he was seeing them for the first time, it was still a lot to handle: the money, the movie, and Jerry's mother, who had been with them all at the World's Fair. A time of mourning and despair full of brothers and sisters and decisions and memories was meet-ing with more and more Superman. And it felt like another life.

So when December 1941 rolled around, the year couldn't wait to be over. Joe was invited to be best man at his cousin Frank's wedding in Toronto. It was cold, so Joe wore his fedora and overcoat. Everyone was glad to see him. It was good to be on his own, he thought to himself. While in town, he also attended a benefit at the Eaton Auditorium hosted by the *Toronto Star* Santa Claus Fund. The highlight of the show was an auction of an original paint-ing of Superman by Joe, with proceeds going to needy children.

Then the planes came low over the Pacific. And the year that was bad somehow became worse in every possible way.

Barely two weeks after Pearl Harbor, the following letter appeared in *The Washington Times*:

> *Please ask Jerry Siegel where was Superman when all the bombing took place at Pearl Harbor. . . . We know he is busy, but this was only a handful of Japanese and they weren't stopped. How come?*
> *EARL BLONDHEIM, aged 14, Washington, Dec. 12.*[39]

When Jerry Siegel read the question, he had no believable answer.

1942

As the world went to war, Jerry and Joe worked like mad. By now, it was impossible to separate Superman from their lives; though they feared for their own prospects in the draft, they were also worried about the character's survival. They tried to make Superman a little more humorous to lighten things up, and though they were still mad at their bosses, they decided to poke fun at them when given the chance. First up was "Case of the Funny Paper Crimes," which was also published in *Superman* #19 in 1942. The story begins with Clark being astonished that Lois reads the funnies: "Lois I didn't realize you were a comic strip fan." Lois plays it off in the cool tone that was perfected by Jerry: "Avid is the word for it." Lois claims that her favorite strip is *Prince Peril,* a scarcely disguised fictional clone of the *Prince Valiant* comic by *Tarzan* artist Hal Foster about knights and chivalry. The artist (John Sikela, with help from Joe)[40] then splashes a whole close-up of the funnies page that Lois is holding, revealing that not only is Hugh Langley the author of *Prince Peril,* but there are other genre strips such as *Detective Craig* by Don Glenn, *Father Imprisoned* by Torgo, *The Solitary Rider* by Cliff Land, *Streak Dugan* by C. C. Cook, and *Happy Daze* by Jim Johnson. The characters, of course, come "alive" under the direction of the villain "Funny-Face," who appears in a loud plaid suit with a smiley face mask. When Superman unmasks the villain, he is a nobody: "Nobody knows me! I wanted to be a celebrity—the creator of a famous comic strip. But no one would buy my strips. My dimensional experimentation enabled me to bring comic characters to life—and I put the strip villains to work for me to gather illegal profits."[41]

In *Action Comics* #55 of December 1942, Jerry writes a *Superman* newspaper script about one of his fellow comics creators: Al Capp, the bombastic writer-artist of the extremely popular *Li'l Abner.* Like *Superman, Li'l Abner* had branched out into all sorts of places, including an RKO movie, a radio show, and some very popular radio songs, mostly about the shmoo or Sadie Hawkins Day, which had become a recognized event on many college campuses.[42] In Jerry's story, "Al Hatt" storms into Perry White's office to hear that the syndication of his cartoon strip *Slapstick Sam* has dropped to five papers and will soon be canceled. Hatt, fat and furious in a bright yellow suit and beret, decides to retreat to his cabin in the woods to think about a new strip. But Hatt is out of ideas and starts pulling his hair out: "So this is the comic business! 'Learn to draw cartoons and lead the Life of Riley'! Ha! Ha! Ha!"[43]

Meanwhile, outside his cabin, local hillbilly "Tiny Rufe" is dismissing the affections of country gal "Maisie Day." Their costumes are the same as Abner's and Daisy's, only in different colors. Rufe says to Maisie, who is getting "too romantical"—"Mah Mammy done tole me a gal's gonna sweet-talk an' give me th' big eyes, but when thet sweet-talkin's done—a gal is a two-faced, a woorisome thing. . . . Keep yo distance!" Hatt hears all this, guffaws, and starts writing it down: "Those kids! They're terrific! . . . what a comic-strip they'd make!"[44]

In the story, Hatt returns to the newspaper with his new strip—"Here you are slavedriver, the strip of the century!"—and it is a huge success. Around a table, the syndicate men pass judgment: "Murray says that in all his years in the syndicate game he's seen nothing to compare with it!" "That goes for me too, Mort!" Jerry writes, thinking of Mort Weisinger, his old acquaintance from the fanzines who was also now an editor on *Superman*. As Hatt's new strip gains in popularity, "rival syndicates issue many weak copies of the original, but without success," including *Tiny Ed* and *Tiny Luke*. Soon, "revenue from other sources pours in, in a golden cascade! Comic books, radio, movies, toys, chewing gum, songs, etc.!" The reader sees Hatt, laughing, standing atop a mountain of cash.[45]

But Hatt finds it is harder and harder to get stories out of Tiny Rufe, so the sneaky creator stages an elaborate scheme by hiring a drop-dead redhead named "Romona Romance" (drawn by Joe) to break up Rufe and Maisie. Romona is so gorgeous that a man falls down when she walks by: "What happened to him? She smiled at him!" Superman gets involved (it is still his strip, after all), and he uses his bizarre trick of "twisting his features" to change places with Tiny Rufe. Soon, Rufe and Maisie see through Hatt's plan and get engaged. Hatt is run out of the county and made a fool, but he returns to *The Daily Planet* with one last great idea for a comic strip based on the very "character" who kiboshed his schemes: Superman. The new strip is, of course, a whopping success. The whole story line is both funny and intricate and shows not only crooked syndicates but creators who do nothing but steal. Jerry makes fun of it all, but not without some truth.[46]

This story line is important not only for its exposé of the newspaper syndication business as a completely crooked farce but also as a means of staging empathy for comics creators—for though Hatt is a fool, it is the structure around him that makes him one. Capp would return the favor much later in 1947, when, in the main *Li'l Abner* strip, a man named Rockwell P. Squeezeblood (who heads his own cartoon syndicate) takes cruel and hilarious advantage of the two creators (drawn as Jerry and Joe, but named "McIntosh and Baldwin") of the superheroic cartoon character "Jack Jawbreaker," who is drawn only as a muscled arm with a helicopter rotor.[47] Capp was sympathetic to Jerry and Joe because he was under a similar contract for *Li'l Abner* until 1947, when he sued his bosses, United Feature Syndicate, for $14 million. The suit was so embarrassing to the syndicate that Capp eventually won control of his own creation.[48]

For all of the back-and-forth between Jerry and Al Capp, which was really done in a shared distrust of the syndicates made public through the medium of the comics, Jerry's initial satire of Hatt (as Capp) was not that far off. Jerry's "Romona Romance" character who made men drop like flies with her monumental beauty appeared five years before Capp introduced a similar character, "Stupefyin' Jones," who arrived in the newspapers on November 5, 1947. Jones was so gorgeous that she rendered men blank and was the single most dangerous creature imaginable to encounter on Sadie Hawkins Day. When *Li'l Abner* was adapted for Broadway in 1956 and for film in 1959, it was actress Julie Newmar who played this part of a "sex-foot-two-inch secret weapon who could turn men to stone."[49] Those ninety seconds jump-started Newmar's career, eventually into the role of Catwoman in the 1966–1968 *Batman* television series.[50]

In 1942, Superman was trying to make leaps into other mediums. One of the first was into so-called real literature in the form of an honest-to-goodness book, *The Adventures of Superman* by George Lowther, a scriptwriter who was in his late twenties when he wrote for the Superman radio show.[51] The story is a retelling of Superman's origin and early adventuring and features sketches and full-page paintings by Joe. The book also boasts a foreword by Josette Frank, the "Staff Advisor for the Children's Book Committee," who compares the Man of Steel to such folk heroes as Pecos Bill and John Henry.[52]

Lowther's story is constructed for its exact target audience: it is full of secret agents and Nazi espionage. The book is also the first time that Superman's parents are named "Jor-el" and "Lara"—a slight spelling change that would stick. Still, there are plenty of additions that do not survive, including the Kents being named Sarah and Eben.[53] Joe's art is magnificent and ranges from pencil sketches at the chapter breaks to full-page paintings. One of the more famous images, of the rocket escaping Krypton's explosion, is a near perfect swipe from a cover of *Science and Invention*.[54]

Though Superman's absence from events in Europe was frustrating to readers, it played perfectly for editorial because it meant serial business as usual. If Superman entered the war, the character might cross a line into reality that would be too hard to retreat from. The newspaper strips explained the problem away by having Clark turn on his X-ray vision by accident during the enlistment test and thus fail to correctly read his eye chart.[55]

WHY NOT

For all of Harry's stern warnings in 1938 that the boys could be easily replaced like so many light bulbs in a Superman machine, the fame of the character had made Jerry bolder. He was also wiser; he knew National couldn't completely hang him out to dry. So when Jerry wrote and asked for another raise, Liebowitz wrote back and again invited him to come to New York to get things straightened out. Harry knew they would—again—have the advantage in their own intimidating, loud, and dirty backyard. It was an exertion of control, just as it was in 1938. But Jerry was prepared this time and accepted his invitation—with Bella, his own secret weapon, in tow. On October 15, 1942:

> *Dear Jack*
> *I was very glad to hear from you. Your invitation to come on to New York to discuss the matter under correspondence was happily received as it will be nice to seeing all of you again. Bella and I expect to leave Monday from Cleveland. And so we should be seeing you Tuesday.*[56]

Money wasn't the only source of tension between New York and Cleveland. National really wanted Lois to figure out Superman's secret identity at this point, presumably because it was so outlandish that she had not already. They were worried that readers would tire of the suspended disbelief. Jerry now completely disagreed:

> *If Lois should ACTUALLY learn Clark's secret, the strip would lose about 75% of its appeal—the human interest angle. I know that a formula can possibly prove monotonous thru repetition but I fear that if this element is removed from the story formula that makes up SUPER-MAN, that this strip will lose a great part of its effectiveness.*[57]

Jerry didn't want the character to fail anymore. He was trying to hang on.
The game they played was a repetitive one: National would overtask

Jerry and Joe to get as much Superman content as humanly possible out of them. Jerry would then ask for a raise. National would grudgingly give it and then proceed to make their lives an editorial hell. It is hard to know if National wanted them to quit or not. Certainly there were internal conversations that life might be easier without them. They figured that Joe was doing little now anyway, but they were still the public faces of the character. They were doing war bond drives and autograph sessions for the effort all over Ohio. And as weird as Jerry was—and New York made fun of him all the time—he somehow had Superman's voice like no one else. So they opted to bicker back and forth over mail like schoolchildren, over a property that was getting to be worth a fortune.

In the beginning, Jerry wrote a script, Joe drew it, and they sent it to Jack to be published. But after the raises, things changed: Jerry's scripts and Joe's art had to be approved by New York editorial, who would then send it all back sometimes with requests for heavy revisions. The red pen of editorial marked up Jerry's grammar and tense like a schoolteacher, in surprisingly flowing script.[58] In a typical set of comments accompanying a returned script, Ellsworth urges in a February 19, 1941, letter: "In the future, may I say again, will you please get the scripts to us far enough in advance so that we can do our editorializing before the artists go to work penciled in." He goes on:

> The artwork on both "dailies" and "Sundays" was again quite bad, along the same lines as my recent complaints to Joe. It was necessary for me to spend the entire day, with my mediocre talents, trying to shorten a number of ape-like arms, and to remove extremely curly forelocks from Superman's forehead, and to de-sex Lois. . . . The magazine releases are even worse than anything I have to say about the syndicate stuff.
>
> All in all, Jack Liebowitz and I are both very much disappointed with the artwork, and we both feel that something drastic is soon going to have to be done. It is possible that we may come out either this week or next, if press of business allows.
>
> In spite of all this, best regards.[59]

There is not one positive word from Whitney Ellsworth, until he says good-bye.

Ellsworth's critique is strange because *Superman* had been getting very positive press, with nothing to suggest that it was too racy for children. An article in *The American Journal of Orthopsychiatry* by Dr. Lauretta Bender and Reginald S. Lourie in July 1941 was being reprinted all over, including in *Print, Youth Leaders,* and *Time.* Bender and Lourie proffer a particular quote that gets fixated on by generations of comics scholars: "The comics may be said to offer the same type of mental catharsis to its readers that Aristotle claimed was an attribute of the drama."[60] At the practical level of the classroom, others noted that "it seems that the level of Superman's grammar is high, his speeches full of vocabulary-building words, like 'imminent,' 'manipulating,' 'destination,' 'cajoled.' "[61] In *The New York Times* in 1943, an article titled "Children and the Comics" states that we can "no more think of taking children 'off' the comics than we do of taking them 'off' candy."[62] The candy analogy—colorful, sugary, capable of easy addiction—was not lost on executives or mothers.

At the same time, Superman was seeping into the darker corners of popular culture as well. *The Plain Dealer* on March 14, 1943, shows the face of a showgirl with a smug, lipsticked smile.

> Jerry Siegel and Joe Shuster have their "Superman" flying over cartoon pages with the greatest of ease but the Roxy's new "Superwoman" is held down to the burlesque stage. She is comely Lois DeFee, six feet four inches tall and strong enough to lift Benny Moore or Lew Fine off the floor with one arm while dancing.[63]

The Plain Dealer later tells its readers about the Boots & Saddle Cocktail Lounge in nearby Bucyrus: "a new chromium and red leather hot spot in the Elbertson Hotel, where Superman Specials are 50 cents."[64] *Superman* was allegedly educational, but it also was being appropriated by strip clubs and bars. There was no stopping him now.

Years later, *Superman* artist Wayne Boring would draw a cartoon to help portray the antagonistic workplace atmosphere at National. In it, Jerry and Joe are drawn as tiny children, almost identically, which was how they were often perceived. Jack Liebowitz has his hands around both their necks. Meanwhile, new editor Mort Weisinger, with pills falling out of his coat, proclaims that he wants to "steal a smash panel" from Bill Finger and "grab a Superman synopsis for a Batman yarn." This was an

old bullpen tale: that Mort would reject a synopsis for one title only to suggest it to the writer of another. Herbie the Muscle is pictured in the back ready to give a vaguely scary "Torpedo" to whoever deserved it. Also pictured is the full-length painting of Superman by Lone Ranger artist H. J. Ward that first appeared in the *Saturday Evening Post* article. Commissioned by Harry, it hung in the National offices for years until it was lost and then rediscovered in 2010.[65] This romantic image of Superman is disgusted by the "odor of this Aegean stable" below him. Whether Boring's depiction was true, not, or just polarizing satire, this was a workplace of rocky personalities.[66]

In *Superman* #14, Jerry tells a story of a young inventor named Chet Farnsworth who has invented an astounding "fire extinguishing powder" that promises to save countless lives. Clark wants to write a story about the young inventor but finds that he has sold the rights to a man named Jim Baldwin, a slick "famous promoter." Predictably, Farnsworth is treated similarly—very similarly—to how Harry and Jack treated Jerry and Joe. In this panel, Baldwin's words can imaginatively be viewed as Donenfeld's:

At the end of the story, Baldwin's own house catches fire. Superman saves the day, but only by forcing Baldwin to give up Farnsworth's rights; Superman actually makes him sign the actual release before he douses the flames.[67] This story could not have been published without editorial absolutely understanding its meaning. Just as Jerry and Joe used people and incidents from their personal lives in their fictional stories, they were now turning to their own lives as comics creators for content.

But this kind of behavior could cut both ways. Another telling comic strip about the National workplace was commissioned for Harry Donenfeld on his fiftieth birthday. Superman does various tricks for his boss but still ends up getting spanked: "Let this be a lesson to you—I'm fifty years old, but you're still taking orders from me!" Superman responds: "And I love it!" Superman is here written, drawn, and portrayed as a completely subservient being. Since Superman is fictional, this makes perfect sense, but in the cartoon he is depicted alongside a real man who has not created him but owns him. Joe gives up most of the work to his peers but is sure to draw Donenfeld's gleeful, unmistakable face as he spanks the subservient Superman.

The whole process was beginning to feel like sadomasochism: Jerry and Joe were drawing a powerful character who could be spanked by Donenfeld, humiliated in front of everyone, at a moment's notice. No matter what they did, they were always reminded of who was really in charge. Above all, Jerry just wanted to have a little more control. He didn't realize he was about to lose all of his freedom. But he would finally get closer to the heroism he so often wrote about. And it would have nothing to do with Superman.

Chapter 18

Private

FAR AWAY FROM THE MACHINATIONS of New York, the people of Cleveland rose with anticipation on the morning of July 4, 1943. Folks laid out their white shirtsleeves and dresses and looked at the calendar in disbelief. There would still be time for hot dogs, a quick dip in the city pool, and fireworks. But this was no ordinary Fourth of July. For thousands of young men, it was the day they were to be officially drafted into World War II.

The event was called the Festival of Freedom and was a colossal patriotic undertaking. Taking place at the huge Cleveland Municipal Stadium, the event rolled tanks, soldiers, and flags across a field usually reserved for smashmouth football. Bob Hope, who grew up in Cleveland, returned home to lend his voice to the event, which was announced by Cleveland radio personality Wayne Mack. Jerry Siegel shifted in his clothes.[1] His muscles felt very un-Superman-like. Still, he was confident that he wasn't going to fight. He hoped. Bella was furious at the whole thing. She thought that the famous writer of Superman shouldn't have to go to war, and Jerry kind of agreed, but what could he do? Local women high-stepped onto the field with stars representing each state, and people roared. They smiled and twirled. Jerry couldn't picture himself with a gun.

Part of him was actually looking forward to it, but at the same time he was dreading it beyond all comprehension. The Japanese had made it to Hawaii once before. And he had no cape. The army also had bad connotations for him. He knew from his father's stories what it was like to be taken into an army against his will. Jerry didn't even know how his dad got out. At least he wasn't going to Europe. He thought of all the other celebrities who had gone over. Jimmy Stewart and Clark Gable were going to fly *airplanes.*

Still, Jerry had known it was coming. Even Superman couldn't fight the U.S. Army.[2]

On June 6, 1943, *The Plain Dealer* ran the story:

> HALF OF SUPERMAN DRAFTED; PARTNER AWAITS ARMY
> CALL
> Jerry Siegel, 28 . . . who writes the continuity and is one of
> two Clevelanders who originated the now famous Man of
> Steel, will be sworn into the army as a feature of the Festival
> of Freedom at the stadium July 4. Married but childless,
> Siegel was inducted Monday. . . . The other half . . . Joe
> Shuster . . . who draws the miracle man, expects to be called
> for service next month. He is single. Both men are out of the
> city and could not be reached for comment. It has been
> reported that both halves of Superman are being considered
> for service with Yank, official army newspaper.[3]

Joe was passed over because of his eyesight, so he would keep watch over the studio and the character. He and Jerry shook hands awkwardly, and Joe stared at him. It was very quiet for once. Jerry wrote as many scripts as he possibly could and left them in Joe's care. They felt like a small body. Jerry wasn't going to let the war—and Donenfeld—take Superman away from him.

Jerry officially enlisted on June 28, 1943, and received training at Fort Meade as an "Airplane Engine Mechanic, a Film Editor, Motion Picture Cutter, Public Relations Man or Playwright (Motion Picture Writer) or Reporter."[4] He did a comic for *The Fort Meade Post* on August 13, 1943, that described his experience a bit:

Jerry Siegel then went to Hawaii a little lighter, with less hair and a new job: staff reporter on *Stars and Stripes*.

MAHALO

Hawaii was so different from Cleveland that it might as well have been another planet. The weather was generally warm and sunny, but once a day, usually in the early afternoons, it rained for about fifteen minutes. Jerry would sometimes stand in a doorway when it happened. He still couldn't believe he was here, with the palm trees and bouncing jeeps. He would step out and look at it with that little half-smile. It was like a movie.

When Jerry entered the U.S. Army as a technician fifth grade, there were some smirky exchanges with a few officers: *Keep it up, Superman!* When he got to Honolulu, though, he was assigned to the only thing he was ever really good at: writing. He knew how lucky he was. And he really was. He was assigned to the Pacific edition of *Stars and Stripes* not only because of his *Superman* experience, but also for his *Torch* work, which Jerry exaggerated repeatedly.

Jerry started doing straight news stories for all three of the major military publications: *Stars and Stripes, Midpacifican,* and *Yank.* For most servicemen, Honolulu was very far from home. It was also exotic, tropical, and welcoming to its ever-growing GI community. Unlike the European alternative, Hawaii meant more beaches, more girls, and ostensibly more fun. The YMCA and USO restaurants were always lined with army men, perspiration on their brows and ready to forget their long separation from home. Or there was the Kaala Club, complete with a lounge, card room, coffee bar, thirteen pool tables, and rooms for reading and writing. The USO girls were there, too, their butterscotch blond hair piled into high curls. The Hawaiian girls could be seen outside, and on postcards in their grass skirts, with a wink and a smile. But there was still a curfew at dark; there was always a fear of sirens.[5]

Stars and Stripes was started during the Civil War by four Union soldiers using a captured newspaper's facilities in Bloomfield, Missouri. In Hawaii, the paper had taken over the second-floor offices of *The Honolulu Advertiser.* The low rooms were filled with wooden filing cabinets, fans, and busy young men in white cotton T-shirts. *Stars and Stripes* was an interesting experiment of a free press during wartime—it was meant to boost spirits, but it was also a source of genuine military news, and army higher-ups were ordered not to censor it. *Stars and Stripes* was for soldiers, by soldiers.[6]

Before long, Jerry found a niche in the paper in a very familiar spot: a skinny column on page two, writing witty short jokes of no more than a few lines. His column, "Take a Break with T/5 Jerry Siegel," ran daily and was a favorite of many Pacific servicemen. He eagerly invited readers to send in their own jokes; and just as he'd made fun of school in *The Torch,* he made fun of the army here. And though he often cribbed stuff from other papers or joke books (sometimes with credit, sometimes not), the whole show was his. It was the "Blow Torch" column all over again, only a bit more grown up. But only just a bit.

In the beginning of the column's run, Jerry showcased certain servicemen who had showbiz connections or ran the kind of standard "G.I. Joe from Brooklyn finally goes home the day his little brother is drafted" stories. But the soldiers loved it, mostly because, unlike *The Torch,* the paper on the whole was far from all fun and games. The first page had war news on it, generally positive by this time but sometimes full of awful statistics and accompanied by gruesome photographs. Page two always showcased several letters from servicemen trying to get explanations about the points system or trying to locate missing comrades from planes that had disappeared somewhere in the Pacific clouds. Casualties climbed to numbers without meaning.

So "Take a Break" needed to be just that. There were already comic strips in *Stars and Stripes,* including *Popeye, Blondie,* Milt Caniff's great *Male Call,* even *Donald Duck*—but Jerry's column offered an inclusive, army-specific outlet for readers. And Jerry took it very seriously. This was not his Superman audience, so he changed his writing accordingly:

> When PFC Wilmer Swift of Downington, PA ran out of his hiding place, somewhere in the Philippines, to aid a wounded comrade, Japs fired. The first shot ripped off part of his pants. The next two shots dislodged the heel of one shoe. The rescued man was saved. Says Swift, "I felt like Gypsy Rose Lee!"[7]

Jerry gave his readers an unspoken promise: *If you laugh at my jokes, I'll laugh at yours.* To add to the appeal of "Take a Break," three to four small cartoon illustrations accompanied each column. These pictures were mostly drawn by cartoonist Clyde Lewis and often pictured beautiful women and hapless GIs.[8]

Jerry also used his column to comment on specific news items of interest to his readers. The atomic bomb was the big talk around Honolulu. For Jerry, it was the doomsday weapons of the pulps brought to searing, devastating life. On the front pages of *Stars and Stripes*, the bomb was explained to soldiers in scientific charts and diagrams. Articles declared that the bomb contained "such unimaginable power as to threaten the end of the world."[9] Jerry responds in his column:

> *We knew the Japs stank, but never thought the UN would use an atomizer on them.*

> *Let's be*
> *Platonic*
> *And not*
> *Atomic.*

> *Those, we promise you, are all the atomic jokes we will print— today.*[10]

Jerry also told a lot of sex jokes in his column, which was smart: he had an audience of mostly captive males, and this was the army. But it also speaks to an underlying culture at Honolulu, which had a thriving sex industry. There were the infamous Rex Rooms in Chinatown where shaky GIs would walk up and stare. There were posters and pamphlets everywhere warning of the dangers not only of venereal disease but of sleeping with the enemy. A different experience was that of the "good time Charlottes," the local, USO, or WAC girls who felt sorry for the men leaving for the swampy Pacific front. This culture, prevalent or not, was food for thought in "Take a Break":

> Her husband told her it was "undercover" work that kept him out so late every night. But when Mrs. Frances Crane of New York checked up, the only thing she uncovered was a sexy redhead her hubby kept covered up in an apartment on 49th Street. Mrs. Crane sued for divorce.[11]

The missus back home is always characterized as the bad guy. And just as the wives back home doubted the fidelity of their husbands, the GIs were worried that the opposite was true. But there was a very aggressive side to this as well:

> A girl asked another girl how to make love to a GI. The reply: "You don't honey. You just stand still and defend yourself."[12]

Separated from Bella, Jerry stared up at the stars and felt the distance on an almost planetary scale. But here he was on a paper again, on his own, in control; it was like high school all over again. He wonders in another column:

> *You tell your girl*
> *That you'll be true*
> *And what is more*
> *You mean it, too.*
> *On double dates*
> *You never go;*
> *You even shun*
> *The USO*
> *What girls you know*
> *Are mere conjecture.*
> *So what do you get?*
> *—Sex morality lecture!*[13]

There are signs of the old Jerry sweetness, writing poems to girls who weren't reading:

> *I wish I were a porcupine*
> *For just a week or two*
> *For then I would have points*
> *enough*
> *To come back home to you.*[14]

Still, he had lost a lot of weight and was fairly famous. Was that unfair?

If there's anything worse than a waffle that's cold
Or mashed potatoes three days old
It's suddenly meeting a fat old birdie
That you loved in high school in 1930[15]

The Tall, Cool, and lovely cashier at the USO Army-Navy Club's restaurant has a heart of gold.[16]

Did Jerry miss Bella or just miss the imaginary old opportunities? He is still the king of a lot of bad, but good enough, jokes:

As the Indian said when he saw the mermaid: "How."[17]

Censor: an expert at cutting remarks.[18]

Today's thought: Didja ever hear of a blind person joining a nudist colony?[19]

She's a nicely reared girl, isn't she?
Yes, and not so bad from the front, either.[20]

Soldier: Hello
Girl:
Soldier: Oh, well.[21]

She was wearing one of those dresses that keep everybody warm but her.[22]

She was indeed a sight to be held.[23]

I would if I could said the frustrated log.[24]

It takes a woman 21 years to make a man of her son; it takes another woman just one night to make a fool of him.[25]

A divorcee is a woman who gets richer by decrees.[26]

Pvt.: I'm forgetting girls.
Cpl.: Me, too. I'm for getting a couple tonight.[27]

I know a corporal who has "Tarzan eyes." They swing from limb to limb.[28]

A woman's best asset is a man's imagination.[29]

A wedding ring is like a tourniquet . . . it stops your circulation.[30]

Girl: an obstacle course with skirts.[31]

In the December 19, 1944, edition of *The Washington Post,* social columnist Leonard Lyons reports on an incident from Hawaii that sounds as though it comes straight from "Take a Break":

> Superman got himself into a helluva fix in Honolulu this month. His creator, Corpl. Jerry Siegel . . . went for a swim, then searched for his clothes and realized that he had absentmindedly undressed in the ladies' bathhouse. . . . After deep thought, . . . he resolved to walk the beach at Waikiki and wait until nightfall to claim his clothing. . . . A bystander finally called an 8-year-old girl, who went inside and retrieved Corpl. Superman Siegel's clothes.[32]

Things for Jerry were very different in Hawaii; yet in some ways they were just the same.

It was on *Stars and Stripes* that Jerry put his stamp on another of the most popular cartoon characters of the twentieth century. Though he never spoke of it in public, Jerry Siegel was instrumental in helping spread the infamy of a very different kind of character. Even now, we know little about him: his origin, his creator, or anything. And his only power was that he was somehow always *here.* His name was Kilroy.

The phrase *Kilroy was here,* complete with its standard droopy-nose-over-the-wall-that-anyone-can-draw face, began to spread sometime during

World War II. The words appeared in latrines, on trucks, weapons, tat-
toos, and fuselages. Eventually, the drawing would allegedly make its
way to the rolls of royal weddings and the top of Mount Everest itself—
and everywhere in between, including song titles, advertising campaigns,
and an infinite number of bathroom walls.

Though Kilroy's first appearance is hard to date due to all of the
hoaxes and claims, his appearance in print is only slightly easier. According to an early source:

> The actual first mention of Kilroy Was Here isn't until **Decem-
> ber 2, 1945** in an article from the *Nevada State Journal,* which
> attributes the origin of the phrase to Sgt. Francis J. Kilroy.[33]

Later, scholar Dr. Clyde Ward of Detroit asks the public for a Kilroy
reference published before June 26, 1945.[34] Kilroy's appearances in "Take
a Break" occur exactly during this time frame.

Jerry did not invent Kilroy, but he is one of the first to write about
him in a way that encouraged a multitude of stories about where he
came from. Early contributors to "Take a Break" note similarities with
other "phantom scribblers" such as "J. B. King, Esquire."[35] After an
article in *Stars and Stripes* titled "Who the Hell Is Kilroy?" servicemen
start writing in with increasingly unbelievable (but entertaining) stories about the origins of Kilroy.[36] Because of the onslaught, Jerry tem-
porarily turns "Take a Break" into a mail column in which dozens of
people write in to comment, debunk, or offer their own stories.
Though it's unlikely that any of these explanations are correct, they
helped (on large scale given the readership of *Stars and Stripes*) to per-
petuate Kilroy as an exercise in storytelling. For those few inches,
there was no mention of loss or blood. "Can anyone tell me more about
this guy?" the soldiers wrote.[37] Some said it was an old railroad scribble
or the work of an irate CO. And every new story sounded better than
the last:

> *Dear Jerry:*
> *I have some information about the "Saga of Kilroy." It seems that
> Kilroy is a dog at Ft. Lawrence, Wash. As a joke, some of the cadre
> put "Kilroy was here" all around camp. The fad caught on right
> quick. Pvt. H. T. Garin*[38]

The new practice of telling Kilroy stories was all about giving a false identity to an absolute cipher. Jerry knew something about that.

"Take a Break" was mostly just great nonsense. Beyond the jokes, Jerry sometimes did news, sometimes Hollywood gossip, and sometimes anything else. He always asked for gags and amusing experiences, and for "payment? Satisfaction that you may bring a smile to someone when he needs it most." And sometimes he just did it himself: "How'd you like to do a good deed? Pfc. John Kulich, now at Fort Bragg, NC has been in the Army for 25 years and hasn't received a letter at mail call in 15 years."[39] Kulich, nicknamed "Pop," was overwhelmed by mail for the next several weeks. Soldiers have always had an interesting relationship with newspapermen, especially in World War II with the great Ernie Pyle and Bill Mauldin. Jerry never achieved this kind of status, but many servicemen read his column every day and smiled. For the rest of his life, Jerry never mentioned his work on "Take a Break" in any public interview.

Jerry did other things—he saw movies at the USO and judged a cartoon contest for the Victory Club (the topic was "Problems of the Point System"). He even slid a few references to Superman in his column:

> While on the subject of Superman, a friend told me, "He tears down buildings, throws everything down that is in his way; goes through the air with the speed of light. But what's so terrific about that? Did you ever see a soldier on a six-hour pass?"[40]

The most disturbing reference is a joke that makes the long distance to Cleveland seem much closer: "Thieves entered a secondhand men's store in Indianapolis, swiped several suits, returned three of them the next night because the pants didn't match."[41] Even when he was thousands of miles away, Jerry's thoughts were never far from the past.

There was also the strange appearance of *Super Sam,* a comic strip in the parallel *Midpacifican* newspaper written by Jerry and drawn by army pal Ben Bryan. In the strip, Private Sam Stupe falls off a cliff. Superman (in a completely unauthorized appearance—which is probably why Jerry did it) shows up and gives him a blood transfusion that gives Sam enough superpowers to complete his grass-cutting detail for the Sarge in seconds. Super Sam is born, the "Dog-face of Steel." It was good for a laugh. There was also *Super G.I.,* a similar strip drawn by Gerald Green with much of the same super-humor, though without the man himself.[42] Superman had a place in the Pacific, but it was only comedic. They had plenty of heroes already.

On August 27, 1944, at the famous army hangout Louise's, Jerry finally met one of his all-time idols: Edgar Rice Burroughs. They posed

for pictures and talked under the palm trees while the soft music played in the background.[43] Jerry had always wanted to be ERB, and he knew he wasn't, but the moment was astounding; Jerry's mouth closed tight over an overwhelming smile. *Midpacifican* covered the meeting and described Jerry as a "modest, almost shy fellow, who gets plenty of good-natured ribbing because of his essential differences from the dashing daring-do of his brainchild." Jerry gave Burroughs a note and a crude sketch that would be one of the only times he would ever truly acknowledge, even indirectly, an inspiration for Superman. It read:

> Best wishes to Edgar Rice Burroughs—the daddy of today's leading heroes—from Tec5 Jerry Siegel—2402 Glendon Rd., University Hts., Ohio

By September 20, 1944, Jerry finally answers the question in *The Washington Post* that had been posed to him after Pearl Harbor:

> Col. Jerry Siegel, creator of "Superman," arrived on a Pacific island, where he immediately was asked why Superman doesn't end the war. He wrote this reply for the *Midpacifican:* Superman realizes it would be an imposition of him to barge in brazenly and singlehandedly win democracy's battle against tyranny and fascism. He understands that freedom is a precious commodity that both individuals and nations should have the right to earn their own salvation. Further, he has the utmost confidence in the ability of the United Nations to emerge triumphant from the conflict. Positive of our eventual victory, he

confines his wartime activities to aiding servicemen and servicewomen in their private difficulties.[44]

Meeting Burroughs and answering the question all happened before "Take a Break" took off, indicating that Jerry knew it was time to try something different. Like many American boys, Jerry had grown up quite a bit during the war, though in different, much less physical and psychological ways. Still, as always, he was the observer, the outsider looking in. But there was a great importance to that role. When it was time for him to leave, in 1946, the paper ran this article:

"SUPERMAN" TURNS BAKER—BY REQUEST
T4 Jerry Siegel, the Stars and Stripes "Take a Break"
columnist and creator of Superman, is wondering whether he
should have called upon the "Man of Steel" to help him with
a Sunday night detail. Currently at the Army Personnel
Center, Oahu, awaiting transportation home and his
discharge, Siegel pulled detail as a baker's helper. "I was
rolling in dough," he quipped in typical "Take a Break"
style.[45]

Even as an observer to war, Jerry had become part of it, which is why the jokes never stopped. When the potatoes were peeled, and he finally got home, there was something new waiting for him in Cleveland. A son.
Two of them.

South Sioux City Public Library
2121 Dakota Avenue
South Sioux City, NE 68776

Chapter 19
Superboy

J ERRY STARED INTO THE FACE of this boy before him. The baby was no longer pink and red but had a face and hair and could walk and say things. While Jerry was in Hawaii, Bella had been trying to teach him "Daddy." Jerry had brought home a small mountain of toys, including a red plastic car. When the little boy ran all around the yard, they called him "Superboy." Jerry remembered when this started, nearly two years earlier on January 29, 1944, in *The Plain Dealer:*

> A SON IS BORN TO SUPERMAN AUTHOR
> Superman is a father—at least his creator, Jerry Siegel, is.
>
> Siegel, now a corporal in the army, arrived home yesterday after his wife gave birth to a nine-pound boy Thursday morning at Mount Sinai Hospital. Siegel is the author of the comic strip which appears daily and Sunday in the Plain Dealer.
>
> He is stationed at Fort Meade, Va., and received a furlough while on maneuvers in West Virginia. His home is at 2402 Glendon Road, University Heights.[1]

Time magazine ran a similar announcement on February 14, 1944: "Born. To Corporal Jerry (Superman author) Siegel, 29, and Mrs. Bella Siegel, 22: their first superbaby [a son] in Cleveland. Weight: nine pounds."[2] So much of Jerry's life could be measured in newsprint. When he was drafted, Bella was, at most, already two months pregnant. The timing here was very common. Jerry runs a joke in "Take a Break" claiming that "vital statistics for 1944 indicate that a lot of people went stork mad."[3]

When Jerry got leave in 1944 for the birth of his son, he got to check in with Joe and the boys. Jerry and Joe had submitted a new comic called *Superboy* way back in 1938 when National was interested in expansion.[4] After it was rejected, Jerry submitted a full script in 1940.[5] It was rejected again, but there was the hint at least that it was a question of timing and that National could possibly move forward in the future. As he always did, Jerry kept tweaking and resubmitting, and he did so again right before he left for Hawaii. The concept itself was as old as *Action Comics #1*, where an infant Clark is shown lifting a chair over his head. Jerry always liked that image and thought a story about a young Superman would be a great opportunity.

While Jerry was in Hawaii, Joe Shuster was doing the same thing he always did: drawing. The city was gray, though there were yellow ribbons around the trees and fewer men everywhere. And lots more babies. But Joe still mostly just drew. But he also wanted to help the effort, so he produced some exclusive drawings for *The Golden Gate Guardian* in San Francisco and did a one-page comic for the Thirtieth C.B. unit of the Thirtieth U.S. Navy Construction Battalion.[6] He also moved the studio back to New York City, at the insistence of editorial. He didn't want to, not really, but without Jerry, National wanted them close and Joe didn't feel like disagreeing. Not now.

In Hawaii, Jerry had gotten a letter from Joe, dated October 1, 1944:

> *Jerry, there is something quite important in the wind here and I want to write about it and give you a firsthand picture. I was assigned to do a 5 page release of the feature SUPERBOY to be used in MORE FUN COMICS. This feature, I know, is one of your original ideas which you tried to get out last summer. . . . Since then, nothing was said about it until the assignment was given to me. I've just finished the job and have been trying to get a copy to send to you.[7]*

Jerry felt angry and instantly very isolated: *Harry had gone ahead and okayed the title without telling him—or paying for it?* He couldn't believe it—but at the same time he absolutely could. But he was also puzzled by Joe's words—"I've just finished the job"—*Joe drew it anyway?*[8]

Superboy was really inevitable, like the stories of young George

Washington chopping down the cherry tree or even the Junior Federal Men. Jerry was very smart—he knew that kids were buying *Superman,* so making a youthful Superman was just good thinking:

> Thousands of followers of the great Superman have asked the answers to these questions: "What is the story of Superman's origins?"—and "What was Superman like before he grew to man's estate—was he just an ordinary boy, or was he a super-boy?" For these stories will deal with . . . Superboy.[9]

Just as Superman was partly inspired by the great strongmen, so was Superboy perhaps shaped by the physical fitness lifestyle. Galen Gough was a famous strongman who was often featured in *Physical Culture.* Gough could supposedly cure himself of any disease by sheer force of will, and his signature act was to let a six-ton truck drive over his chest. He also circled the Washington Monument from a plane, dangling from a wire clenched between his teeth. He once, notoriously, went on a beer-only diet for over a month. After retiring from the circuit, he became a painter and showed his work in galleries in New York. Galen had a son, Wallace, born in 1937, who was billed as the "world's strongest baby." Wallace, "a muscle-man in three-cornered pants," reportedly "learned how to stand within days of his birth and swing on a homemade trapeze within weeks. . . . When he was two he could tear a telephone book in half." His story was picked up by the Associated Press and was the subject of a newsreel. "We'll make him a Superman," his daddy said. Soon they started calling young Wallace "Little Hercules" and "the Superboy."[10]

So when the first official *Superboy* adventure was published in *More Fun Comics* #101, the first portion of the story is Jerry's script with Joe (and the shop) providing art. But then, abruptly, the tone changes as writer Don Cameron is brought in to finish the rest. National published Jerry's initial submission; they counted it as a work-for-hire, and therefore they owned it. But they never entered into an actual agreement with Jerry. This would prove a costly mistake.

As soon as Jerry got home, he made plans to move the back to Cleveland again and resume his duties. National said no. Jerry couldn't understand why. As far as *Superboy* went, National claimed they published it to placate Jerry, but since they were at the same time claiming ownership of it, Jerry was furious.[11] They had done it to him *again*. But this time Jerry wasn't going to back down. He felt lean and stronger after being in uniform for so long. So in April 1947, Jerry and Joe sued National for $5 million and the rights to both Superboy and Superman.[12]

Jerry had a hard time convincing Joe to go along with it, but eventually Joe fell victim to Jerry's sway. After weeks in court in a white building in Westchester, New York, the decision by J. Addison Young on November 21, 1947, was as follows:

> It is quite clear to me however, that in publishing Superboy, the Detective Comics, Inc. acted illegally. I cannot accept defendants view that Superboy was in reality Superman. I think Superboy was a separate and distinct entity.[13]

Publishing *Superboy* was a mistake for National, as the evidence revealed it had clearly been originated by Jerry. But the judge ruled that National still owned Superman as a *separate* entity.[14] The case brought forth stories of Jerry constantly asking for raises and accusations of him even buying plots from ghostwriters.[15] Joe was barely drawing anything at this point, and it came out that Harry had paid for an eye operation for him. But in the end, it came down to the law: the boys had officially sold them Superman, but not Superboy. Both sides appealed into the next year. The case, which involved a lot of talk about the timeline of what was submitted and when, was settled with the help of someone Jerry met in the army named Albert Zugsmith. He was not their lawyer, or even a lawyer at all, but Zugsmith convinced Jerry that he could speak for him.[16]

Time reported that "Siegel & Shuster filed a super-suit for $5,000,000," demanding "the rights to their creation." By now, the general plight of the comics artist was well-known enough that only a short explanation was necessary: "(Like most comic-strippers they had signed away all rights.)" But the case had an unexpected outcome: Albert Zugsmith, a "newspaper broker" who acted as their representative, helped the parties reach an agreement whereby National Comics Publications, Inc., paid Jerry and Joe $100,000 in exchange for Superman and "a comic called Superboy."[17]

Jerry and Joe were in debt, needed cash, and may have been advised by Zugsmith that National might win an appeal. So they settled, losing both

Superboy and Superman. But the money went to paying their legal team and presumably Zugsmith himself. Jerry and Joe got a final check—and were promptly shown the door by National.[18] During some of the court proceedings in Westchester, Jerry would sometimes imagine Superman standing or sitting in places near him, kind of like a ghost. When they left the courtroom, they left alone. Superman had been, in the judge's own words, "separated" from Jerry and Joe. The creation that had brought them fame, houses, money, and respect had been cut from their lives like an arm or a leg or a heart. The result was a moral victory for the Superboy issue, but the settlement was emotionally hollow. For the past ten years, both Jerry and Joe had been the secret part of another, larger identity. All they had left, they felt, was what they had started with: that feeling of being small, meek, and alone. In their minds, they had nothing. Nothing.

HUMAN

Jerry Siegel found himself looking at a balloon drifting slowly across the Waldorf-Astoria's main ballroom. Someone had taken a marker and sketched a face on it. It grinned stupidly as it bumped up against the columns. From the floor, somebody pointed and laughed uproariously. Men in rumpled tuxes drank from glasses of brown Scotch, smoked fat cigars, and belly laughed around circular tables with clean white tablecloths. Very few of them danced. It was April Fools' Day 1948, and this was the Cartoonists Ball in New York City.[19]

Jerry was in a daze. The settlement had lined their pockets a bit, but there were lots of bills to pay. He glanced around nervously. He knew everyone there was talking about him. He thought he saw Al Capp. He could almost see the famous movies that had been filmed here. He had heard Marlon Brando might actually be coming to judge the costume contest. Jerry sipped his drink and felt he was going to choke. His eyebrows went up. He was trying. He checked again. He felt as though his heart were beating in his fingertips; *am I having a heart attack?* This was a common thought for him lately.

Excised from Superman, Jerry and Joe had convinced themselves they could do it again with *Funnyman,* their new big comic book about an unlikely hero who used comedy gags to defeat his enemies. They even pitched the idea to Jack Liebowitz, who turned it down.[20] They then took it to their old editor Vin Sullivan, who was now at Magazine Enterprises.[21] In *Funnyman,* they tried to change the superhero paradigm completely, and in some ways, the character prefigures the Silver Age. But people weren't ready, and in some cases the jokes were just not that good.[22] There had not been a lot to laugh about lately. The book would flop in a month or so, only to be replaced by a syndicated newspaper strip that would last a bit longer before it was reimagined as *Reggie Van Twerp.*[23] But even with all the good Joe art (especially in the newspaper version), it just wouldn't fly. It's not that it was bad, it just was not *Superman.* To make matters even worse, a fifteen-part *Superman* movie serial from Columbia starring Kirk Alyn was set to debut later that year. It was going to be the first time Superman would be played by a real person on the big screen. Jerry knew that Whit was somehow involved and no doubt making more money.[24]

Jerry stared up at the ceiling again and his head was pulsing. He couldn't even think of facing Bella. He looked around again, trying to avoid everyone else's eyes. Joe was also coming to the costume ball, but not alone.[25] He was bringing Joan Carter with him, the girl who all those years ago posed at Joe's house as Lois Lane. She had changed her name again, but just a little, to "Joanne." Joe had kept in touch with her for many of those years, writing back and forth as she moved across the country. During World War II, Joanne worked in California building battleships. *Lois the Riveter,* Jerry thought. He had heard she had been in Miami last.[26] He thought of all the little references to her they had put in their comics and wondered if she had seen them. Tonight, he would find out.

Jerry felt a single finger on his shoulder and turned around and stopped: there was Dixie Dugan, the cartoon character, come to life with a pixie haircut and a beautiful dress. Realizing it was Joanne in costume, Jerry said something, or he hoped he did. She looked like a movie star. Joe had taken her to the Brooks costume company and rented an enormous ball gown for her.[27] Joe had moved back to New York permanently, so he knew all the places like that. Joanne did not look the same. Her smile was wide and her eyes were bright, though there was a sadness there. *Was this happening?* They played music. There was dancing. And Joe was somewhere. And then he was not. And then the night was over in a blur of laughter and promises. And Jerry and Joanne were talking and laughing, together. It was like a movie. And Jerry was still married.

On July 15, 1948, just over three months later, Bella Siegel sued her husband for "gross neglect of duty and extreme cruelty."[28] About ten days later she filed for divorce, citing "differences which have arisen between them, rendering it impossible for them longer to live together as husband and wife." Their assets were listed as $15,000 in savings bonds, a 1947 Chrysler, $25,000 on deposit in New York, life policies at $30,000 ($5,000 for the baby), and "personal effects such as typewriter, Dictaphone, etc., used by Party of the second Part." The document also mentions that *Funnyman* was forthcoming and the plaintiff "will receive a remuneration in the future." The document mentions that though Jerry got $29,000 in settlement from the Westchester case, he still owed Uncle Sam $24,000.[29]

In Cleveland, Bella didn't care about the money. She spat curses and stamped her feet and cried her eyes out. She looked at her young son and her face fell. *He is a bad man,* she said. *He will never have you. He lost his chance. He wasn't good enough. He will never have you.*

Three months later, *The Plain Dealer* ran another, very different announcement:

SUPERMAN CREATOR WED
Siegel Takes Model as Bride in Ceremony Here
    Cleveland. Jerry Siegel, original creator of Superman, and
Miss Jolan Kovacs, a model known professionally as Joanne
Carter, were married at Hotel Commodore yesterday
afternoon at 2 by Justice of the Peace William J. Zoul. Siegel,
a Glenville High School graduate, gave his age as 33. He was
recently divorced by his first wife, Mrs. Bella Siegel of
University Heights, who sued for a decree July 15 charging
gross neglect of duty and extreme cruelty. Miss Kovacs, who
gave her age as 25, was divorced in 1945.[30]

Joanne and Jerry fell in love and married within seven months of the Cartoonists Ball. For Jerry, it was as if his stories had became real. They had their ceremony at the courthouse at 1214 Ontario Street. Joanne were a corsage. On their "Application for Marriage License," dated October 13, 1948, they are both listed as living at the Commodore, a nice residence hotel on Euclid Avenue. Joanne lists her occupation as "Asst. Writer and Model."[31] They were teenager happy. Joanne was also coming out of a period of great personal pain: her mother had died of lingering breast cancer in March of the same year, having been hospitalized in a state hospital for fifteen years.[32]

Jerry did not fight the divorce, so sole custody of their boy was awarded to Bella. Jerry was ordered to pay $25 per week in child support until his eighteenth birthday and 20 percent above any annual income over $10,000.[33] Bella had many claims:

> Defendant has absented himself from their home in Cleveland for long periods of time without giving any excuse or reasons for same and that during the short periods of time he was at home in Cleveland, he displayed a moody, quarrelsome and argumentative attitude toward the Plaintiff.
>
> Plaintiff further avers that Defendant has been guilty of other and additional acts of Gross Neglect of Duty, the evidence concerning which will be presented at the trial of this cause.
>
> Plaintiff further avers that she has at all times conducted herself as a faithful and dutiful wife and has performed all of the duties incumbent upon her.[34]

When Jerry's cousins would later run into Bella and her little boy down at a department store, Bella would pull him into the folds of her coat and rush out the door.[35] And just like that, another Siegel father disappeared.

STARS

Joe had been living in New York since the war. His sister, Jeanetta, was now known as Jean and was coming out to the city to be an actress, so the whole family moved—Joe bought them a house in Forest Hills.[36] Out from under Jerry's shadow, Joe had a freer lifestyle. He and his sister would often pal around town together. Jean would join him in wide-eyed amazement as they went to the Latin Quarter. Milton Berle would often be there, and when he recognized Joe, he said, "I want the creator of Superman!" and Joe stood up and took a bow. They went to the Riviera, where Desi Arnaz and his orchestra played, full of cymbals and pushing horns. They sat next to Lucille Ball's table. When Lucy and her friends got up to go to the ladies' room, Jean sneaked into the bathroom just to see what they were doing. The bathroom was big, with mirrors and chairs and perfume.[37]

They went to see *The Red Mill*—an operetta about two young Americans trying to get out of poverty—and Joe couldn't take his big eyes off one of the lead girls. So after the show, he went backstage with some flowers and asked her to dinner. They went out for a while; he would take her out every night and bring her flowers or little transistor radios. Jean even went with them on a double date. The girl was tall and gorgeous. But, as his sister said, "it wasn't anything serious."[38]

After the Superboy fiasco happened, Joe wondered if he should have handled it differently. His eyes weren't good and he had to wear a stiff leather glove because his wrist hurt so much. Things got worse when his father, whom he was named after and who had always supported him in the best ways that sons remember, died of lung cancer in 1948 just shy of his sixtieth birthday.

And Joanne came to New York again, which was a wonderful surprise.

And so Joe asked her to the ball. But afterward, she was with Jerry.

And Joe went home alone.

Chapter 20

Fifties

THE MAIL WORKER IN WASHINGTON, D.C., dumped out a white cascade of stiff envelopes onto the steel table. The man sighed—it was like this every day, letters from nut jobs and paranoids all over the country. That's the kind of mail the FBI was getting in 1951. Peeking out from the pile was a letter with a return address from Long Island. By the time this particular letter was read by a screening agent, it was alarming enough to be not only kept but forwarded to the director for a closer look.

The letter begins "Dear Friend," as the writer praises the FBI for their frequent articles against comics. But the writer wonders why the FBI never looked into "the background of the publishers." The writer admits that he used to write comics himself and piled them high with "hair-raising excitement and blood-shed" only because it would "sell to the kids. We knew it paid off in big money."

The writer tries to lure the FBI into digging deeper into National Comics by insinuating that before they got "on the comics gravy train," these publishers had sordid pasts, including "criminal or communist records . . . and publishing lewd magazines with titles like 'Hot Stories' and 'Paris Nights.'" He even claims that National's publishers paid off educators to write "pro-comics articles."

The writer personally laments that these men

> have maneuvered me to a point where I am destitute and they continue
> making enormous profits from my creation. Any day I expect to be extra-
> dited and prosecuted for non-support of my child due to lack of funds.

He closes with a hope that when people see "SUPERMAN the symbol of glorious justice," that they "think of me, his destitute creator." It is signed, "Jerry Siegel," and is followed by the complete home addresses of Jack Liebowitz, Harry Donenfeld, and Paul Sampliner.[1] The naming names mind-set of the Cold War was becoming an easy tool for anyone with a grudge. The lawsuit had been settled, *Funnyman* had failed, and the money was largely spent (as it always was). Jerry wanted revenge against Liebowitz, Donenfeld, and even Sampliner for all the crimes he felt they had committed against him.

Jerry thought this information would be enough to start a formal investigation of Harry. Someone important at the FBI wrote him back:

> *Dear Mr. Siegel:*
> *I have read with interest your recent letter, which was received at this*
> *Bureau on November 28, 1951, and I appreciate your letting me*
> *have your observations in connection with the matters you discuss.*
>
> *In view of your expressed interest, I am enclosing some material*
> *which reflects my own views regarding the relation of unrestrained*
> *"crime comics" and the alarming juvenile delinquency rate with which*
> *the nation is faced.*
>
> > *Sincerely yours,*
> > *John Edgar Hoover*
> > *Director*[2]

On the FBI's copy, there are scrawled notes from the agent in charge of vetting the letter:

> ATTENTION SAC: Correspondent is not readily identifiable in Bufiles.
> They can't identify him one Communist Activities in NY another in Ziegfeld Follies and another in Brooklyn in 1949 who urged Senator Ives against ratification of Clark to the Supreme Court. Is the signature his???

The FBI not only didn't care, they didn't even know who Jerry was. The highest intelligence officer in the country, perhaps even the world, didn't know Jerry's name, yet all over the country people were consuming Superman. That same year, Robert L. Lippert released the full-length feature *Superman and the Mole-Men* in black-and-white, starring a stocky actor named George Reeves who had a wonderful Superman smile. For generations, he was what people would think of when they heard "Superman."

On September 12, 1952, in a congressional hearing room, William F. McDermott stood in front of a committee and took up the issue of how existing law could affect the avalanche of what they termed "lurid magazines" that were littering the stands and minds of America. This wasn't just comics, but paperback fiction as well—a certain John O'Hara book cover subject was singled out because "she had no face. Only legs."[3]

Back in Cleveland, these protests had begun some time earlier. On March 19, 1952, *The Plain Dealer* reports:

> Vigorous protests against "censorship were voiced yesterday at a Council meeting hearing on Councilman Joseph E. Flannery's proposed antismut, anticrime publication ordinance. Flannery . . . was the sole speaker in favor of his measure. . . . March Hambers, high school senior, petitioned with 11,000 signatures in support of the ordinance. L. Quincy Mumford, head of Cleveland Public Library, was one of several speakers in opposition.[4]

Flannery was young, with slicked-back hair and a bow tie. He looked believable. Cleveland was actually one of the first cities to crusade against comics. On the cover of the May 14, 1949, *Plain Dealer* two detectives are pictured mowing through a stack of comics and pulps:

> For several hours . . . members of the police department, accustomed to remaining cool under harrowing conditions, grappled with quick shooting desperados, dagger-armed toughs and threats of wholesale destructions. Patrolman Donald McNea and Policewoman Margaret Kilbane simply leaned back in their chairs and turned more pages in their comic books. Pictures of flame-spurting pistols, intended to stir the emotions of comic book addicts, intensified the seriousness of their assignment.[5]

The article reveals that the two detectives were charged with studying, at the Police Women's Bureau,

350 so-called comic books for possible violation of a new city ordinance banning sale of volumes containing immoral or obscene matter. . . . "I have no intention of carrying the comics to my living room," said Kilbane. "Comics are a good thing generally," said McNea, "but when these books portray violence against the police, use of vulgarity or torture they have gotten out of hand."[6]

Jerry sent another version of his angry letter to the U.S. Science Service on November 26, 1951. President Watson Davis read it and shook his head. He attached his card and wrote in pen: "Who is campaigning against comics?" One of his colleagues answers below in pencil: "I dunno!" The name "Siegel" is circled. Davis asks more seriously: "Do you know anything about this?" The penciler responds: "This man seems to be like Rose O'Neill. Cut out of the profits on his own artistic invention. And he is sore!" O'Neill was the famous artist who created the incredibly popular image of the Kewpie doll—and whose first husband stole all of her money. Davis responds: "I know nothing about the situation." Davis's job as president and editor of the U.S. Science Service was to popularize science as a field of study (he would later go on to revolutionize libraries by transferring resources to microfilm). He didn't know what to make of this guy.[7]

During all of this, Jerry was still desperately trying to make comics. Ironically, he actually turned to the subjects that the comics crusades were targeting. In 1950, he was writing the syndicated newspaper strip *Tallulah,* which was an unauthorized portrayal of celebrity sexpot Tallulah Bankhead, though her last name is (smartly) never used.[8]

The entertainment columnist Walter Winchell, whom Jerry always read in *Variety,* makes note of *Tallulah* on May 9, 1950:

Tallulah—the Bankhead of the stage and screen—is fired at The Tribune.

Among other newspapers, that is. She frowns upon all newspapers that publish the new comic strip, "Tallulah," that blonde siren of the typewriter keys who wisecracks each day at the top of the Trib-Strip double page.

Tallulah, the actress, is quoted by her attorneys as saying she intends to sue. That's HER name, she says, and its use on a comics strip is "offensive and humiliating."[9]

Jerry was adopting the same tactics as the companies who sought to cash in on Superman rip-offs. Though the strip would be renamed *Jezebel* for a time, it didn't last long after that.

Since Jerry wasn't writing big superheroes, he had to cherry-pick freelance jobs with the outlying publishers: *Jon Juan* for Toby Press, which featured Alex Schomburg on art and proudly advertised its author as "the Creator of Superman." Jerry also did the space opera *Lars of Mars* with Murphy Anderson at Ziff-Davis in May 1951.[10] Back on the home front, he wrote the first comic book titled *G.I. Joe,* which took place in Korea. Ziff was so impressed with Jerry's pedigree that they made him a very generous offer to edit their new comics line. Their offices were in the Empire State Building, and their imagined potential was limitless. When someone at a meeting asked, "What about Shuster?" Jerry looked out the broad window and replied: "We'll find work for Joe if he wants it. . . . I'll be the editor and part of management. Frankly, at this point, Shuster's not involved."[11] The people in the room wondered if they were even friends anymore. Ziff published a number of titles and had star artists but stopped work after about a year. Once again, Jerry Siegel was out of a job.

Jerry's life with Joanne was day to day, schlepping for work in the comics business and living on Long Island. They spent the Christmas holidays and some long summer days on the beach with his old Glenville friend Bernie Schmittke and his family in New Jersey.[12] Things brightened even further on March 1, 1951, with the birth of Jerry and Joanne's daughter, Laura. She was a blessing, but they worried how they would provide for her. This question took on new anger when Jerry heard about a new *Superman* television show. The films had done so well that there was going to be a Kellogg's syndicated program called *Adventures of Superman* starring George Reeves. The show would run until 1958 (and evolve into color) with Reeves in the lead and Phyllis Coates and Noel Neill as Lois Lane.[13]

Adventures was going to be produced by Robert Maxwell and his old acquaintance Whitney Ellsworth. Jerry knew the show would be a gigantic
hit and that Ellsworth would make a fortune.[14] But he was also jealous
simply because Ellsworth would be involved.

At this point in his life, with a new baby and completely separated
from the one thing that should have been making him rich and happy,
Jerry did something even more dramatic than his *Torch* poem to Lois
Amster: he went on a public hunger strike. The bigger newspapers ig-
nored it, but the Long Island locals ran it. The article, which told how
Jerry was broke while Superman was about to make millions on a television show, contained the one thing it absolutely needed to have: a small,
sad photograph of the young family. National knew that if his hunger
strike did continue, the photo—of a father almost saying good-bye to his
baby daughter—would be everywhere. So when the mail came, Jerry
started seeing checks for $250 a month, then later $135 a week.[15] He
started eating again, though it is unclear if he ever stopped.

The other event that set Jerry off also had to do with television but had
no connection to National. On May 25, 1952, Jerry tuned in to NBC's
Goodyear Television Playhouse, which was an hour-long program on Sunday nights. He was amazed to see "The Lantern Copy," a story about the
shady world of cartooning that was written by David Shaw. *Variety* said
the show, about "the moral breakdown" of a man driven by "greed and
vengeance," was "sharply realistic." The comics writer in the story, a
"one-time idealist," is driven by the "dog-eat-dog" comics industry to
destroy the career of his former artist.[16]

Jerry was sure the story was based on him. Besides painting the writer
as greedy, it showed him as being utterly ruthless to his artist. Jerry was
so angry that he sued NBC. As *Editor and Publisher* reported:

> A $1,000,000 damage suit was filed in New York State Su-
> preme Court this week against the National Broadcasting
> Co. . . . by Jerry Siegel, who in 1935 originated the "Super-
> man" comic strip. Mr. Siegel's complaint charges that the plot
> of a television play called "The Lantern Copy" broad-cast May
> 25 closely parallels his own career to a point, but portrays the
> cartoonist as "a person of immoral, vicious, disreputable and
> criminal character and nature."[17]

Making everything worse, *Adventures of Superman* finally hit the airwaves, and it hurt like an invisible death ray. Later, on a cold day in New York, Joanne and Jerry, huddled close, watched as George Reeves walked right by them. Joanne had been friends with George years earlier when she worked in a Hollywood nightclub. She urged Jerry to speak up and tell him his story, but Jerry's voice lost all of its breath.

NEW YORK HORROR

Across the bridge in Queens, it was getting dark outside. The noises in the hallway had finally stopped, for the most part. The man upstairs had dragged his heels to bed. Joe sat at his table and sighed, remembering older dining room tables long ago and far away. He wondered who lived in the old house back in Cleveland now.

His sister, Jean, was doing well. She was on her way to Miami to do a one-woman comedy music show.[18] Joe lived with Frank, who had settled down somewhat and would get a good job working for Nielsen doing the TV ratings charts. He had the Shuster creative streak as well. Joe still felt it was his job to take care of his family. In *The New York Times* on November 23, 1954, almost twenty years to the day of his Thanksgiving cartoon triumph in *The Torch,* the following ad ran in the classifieds:

Artist—Creator of Superman
Accepting limited amount advertising, television and
educational-comics.
D200 Times.[19]

And then on December 20:

For Advertising, Sales Promotion, Education and Information
Comics-Cartoon Productions top
Art Director: Joe Shuster
Comadic Productions
31 Park Row, New York 38 NY

Season's Greetings to all our Friends, everywhere.
The best . . . at piggy bank rates[20]

Whether it was through this ad or not, word got to Joe that someone wanted to hire him. He listened carefully but shook his head. As desperate as he was, he turned it down.

Eventually, though, Joe changed his mind. So he got out his paper and pencils and started. He stalled by spending a lot of time on the background with shaded walls and shadowy corners. He drew in some furniture and windows and tables. He then started on the figures with the old familiar shapes: a block for the chest, long circular ovals for the arms, shorter ones for the fingers, and a small oval for the head. Then he did the detail work, stopping at points to add depth. There was the chiseled chest, the ears, the chin, and that thick shock of hair. And those set, lined eyes. He couldn't help but smile, even now. That's why he did it. But he knew what was coming next. He had stalled long enough. He checked the notes to make sure and got started. He drew a whip in the hand, brandished at the nude woman he had drawn previously, who looked just like good old Lois Lane. Then he drew a devil, shaded heavily in black with an eerie sneer. He was glad his mother couldn't see this one. He hunched over the table, just in case. Hours later, the inking mostly dry, he looked at it.

After slipping the art into his case, Joe left the next day for Times Square. Frank didn't know where he was going; no one did. He walked into the store, his peripheral vision on overdrive. The man looked at the pictures quickly: *You can go in back. These look great.* Then: *Here's your money. I got some new stories for ya.* Joe took it, stuffed it in his pocket, and left.

As the months went on, Joe would illustrate dozens of dirty stories for a variety of under-the-counter magazines, most notably the *Nights of Horror* series. They were small, thin paperbacks with one-color printing. The stories were awful. The whole thing was bad, and Joe knew it, but at least he was drawing again. The *Nights of Horror* books would later be linked to a series of horrific murders in Brooklyn, but when Joe was drawing, it was just a secret new identity.[21] For one, all theories of Joe having lost his eyesight by the end of his Superman tenure and having to rely on ghost artists for everything must be completely dismissed by these drawings. It may be unnerving for some to see Clark, Lois, and Jimmy involved in weird acts of bondage, but there is no mistaking the pedigree. Joe might have looked at it as the ultimate revenge against National. Something made him put so much work into it.

The publisher of *Nights of Horror* was Eddie Mishkin, the owner of some of the seedier bookstores in Times Square. In 1959, the police started intense surveillance of Mishkin's secret warehouse. Mishkin, his printer, and at least two writers were among those detained, including a writer whose alias was "Justin Kent."[22] The court case revealed that Mishkin had made a lot off his books. He paid fairly well, too: for a single drawing, artists "got $30 or $35" for a cover and "$10 or $15" a page for interiors. Mishkin dealt only in cash, at either one of his bookstores or a bar he owned on Forty-second Street called Dino's.[23]

If he wasn't contacted directly, Joe might have initially heard about Mishkin at the Cartoonists and Illustrators School on Eighty-ninth Street. Now called the School of Visual Arts, Joe taught there once in a while. Artist Dick Ayers would remember that Joe would come in "not just to talk; he came in and he sat beside you and chatted with you, real nice. He'd just come in and visit like a regular guy."[24] It is here that he may also have met Eric Stanton, who attended the school with studio partner Steve Ditko, who would go on to co-create Spider-Man and the surrealist magician-hero Dr. Strange. Stanton, who would become a significant fetish artist himself, was one of the first to sell work to Mishkin.[25]

Joe also did similar drawings for magazines other than *Nights of Horror,* some of them even signed. He didn't have to, he knew, but he did anyway, almost as if the picture were daring him. In all the years of Jerry coming up with ridiculous pen names, Joe had been party to it only once, in the early days of Legar and Reuths. But this was different. Still, he would keep it simple. He wouldn't dig out archaic cousins or old pulp names. Maybe he even wanted someone to figure it out. So he took his name and shortened it: "Joe Shuster" squeezed together to become "Josh." And he finished his signature with his trademark tail.

Joe also did work for the illustrated magazine *It's Continental,* which may have lasted only one issue:

 **A WOMAN'S WORLD**

The essence of cartooning is simplicity for the sake of exaggeration. Based on hair, the hint of a costume, and the unavoidable muscles, this is Lois about to whip a bound Superman.[26] Given that Joanne married Jerry, Joe, who always drew parts of himself into Superman, might have felt he was being punished. Or punishing himself.[27]

A very interesting *Continental* cartoon titled "Judge's Ruling" depicts a stern-faced judge ready to deliver a sentence—on the reader.[28]

Joe may have been thinking here of the 1947 court case—or the fear that he would go before another court for drawing these very cartoons.

Doing these sorts of comics, especially in the mid-1950s, was risky. But Joe did it anyway. And just as he and Jerry always did, they used the truths of their own lives to make their art. Joe punished Superman in these drawings as an act of self-flagellation—did Joe feel responsibility and regret for losing Superman, too? At arguably the lowest point of his life, drawing dirty pictures in semianonymity, Joe was taking stock. In a four-page comic he does for *Continental,* he introduces a spy, "Secret Agent Z-4," who slinks around in black leather and tantalizes everyone she meets. Her name is very familiar to Joe, the name of his old girlfriend, Annette.[29]

A few weeks after turning in some of his work, Joe got a letter from his sister, Jean. She had made the westward move from Miami, and she and her boyfriend were going to be married shortly. *She sounds happy,* thought

Joe. *Finally.* She was a good singer, but show business lasted only so long. Now she could have a real life. Jean closed her letter that day thanking Joe from the bottom of her heart for taking that secret job he had hinted at but never told her about—and for the large amount of money he had sent her to get settled. Jean and William Peavy would have a long and fruitful life together in Texas; he would write a bestselling book entitled *Super Nutrition Gardening.* Jean would teach classes on food and exercise for two decades. They would have two children, Warren and Dawn. Jean didn't know all of this yet, of course, but she had a feeling, as she often did. So she thanked her dear brother yet again. When she would find out, years later, what the job actually was, she cried at what her brother had done for her.[30]

On February 6, 1958, Joe declined an invitation to the Alexander Hamilton thirtieth anniversary reunion in Cleveland.[31] He said he was working on something he couldn't get away from. He sent his regrets and closed the door to his apartment slowly. He felt it wasn't going to be possible to go outside for some time; he felt very tired. Joe began to retreat. He began to disappear. The Brooklyn thrill killers had been caught and tried a few years earlier, but it still made him uneasy. The papers had covered every lurid detail of how four underage boys killed two people and tortured others in ways possibly inspired by the *Nights of Horror* illustrations.[32] The leader of the gang sported a sad, half-Hitler mustache and was the exact opposite of Superman.[33] Joe stopped drawing for a little while then, for maybe the first time. Though other writers were held as material witnesses for months and Mishkin eventually went to prison, Joe escaped scrutiny, which was a testament either to Mishkin's loyalty or to Joe's own increasing anonymity.[34] Though the evidence was shockingly unmistakable, no one had any idea who Joe, or "Josh," really was.

At around this time, another story goes that Joe was found sleeping on a park bench:

> A policeman picked him up, took him to a lunch counter and bought him a hamburger and coffee. "He asked me what I did for a living. I told him I was a cartoonist. I was too embarrassed to say I drew Superman. He asked me to draw some pictures on the back of a menu. He was amazed. Then the waitress came over. Then kids at the counter. After a while, they wanted my

autograph. I used to sit in Central Park in summer, watching kids read Superman and wondering if anyone would believe me."[35]

On the same day this story would be reported, years later, a *Peanuts* cartoon ran in which Linus sits with a classic Schulz frown. Peppermint Patty asks him, "I don't understand this blanket business, Linus. . . ." Linus stands up, his hands over his stomach. She questions him: "Like, now . . . what do you do when your blanket is gone?" Linus answers, "You suffer a lot, and you look for substitutes."[36]

Chapter 21

Invisible Kid

S EVERAL SUBWAY STOPS AWAY, Jerry shuffled his feet in desperation. Determined to stay in comics, he had been doing more outside work as well, this time for the publishing company Charlton. In 1956, he did two issues of *Mr. Muscles,* a comic about a wrestler named Brett Carson who gets superstrength and fights crime. He had a costume of red and black with a garish yellow "M" on it.[1] Jerry also did *Nature Boy,* about a guy in shorts who is granted the powers of the four elements.[2] He had another newspaper strip appear, the 1954 private eye thriller *Ken Winston,* with artist Ogden Whitney, though it too was short-lived.[3]

In early 1957, Joanne went home to Cleveland. Her father, Mike, who had been living in a home, suffering from cancer, passed away on February 24.[4] When she came back to Long Island, she made a call to a place she and Jerry never really talked about. She made a call to an office in Manhattan: National. She was taking charge.

Jerry was mad but accepted it, eventually. He was soon on the subway, because he knew that no matter how mad he was, something had to change. He was, unbelievably, going back to National.[5] It was a very long ride on that train and up that elevator, with the steady yellow light and just the hint of music. There were still members of the old guard there. When he saw Jack Liebowitz again, a little fatter but not by much, Jerry forced a smile. Even after taking him to court and causing a mess over Superboy, Jerry went back to Jack. It might have been the most humiliating thing he had ever done, but these were people who dealt in serial adventure—things always moved forward. They had to. Jack hired him back on the spot. *It was business,* they said.[6]

The plan was that Jerry would go to work immediately on scripts for the Superman titles. Another smile came, this one more genuine. Jerry would be paid the standard rate and would be given a lot of work, but he would get none of the extras and raises that he had ten years ago. And he would never get a byline. He would report to Mort Weisinger, who was now editing the Superman "family," as it was then called.[7]

The hardest thing about seeing all these people again was realizing how they had surpassed him in the genre he had invented: Julie Schwartz, Otto Binder, and Edmond Hamilton all had positions of power at the new National. Even the scary, lumbering Herbie Siegel was still there, snoring away at his desk. The irony of the whole situation did not escape Jerry. He was going to write Superman's adventures again—in complete disguise.

At the time of Jerry's rehire, superhero comics had taken a fairly drastic swerve from the last time he had written Superman. The moral, slightly subversive drama of Jerry's time had given way to a level of science fiction that was completely ridiculous. This era of comics, past the horror scare of the fifties (and in part to assuage it), was dominated by sight gags, play-it-straight absurdist romance, and bright, multicolored craziness. This was the Silver Age of comics. It was here, stripped of all identity, that Jerry Siegel perhaps did the best work of his writing career. For though he invented Superman with Joe, it was here that so many elements of the modern Superman came into full being: Superman's cousin Supergirl, the silly Bizarro, the alien Braniac, the noble Legion of Super-Heroes, Superboy, and even Krypto the Superdog. Jerry had an invisible hand in the growth of all of them.[8]

Jerry worked mainly from his home in Long Island.[9] He took the train into the city only when necessary. When he did, he would look down at his hands as they passed through Queens and wonder what he would do if Joe walked in off the platform. He heard the doors push open and felt the cold air rush in as it wrestled with the warmth inside the train. He wondered what he would do.

So Jerry worked instead of wondered. The new stories were almost polar opposites of the smirking *Action* #1 Superman who beat up cowardly husbands and terrorized corrupt lobbyists. Whereas *Action* was trying to wrest itself from the Depression in anticipation of World War II, the Silver Age mirrored the falseness of the fifties: domestic perfection as a disguise for all the underlying tensions. Stuck at home with a baby and unsure of his place in the world, Jerry was the perfect person to write the Silver Age. And Superman was the perfect vehicle.

GLINT

The Silver Age Superman was now active in only one important mission: fighting off man-crazy Lois Lane and his old childhood sweetheart, the red-haired Lana Lang.[10] These two women would try everything in their power not only to uncover Superman's secret identity but to get him to propose. The letter columns were filled with statements like "Why do you have Supergirl with a red skirt sometimes and other times a blue one? Please explain. Bill Mason, Ontario, Canada." Editorial responds that her skirt is reversible to "avoid the monotony."[11] Jerry was good at this kind of humor and good with writing to an audience, so he fit in quickly. Though Weisinger himself would claim that he basically wrote all of Jerry's stories for him, there is too much of the old Jerry in the actual stories to ignore. So the first time Mort said something snide or tossed a script out a window, Jerry thought of his wife and shut up. And wrote and wrote and wrote.

Jerry did particularly well with the so-called Imaginary Stories that were popular at the time. These were Superman stories that occurred outside of the accepted continuity. This loophole allowed writers to tell new, previously off-limits stories that might not be possible because they would alter the basic principles of Superman—Clark, Superman, and Lois—to an unfixable degree. Jerry loved this type of thinking. In "The Unwanted Superbaby" in *Adventure Comics* #299, the premise is really a question: What if Superboy (who was now very popular) used his powers in public *before* the Kents were able to take him in? The results are disastrous: baby Kal-El is first captured by the government, then escapes, only to find the Kents don't want him. He ends up in an evil dictatorship until years later, as Superboy, he encounters a gold meteor in space, which is really gold kryptonite. The meteor (just as in the K-metal story) takes his powers away; he now needs glasses for real. The Kents finally adopt him, but he is forced to live the life he formerly only pretended to as a normal human being.[12] Just like the anonymous Jerry.

Supergirl was another addition to the mythos that Jerry really liked.

Kara Zor-El, Superman's cousin, arrives on Earth after her home colony, Argo City of Krypton, is destroyed. Adopting the identity of Linda Lee, Supergirl lives at an orphanage before being adopted. All the while, she works with Superman—in secret—until she is ready to go public. Jerry writes good dialogue for her, perhaps inspired by his feelings toward his own daughter. In another Imaginary Story, "The Bride of Mr. Mxyzptlk!," the dastardly imp gives Supergirl a gift by bringing her Kryptonian parents back to life. There is plenty of humor in the story, especially when Mr. Mxyzptlk changes Metropolis to a Bizarro City (complete with a store named "Oldest Fashions from Paris"). But the turning point of the story is the exact opposite of humor: after several scenes showing Supergirl enjoying time with her real parents, Mxy reveals that it was all a big prank and her parents are not real. Supergirl yells at him in a very ten-year-old voice: "I think you're an irritating, aggravating, annoying pest! I hate you! You're the greatest creep there ever was!"[13] It is a cruel story for the Maid of Might.

Supergirl was, in Superman's own terms, a "secret emergency weapon."[14] But over time, Superman believes it is time to announce her to the public. In *Action Comics* #285:

> She's every bit as powerful as Superman!
> She's terrific! Cute, too!
> What a Super-doll!
> She's gorgeous![15]

Superman uses a television broadcast from his Fortress to tell the world about his young cousin. The world rejoices as President Kennedy welcomes her mission to "preserve peace."[16]

Jerry also explores his familiar topic of proud fatherhood mixed with loss in *Superboy* #77. Clark and his father, Jonathan, are rummaging around the attic when Jonathan finds a marionette given to him by his father, Hiram. This launches a flashback sequence where Superbaby (his actual code name) makes up "cute feats" to wow an audience of adults. It is a good memory, though a lost one. In *Superboy* #78, "The Ghost of Jor-El," Superboy is confronted by his dead Kryptonian father: "Great Scott! It's the ghost of my father Jor-El, who died on the planet Krypton! He's . . . trying to say something!"[17] But it is really the imp Mr. Mxyzptlk (again) who taunts Clark with the illusion of Jor-El's ghost. The fourth-dimensional trickster revels in the deed: "Hee hee! I've got him this time! I've hit Superboy right where it really hurts . . . in his vulnerable heart."[18]

Jerry wrote stuff like this for years. He was quietly molding the Superman universe back into his own shattered image in complete secrecy. It was just like the flimsy disguise of Clark that always fools Lois and Lana: Jerry was almost trying to get people to recognize him—but they didn't.

THE TEENAGE DREAMS

The late fifties and early sixties also gave American culture other characters it had never really seen before: teenagers. Not docile, stay-at-home creatures, but ones who did weird things with their hair, took the car after school, and wore short skirts. Comics, the good ones, picked up on this and went to town. Though he did not create the concept, Jerry created much of the early history of the Legion of Super-Heroes. The initial concept by Otto Binder and Mort Weisinger was that teenage superheroes in the thirty-first century idolized the twentieth-century Superboy—and thus became heroes themselves. It remains one of the great new ideas in comics, but Binder left comics after the Legion's first appearance when he and a group of fellow creators began asking for basic health benefits. So in stepped Jerry.

The list of characters that Jerry introduced to the Legion included Bouncing Boy, Brainiac 5, Computo, Cosmic King, Duplicate Damsel, Glorith, Invisible Kid, Matter-Eater Lad, Lightning Lord, Phantom Girl, Chameleon Boy, Saturn Queen, Spider Girl, Sun Boy, and Ultra Boy, among many others.[19] The Legion was a high school sitcom in space years before *Happy Days* or *American Graffiti*: crazy teenagers in colorful costumes with yellow flight rings emblazoned with an "L" that allowed them to fly. They had a clubhouse, secret crushes, and almost unbearably innocent code names. Each member represented a different planet and had a different power. They were the ultimate Junior Federal Men Club—but with superpowers.

One of the most enduring of Jerry's creations was Chuck Taine, who first appeared in *Adventure* #329.[20] Chuck, an errand boy, mistakenly drinks a bottle of "liquid super-plastic" because he thought it was "soda-pop" (Jerry's use of "pop" belies his Ohio roots), and he transforms into the round, superelastic Bouncing Boy.[21] Like human Flubber, he is perhaps partly named after Chuck Taylor, whose famous rubber shoes were meant to give schoolyard athletes some bounce in their jump.[22] Bouncing Boy, who was overweight and a jokester, was the first slacker superhero and very much mirrored Jerry's new attitude toward comics (and his own middle-aged girth). In terms of comedy, there was also Matter-Eater Lad, who had the power to eat anything, including iron bars and ray guns. His home planet was named "Bismoll."[23]

One of Jerry's more intriguing creations for the Legion was Brainiac 5. Brainy, as he was called, was the nerdy boy scientist from the planet Colu with green skin and blond hair who created time bubbles and was sweet on Supergirl and who was able to join in the Legion's adventures through some old-fashioned time travel.[24] The Silver Age was marked by its long, breathless thought balloons about one character's unrequited love for another, often punctuated by heartfelt sighs, chokes, and sobs. The most fascinating aspect of Brainiac, though, was the nomenclature "5"—Brainy wonders, in several Siegel tales, if he is related to one of Superman's greatest foes, the evil alien Brainiac, who had been a part of the Superman mythos since his introduction in 1958. Unlike his possible villainous ancestor, the Legion's Brainy was smart and detached and fought for good. He was making his own way, regardless of his parentage.

Jerry also wrote some very dramatic stories for the Legion that struggled against the silly confines of the Silver Age. In "The Stolen Super Powers!" from *Adventure Comics* #304, Saturn Girl reads a calculation from a "super-computer" that says a member of the team will die in battle with the alien Zaryan the Conqueror. Horrified by this, Saturn Girl, as team leader, tries to satisfy the prophecy and save her teammates—by planning heroically to sacrifice herself.

But Lightning Lad discovers her plan and dies in her place. His last words to Saturn Girl are: "Don't cry, Saturn Girl! . . . Better me . . . >gasp!< . . . th-than you . . . Goodbye . . ."[25] Emotionally wrought, Saturn Girl and the other members attend Lightning Lad's touching funeral. The readers couldn't believe it. The letter columns were filled with speculation:

> *Dear Editor: Who are you kidding? You've got all of America's comic*
> *book fans crying their eyes out, grieving at Lightning Lad's death,*
> *except that you and I know he never really kicked the bucket. I call*
> *the attention of your readers to the story, "The Legion of Super-*

*Villains," in SUPERMAN No. 147, which shows LIGHTNING
MAN in one of the sequences. Since he is our deceased friend,
Lightning Lad, grown up, obviously he will be brought back to life,
Right? Caroline Dove, Wildwood, Neb.*

*(Right! Ever since we published the story which told how Lightning
Lad died, we received hundreds of letters similar to the preceding from
sophisticated readers who guessed that Lightning Lad's demise would
only be temporary. We did not print any of these letters so that his
revival could come as a surprise bombshell. Now, however, we are
happy to announce that the next issue of ADVENTURE will
feature a great two-part story which shows how Lightning Lad will be
brought to life. However, there is one great drawback. In order for
Lightning Lad to be revived, one of the Legionnaires must sacrifice his
or her life in his stead. This is exactly what will happen in the next
issue, and we defy you to guess which member volunteers to die in his
place! —Ed.)*[26]

As it turned out, Lightning Lad was actually only struck by a "freeze-
ray." Jerry obviously planned on bringing him back, but he knew what
this level of interactivity would do to readers. By giving readers room to
speculate, they got more into the stories. Jerry had seen it before with
Kilroy. Lightning Lad was one of the first comics superheroes to be killed
and then resurrected, setting the stage for hundreds more to come.

In "The Secret of the Mystery Legionnaire!" from *Adventure Comics*
#305, a new, masked Legionnaire named Marvel Lad joins—only no one
knows who he is. The Legionnaires are suspicious (especially since he is
named after the competition), but he eventually fits right in. After the
obligatory high jinks, the mystery Legionnaire (who is also called "Legionnaire Lemon" in what is to be another Jerry anagram) is revealed to
be Mon-el, the most powerful Legionnaire, with Superman-like powers
from the planet Daxam.[27] Mon-el is eventually banished to the Phantom
Zone, a transparent limbo outside of the real world. Jerry takes a reflective glance to the reader in the form of a clue: Just like Marvel Lad, who
is the mystery writer who has provided all of these stories and adventures from a separate dimension? You may never know.[28] Three issues
later, in *Adventure Comics* #308, a letter in the "Smallville Mailsack" letter
column reads:

> *Dear Editor: I can't tell you how thrilled I was to see MON-EL*
> *finally liberated from the Phantom Zone. His reunion with the*
> *members of the Legion of Super-Heroes was very touching; this was*
> *absolutely the greatest Legion story you've ever published. My*
> *sincerest congratulations.*
>
> *Ben Conner, Sherman, Tex.*
>
> *(Thanks for your kind words. We'll pass them on to author Jerry*
> *Siegel, who wrote this story. —Ed.)*[29]

Whether this was finally credit for a good story told or a joke about the
Phantom Zone is not really certain.

Jerry's situation as the mature, returned creator from the past was the
talk of everybody at National. In *Action Comics* #270, Otto Binder begins
a tale called "The Old Man of Metropolis" with Superman waking up in a
strange future where his young cousin Supergirl is now the fully grown
"Superwoman" and in easy control of protecting Metropolis. Superman
has no more powers and is frail, bent, and gray. His legacy isn't great:
"I'm the forgotten Superman!"

> "M-my super-career is over," he says, adjusting his tie in an
> alley. "I can't fly back over the time-barrier to 1960!! Well, I
> can still carry on as Clark Kent, reporter! Nobody at the Planet
> will know that I'm the old Ex-Superman!"[30]

The future has moved on without him. His old friend Perry is long
gone, and Jimmy, now with a family of his own, is editor in chief. Lana
Lang is married to a millionaire, and Krypto, scrounging for food in the
trash, gets dragged to the pound. So Clark wanders the streets, his costume in full view, but no one seems to care. A boy and his grandmother
walk by: "'Granny! Who's that strange old man?' 'Hmm I've seen him
somewhere before, years ago.'"[31] No one really recognizes Superman
anymore. This is Superman as Jerry Siegel, who has to use his "pension
money" to buy a cheap, used rocket-car that will get him to his Fortress
of Solitude. When he finally arrives, he finds that Superwoman has completely taken the place over with new artifacts and decorations. Superman's stuff has been pushed into a dark closet: "All my trophies . . .

covered with dust and cobwebs . . . are forgotten, like me! Well, I had my hour of glory . . . it's Superwoman's turn now!"[32] The forgotten Superman now seems to accept that his time is over. He finds a kryptonite meteor that has fallen onto the street and smiles because he knows that since his powers are gone, he can help Kara by disposing of it for her. But when he picks it up, a cop is all over him: handling kryptonite, because it can hurt Superwoman, is illegal. The old Superman protests:

> But, officer! I was going to get rid of it! You can take my word
> for it! You're old enough to remember me, Superman!
> Ha, Ha! A lot of old geezers like you say that!
> I'll prove it . . . look—
> Come along, you old faker! You'll pay a $1,000 fine or spend
> 30 days in jail for possessing kryptonite.[33]

This scene is reminiscent of the story about Joe from the old *Post* article: that he was once almost arrested in Miami for vagrancy but proved his identity by drawing a picture of Superman.[34]

But that shtick doesn't fly anymore. Superman goes to jail and shares a cell with a sad Bizarro: "It's no use Bizarro. In the old days either of us could have smashed the whole jail apart! Now we're both as weak as kittens!"[35] In the final reversal, Superman is bailed out by Lois—who has been waiting for him these many years. In some ways, Binder's story prefigures the so-called last Superman story, "Whatever Happened to the Man of Tomorrow?" which Alan Moore would write in 1986, an opportunity that Jerry Siegel allegedly turned down.[36]

Maybe the worst part of the story is when Superman finds out that his old (now literally so) nemesis Luthor is "reformed and was pardoned when his Luthor serum became a cure for cancer! He's the mayor of Metropolis now!"[37] At this time in his life, Harry Donenfeld was retired, incredibly rich, and directing all of his money toward cancer research. In *Superman* #149, written by Jerry, Luthor is in prison and tells the warden that he needs some lab equipment to cure cancer. He promises: "Cancer is mankind's deadliest disease! In view of my great scientific background, you can't refuse to let me try. . . ." But the warden is skeptical: "All your life you've tried to crush and rule mankind." This panel shows Luthor in front of a full-length portrait of Superman that looks just like Harry's prized Ward painting.[38] Like Luthor with his "serum," Donenfeld was "president of National Tonics, Inc.," which was dedicated to "establishing [a] cancer-care program." He had built a huge "American Medical Center" in Denver devoted strictly to cancer. Donenfeld said to the papers:

> Although it costs much more to care for cancer patients, this is a field we gladly enter on a full-scale basis, for there is great need of a cancer facility such as ours where patients can be treated with no cost whatsoever to themselves or their families.[39]

Had he reformed? Or was he ever really the evil genius Jerry made him out to be? Years later, after a night of drinking, Harry took a nasty fall in his apartment and hit his head on his television set. He suffered a brain injury that sadly robbed his memory and left him largely unable to communicate, except for a few lucid moments and conversations about the 1923 Giants.[40] When he died on March 5, 1965, his estate would sell its shares of National shares for $21.50 a stock. Before taxes, his estate made $3.2 million.[41]

At home, Jerry touched through his mail before walking into Laura's room. There would still sometimes be letters from fans, but they were few and far between and even then mostly from people wondering if he had any old comics to sell. He had plenty of comics at one point, but torrential Long Island rains swept into his basement and washed most of them away.[42] When the market for old comics began to pick up, Jerry could never think of this without sighing. But now he stopped, his eyes moving over the return address on the final letter in the pile . . . more of a half-crumpled piece of paper, really. It was from Cleveland. He opened the letter, almost in disbelief. He blinked his eyes and moved closer to the hot lamp. Outside, his small street was quiet as he was framed in the window above the lilacs. He read the letter quickly. He looked down at the signature at the bottom. It was the same name as on the return address. He started to feel dizzy. There was an enclosed script. The letter was signed a strange name that was still very familiar to him.

Bernard J. Kenton.

Chapter 22

Bizarro No. 1

THE SIXTIES WERE A TRANSFORMATIVE TIME for science fiction. The groundswell of fan support that helped shape the hesitant niche of the 1930s and 1940s was now a full-fledged genre phenomenon; it was the decade that gave us *The Twilight Zone* and *Star Trek*. The weird magazines were still around, but they were shorter and for a more sophisticated, college-educated crowd. But comics were still pulp science fiction. One of the more popular Silver Age Superman characters was Bizarro, an "imperfect clone" who looked like Superman but with white cracked skin and a shock of black hair. In some ways a foolish humor device, Bizarro is also downright eerie because his value system is the opposite of Superman's. He is the Superman idea that didn't work out. He is powerful and frustrating. He is also completely unpredictable, like Bernard J. Kenton.

Clues to the identity of Kenton and how Jerry ended up receiving a physical letter from his own alias begin with another strange letter that appeared in the back of the new sixties incarnation of *Amazing Stories*. The magazine runs a letter asking for help in locating "the man who **created Superman**." The writer says that "G. Bernard Kontor Ries— Kantor Promotions" of New York is looking for Jerry Siegel, who "happens *merely to be none other than*" the famous "creator, with Joe Schuster, of Superman." The company is seeking out Jerry, "the writer with the $1 00000000 brain," because it has an old manuscript of his titled "Miracles on Antares." The letter is signed "G. Bernard Kantor."[1]

The name sounds and looks a lot like "Bernard J. Kenton," though it is not a perfect match. Was Jerry using his alias to plant a letter in his old favorite magazine to generate interest in himself? "Miracles on Antares" is the same story that the old *Torch* article written by Jerry said Kenton had sold to *Amazing Stories*. The "Ries" that the letter mentions is actually Al Ries, who became a legend in Manhattan advertising and a bestselling author. Ries has never heard of, dealt with, or worked with any Bernard Kantor or Jerry Siegel.[2] But the script was real. *Famous Monsters* #7 of June 1960 told of an upcoming science fiction film of the same name.

In a short news bit titled "Return of a Superman," the editor reveals how "an ambitious youngster named Jerome Siegel," before he created Superman, wrote a story called "Visitor from Antares," which was sold to *Amazing Stories* but "never saw print." But now, the story has been turned into a script and "a Cleveland-Chicago syndicate plans to film it" using "the most incredible cast in the history of film-dom!" The editor teases that genre starlet "Faith (THIS ISLAND EARTH!) Domergue" will be asked "to star in the Siegel scientifilm!"[3]

This article seems to confirm that it was Siegel's "Antares" script that was originally sold to *Amazing Stories*.

In a few of Jerry's old letters to the magazines in the 1930s, he mentions "Bernard J. Kenton" writing similar letters to the pulps. One such letter from the Kenton name does appear in a 1932 *Amazing Stories*:

> *After reading Jack Williamson's recent "opus magnum" entitled "The Stone from the Green Star," for the eighth time, I sat down, rested my eyes in meditation, and spent an hour contemplating his fallacious supposition of rejuvenation. . . .*
>
> *Primarily, the intrinsic case of old age is due to sedimentary deposits in both the arterial and venous structure, this condition influencing the inelasticity common to old age. If the formation of these deposits is not checked, adjacent parts of the anatomy will inevitably follow. . . . So far as biological interpretation extends corporeal senescence constitutes a major involution, in direct opposition of the evolution of the life-cycle, which transpires normally in the latter half of the third decade. . . . For the past three months I have been engaged in obtaining a protoplasmic formula for synthetic haemoglobin, contrasting the previously highly significant investigations of P. Schuyler Miller and Dr. Walter Elkington . . . if successful, this unprecedented formula may increase the longevity of the human race to an astounding extent.*

*O Zeus! In writing this extensive anatreptic communication I have
acquired the anathema of all writers—anapeiratic paralysis of the
digits!*

Bernard J. Kenton
416 Frankfort Ave.
Cleveland, OH[4]

The language and tone in this letter are very different from those in
any of Jerry's letters. Moreover, there are no personal clues—which Jerry
always included in all of his *Torch* work—to give himself away.[5] All of
which leaves us with a startling question: Who or what was Bernard J.
Kenton?[6]

UNDERVERSE

Arnold Drake was a *Plain Dealer* beat reporter of the old school. He
pushed for good quotes, his shoes always wore out faster than his suits,
and he thought most of the people he dealt with were either crooks or
idiots. He sat at his desk and stared at the pamphlet that someone had
given him. He checked the clock and eyed the coffee machine across the
room.

Sitting down with an afternoon cup of coffee, Drake looked at the
small pamphlet in front of him. The title was *SUCCESS Simplified!* It was
put out by the Success Society of America. *Where do they get these names?*
Drake had gotten a number of complaints over the pamphlet. He picked
up the phone.

After a few calls, Drake wrote up his article and sent it to copy, and the
next day, February 18, 1952, on the front page:

SIDEWALK PHOTOGRAPHER DEVELOPS VISIONS OF "SUC-
CESS SIMPLIFIED"
The ad promised that by paying the registration fee of $3
followed by $3 a month, in a short time you can compare
favorably with the most profound followers of erudition.[7]

Drake was used to these scams. These people always promised money,
but never directly. Drake scowled. They also always promised some

vague intellectual skill that you could learn that *might* lead to money, but it was never the thing itself. Darke quotes the pamphlet directly:

> There are many obstacles preventing every person from attaining great wealth: once you understand them, it becomes a question of scientific behavior to surmount these obstacles. . . . In time, you ought to be able to hold your own in a group of college professors, and squash their arguments into the bargain. You could eventually point out flaws in the Einstein theory. Become a financial wizard; a mental giant; an athletic Superman; a romantic magnet; an expert in any field![8]

Drake also quotes the pamphlet's last line: "A personal message from the executive director, G. Bernard Kantor."[9]

Drake had called the Better Business Bureau and found out they had four fat files on Kantor; *big surprise.* Apparently, Kantor was always one step ahead in his harebrained moneymaking schemes. Drake knew of him a little but had never seen him—he was a well-known street photographer who worked the Playhouse Square corner. He would run up, snap your picture, ask for payment, and then give you a little tab to send away (with a check) for your priceless memento. He did it so quickly that you could barely respond, much less remember his face. Happy couples would send in money but never receive their photograph. Drake doubted he even had film in that black camera of his. Kantor, it seems, had a reputation for "nimble leaps from one promotion to the next."[10] Drake smiled when he typed this.

The previous summer, Kantor had been running a sham company called National Evaluators, Inc., that encouraged people to submit old stock certificates for reappraisal. The SEC found out and a federal judge ordered Kantor to cease and desist.[11] *He got lucky there,* Drake thought. And last December, Kantor was advertising for 150,000 contributions to start, of all things, a new comic book. Kantor claimed a writer named Jerry Siegel as a sponsor. But according to the BBB, "all [Kantor] had was a noncommittal letter from Siegel explaining how much it would cost to start such an enterprise." Drake notes that "Siegel's name is used frequently by Kantor":

> In 1949, complying with a science magazine's request for references before an advertisement would be published, Kantor

named Siegel and a group of lawyers and bankers. He added coldly: "It would be impossible to provide a veritable compendium of personal and business references."[12]

Kantor often wrote letters to the newspaper on bizarre topics, was sometimes associated with the Communist Party, and could not be pinned down to a single address. Drake found nothing but an endless string of post office boxes and empty rented rooms. And he couldn't find a picture of him, no matter how hard he tried. Drake thought that Kantor had grown up near Glenville, maybe near a candy store. Kantor had six tax liens against him. Drake almost felt sorry for him. *Almost.*

A few days later, Kantor showed up in the *Plain Dealer* bullpen, waving the article that Drake wrote and shouting like a crazy person. Drake wasn't there, so he couldn't see his face, but he heard he made a big racket. He was sort of sorry he'd missed it.

Kantor was what they called a "pitchman," and he was always looking for an angle. In *Billboard* magazine on September 9, 1957:

> Bernard D. Kantor, writing from Cleveland, says he will take off by plane for England soon to attend the World Science Fiction convention. Kantor will combine business with pleasure, having set plans "to pitch watches, gyroscopes and cigarette lighters in a whirlwind campaign in London." Looking far ahead, Kantor also says he will "attempt to sell shares in Space Trips, Inc. In my opinion, if we can set up the trips and leister on the Moon, Mars, etc., a $10 million score would be simple."[13]

On November 4, 1957, the following appears in the same trade, in equally small type:

> "GLAMORIZING . . . The American pitchman" could be the slogan of a new project Bernard D. Kantor of Cleveland and his associates are in the process of developing. The project is a comic strip to be known as "Tripod Taylor." Planned for comics magazines at first and newspaper syndication later. "'Tripes' will travel a route consisting of the earth, moon, Mars, and Venus," said Kantor. "Episodes will be both funny and educational,"

said Kantor, "as Taylor pitches gyroscopes on the moon, knife sharpeners on Mars and perfumes on Venus. We contemplate the co-operation of Jerry Siegel and Joe Shuster ('Superman' creators)."[14]

The connection of Kantor with not only Cleveland but Jerry and Joe is certainly curious. In the same magazine on February 24, 1958:

PIPES FOR PITCHMEN
WRITING . . .
From New York, Bernard D. Kantor said that a record 45-minute discussion there with Jerry (Superman) Siegel indicated phenomenal profits for the pitch trade in space toys, dolls, rockets, etc.[15]

Kantor seemed to be involved in moneymaking schemes of any and all varieties.

On January 12, 1960, Drake exposed another Kantor scam that even he couldn't believe. Drake quotes the new pamphlet:

Save Earth, Save Moon, Send Money
Greater Clevelanders are being solicited by mail for funds to help save the moon for America. A yellow card, the size of a postcard:
American moon Campaigns
310 Caxton Building
YOU CAN HELP SAVE THE EARTH!
Exploring the moon is the world's most important project!
If another nation conquers the moon FIRST, the United States may be reduced to a primitive subservient territory
We may be forced into a 70-hour week!

The card gave no hint how the saving of the Earth might be accomplished.

The guy has guts, Drake thought. And this did sound like a lot of Superman stuff. But Drake winced as he had to force himself to write the last, extremely painful line:

Efforts to find him were unsuccessful.

Bernard Kantor died in Cleveland on January 13, 1967, of a painful cancer in a downtown nursing home. He had no offspring, was never married, and listed no relatives. He was born in Brooklyn and grew up in Cleveland. He was a real person. He was fifty-four years old.[16]

All of the books and articles written about Jerry Siegel afford a thin sentence to Kenton as being a well-used alias for the Superman writer. One of the first fan historians of the early days of science fiction was Sam Moskowitz, who may even have been the first to mention Kenton as an alias. In his book *The Immortal Storm,* Moskowitz wrote that "Siegel himself wrote under the nom de plume of Bernard J. Kenton." So it stuck. But later in his career, it seems that Moskowitz himself rethought that claim. In a small comics trade magazine, comics dealer–turned–historian Robert Beerbohm writes in his article "The Big Bang Theory of Comic Book History":

> Sam Moskowitz tracked down Bernard Kantor many years ago. He came away with 1939 correspondence between Jerry [and Kantor] . . . specifically commenting about $50 the former was paying the latter for a Superman plot. In a letter dated October 8, 1939 (when Jerry was located at Electra Court, Apt A-38, 40-15 81st Street, Jackson Heights, L.I., N.Y.) he wrote to his long-time friend and collaborator in Cleveland. "Enclosed herewith please find a fifty dollar bill which is payment for the assistance I received from your Superman plot. . . . I'm glad that I got in touch with you at this time when you will be able to use the income from selling me Superman plots. Payments will always reach you just as promptly as I can ascertain whether my version of your synopses are acceptable to the editors."[17]

According to Beerbohm, Jerry also apparently tells Kantor in this letter that he had "a new fantastic character strip, The Spectre," and "if he has any possible plots to please pass them along."[18] According to Julie Schwartz, whom Moskowitz also claimed to confer with, "Jerry stopped buying Superman plots from Kantor because Kantor had tried to put one over on Jerry by naming a character 'Bordello.'"[19]

Versions of Kantor's name appear in almost every comics title Jerry ever wrote, both with and without Joe, in a strangely parallel but sadly negative way. Words and names resonate in an echo that links 1938 with the late 1960s. A letter to the "Metropolis Mailbag" in *Superman* #140 asks:

> *Well, I am wondering about the numerous K's you have given us.*
> *For example, Kryypto, Krypton, Kryptonite, Kryptonese, Kent,*
> *Kandor, Kal-El and Kull-Ex. Can you explain this phenomenon?*
> *Bruce Minzer, Manhattan, N.Y.*
>
> *(It must be a Koincidence. —Ed.)*[20]

But some of it was not. Even with a background like Jerry's and a similar interest in science fiction writing, Kantor was in some ways Jerry's opposite. But for all of Jerry's ups and downs, Kantor was the one who really didn't make it. If he wrote scripts for Jerry, had him as a friend in Glenville, or was just left behind, Kantor remained Jerry's worst fear: someone who was invisible, anonymous, and alone. Kantor was Jerry's friend at one time, but he turned into his Bizarro, yet another identity to hide behind a flimsy disguise.[21] What Jerry and Joe did with Superman was not unlikely; it was nearly impossible. The shadow of Kantor in Jerry's work was perhaps Jerry's secret way not only of keeping the name of his old friend in print (or of giving thanks to someone who was still helping him), but also of never forgetting the far side of success. So Kantor became Kenton and thus, quite possibly, "Kent," the ultimate secret identity.[22]

Chapter 23

'Nuff Said

JULIE SCHWARTZ WAS IN HIS OFFICE all morning looking at the new cover for *The Flash,* which was a comic he had brought back from nothingness. He stopped and cocked his head because he could swear that he heard Jerry Siegel, out in the hall, say that he was going to kill Mort Weisinger.[1] Julie, the editorial mastermind who had also immigrated to comics from the old fanzines, laughed out loud. Not that he could blame him. He knew Mort was pushing Jerry hard, but he also knew Jerry was kind of losing it. He thought he heard Jerry say once that Mort had spies in the elevator to find out when Jerry was in the building.[2] Julie was a good friend to Jerry and felt sorry for him. He rolled back in his chair and got back to the *Flash* script.[3] Years later, Mort would describe Jerry as "the most competent of all the Superman writers . . . what his successors did was just embroidery, including my own contributions. Siegel was the best emotional writer of them all."[4]

Jerry had been told that because of new laws he could reapply for the rights to the Superman copyright. This was a onetime legal opportunity, but he knew the ramifications would be immediate. Jerry really liked writing Superman again, despite the friction with editorial. But he had to try the courts. Once National found out about the new lawsuit, Jerry was let go.[5] Some readers may have noticed a difference in the stories, but because of his anonymous status, most probably did not. The court found that Jerry and Joe had indeed given National back all of their rights, not in the 1938 agreement signed on the back of a check, but in the 1947 settlement.[6] The court also ruled that the original *Superman* was a work-for-hire for National, even though Jerry and Joe had created the stories well before National bought them. They appealed. The court reversed the lower ruling and declared that *Superman* was not a work-for-hire but that they had signed away their rights to reapplication.[7] Appeals would continue.

Jerry, distraught again, could not go back, so he had to go forward. He went to Stan Lee, the editor at Marvel Comics who was rearranging the comics landscape with his hipper, more youthful take on superheroes designed around Cold War space anxieties and radiation paranoia. Jerry had been doing some short work for Marvel Comics in the past few years. In 1963, he wrote and co-created the character Plantman for *Strange Tales* #113. His credit, with Stan Lee, was "Joe Carter," a masculine version of his wife's old modeling name. Jerry wrote a couple of Human Torch stories for *Marvel Tales* and later did two backup stories starring the X-Man Angel in *Ka-Zar* in 1970 with the great penciler George Tuska.[8] But Marvel was pretty stacked with talent at this point, and Stan's youthful vision may not have been the best place for an old-timer like Jerry. Stan had given Jerry the earlier shots at writing, mostly out of respect. But Stan Lee, mustached and tall, knew they could find a spot for him somewhere.

Marvel was getting into the animation game in 1966 and was putting its name to a series of jerky, cutout cartoon shorts of Captain America, the Sub-Mariner, Thor, the Silver Surfer, and others. They looked nothing like a traditional cartoon, but they had a certain modern flash with those Jack Kirby faces and energy crackles popping across the screen. Marvel would ultimately produce sixty-five episodes to air in afternoon syndication. Up in Boston, WNAC Channel 7 had decided that they would lead each block of the Marvel cartoons with a live-action master of ceremonies—who would be dressed up as Captain America. Marvel liked the idea because it would be a daily platform to extol the virtues of their heroes (and their comics) to a substantial captive audience. But they needed someone to write Cap's dialogue in an exciting, bombastic way. They called Jerry.

Boston had settled on actor Arthur Pierce for Cap, mostly because he was already doing the voice-over work in the cartoons. Jerry didn't know Pierce but got right to work in Long Island at writing words for him. What Jerry wrote was completely over the top in terms of singing the praises of the Mighty Marvel House of Ideas. It went beyond talking about the characters to talking about the company itself—and Marvel loved it. And Jerry knew his stuff: he used all the little catchphrases—*Hi, True Believers! Excelsior!*—that Stan used to help make Marvel a comics of the people rather than of old bald men. This, in 1966, was why Marvel was so vibrant. And unlike DC at that time, Marvel had the attention of the kids on the floor. To Jerry, it felt like 1938 again.

So kids in Boston ran home from school, threw their knapsacks and Red Sox hats over the sofa, and tuned in to Channel 7 every afternoon. Eyes forward, hands on chins, they saw the spinning logo push forward as if it were coming right at them: "The Marvel Super-Heroes!" buzzed out of the tiny speaker as the screen lit up with images of their favorite Marvel characters. Then, as if on a national feed addressing the nation in a time of crisis, Captain America, with a decent-looking costume and shield (shot midchest up), started talking in a deep, resonant voice:

> *To be or not to be a Marvelite*
> *That is the question*
> *Or to take up arms against the sea of super-hero competitors*
> *By opposing to ECHHH read them*
> *To enjoy to view to snore*
> *To perchance dream*
> *Aye there's the super-action!*[9]

This was superhero shtick that sounded like *Hamlet*. And the kids—young and older—ate it up. This was superhero camp long before Adam West's Batman would show up on television walking up the sides of buildings.

At Thanksgiving, the station invited Jerry and Joanne to come visit the set. At showtime they had not yet arrived, so they ducked into a department store to see it for the first time. They saw Pierce, heard his voice, and watched him jump up and down across a whole row of television sets. They howled. College students especially loved the craziness of Cap's delivery followed by Kirby's animated insanity. Jerry and Joanne met Arthur Pierce, and he told them that every time he went out he was mauled by kids. He thanked Jerry. He would later come out to their house for dinner. The show paid the bills for a year.

CRUSADE

Comics were good business again, especially in superheroes. This was due largely to the success of Marvel Comics, which began as a small imprint and quickly started cranking out new titles that seemed positively revolutionary compared with the stories at National, where Superman was still being turned into a baby. Marvel, behind the genius of Jack Kirby, Stan Lee, Steve Ditko, and Joe Simon, gave birth to the Fantastic Four, the Hulk, Iron Man, the X-Men, and Spider-Man, all featuring snappy patter, outrageous science, and a new type of imaginative realism.

It was the beginning of the Marvel Age of comics, and other companies wanted in. One such company was Archie Comics, which started out as a cooperative between Maurice Coyne, Louis Silberkleit, and John Goldwater. Their first success was 1941's *Archie,* about the ongoing love triangle between Archie Andrews, Betty, and Veronica, which remains one of the most successful comics ever made. Archie Comics got into superheroes in the 1940s, but they stopped being popular after the war. Now, in the 1960s, the company wanted to try again. So it brought back some of its 1940s characters in shinier versions—and, in true comics fashion, relaunched them.

Jerry's main contributions to Archie's Radio Comics imprint were the superhero series *The Web, The Fly, Steel Sterling* and the Justice League rip-off book *The Mighty Crusaders,* which was inspired in part by a fan illustration that grouped them all together.[10] The art was done in the long Marvel style courtesy of the underrated Paul Reinman, who was Jack Kirby's inker for some of the first issues of *The Incredible Hulk* and *X-Men.*[11] The Crusaders were legacy heroes, based on older heroes of the forties, which is exactly what Marvel had done, reaching into its own past to pluck out the Sub-Mariner, the Human Torch, and Captain America.

Among the Radio Comics characters was John Raymond, the Web, a criminologist (and son of the original Web) who had a high-tech suit that he used to fight crime. He was joined by shapely heroine Pow Girl. The brilliant twist by Jerry was that the Web didn't know that Pow Girl was really his lovely wife, Rose. In *Fly Man* #36 of March 1966, Raymond begs his wife for permission to become the Web again. This argument continues for the next few issues as he fights off villains even as he promises his wife he is giving up crime fighting. In *Mighty Comics* #40, he finally has to justify his career to both his wife and his mother-in-law—and gets their blessing to continue as a superhero.[12]

In *Fly Man* #32, the titular character teams up with the Shield, the Black Hood, the Comet, and Fly Girl against Eterno the Tyrant, and they consider calling themselves "the Mighty Crusaders." They later meet at a "Comic Book Fans Convention," where they overhear some of the fans, who are costumed themselves in homage to their favorite characters:

> "The Golden Age of Comics was great!"
> "Yes, but there are some comic masterpieces today, too!"
> "I'm for reviving more hit heroes of yesteryear!"
> Watch Radio Comics! They're doing just that![13]

Jerry's *Crusaders* comics were very self-aware of the universe that read them, and this was not just a Stan Lee impression, but Jerry bringing in his experience as both a teenage letter writer and an instigator of Kilroy mania. The editor raves:

> Letters are pouring in . . . judging by your enthused reactions,
> it struck the newsstands with the impact of a billion H-bombs
> and the comic book biz will never be quite the same again![14]

A cover page credit panel lists the "Dazzling drawing by Paul Are" and "Superb Script by Jerry Ess." Just as in the old *Science Fiction,* the editor promises:

> More is yet to come!
> You'll scream as Jerry Ess smashes his typewriter to smithereens, because it's revolting against its master! You'll gape aghast at the spectacle of Paul Are running out of ink with the deadline but instants away!
> Till next we meet, hippies, *send letters!*[15]

The editors promise great characters, such as Steel Sterling, using some very familiar language: "Until you've seen the Man of Steel put down criminal geniuses galore, in his inimitable fashion, you just haven't lived!"[16] There would be Fly Girl and the Shield, with his invulnerable uniform emblem. In a particularly touching issue, the current Shield faces his father, who was turned to stone by a villain many years ago.

> The Shield of today, faces The Shield of yesterday. . . .
> You are avenged . . . Father!
> No one knows The Shield had a son . . . and that now that I've grown to manhood I am carrying on your career in the great tradition **you** established! I am wearing one of your spare Shield uniforms!

> I swore to make your assassin pay! But I also swear this! Some-day, somehow, I'll find a way to restore you to life. Then there'll be two shields, to continue your great battle against evil! . . . Yes, Dad . . . I'll carry on in your superb tradition.[17]

This was the old, familiar, but still very poignant, Siegel theme: the father is gone, but the son vows to carry on for good. As it did with *Super-man,* this level of emotional realism struck a chord with fans:

> *Dear Editor: Remember a few years ago, when Marvel Comics made a rise from nothing to a top rate company. It's happening again, right now, by Mighty Comics. I just read Mighty Crusaders No. 4, I was startled by the way Jerry Ess handled it perfectly. Soon, you will have a Company rivaling D.C. in volume, and your heroes are ten times as good.*
>
> *—Allan Rifkin, Brooklyn, N.Y.[18]*

Cleveland policeman William Corrigan (Courtesy of Craig Corrigan)

Jerry Siegel and Joe Shuster at war bond drive in Cleveland, 1940

ABOVE: Joe Shuster doing a sketch for Marian Henderson at Fenn College, 1942 (Courtesy of *The Plain Dealer*)

AT RIGHT: The Shuster apartment at the corner of Parkwood and Amor, 1959 (Courtesy of Cuyahoga County and Marc Tyler Nobleman)

BELOW: The Shuster shop at 10609 Euclid Avenue, 1939 (Courtesy Cleveland State University)

TOP: Jerry Siegel, c. 1940
(Author's collection)

ABOVE: Joe Shuster, rolling up his
sleeves, c. 1941 (Author's collection)

AT LEFT: Frank Shuster, c. 1941
(Courtesy Jean Shuster Peavy)

Masters Of Imagination Meet In Waikiki

Historic Conclave Characters created by these three men have captured the imagination of America. Left to right, Mr. Edgar Rice Burroughs (Tarzan), Maj. Laurie York Erskine (Renfrew of the Royal Northwest Mounted Police), and Cpl. Jerry Siegel (Superman). Midpacifican's Sgt. Jim Mooney got this historic picture when the three masters of imagination met each other for the first time the other day in Waikiki. SIGNAL CORPS PHOTO BY SGT. JIM MOONEY

ABOVE: Jerry Siegel meets Edgar Rice Burroughs (left) in Waikiki, 1944

AT LEFT: Jerry Siegel and his son, c. 1945 (Author's collection)

BELOW LEFT: Bella and Jerry Siegel bundle their son into a sled, c. 1946 (Author's collection)

BELOW RIGHT: Jerry Siegel and his son, c. 1947 (Author's collection)

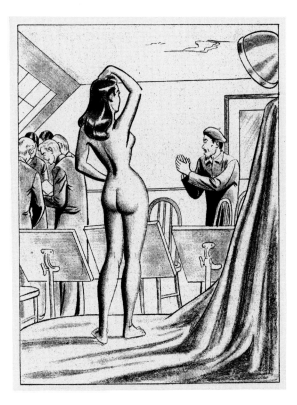

Joe Shuster, unsigned illustration
in *Merry-Go-Romp* digest, c. 1961
(Courtesy of Jim Linderman)

Joe Shuster, unsigned illustration
from *Nights of Horror*, c. 1953
(Author's collection)

Jerry, Joanne, and Laura Siegel, 1975
(Courtesy of Alan Light)

Christopher Reeve, Jean Shuster Peavy, and
Joe Shuster at the *Superman* movie premiere,
1978 (Courtesy of Jean Shuster Peavy)

Restored Jerry Siegel house at 16022 Kimberley Avenue, Glenville, 2009. Ordinary fans from all over the world raised more than $100,000 for this project with help from novelist Brad Meltzer and the Siegel and Shuster Society in Cleveland. Fence by Derek Gelvin. Landscaping by Dean's Greenhouse. (Photography by Jim Bowers, Capedwonder.com)

Commemorative fence at Shuster site, 2009. Produced by Vista Color Imaging. Installation by David Boyer. (Photograph by Jim Bowers, Capedwonder.com)

Interior of the Wayfarer's Lodge in Cleveland, c. 1930
(Western Reserve Historical Society)

Drawing by Joe Shuster. Superman is carrying Jerry (left) and Joe (right),
pictured as their younger selves. Note their terror.

The letter writers, as always, were smart. They soon figure out who is who:

> *One of the first comic heroes (and I noticed you said "super-hero," not your usual "ultra-hero") was SUPERMAN. His writer was Jerry Siegel, so that's who I say your writer must be since "he set the pace. . . ." Also, in your credits, you call Paul Reinman, Paul Are, so Jerry Ess must be Jerry Siegel.*
>
> —Patrick Stout, East Moline, Ill.[19]

By August 1966, in a story titled "Blackest Night," Jerry starts using "Jerry Siegel" outright in the credits. But though the Crusaders and their heroes had a very loyal fan base, they could not be sustained in the two-party system of comics. So Archie backed off, deciding to focus on Riverdale full-time. In the last panel of *Fly Man* #37, the Shield walks off alone into the sunset:

> Since I haven't wings like Fly-Man, or a flight helmet like the Comet . . . and there's no auto traffic in this deserted area, I've gotta walk all the way back to town! Oh, my aching feet . . . ! Some ultra-heroes have **all** the luck![20]

From Archie Comics, Jerry went on to do *The Owl* for Gold Key comics, another revival of a 1940s Dell, Batman-like character. Though it lasted only two issues over one year (April 1967 and 1968), the Owl (Nick Terry) and Owl Girl, a blond reporter whom Jerry names Laura Holt—probably after his own daughter—fought mod villains "the Terror Twins," who attack the Owls with souped-up guitars.[21] Jerry also did some work on European comics, most notably on *The Spider,* the British newspaper comic strip that ran in *Lion* about an evil criminal genius who uses bizarre gadgets to build an "Empire of Crime."[22] Once Jerry took over, he had the Spider turn against crime a bit, though he retained some of his more ruthless characteristics. Jerry even had a long tenure from 1972 to 1979 writing for the Italian comics versions of *Huey, Dewey, & Louie* and the *Junior Woodchucks.*[23] Jerry Siegel, at any age, was able to find authorial possibility in every corner.

Jerry's association with Grantray-Lawrence, which produced the Marvel cartoons, enabled him to get some more work in animation, specifically

Hanna-Barbera's *Frankenstein, Jr.*[24] The story centered around a boy genius named Buzz Conroy and his scientist dad, who build a super-robot called Frankenstein, Jr., to fight off evil villains such as Dr. Spectro. The show ran from 1966 to 1968 but actually got into trouble for being too violent. The show would be recycled in later episodes of the popular cartoon *Space Ghost.*[25] At Hanna-Barbera, Jerry worked for a time under Jack Mendelsohn, whom he had once edited at Ziff-Davis. Jerry did some writing but mostly wasn't sure what to do. When Jack invited Jerry over to his house to have some of his wife's chicken soup, Jack tried to talk him out of his lawsuit against National, which was still creeping along in endless appeals. But Jerry would have none of it. Jack later claimed that Jerry listened to self-help tapes under his pillow at night in order to feel more successful. But once the lawsuit was over and he was fired by Hanna-Barbera, Jerry felt little need to continue.[26]

As the 1970s began, Jerry had few things to look forward to. He wrote a story illustrated by Ralph Reese called "Let the Dreamer Beware" that ran in the creepy magazine *Psycho* #5.[27] Reese's gorgeous art depicts a skinny, balding man named Alex Nimbo, "who is afflicted with one of the most loathsome maladies that ever beset mortal man—a lazy, nagging wife." Jerry's portrayal of the slippered wife, Florence, is brutal: she tells Alex to eat sardines, refuses his "normal physiological urges," and tells him if he wants a divorce, she will "have one of my brothers break every bone in your stupid body." Alex is miserable until he has a dream about a slinky blonde in a purple dress named Dileeth. She tells Alex that she loves him "supremely, totally," and informs him that if he wants to come to her "extra-dimensional plane" where "everyone is radiantly attractive," he will have to get rid of his wife. He does so, with rat poison, and Dileeth indeed transports him to her world—but turns into a half-snake demon who dissolves Alex in acid for his horrible crime. All that is left is his skeleton, stripped of its outward identity.[28]

Part Three:
Steel

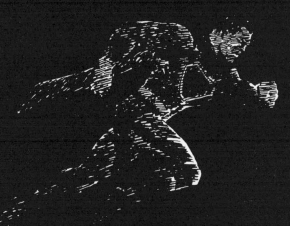

Chapter 24

Fortress of Solitude

THE SIGN ON THE DOOR downstairs read, "Furniture for Sale. Also Records. Best Quality." People trudged up the stairs to take a look and were greeted by a short man with graying hair and large glasses. He seemed very sad and sat silently in a chair as people came in and looked his things over. And only when they asked did he slowly show them his records. When they too were taken away, he tried not to watch.

When the sixties came, Joe wasn't working nearly as much as Jerry. He did a few covers and interiors for *Startling Stories, Crime and Justice,* and *Hot Rods and Racing Cars.*[1] Earlier that year, Joe heard that a Superman musical was opening on Broadway at the Alvin Theatre. So he walked down and stood on the sidewalk. He stood there almost every night and saw lots of people go in. Even Frank Sinatra. Joe never saw the musical itself. He couldn't afford it.[2]

In the comics, Lois, Clark, and Superman were constantly beset by foes, but the two reporters still returned to a happy inertia at the end of each issue. Not so in real life. In New York, Joe was so broke that he had to sell his furniture. He would get a check for fifty bucks from National every once in a while, but it was never enough. His high bed was wedged into a small corner of his apartment next to a bright light and easy chair.[3] He worked as a cashier and even as a stock boy. He looked at the phone. He was living with Frank, who was working. His mother had died right before Thanksgiving in 1974. He had been taking care of her. Now there was no one to take care of him.[4]

On the other side of the country, things were darker than they looked.

Jerry had finally moved his family to California in 1968, but no one was calling him back. After Joanne had a serious bout of pneumonia, Jerry later admitted he was "close to suicide."[5] To pay the rent, he got a job at the California Public Utilities Commission typing and sorting mail.[6] Joanne sold Chevys in Santa Monica and folded bathing suits in a clothing store.[7] They lived in a one-bedroom apartment. They sold off what little Superman stuff they had left. Their daughter, Laura, in school, was trying not to notice.

One day Joanne looked at the phone. It didn't make a sound. So she did. Again.

By now, National was owned by the Warner Brothers entertainment corporation and called itself DC Comics, though that title would not be official until the late seventies.[8] Most of the old guard was gone, having made their fortunes and retired to the board of directors or passed away. But people there knew who the Siegels were, even if the general public did not. Though Jerry's legal options were, for the time being, exhausted, his very name had a potential energy that the suits were aware of.

Joanne finally got through to New York and asked, in effect, if it would *look good for DC to have the creator of Superman die of starvation?* There was a pause on the end of the line, high in the skyscraping offices of DC, where pictures of Superman were plastered all over the walls. It was essentially a replay of Jerry's earlier grandstand on Long Island before he was hired back. But this was a different regime, and Joanne was very convincing. And there was television to think of, though it is unclear if anyone even thought of that. For many reasons, different for many people, Joanne had a good point. So on the other end of the telephone line, someone finally listened.

After weeks of calls and letters, there was a knock on the door in California and a smart-dressed man asked Joanne who she was. He told Joanne that if she wouldn't make any more calls, he would give her money. He was an attorney. He handed her a check for $50 and walked away. There would be more.[9] Joanne was convinced they had an ally somewhere in the company. She was determined to find out who that person was.

Joanne kept making phone calls, finding a time during the day when she would be undisturbed and careful to calculate the time difference. Soon the Siegels started getting a steady $100 a week. *It's time,* she realized. *We have to call Joe.*

She navigated Jerry's desk and found a number scratched on a piece of paper. Jerry may have been sleeping in the next room or at work. Joanne sat down, took a breath, and made the call. Joe answered and his voice brightened. There was a pause. It didn't last long.

Whatever it was that separated Jerry and Joe for a time, and whether it was just a break or a genuine falling-out over Superboy and the 1947 court case, Joanne, or something else, it disappeared almost instantly.[10] Joanne filled Joe in and he started making the same calls to DC.

Someone might have felt sympathy for the pair. Or someone was trying to pay them off before it got worse. What Joanne didn't know was that preliminary preparations were under way to begin work on a full-length, big-budget Superman movie. The higher-ups knew Jerry and Joe could cause trouble, just as Jerry had before the television show debuted.

Which, of course, Jerry did.

TURN

In 1975, a kid named Alan Light—jeans with a belt, hair over his ears— was the publisher of the weekly *Buyer's Guide for Comic Fandom,* an advertising magazine (later known as *Comics Buyer's Guide*) for comics that also contained some must-read news columns for fans and retailers. One of his regular contributors was a kid named Murray Bishoff—with a goofy hat and a constant smile—who wrote a column for the magazine. In 1975, Murray got an anonymous letter in the mail containing a photocopy of a summary of the Superboy court case. Murray stopped smiling and ran to Alan. They both agreed they had to run it, and on April 1, 1975, Murray's column ran with the story, which he claimed was "the only published account of the story anywhere."[11] Though the case had happened years before, it was unknown to the generation of comics fans in the seventies who were reading titles such as *Warlock, Heavy Metal,* and *New Gods.* Since it was about Superman, the story struck deep.[12]

After reading Murray's column, a guy named Shel Dorf blinked his eyes and wiped them. Shel had worked in comics here and there but was now a promoter. Shel was one of the first to realize the appeal of the comics convention, which could be held in a small hall or hotel almost anywhere near a big city. Shel found that if you filled a room with comics and maybe got an artist or two to sign stuff, people would come out of the woodwork. After having great success with these conventions in Detroit, Shel moved out to San Diego and started staging one-day and then three-day shows at local hotels. These events would grow and evolve into what would become the genre juggernaut known as San Diego Comic-Con International, where attendance is now more luck than ease. But back then, Shel read Murray's column and just reached for his phone book. He already had Jack Kirby coming in, but there was always room for more.

In 1975, Comic-Con was held at the El Cortez Hotel in San Diego from July 30 to August 3. They gathered out by the blue pool and in small, hot rooms. Stan Lee talked about Marvel as if it were some sort of futuristic time machine. Chuck Norris gave a sad but bizarre demonstration to show how Bruce Lee had accidentally died in 1973. Marvel had, relatively speaking, a fairly big presence: Kirby, back at Marvel at this time, was the main guest. When he got a standing ovation, he lowered his eyes with a smile. National had sent no one. Their only representative, sort of, was a man at a table in the corner. As *The Los Angeles Free Press* notes:

> The weekend was star-filled, though National Comics, the big #2 company, was only represented by its ex-employee Jerry Siegel, the creator of Superman, the man who started all the superhero stuff, who tried to remain anonymous, begging at least one sharp-eyed fan not to let on he was there. When someone recognized him as Jerry Siegel, the old guy begged him to keep it quiet.[13]

Jerry was incredibly uncomfortable. There were people he knew: Stan, Jack, even his old pen pal Forrest Ackerman. All of them were getting top billing. Jerry didn't know where he fit or even why Shel had invited him. Jerry had brought Joanne and Laura with him, expecting a big splash. But it wasn't at all what he'd expected. They gave him something called an Inkpot Award and it made him smile, but he wasn't sure what it was for.[14]

At the Con, in a private room, Jerry walked in and met Alan Light and Murray Bishoff. Jerry smiled because he liked these kids—a lot. He was really impressed with Murray's column about the court case. The truth was, these kids reminded Jerry of himself a bit. Him and Joe. Alan and Murray wanted to interview Jerry. He agreed, but he wanted Joanne and

Laura to be there. It was the first big interview he had done since 1941, really. He took a deep breath.

By the end of the interview, Alan and Murray looked pale. But they were excited. Murray later remembered:

> I found Jerry Siegel to be a deeply injured man emotionally; not bitter, for bitterness poisons one's viewpoint about everything. He was bitterly disappointed, let down by those he had trusted. He'd carried this hurt for over 20 years, from the time he hadn't been able to bring himself to speak to George Reeves on a New York sidewalk, leaving the industry, then later swallowing his pride to return to work for the very people he felt had abused him. Though his voice didn't get very loud, he was articulate, unwavering in his narrative, stopping occasionally as he'd get tears in his eyes, recalling how he'd been treated. We never got much insight into his creative process. It seemed the characters and adventures he wrote simply flowed effortlessly out of him. We also found his wife Joanne and daughter Laura to be utterly charming. Joanne was the strong one, the rock that obviously kept Jerry steady, and much more talkative.[15]

Jerry's story of growing up in Cleveland, meeting Joe, and creating a character they would sell for only $130 was mesmerizing to the two young comics journalists. Alan and Murray were determined to tell it to others, which they did, by pressing an LP of all their interviews and offering it to buyers. People put it on their turntables and listened to Jerry's voice, still high and cracking with sadness. They stared at the black circle. But what really resulted from this interview was not that the story was out again, it was that Jerry felt empowered to speak it more loudly.

Chapter 25

Motion

B Y 1975, their ongoing lawsuit to reclaim the copyright was finally over, its last stop being the Second Circuit Court of Appeals. The case took twelve years and was being handled solely by
the lawyers. According to *The New York Times,* the law firm, Coudert
Brothers, "advised them not to take the case to the Supreme Court."
They hinted strongly that National "might work out some financial settlement . . . if they dropped the case."[1] So they dropped it, to deafening
silence.

Ilya Salkind was a Mexican American film producer who, after producing *The Three Musketeers* in 1973 to great success, asked a question that
fans had been dreaming of for years: *Why not a big Superman movie?* So
Ilya got to the long, thoughtful work. It would take a long time—and
lots of money—to negotiate the rights, settle on a script, and somehow
cast an impossible role. It would all turn out perfectly in the 1978 *Superman,* but in the early stages, with the case over and National sending small
bits of cash, Jerry heard only one, red word: "movie."[2]

The boys had grown up on movies, and Superman himself was in
great debt to many afternoons spent in those dark Cleveland theaters. But
if there was going to be a Superman movie, Jerry thought he and Joe
should be involved. Jerry pushed a rusty steel cart in his job. He had to
wear a short-sleeved white shirt with a name tag that read, "Jerry." *They
were making a movie.* So Jerry went home that night and did the same thing
he used to do back in the 1930s after he saw a movie with Joe and thought
he could do better. He got out his same typewriter and rolled in, on re-
flex, the first sheet of clean paper.

What Jerry wrote was what he referred to as a "curse." The word has a biblical connotation, in passages like Deuteronomy 28:63:

> And it shall be, that just as the LORD rejoiced over you to do you good and multiply you, so the LORD will rejoice over you to destroy you and bring you to nothing; and you shall be plucked from off the land which you go to possess.[3]

Jerry learned how to write big talk from the pulps, the Major, and the movies. This was to be his biggest claim of all.

11711 Mayfield Avenue, Apt. 14
West Los Angeles, California 90049
FOR IMMEDIATE RELEASE

SUPERMAN'S ORIGINATOR PUTS "CURSE" ON SUPERMAN MOVIE

It has been announced in show business trade papers that a multi-million dollar production based on the SUPERMAN comic strip is about to be produced. It has been stated that millions of dollars were paid to the owners of SUPERMAN, National Periodical Publications, Inc., for the right to use the famous comic book superhero in the new movie. The script is by Mario Puzo, who wrote "The Godfather" and "Earthquake." The film is to have a star-filled cast.

I, Jerry Siegel, the co-originator of SUPERMAN, put a curse on the SUPERMAN movie! I hope it super-bombs. I hope loyal SUPERMAN fans stay away from it in droves. I hope the whole world, becoming aware of the stench that surrounds SUPERMAN, will avoid the movie like a plague. Why am I putting this curse on a movie based on my creation SUPERMAN? Because cartoonist Joe Shuster and I, who co-originated SUPERMAN together, will not get one cent from the SUPERMAN super-movie deal. SUPERMAN has been a huge moneymaker for 37 years. During most of those years, Joe Shuster and I, who originated the character SUPERMAN, got nothing from our creation, and through many of those years we have known want, while SUPERMAN's publishers became multi-millionaires. Full details are in the enclosed news release. Read

*the enclosed material and you will get some idea of how it feels to
create one of the most successful fiction characters of all time . . . and
be cheated out of your share of its profits. The publishers of SUPER-
MAN comic books, National Periodical Publications, Inc., killed my
days, murdered my nights, choked my happiness, strangled my career.
I consider National's executives economic murderers, money-mad
monsters. If they, and the executives of Warner Communications
which owns National, had consciences, they would right the wrongs
they inflicted on Joe Shuster and me.*[4]

Jerry goes on to personally call out Jack Liebowitz, whom he claims
got "extremely wealthy" from Superman. Jerry then quotes from the letters he had always saved to provide evidence that they had been strung
along since 1938. Their legal avenues were now closed, so Jerry tried to
appeal to the same things Superman did: the inherent humanity of the
audience. In some ways, Jerry had always done this. He noted that Liebowitz adopted an almost paternal personage at times to "protect" "the
boys" and their "best interests." Jerry found this incredibly false and con-
descending. Their whole life they had been called "the boys," as if they
were only one person, and children at that. They were not. They were in
their sixties now. Jerry notes that Liebowitz referred to him first as an
"inexperienced young man," and once he fought back, those references
turned to "cheat," "swindler," and "highbinder."[5]

Jerry sent these fiery pages to every news outlet he could find an address for. It reminded him of when he looked up syndicates to send the
Superman proposal to all those decades ago. And just as with those old
proposals, no one wrote back.

FIRESTORM

The national media didn't really know who Jerry Siegel was, so most of
the reporters and papers dismissed his press release as the work of a crank.
But Phil Yeh, a bushy-haired cartoonist who published a small Bay Area
arts magazine called *Cobblestone,* was a comics guy and did know who he
was—and could not believe what he was reading. So he took a chance
and gave Jerry a call. After an interview, Yeh and his publishing partner,
Randy Kosht, ran it as a story called "Supersham!" that told the "new"
story of Jerry and Joe and how they had lost out on the financial successes

of their creation.[6] There were some similarities to the old *Saturday Evening Post* article, but the tone had completely changed to nothing but empathy. Yeh agrees with Jerry that they had suffered a "great injustice" and closes with a strong call to arms that was the real first shot across the bow:

> We, as artists and writers ourselves, should find enough moral courage to see that justice is done in this situation. Write to National Periodical Publications, in care of Carmine Infantino, Publisher, at 75 Rockefeller Plaza, New York, NY 10019 and ask what efforts are being made to see that something is done for the men who created a character that has dedicated his life to "Truth, Justice and the American Way, Superman."[7]

Cobblestone was a small, free magazine. But it had a steady audience of liberal-minded people who believed in social justice for the underdog. It got things rolling.

On October 29, on the other side of the country, *The Washington Star* ran a front-page interview of Jerry and Joe by reporter John Sherwood. Soon, *The New York Times, The Washington Post,* and other papers ran similar articles, mostly inspired by Sherwood's piece. Now everyone knew. Bob Greene, working at the *Chicago Sun-Times* and already very popular as a syndicated columnist, spoke with Jerry and reports that he just "tries to keep from going crazy" over all of this.[8] Greene writes from the perspective of the 1970s and a growing mistrust of corporations (and government) at the expense of the working individual. Greene also gets a quote from Jay Emmett, the executive vice president of Warner Communications:

> Of course, we have no legal reason to do anything for Mr. Siegel or Mr. Shuster, Emmett said. He added, however, that for reasons of "morality and compassion," Warner Communications was considering making some sort of offer. They are, indeed, destitute and they did, indeed, create Superman, Emmett said.[9]

Greene lets Emmett's words speak for themselves. Jerry's last quote in Greene's article bears this out: "My spirit is broken. I will admit it, I've contemplated suicide. I brought Superman out of my own heart. I hope people remember that after I'm gone."[10]

The story was getting legs not only because of the times or its resonance with people who grew up on Superman, but because a few people were working behind the scenes to make sure it wouldn't go away. One such man was Bobby Lipsyte, who was a writer for the ABC show *Saturday Night Live with Howard Cosell* when he heard the story. Like most people, he was disgusted with the version he was hearing that was painting Warners as monsters. So Lipsyte wrote a skit where Howard, dressed as Superman, would welcome Jerry and Joe as guests. Then, out of nowhere, the head of Warners would walk in and announce that they would get $10,000 for life, ending the feud in a matter appropriate to the upcoming holiday season. Lipsyte thought it would be great television and made the call to someone at Warner Brothers. Their response was simple. According to Lipsyte, they said: "You have to be fucking joking."[11]

Now really angry, Lipsyte arranged for Jerry to come out to New York anyway, where he put him up in a nice hotel. He would at least book them as guests (Joe was still living in Queens). But Howard saw them in rehearsals at the Ed Sullivan Theater and said they were "too unattractive for TV." Lipsyte stared at Howard for a good thirty seconds, right at his unmistakable mug, to let the irony of this statement sink in. After telling Howard that he would quit if they did not get on the show, Howard guffawed and compromised—Jerry and Joe would sit in the front row and Howard would visit with them during a segment to get their story. It went rather poorly though, especially when Howard greeted Joe as "John" Shuster. It looked like their fifteen minutes was up.[12]

Luckily, however, at the same time Lipsyte was inviting Jerry to come to New York, Jerry and Joe also heard from the person who would become their staunchest advocate: Neal Adams, the popular comics artist who drew realistic, lean figures in *Batman* and *X-Men* that were the evolution of Joe's original Superman. Adams, cocky and young with a mess of dark hair, was the outspoken president of the Academy of Comic Book Arts and though he didn't know Jerry or Joe personally, their story filled him with outrage. Adams and others had worked hard for basic rights for artists, including the returning of original art and the onset of royalties. But Jerry and Joe were from an older, unluckier time. So Adams wrote, then called Jerry and Joe, and boldly said he wanted to represent them. Jerry told him they had no more legal options, but he said, "No, no, I can represent you to the people . . . I don't know what I'll do. But if you let me do it, I will do it. I will get publicity, I will get attention, and I will try to turn this around." They said *okay*.[13]

Lipsyte had gotten Jerry to New York, and Adams made the most of it, personally driving the boys around to as many news outlets that would talk to them. But after the Cosell show, Jerry was broke and had to go home. Adams knew that Jerry needed to stay in town in order to stay in the public eye, so he ingeniously convinced the television stations to pony up for the hotel expenses. In return, Adams succeeded in booking Jerry and Joe on a number of influential shows, including *Tomorrow with Tom Snyder.* The response to these appearances was overwhelmingly positive. But after a few weeks, the media grind was taking its toll on the elder creators. Adams then called someone he knew only by reputation: Jerry Robinson, the legendary early Batman artist, and past president of the National Cartoonists Society. Adams met with Robinson and the society in a large ballroom in the Allied Chemical Tower building. But the best they could do was to draft a formal letter of protest. Adams lit into his colleagues, many of whom owed their livelihood to the two old men from Cleveland: *Is this all we can do? Really?* He walked out, furious. As he was leaving, a small man with an Irish accent stopped him at the door and told Adams that they should instead have a press conference, especially since the building they were meeting in was also the home of the Overseas Press Corps, of which *I am the President,* the man said, smiling. Adams eyes lit up. So on the following Tuesday, a packed room of newspeople heard Jerry and Joe's story and told it to others. Exhausted, Jerry had to finally go home to California as Joe retreated to Queens. But Emmett, and Warners, couldn't wait for the story to just go away. Not anymore.[14]

Jay Emmett was a Korean War vet and a young executive just doing his best for the higher-ups who didn't want to deal with this sort of public relations nightmare. As Adams saw it, Emmett's job was to talk him out of helping Jerry and Joe. Adams said, "His goal was nothing, my goal was something."[15] Throughout those long weeks of negotiation, Emmett and Adams went back and forth as Adams tried to convince Emmett that all they were asking for was a secretary's salary. In an AP article on November 25, 1975, Emmett publicly acknowledged that "We do have a compassionate and a moral obligation and we will certainly do something."[16]

One day over the phone, Emmett told Adams that what they were doing didn't matter anyway since Warners was going to sell National because it wasn't making them any money. Once Adams heard that, he knew he had him. He told Emmett:

Jay, you're the nephew of the man who basically was the accountant and held on to DC Comics. You came back from the
Korean War and your uncle gave you the right to do the licensing for DC Comics . . . you made millions of dollars.[17]

Adams pointed out what the papers had thus far missed: that Jay Emmett's uncle was Jack Liebowitz, the sharp accountant in the Harry Donenfeld outfit that originally engineered the acquisition of Superman for
Action Comics #1.[18] Jack was still alive and incredibly rich. Adams's sharp
point to Emmett was that "You, more than perhaps anyone in the world,
know how valuable Superman and all these comic book characters are."[19]
There was a slight hesitation in his voice as Emmett said, "Let's change
the subject."[20] Adams smiled.

Gotcha.

Adams knew that Warners would never sell off Superman. Emmett,
who was in a terrible position already, trying to negotiate between corporate desire and rising public opinion, had just lost his teeth. On December 10, 1975, *The Washington Star* reported that an offer was made to
Jerry and Joe, who "have until Thursday to accept the company's offer"
of $15,000 per year. The unrelated public service ad below the article was
an ironic coincidence: "Please help fill Empty Stockings."[21]

After getting the latest offer from Emmett, Adams put the phone
down, stood up and made a long cup of coffee, called back, and refused,
without even running it by Joe and Jerry. There was a pause on the line.
He gave him a number. They were getting close. Adams got the settlement money moving upwards, but was still getting resistance over something he felt was immeasurably important: the restoration of Jerry and
Joe's names to the Superman byline. So Adams decided he should leave
town. Emmett, frustrated that he couldn't reach him, called Robinson
instead, who convinced Emmett to capitulate and give them the byline,
as well as a starting bonus and expense payments. They called Neal Adams in Florida, who had subtly shaped the events of the past months just
as skillfully (and instinctively) as he could draw an action hero. When
Adams heard the news coming over the line, he smiled and looked up at
Jack Kirby, who was seated right across from him. But that, as they say, is
another story.[22]

★ ★ ★

Things finished up by Christmas Eve. Jerry's quote in the papers was priceless for anyone who still believed in Santa Claus: "After more than 30 years we are overjoyed at being reunited with Superman." Glasses clinked and hands clapped. On the *CBS Evening News with Walter Cronkite* on Tuesday, December 23, 1975, reporter Sam Chu Lin reported that Jerry and Joe would henceforth receive $30,000 a year.[23] This number had been negotiated up by Adams from $10,000 and also included fine print for continuing payments to their families when they both died. It also—at Adams's insistence—restored the "Created by Jerry Siegel and Joe Shuster" byline to every Superman publication.[24] When *Superman: The Movie* finally debuted in 1978, comics fans and professionals cheered openly as Jerry's and Joe's names pushed at them from the screen, in crystal blue type from beyond the stars.[25]

The New York Times quoted Joe: " 'Now we can start living again,' Mr. Shuster said. 'This will be a wonderful Christmas, a wonderful Christmas.' " The report notes that "Joe is still in Queens with Frank" and that the contracts were signed at the offices of Edmund Preiss, their new lawyer, "at 680 Fifth Avenue with other parties present."[26] Afterward, there was a party at the home of Jerry Robinson, the longtime *Batman* artist, who continued to champion comics and their creators until his death in 2011. Joe is photographed in a suit, lifting a glass of champagne.[27] The next day, Joe walked into a bank and deposited a check for $17,500, which Warners had given him to help with his debts. When he filled out the initial paperwork at Preiss's office, Joe noted that it was the first time he had needed to use his Social Security number in fifteen years.[28]

The Oakland Tribune picked up a different story on January 12, 1976, how Clark in the comics was becoming a TV newscaster, and went to DC publisher Carmine Infantino for comment. But the conversation turns to the settlement. Infantino, who made his name as the definitive modern artist of *The Flash,* says: "Those guys told a very sad story, but they made a million dollars off Superman. They spent it all. They were making $50,000 a year apiece in the '40s, when that was a lot of money."[29] Some people saw a problem with this inequality, while others believed that a contract was a contract. Regardless of legalities or even ethics, the story that had spread itself through every major newspaper and television outlet for the previous three months—during the holidays—did so only because the irony of Superman being associated with injustice hit a raw, American nerve.

About a week later, on January 19, 1976, a piece appeared in *The Village Voice* written by Elliot S. Maggin, who was writing Superman stories for DC at the time. Maggin, a fan favorite of readers, was very critical of his profession: "The current setup of the comic industry would do King John of England proud."[30] Maggin not only suggests that comics artists be allowed to unionize but relates several personal stories that do not paint the industry in a very favorable light. Maggin tells how he wrote a story about a character named "Joey Jerome," who is stranded on an island for thirty years and creates a superhero in his mind. When Maggin wanted to dedicate the story to Jerry and Joe, he "was told that National does not publish their names."[31] In his essay, Maggin is unapologetic about his respect for the creators of Superman, calling their work his "graduate school education." He wishes things were better in terms of creators' rights but is sure to end with the truth that Warners "after all, acted in good faith and exceeded its legal obligations in the agreement." Maggin posits that Warners must be happy with the outcome of all of this, especially since they "have made roughly twice as much money on Superman in the past 12 months than Siegel and Shuster will be paid if they both live to be 100."[32]

In 1979, after the movie had come and gone, the last word on this incredibly fast portion of their lives was given in a publication that had been started by the son of the person who helped buy Superman: Charlie Gaines's son, Bill.[33] Since the 1950s, *MAD* magazine had been employing a Superman parody named "Superduperman." But in July 1979, the usual gang of idiots decided to spoof the film. In the last panel of the story, "Cluck Kennt" turns back the Earth for "Lotus Lain" (just like in the movie, sort of), not to save her but because he "heard a chorus of voices! They convinced me to do it!" Lotus asks: "Who were they?" Cluck answers quickly: "The executives at Warner Brothers! They reminded me that without Lotus Lain, there's no *Superduperman II*." The story ends with Cluck looking up at four bodiless phantom faces: all sitting executives of Warner Brothers.[34]

Chapter 26

Bachelor No. 2

JOE COULD SEE NOTHING but sun. San Diego stretched out across both sides of the bay. The ocean was full of white, winking lights. It was so much quieter here than New York. And so much brighter. Next to him, a pretty woman with long blond hair in a green pantsuit smiled at him. Her mascara set off her eyes as she squeezed his hand. Joe, at sixty-two, had finally left New York, and things were looking up. It was like a dream.

After the 1975 victory, Joe heeded Jerry's cajoling and moved out west. It was hard to leave his brother, Frank, but he didn't want to be a burden anymore. It was time for a new start. He decided on San Diego for a variety of reasons.[1] Whispers began circulating among Jerry, Joanne, Frank, and finally Jean. Joe, the shy boy, even as a grown man, found it hard to say that he had met a girl.

Her name was Judy Calpini. She had an otherworldly presence and a smile that made Joe look at his shoes. She was really nice, especially to Joe. Beyond her physical attractiveness, she offered something else that Joe desperately needed: an empathetic ear. Joe, with a lifetime of sad stories that he never told anyone, wanted to finally grow up and share his life in blissful retirement. She listened to everything he said.[2]

Joe gave her greeting cards all the time, even for no occasion at all. The cards, dressed with big, colorful flowers, were signed in perfect script. "With warm, affectionate thoughts of you—Joe," complete with his signature tail.[3] This was finally something he enjoyed signing. Judy had been a showgirl earlier in life, had been married, and was now an aspiring artist of her own.[4] She was also a devoted member of the Fraternity of the Hidden Light, which was abbreviated as "L.V.X."[5] This group was one of the many mystery-based religions that were so popular in 1970s California.[6]

The central tenet of the L.V.X. was that all life contained a hidden spiritual power. Access to this energy could be had through a numerological system that would reveal the "Hidden Light" in the forms of peace, prosperity, and power. In the seventies, alchemy and the tarot were becoming similarly modernized toward more practical concerns. L.V.X. members were urged toward "unselfish service to humanity" in order to "help herald a universal brotherhood on earth."[7] They had ties to the Rosicrucians and followed the teachings of the mystic St. Germain, the alleged ascended form of Francis Bacon, who was known as the "Wonderman of Western Europe."[8] The group met in the San Diego canyons at a place called the White Lodge, named after the mystical Himalayan retreat of their texts.[9]

The leader of the L.V.X. was Mother Elizabeth Clare Prophet. She would become an incredibly influential New Age leader, author, and television personality who would later predict global nuclear disaster. At the time she was in San Diego, her role was more maternal. She preached that "the goal is for us all—men and women alike—to realize ourselves as the Mother. And then, through the Mother, we can become the Christ."[10] Judy was very deep into the system, which combined the spirituality of the landscape with Californian desires for practical success. In a long letter to Mother Elizabeth, Judy describes (and confesses) that she thinks Joe's rescue from anonymity and despair is a true sign of the Creator's plan, that when he told her "his remarkable life story, tears of joy rolled down [her] cheeks" as she "understood how he has been a channel for the Masters," those spiritual leaders of the past who could still guide the earthly; among their number were Buddha and Christ. Judy goes on to explain how the "forces of evil" forced Joe "to accept demeaning work" to provide for his family. Judy sees Joe and Jerry's recent settlement "clearly as a victory for St. Germain" and a "miraculous story." She is clear about her feelings for Joe: "We have fallen in love." She mentions that Joe is a man of "great faith," which he learned from his mother. Judy tells Mother Elizabeth that she loves Joe deeply and hopes that she will marry them this coming Christmas. She also reveals that Joe himself went in front of an L.V.X. group and confessed himself to St. Germain.[11]

The letter is marked "Confidential."[12] One L.V.X. book claims that "man is capable of attaining superpower, not as a result of directing a magical force not based on order, but by bringing into activity the unlimited, though dormant, God-like potentialities and possibilities resident within himself [he] becomes the potent *son* of God."[13]

Joe Shuster and Judy Calpini were married in San Diego and had their reception at the Atlantis restaurant on Christmas Eve in 1976, the one-year anniversary of the agreement with DC. They had a three-tiered wedding cake. Judy wore a long-sleeved pink gown with a high neck. Joe wore a snappy navy suit with a gray tie, his salt-and-pepper hair slicked back and his pocket handkerchief visible. He couldn't help remembering how his mother had forbidden him, all those years ago, to marry Francine just because she was Catholic.

Off to their left, Jerry and Joanne smiled. The old grudge, whatever it was, was gone. They got to act like the popular kids. They smiled and laughed and made jokes at how much taller Judy was than Joe. Jerry was trim, wore a red power tie, and carried a drink, walking through the room like a superstar. Pieces of cake were crushed in the happy couple's mouths as flash bulbs popped. Jerry and Joe were enjoying their second burst of fame. They were being discovered by a whole new generation of people, some of whom worked at colleges and universities. People wanted to talk to them. The two couples could go out together and have dinner parties.[14] They had lots of in-jokes. When Jerry and Joanne went to their house over Christmas, Jerry would sneak a card off the mantel, cross out the sender, and sign his own name instead.[15] This was the colorful life they had dreamed about.

But the increasing physical and financial demands of the L.V.X. quickly took a toll on Joe and Judy's marriage. On May 24, 1977, Jean writes Joe a letter, worried that her brother is "dissatisfied with this marriage" because of the "burdens it has brought." Jean looks out for her brother and is fearful that, for Judy, "being married to Mr. Nice Guy" gives her "freedom to pursue her religious interest and hopefully pay for it as well." As little sisters have done for centuries, Jean questions her brother's wife's motives. She is only trying to help. Jean tells her brother that "my heart is with you" and that he should call her on Friday night.[16]

Jean, always the little sister, looks out for her big brother and gives him a number of suggestions on how to either save the marriage or move on. But Joe wanted to keep trying. He left greeting cards, yellow and flowery, that read, "Remember the sunshine when raindrops must fall. Remember the blue skies, and then . . . Remember the raindrops don't stay for too long, And watch for the sunshine again." And on that Friday, the day he was supposed to call his sister, Joe had a stroke.[17]

After several days in the hospital, Joe went home. Jean called it an "emotional breakdown." Either way, Joe knew that the marriage was too much. So when Judy was out of the house, he wrote her a simple, sad letter on yellow lined notepaper. In the note, Joe writes that in emotional moments Judy had suggested separating and he has "finally come to the conclusion that it would be best to take your advice." Signing the letter that he is "deeply sorry," Joe writes, on a new line, that he will be moving to a "separate apartment."[18]

Joe enclosed cash and his lawyer's number—and quietly, slowly, moved out.[19] But they stayed in touch, and when December rolled around, they began seeing each other again. Jean writes Judy on December 13, 1977, and is much more optimistic about the couple. She is "so happy to know that there may be reconciliation." But Jean is still worried about Joe's money and advises that only "if the financial burden was lifted off him" could she see a future for them. Jean is very straightforward about her brother's state: "He can't handle responsibility well," which is why, Jean speculates, he is "broke emotionally." She appeals to Judy that since "he is a little weak emotionally . . . we have to help him out in that area."

But Jean is confident that "in the long run, love always wins." She thinks that if Judy can earn some money, everything will be okay.[20] The couple did get back together and things were good. But then it was over again, and Joe dropped his head and moved north. He rented an apartment just around the corner from where Jerry and Joanne were living. Just like old times. Joe was an emotional sort who believed in love as much as Clark Kent did. But just like Clark, and so many of his fans, Joe knew what it felt like to be alone.

AFTER

In the February 12, 1979, issue of *People* magazine, a back article on Jerry, Joe, and Joanne by Laura Stevenson states: "Aren't Jerry and Joe pleased?

Well. No, as a matter of fact: They're mad as hell." The article is paired with a wonderful photo of the three dressed as their fictional counterparts: Joanne has a notepad, Jerry is pulling his shirt open to reveal a Superman T-shirt, and Joe, with his glasses, is Clark Kent.[21] The point of the article is again one of eliciting sympathy: "How would anyone feel in our shoes?" Jerry asks. He goes on: "Everywhere we go, it's Superman this and Superman that and we don't have anything." They were getting their pensions but felt they deserved more. Only this time the story didn't catch fire. It was the dawn of the eighties and the underdog seemed less believable. There was not even a spark.

On February 3, 1984, the space shuttle *Challenger* launched successfully into space. The CBS Evening News interviewed Jerry and Joe about it, and they praised the brave astronauts.[22] Man had made it into space during their lifetimes, and in some strange way, they were being acknowledged for it. Jerry and Joe often got together for lunch, talked on the phone, and did events and interviews once in a while. They talked about that space shuttle more than once. *That was something.* They could still complete each other's thoughts when they needed to. They lived three blocks apart.[23]

In 1982, Joe had had eye surgery for a detached retina. In June 1983, DC's *Action Comics* reached its milestone #544 issue, which was advertised as the forty-fifth anniversary of *Superman*. In the back of the issue, Joe contributed a beautiful side view of Superman leaping into the air in full color on a yellow background. Joe wrote to all his readers:

> *Since this may be the last SUPERMAN drawing I will ever make,*
> *due to the condition of my eyes, I have decided to keep the original.*
> *It has a very special and sentimental meaning for me.*
>
> *Sending my best personal wishes to you and all the staff at DC*
> *Comics.*
>
> *Warmest regards,*
> *Joe Shuster*[24]

As always, the inventor of the superhero signed his icon with his trademark perfect handwriting and a long running tail at the end of his name, something he had been doing since he was sixteen. Joe gave an interview on April 26, 1992, to Henry Mietkiwicz of *The Toronto Star*, the paper that his younger self used to read and sling. Visiting Joe at his apartment, Mietkiwicz notes that "memories are all that remain for the frail, 77-year-old artist, who neatly tucks his most cherished moments into the dozens of scrapbooks and photo albums that line his simple, one-bedroom apartment."[25] Joe would sit on his couch and bring his photos and pictures very close to his eyes. He listened to classical music and operas almost all the time and spent his money on the best audio equipment. He had also replenished his record collection, which made him very happy indeed. He coughed and wheezed a bit through the interview but was clearly pleased to be talking about Toronto, a place he had not seen since 1941. Mietkiwicz would write another essay where he states that "Shuster is often denied the credit he deserves as an artist, because of the 'deceptive simplicity' of his style . . . a simplicity that goes hand in hand with the innocence of humor."[26]

Joe also talked to his sister all the time. He enjoyed a few visits from his nephew, Warren, whom he would sit and talk with. Joe was happy and closed the *Toronto Star* interview with something that brought him peace: "There aren't many people who can honestly say they'll be leaving behind something as important as Superman. But Jerry and I can, and that's a good feeling. We're very, very proud and happy and pleased."[27] He bought sports jackets and smiled in the sun. These were good years. He was telling the truth.

On July 15, 1992, Joe died.

The *Los Angeles Times* reported that he passed away at his home in West Los Angeles of "congestive heart failure and hypertension." "The comic-book field has lost a great artist and a true pioneer," Jerry said. "I've lost a lifelong friend and partner. He'll be sorely missed." The rest of the piece talked about the lawsuit and Superman's popularity but said nothing of Joe's life.[28] Later that same year, DC Comics did the unthinkable and killed Superman in a battle with the monstrous Doomsday. The news flooded the country. Specially bagged issues included a *Daily Planet* obituary and a commemorative black armband with the famous "S" done in scarlet red.[29] Superman would return from the dead a year later.

One of the last things Joe had worked on was a cartoon pitch called *Kosmo the Whiz Kid*. He had been working on it for years. At one point, he enlisted the help of his old comics pal Sid Couchey, the longtime artist on *Richie Rich,* to help design the character.[30] His first iteration was Golly Galloo, a genielike kid who was always looking for adventure.

GOLLY GALLOO

After moving to California, Joe adapted some of his ideas for a new character named Kosmo. In his handwritten script for the first episode of *Kosmo,* on the same kind of paper he used to write to Judy on, Joe describes the character's Pinocchio-like origin: "A lonely old man . . . spent long hours in his workshop, making drawings, plans, calculations," on a model he was making of a little boy, which, "of all the machines . . . was really his favorite." The man wishes the boy were real.[31]

One night, after [he] had gone to bed in the rear of the workshop, he was awakened by the sound of a terrific thunderstorm—the room is lit by flashes of lightning and the sound of thunder. He sees a bolt of lightning strike the mechanical little boy—and then <u>miracle of miracles</u>—Kosmo becomes <u>alive</u>![32]

The man is ecstatic: "After all these years—I finally have a son—I'm so happy!" But Kosmo has a reaction and his heart stops beating. Luckily, he is revived by a miracle drug. He looks up at the man who created him and asks if he is real. The creator responds:

The cosmic forces have given you Life—but to prove yourself a <u>real</u> boy you must first learn all life's lessons. The world is full of temptations—you've got to choose between right and wrong.[33]

Kosmo asks: "How will I know?"

"You must have faith," the man says, "—and believe in yourself!"

This was the philosophy of Joe Shuster. Faith and belief in his own abilities are what he drew into those early panels of *Superman* as he carried Lois in silence over soft, sunlit vistas. And lifted a car over his head. No one could write that—it could be expressed only in images understood *as is* with the lean toward the ideal. Joe never had children, but somehow that didn't ring true. When he had become famous (or famous enough, he thought), one of the first things Joe did was paint a picture of Superman and send it to his old art teacher at Alexander Hamilton. He knew she was long gone by then, but in the last years of his life, he wondered if the painting was still there.[34]

THE STARLING

Just as Joe was working on his cartoon scripts, so too was Jerry busy during the eighties and early nineties. Jerry had been trying to get work at other comics companies—not only for the money but because he thought the timing was good. Comics were big business again, so there were lots of small, independent comics publishers trying to carve out their own slices of profit. Just as he did as a teenager, Jerry started sending things out to astonished young editors. He contributed a story to *Near to Now* #1 in 1987 with a character called "Space Cop."[35] The editor, Scott Johnson, remarks in the inside front cover: "We had received a package of several scripts by *Jerry Siegel*! Would I be interested in tackling one? he asked. Would I? I told him I'd do *'The Maid of Might Meets Jimmy Olsen's Sister'* if it was written by Jerry Siegel!" The story itself is strange; it involves an alien supercop fighting another alien who creates the giant illusion of Hitler's ghost to terrorize Brooklyn.

Another independent company active in the eighties was Eclipse Comics. They were readying an anthology comic called *Destroyer Duck,* the "Marauding Mallard of Vengeance," to raise money for *Howard the Duck* writer Steve Gerber's lawsuit against Marvel Comics.[36] The art would be by Jack Kirby himself, inked by a slew of contemporary comics all-stars. Jerry submitted a treatment to Eclipse publisher Dean Mullaney, and it was approved as a backup for *Destroyer.* Jerry was teamed with artist Val Mayerik and they got started on *The Starling.*[37]

The Starling is, though its editor vehemently denied it,[38] an adult take on the Superman origin. In it, a young woman named Irma Zane is accosted by a group of thugs. She is rescued by a golden alien being who appears and fends off her attackers. Irma and her alien savior—in a very psychedelic sequence—make love, after which the golden man promptly leaves for the stars. Irma's shirt is ripped in two as she cries out, "Where are you?" Later, it turns out that Irma is pregnant and she delivers a son named Robert, who is half-alien in heritage. Irma raises him by herself and struggles to make ends meet, until she develops a successful career as a romance novelist. As Robert grows up, he finds that he can change into two different forms: a golden muscular man (like his father) or a hideous misshapen monster: "I don't get it! I changed twice—from something uglier than sin to something that looks like a god!" Irma meanwhile is in therapy, wondering, "What if Robert is something inhuman—like his alien sex fiend of a father?"[39] As Robert grows up and begins to ask about his father, Jerry imagined his own son doing the same.

At the time of *The Starling,* Bella Siegel was still in Cleveland, having never remarried and having raised her and Jerry's son by herself. At heart, *The Starling* is Jerry trying to imagine the life that Bella and his son had to live without him. It is a story about guilt, wonder, and fear. It turns out the golden superalien who fathered the child was only in disguise— and that a darker plan may be in place to conquer the planet. *The Starling* is not so much about an absent father as it is about the experience of a young boy questioning why his father left him in the first place. In this way, near the end, Jerry found common ground with the son and wife he had left behind.

Unfortunately, *The Starling* was never fully completed and the additional two volumes Jerry had planned went unpublished. Jerry worked on some other one-offs here and there and began work on his autobiography. He was always typing away, even when it looked as if he wasn't. In a thin drawer at the Library of Congress lies a stack of full-length scripts he copyrighted, though he never mentioned them to the public.[40] They lie there still, waiting.

Mostly, though, Jerry very much enjoyed life with his wife and daughter, Laura, who now had two sons of her own. He was immensely proud of his daughter, who had been a teenage actress and another real-life Lois, having won numerous awards as both a newscaster and producer.[41] Jerry would welcome visitors and beam at the letter sent to him by the president, which congratulated him on the appearance of Superman on a postage stamp. But his wife and daughter made him smile even more than that. Jerry slept a lot these days, finally, but that was okay. After Joe passed away, Jerry thought a lot about the way Joe would draw on his mother's breadboard as he would pace above him in that little dining room so long ago.

Sometimes Jerry and Joanne would just get in the car without telling anybody and drive out to Laguna Beach, where they could enjoy being together, alone in the sun and under the endless blue sky. Not like Cleveland at all.

Jerry died on January 28, 1996, of a heart attack, having suffered from cardiac disease for several years, even after having a bypass operation. Several years after his comic book death, Superman would finally be married to Lois on TV after a tumultuous engagement on the show *Lois & Clark: The New Adventures of Superman*.[42] The two characters would be married in the comics the very same week in the DC Comics one-shot *Superman: The Wedding Album*.[43] In the elaborate two-page splash of the ceremony itself, the officiating priest is drawn to look like Jerry.[44]

There was a memorial ceremony for Jerry by DC employees in New York; Julie Schwartz gave a funny, poignant eulogy.[45] Later, back at his office, Julie remembered something he had somehow forgotten. He rummaged through his monstrous desk that was more like a petri dish for a parallel universe and found a plain manila folder that had been sent to him months before. In it was a script for a full-length comics novel. It was called *Zongolla*.

It was the last story of Jerry Siegel.

THE OTHER SIDE

The 122-page *Zongolla the Ultroid* is a sprawling mixture of *Star Wars, Barbarella,* and Jack Kirby's *Fourth World* series of comics. It begins with a worthy galactic enemy delivered in a vintage Jerry Siegel voice, focused like a laser straight from the 1930s:

> If you are the OVERLORD of THE NECRO EMPIRE in
> the year 2113 A.D., you can greedily smack your lips with

much enjoyment! You have the BEST! You eat the BEST! You squander the BEST! And why not? You EARNED it! By outwitting and cheating and/or bribing anyone who could be USED FOR PROFIT who crossed your devious path![46]

The evil Justice Lombroso tortures everyone he meets and rules the planet as an overlord of pain. But on the street below walks Zongolla, "tall, strong, and handsome," who is headed toward a monastery. "Next stop: PURITY! NOBILITY!" But he sees an old costumed speaker preaching against Lombroso: "Overcome vile brute force with LOVE!" Lombroso's savage Law-Wolves enter and rip the man's chest open. Zongolla is stunned: "The death of that peace-loving old man cries out for VENGEANCE!" He fights back but ends up in Lombroso's pits, beaten and lost:

> They CONFISCATED all I had:
> They STOLE my life!
> They SCORN me! BEAT me!

He collapses and has "no heartbeat."[47]

But thanks to a strange pool, Zongolla returns to life: he feels "NO MORE PAIN! I feel . . . INDESTRUCTIBLE! I am SUCH A ONE. I can defend myself against ANY onslaught in BIZARRE WAYS!" He fights his way back to Lombroso but decides at the last moment to use his strange powers . . . for evil. Here, at the end of his career, Jerry conducts the great experiment: What if his character in 1933 had chosen another path? Zongolla goes on a rampage of wanton, surrealist sex and violence with bizarre Jerry-created characters such as Serpentina and Cheeta. But Zongolla hears that his mother is dying and rushes back to see her. He repents to her, admitting that "EVIL CREPT CLOSE! It made me . . . like THIS!" His mother forgives him, and Zongolla sees Death itself as he races to save his mother—but fails: "I'm sorry I wasn't a BETTER son. . . ." He vows, "From now on, I will be a SUPERHERO!"[48]

At the end, Zongolla confronts his own younger self in an "arena of the ID" and finds that he hates what he has become. But he spares Lombroso's life, and a woman named Zyra—which end-rhymes with Bella—forgives his enemy, as does the spirit of his mother. He eventually forgives himself by doing good for others. Near the end of the story, a soldier remarks to Zongolla, "This is REAL LIFE, not some morality play!"

Jerry Siegel died a happy man, according to his friends and acquaintances, surrounded by letters from presidents and spending his days in a good easy chair.[49] He had finally achieved the recognition he had struggled for over Superman. Yet this, like much of the story, is romanticized. The truth is that Jerry also died after ten years of suffering from heart disease, no one publishing his scripts, and his best friend being gone. And like anyone—everyone—facing the last page of his or her life with the gift of some time to think about it, he still had his own regrets.

This was human, after all. The truth that placed its hands on Jerry all those summer nights ago was that a hero could also be funny, ugly, or awkward; he could be human by virtue of being alien. Superman began the nation's cultural fascination with superheroes not because he could jump and punch in perfect pitch but because we were in on the secret from the very beginning: He was not perfect; he was really *just like us*. He had to put on a suit, he had to go to work, and the one he loved was always walking away. This important layer to the story that would define the genre was accomplished—in the new, colorful, and bizarre medium of superhero comics—only by using autobiographical elements as a sort of science of the imagination. Reading about Superman, we never knew these personal secrets, but we could still recognize the truth of them. This is what Jerry realized at the end: The truth made things stronger, not weaker. The truth was Clark. The truth was Jerry.

Chapter 27

Both Sides

YOUR LEFT FOOT, braced by a cushion of rubber, pushes down on the square metal pedal. You hear the metal clicking and move forward, over the hump of gray concrete and into the street. The silver spokes turn. You ride up to the drugstore sometimes twice in one day. You walk in and wonder if they notice you again. You walk long laps before settling on the aisle where you see the white metal spinner rack, ready to squeal and spin. The light above pulses. You look around: *Are there new ones?* You grab the double-sized issue #200 and try to find the tiny price. When you take it up front, your cents and bills scatter on the black rubber mat. You are twelve cents short. The lady in front of you spots it and smiles, digging into her pocketbook. You go red, pick up your comic, and walk out. Your bike lies on the ground. You fly home in a minute. You hide it under your shirt so your mom doesn't know you went up there again. Your dad is at work. Upstairs you place it on the bed and make sure you didn't bend it.

Comic books, for all of their rhapsody, can really be understood only by context: historically, culturally, and personally, over issues and between panels. Something happened before, and something happens after. The adventure itself is an interior one framed by a secret origin and a cliff-hanger, the space that lunges out from the last panel into those empty days before the next issue. They are like summer vacations. After you read the story, these are the spaces, before and after, where you can remember, think about, and imagine. The same goes for the story of the creators: once you reach the last panel, there is a real urge to look at both sides—before the beginning and after the end—to try to find some context. We don't know much about that first group of kids who bought, begged, or stole *Action* #1, but we know one thing for sure: They didn't read it just once. There is still truth to be told.

SECRET ORIGIN: OLD GHOSTS

In the comics, Superman's secret origin—as Kal-El of Krypton—is one he cannot remember, as it starts before he is born, with his father on a distant world. Similarly, Jerry Siegel's father was born on July 1, 1872, far away and with an alien name, as Mikhel ("Michel") Ianke Segaliovich in Vilijampole, Lithuania, near the city of Kaunas.[1] The word *kaunas* means "fight." The area was also known as the Pale, an expanse between Lithuania and Poland that was designated by Russia for Jewish settlement. The world that Michel was born into was one of bustling marketplaces, confusing languages, and secret glances. Local towns were ruled by councils of elders, who would pass judgment on matters both religious and political with solemn faces framed by long, draped clothing. Jewish identity was strong in Lithuania, but deep internal pressures also challenged some of their older, more traditional ways. The Pale was a bleak place of constant incursions and eroding freedoms. It bubbled with unease and arguments, ready to explode.

Michel received apprentice training in a skill, but not a lengthy, formal education. He married Sora on October 15, 1898, and they quickly had two children, Rokhel in 1899 and Mina in 1900.[2] As the head of his family, Michel looked toward America because there were things worth escaping in his homeland. For Jews living in the Pale, Russian army conscription was almost a mandatory way of life. Michel himself served for a short time under the whims of the czar's commanders. How he got out (the usual term of service was twenty-five years) is not known for certain; he may have been bought out by another family member or been replaced by another Jew. He may have even escaped; others even killed to do so. In posed photos as a soldier, Michel is in uniform and holds a dirk. In later pictures, outside the home on Kimberley, he is seen in a tank top undershirt in his front yard. The change is remarkable, but the eyes are the same.

The army experience for young Jews was particularly hard; they were often forced to do things like kneel on dried peas for hours while Russian officers implored them to accept the Orthodox Christ, who was seen as both human and divine.[3] Jews like Michel were given bad food and verbal dressing-downs in an attempt at forced conversion. Like the violent pogroms, the banning of a free Jewish press, and the awful cartoons that depicted thick snakes with dark-eyed faces, the Russian army served as yet another form of nationalism whereby Jews were treated as inhuman aliens.

When Michel finally got out of the army, he knew he had to leave Lithuania. The world was crumbling around him. This was his home, but it certainly was not a place to raise his family.[4] So Michel, like approximately two million of his brethren, emigrated as the century clock turned. It was certainly good timing, because a few short years later Lithuania would become embroiled in World War I and eventually be overrun by the Nazi horde that would reduce the Jewish population to an unimaginably sad fraction. Kaunas itself was devastated by a horrific massacre of Jews in 1941.[5]

Michel brought all of this invisible baggage across the gray Atlantic. He landed in New York on November 8, 1900.[6] When he got to Cleveland—a smart choice, because it likely held more opportunity than an already overcrowded New York—he settled in a small wooden house in the Jewish neighborhood of Woodland.[7] Like his father, Michel was a skilled tailor; he could cut and sew fabric, fix holes in knees, and adjust seams in and out. So he made a sign for the front window and got to work. Eventually, he saved enough money to bring in Sora (now Sarah) and his two children. They were, of course, fascinated with the world he had opened up for them. But there was still work to be done. He had to take care of his family. When the sun disappeared, Michel would still think of home. It never really left him. He had just heard that back home, his younger brother Movsha had died of pneumonia, at the age of two.[8]

Siegel, like many immigrants in the 1930s, reinvented himself in different shades of the same profession in an attempt to outwit the Depression. Part of this strategy included him adopting an Americanized version of his name, "Michael," which appears intermittently in the historical record of his life.[9] Michel Siegel was creative in his work—if he could fix clothes, why not mend old ones and sell them? He ended up buying a building on Central Avenue, a freestanding wooden structure that had a residence in the back he could rent out. His store would go in front. There was already a clothing store called Siegel's in Cleveland, so he went with the simple, more utilitarian "2nd Hand Clothing."[10]

Clothing was important business during the Depression, perhaps especially so. The major newspapers of the time—*The Plain Dealer, The Cleveland News, The Cleveland Press*—ran pages and pages of clothing ads, mostly from the giant department stores such as the May Co. and Halle's. Men wore sharp wool suits and dark hats at plunging angles to work, church, picnics, and baseball games. The area around Central was quickly being occupied by lower-income residents, mostly blacks, who were filling the void left by Jews moving farther east and who were struggling to get their own piece of the American "pie". Michel then had two sets of eager customers: those who wanted to sell clothes and those who wanted to buy cheap ones. From his table in the back, he saw plenty of people selling clothing that did not originally belong to them. Cleveland at this time was rapidly earning its reputation as a city of crime on both sides of the badge: the newspapers of the week leading up to Michel's death are riddled not only with grisly stories of robbery and murder, but also with several editorial cartoons showing police being bought off.

The store did so well (and the Siegel family grew so quickly) that Michel bought a house in the eastern neighborhood of Glenville. He was proud of all his children, when he wasn't yelling at them. And then there was Jerry, the youngest. Michel knew Jerry's grades were bad and that perhaps the store would be his someday. This was something he tried not to think about too much; it caused heartburn sometimes. But Jerry was his youngest, and Michel could not help thinking of his own younger brother when he held him in his arms. When Jerry was little, Michel would bounce him on his knee. Decades later, Jerry would remember these scenes without sound, deep in the past, and describe them as "bliss."[11]

The Plain Dealer and *The Cleveland News* offered no mention of the robbery at all. Clearly Michel, a Jew on Central Avenue with his racks of musty clothes, could not compete with the latest exploits of the dashing Charles Lindbergh or the more macabre death penalty cases going on in Cleveland at the time. His obituary finally ran in *The Plain Dealer* for two days over the weekend. It read:

> Siegel, Michael, 10622 Kimberley Ave., beloved husband of Sarah, father of Harry, Leo, Jerome and Isabel Siegel, Mrs. Rosalind Spanner and Mrs. Minerva Levin, grandfather of 2. Services Sunday at 2 p.m. from Berkowitz Chapel, 818 E. 105th St.—June 2, 1932, age 59 years. Mt. Olive (Jewish) cemetery, Solon, O.[12]

The obituary was, like most, both rich in facts and poor in details. Luckily, Cleveland was a newsy town filled with suited reporters eager to hound the truth, though they were often younger than the printing presses that ran the ink. In Cleveland, one such man was Louis B. Seltzer, infamous editor of *The Cleveland Press,* which started publication in 1878. Seltzer was the kind of cigar-chomping editor who rolled up his sleeves, barked at his reporters, and knew exactly what phrase to lead with. In his autobiography, *The Years Were Good,* Seltzer writes about what he wanted his paper to be:

> Even though you were born in the city in which you have made up your mind to live all your life, it is not possible at any moment to say that you know it. You don't. Under the impact of the swift and steadily accelerating change that is taking place in a fermenting America, it is imperative, at all times, to keep at the business of knowing your home town.[13]

True to its editor's word, *The Press* delivered, and on the front page on June 3, 1932, Jerry Siegel and the rest of the world read the true cause of his father's death, which for years after was whispered, passed on, and even published, many times, as a gunshot.

DIES AFTER ~~ROBBERY~~

Coroner Says Heart Disease Caused Death of Merchant

Coroner A. J. Pearse today said Michael C. Siegel, 60, owner of a clothing store at 3530 Cedar avenue, died of heart disease shortly after being held up by three robbers there yesterday.

It was believed the robbers might have murdered the merchant, but Pearse said that his was a natural death brought on by shock. Mrs. Sarah Siegel, 10622 Kimberley avenue, said her husband had suffered from heart disease.

Michel Siegel was not murdered in a hail of gunfire. He died of a heart attack.[14]

The coroner was quoted in the paper, but the signature on the death certificate was that of Wilson S. Chamberlain, who filled out the report and signed it on June 4. Chamberlain listed the cause of death as "acute dilatation of heart. Collapsed in store after two men stole suit of clothes" (which conflicts with the paper's account of three). Contributory causes are listed as "chronic myocarditis" (which was confirmed by "Exam")—a catastrophic inflammation of the heart due to either chronic disease or enlargement.[15]

Later that night, Detective Lieutenant Gloeckner of the No. 3 Reserve Squad sat down and plunked out his police report. He wrote that "unknown colored men," described as "No. 1," "No. 2," and "No. 3," all averaging five feet nine and 160 pounds, give or take, came into the store and asked to see a suit of clothing, when same was shown to No.1 man he walked out of the store without paying for it, the victim became excited, about 5 minutes later and fell on the floor in a faint, he was immediately taken to Charity hospital by No. 3 Emergency where he was pronounced dead on arrival . . . death was due to natural causes.[16]

In the attached letter to Cornelius Cody, the chief of detectives, Gloeckner wrote:

At 9:20 pm after the receipt of a man shot at East 36th street and
Central Ave responded to the scene. Upon arrival learned that a man
named Michael Siegel who conducts a second hand clothing store at
3530 Central Ave had fainted. . . . I went to Charity Hospital and
upon my arrival learned that Siegel was dead.[17]

This may have been where the story of a gunshot began. Gloeckner
specifically noted that he "failed to find any marks of violence" and "at
no time were any blows struck or any weapons used."[18] Still, the detective noted that "his neck appears as tho [sp] there may be a dislocation."
There was bruising and an awkward look to it. It was a scary scene.[19]

Where did all this information come from? There was an eyewitness:

According to John Ewing colored and living at the Wayfarer's
Lodge 3 men (colored) came into Siegel's store. . . . Siegel followed him to the door but his progress was blocked by the
other man in the store. Siegel then walked into the store and
fell over in a faint. . . . At no time were any blows struck or any
weapons used. . . . [20]

Located a few streets over from Central on Chester, the Wayfarer's
Lodge was a long, low building with a massive common room. Very well
organized and unfortunately well occupied, the Lodge offered a place for
out-of-work men to stay during difficult times. Ewing must have returned
to the Lodge that night half-afraid he would run into the very men he saw
rob the store. Or had he already known them and thus refused to identify
them because he feared reprisals? Was there a gunshot and he didn't want to
rat? No one ever knew. Ewing did tell police in the criminal complaint
that "all can be identified."[21] A few years later, Ewing died while renting
a room in East Cleveland. He succumbed to pellagra, a vitamin deficiency
that caused his eyes to sink and his hands to explode in dozens of sores.
Ewing died without ever identifying the robbers, at least to anyone who
bothered to write it down or remember it.[22]

The Cleveland police have no more records of the Siegel robbery, so
whether there was ever an ongoing investigation or any suspects is both
unknown and unlikely.[23] For Michel Siegel, any questions of justice in the
real world probably ended with the coroner's report. Who was responsible?
The robbers? The police? Or just his own poor health? At the end of his

report, Gloeckner noted the standing truth of the case: "Search 1 being conducted for the three men but up to this writing they have not been apprehended."[24] The crime would never be solved. There is some doubt whether it was even pursued.[25] Gloeckner had a lifetime in police work, beginning in white-glove traffic control; in 1927, when Sacco and Vanzetti were executed, Gloeckner single-handedly stopped a rowdy demonstration on the steps of the criminal court building. Gloeckner waited inside the front doors of the building on his motorcycle; when the execution was announced, he roared out, grabbed the leader of the rally, and sped off. He was on a constant search for evenhanded justice in an area that was inhabited by people of fifty-seven national, racial, and religious backgrounds. He had slicked-back hair, spectacles, and a hard-line jaw.[26] He worked out of the same station as another cop named Corrigan.[27]

Michel Siegel's burial cost $381, which included ads in the papers, a night watchman, a limousine, and an actual casket instead of the other choice, a simple "rough box." The funeral was paid in full. His assets, which included half-interest in both the store and the Kimberley home, totaled $3,131.[28]

Back in 1932, right after his father died, Jerry wondered briefly if he would be asked to take over the store. But he knew he was too young and that it wouldn't really work. Everyone kind of knew that. When he finally got into the store to help his mother and brothers clean it out, it was hard seeing his father's things: scissors, measuring tape, a grease pencil here and there. He stared at his dad's markings on scraps of paper and then quickly looked away. He looked back. The letters were very still. He didn't like walking through the front door. The building was going to be sold and indeed would be demolished soon. Years later, he would wonder how much his life would have changed if things had gone differently.

Jerry looked around uneasily. He also couldn't help but think there were clues.

On June 9, 1932, there was another murder in the area. Someone named Isaiah Johnson killed a grocer named Harry Friedlander. *The Plain Dealer* had most of the facts: "Resisting a holdup in his grocery store at 2366 E 39th St., Harry Friedlander, 41, father of three children, was shot and killed by a gunman today."[29] Two children playing outside looked in and watched and saw Friedlander struggling with the robber. But the robber tore his gun hand free and fired at the grocer. Friedlander had been running his store for fourteen years. Jerry focused his eyes on the article: "A short time after the murder, two armed holdup men entered the Consolidated Fruit Auction Co., 3716 Croton Avenue, forced the proprietor and five clerks to lie on the floor and robbed the safe of $1236.54, police say."[30] Were these crimes related to the robbery of his father's store? They sounded so different, but Jerry's emotional imagination was so heightened that *could they be?* Before trial, on August 10, 1932, Johnson admitted to killing Friedlander and turned state's evidence for a shorter stint in Mansfield. Johnson gave up information on a number of other holdups all over the area, including another murder by someone named Louis Harrison. Johnson told police that he could probably tell them about dozens of other "little crimes" if he wanted to. The group he turned in was named "the Crime Club." The Crime Club, it turned out, was a vast network full of "known underworld characters" who dealt in extortion, burglary, and murder.[31] The club also had a secret hideout:

> It is a second-story suite, he said, over a store room, and is reached through a narrow alley and a dark stairway. Three or four rooms were given over to gambling activities, he said, in which the "house" got a cut. Several other rooms were used as a place to "check" weapons and clothing used in criminal activities, he said, and one of the prisoners being held is suspected of being the man who had charge of concealing these weapons. The men who made up this gang . . . are of the most vicious type. They are absolutely ruthless. They kill at the slightest provocation, and this is the more pernicious because it is not each other they kill—as most gangsters do these days—but honest citizens unfortunate enough to live or do business in their bailiwick.

Their headquarters—full of smoke, booze, clothes, cards, contraband, and criminals—was at 3535 Central Avenue—right next door to Michel Siegel's clothing store.[32]

The young Jerry studied the papers but could not find out if any other members of the Crime Club were ever caught and confessed to the robbery of a clothing store. Most of them took off once Johnson started singing, so any trails went quickly cold. Jerry, who read the paper every day, probably found it hard to believe that criminals, coming and going next door, wouldn't look at his father's store with a sly, opportunistic eye. In the *Torch Style Guide* that Jerry would also absorb in equal amounts, reporters are told to "constitute yourself a news blotter, absorbing all information you can."[33] Jerry kept looking, but he couldn't see a solution. He couldn't find a single criminal, so he would have to face them all.

Jerry Siegel's Superman is as much veiled autobiography as it is national need. A very specific allusion Siegel makes to his father's death occurs in *Superman #2*.[34]

Superman, with that incomparable Shuster face, in a knowing, scholarly pose, confronts a crook who faints dead away. Superman then makes a comment from Siegel's script that sounds like a medical diagnosis: "The

excitement was too much for him." That the criminal dies of "heart-failure" speaks for itself, but that it is a *criminal* who dies makes it more complicated. Part of this reversal echoes Siegel's possible anger at his father for not being able to handle the "excitement" of the robbery that kills him. Indeed, that same week, *The Press* reported in a towering headline, BANDITS FLEE HER WRATH, that a teenage girl named June Ludwig single-handedly foiled four robbers at her father's store. This frustration on the part of Jerry echoes the screaming, jumping Superman who in *Action* #1 yells at a crook, "You're not fighting a woman now!"[35] Why couldn't Jerry's dad do what even a teenage girl could? Somewhere in the ugly mix of introspection and hormones that is the teenage mind, Jerry must have felt disappointed. In the final panel, Superman completely overshadows the criminal, who is reduced on panel to a simple pair of shoes.

In *Superman #3*, Clark Kent, in his obligatory bright, shiny blue suit, arrives to surprise Lois at her home, after apparently drowning at sea.[36]

Here we see the fantasy of Superman as a replacement for Jerry's father: after having replaced the criminal, cowardly version who dies of heart failure, Clark Kent returns to Lois's front door "ALIVE!" Superman here is not only a response to, he *is* Michel Siegel, who will return (apparently forever) "each and every month" in the colorful pages of *Action Comics*. Armed with a fantastic, fictional story—he even manages to "phone in" his assignment—the amazingly dry Clark says, "Surprised?"

and surely we are. Lois buys his incredible explanation because she too is charged with keeping the fictional drama alive. Just as readers are in on the secret of Superman's secret identity, so too is Jerry (and perhaps Joe) the only one in on his third identity as the figure of Jerry's father.[37]

There is another kind of resurrection going on here. Jerry the writer removes his father (the scared criminal) and replaces him with his avatar, Superman, who is not only better and more interesting but wears a nice blue suit eerily symbolic of the one that was stolen.[38] As Freud puts it: "The murder was not remembered: instead of it there was a phantasy of its atonement, and for that reason this phantasy could be hailed as a message of redemption."[39]

Superman, like Hamlet's father, is a "GHOST!" who defies rational explanation and drives the rest of Jerry Siegel's professional (and perhaps personal) life.[40] Just as only Hamlet and the audience can really see the ghost and understand it, so too is Superman's identity a shared secret.[41] In *Superman* #1, Clark's foster father, Jonathan Kent, even warns him: "This great strength of yours—you've got to hide it from people or they'll be scared of you!"[42]

Another connection between Jerry Siegel's life and the Superman comics he wrote occurs in the obvious character of Superman's alien father,

especially in the first newspaper proposal that made the initial rounds.[43] Jor-L is the perfect father: a handsome scientist whom everyone in the world—literally and wrongly—is set against because of his wild theories about Krypton. The first time we see him he is running through a door to reach the bedside of his wife, Lora, and a young Superman, known here only by the first version of his Kryptonian name, Kal-L.[44]

Like Clark Kent showing up at the door of an awestruck Lois Lane, Jor-L is a welcome, and surprising, appearance. The young Kal-L[45] and his fetching mother could not be more pleased. The fantasy continues in the next panel as his wife explains the reasons for her summons. Kal-L (who immediately reaches for his father) is apparently a chip off the old block: "just like your dad," he is a "roughneck" and "gave the doctor a discolored eye."[46]

This is not the father who dies of heart failure diagnosed

by a "doctor": Jor-L scoffs at doctors and other such enemies. Kal-L wants nothing more than to *be* Jor-L, the perfect idealized father. Part of the fantasy is also that the son is the source of the father's happiness. Kal-L is suspiciously nowhere to be seen in the last panel, as he is sublimated into Jor-L himself.

But disaster is just a panel—and a heartbeat—away. A massive earthquake cuts off the Ls' blissful happiness as Krypton begins to show signs of its imminent destruction. Jor-L sets himself on finding a way to halt the inevitable destruction. But try as he might, he can't find a solution that will save them all.[47]

Lora (which rhymes with Sarah) comes across the distraught Jor-L, his hand to his brow, and says: "You're terribly pale, dear—I know there's something's wrong. What is it? Tell me!" And we are left to wonder if this isn't a scene Jerry might have overheard, or at least imagined, of his mother confronting his father about his obvious poor health, which he may have tried initially (and, in Jerry's eyes, heroically) to hide from her.

In one of their earlier *Popular Comics* strips, *The Pinkbaums,* Jerry portrays a mother with similar worries for her husband.

But Michel/Jor-L cannot lie and tells the sad truth: Krypton is doomed, it will "explode into fragments." So Jor-L concocts the plan that everyone knows by heart: Build a ship and send his only son to another world.[48]

Jor-L launches his son into space and dies as Krypton explodes, forcing Kal to make the long trip through cold space alone—in a long, tight ship that looks like a coffin. This blazing, highly dramatic act of self-sacrifice is again perhaps a carefully constructed mythology

through which the young Jerry can attempt to understand his father's death. Jerry must have wondered if the time and effort he put into his creation of Superman was a response to his father leaving him. And he must have had mixed feelings of despair and gratitude, which play out in the origin story: Jor-L *had* to send him away; he had no other choice.[49]

It is Jewish custom that the headstone be unveiled a year after the person's death. In that year from 1932 to 1933, Jerry took a very different approach to mourning his father. Faced with enormous emotional and economic pressures, Jerry—along with his friend Joe—attempted a solution that was both fictional and practical, that connected the real world with an imaginary one, in order to solve all their problems at once.[50] It was a long, yet quick year. But now, staring at the black marble headstone and the tiny black-and-white photo of his father, who was both the strongest man he knew and the meekest—who had fainted while being robbed—Jerry wanted to bring his father back as the person he felt he remembered, or should have.[51]

This scene is echoed in the comics at the end of Superman's new origin in *Superman* #1, which was done a year after the one-page explanation in *Action* #1. The editors felt that readers should know more about why Superman was Superman. We watch in silence as Clark stands at the resting place of his earthly parents as he vows to be a good hero, and we understand both origins: the public one and the secret one. Their deaths "strengthened a determination that had been growing in his mind."[52]

When Michel Siegel's affairs were finally settled in probate, the value of his clothes and bank account was $131.00, one dollar more than what Jerry and Joe got for Superman.[53]

Chapter 28

The House of El

SIXTY-SEVEN YEARS LATER, Joanne Siegel stares at the glassy eye in front of her. It is black with a slight sheen of blue. The video-camera is on a heavy tripod and looks immovable. Someone stands behind it. The office is warm, even for Southern California. She thinks of Jerry. And where she is. And why she is here. And how much she misses him. This isn't how she imagined it. This is a deposition, an attempt at discovery—of information, of evidence. In the absence of all superpowers, all that remains is the great domain of the reporter: the so-called facts themselves.

Almost ten years earlier, on April 3, 1997, a little over a year after Jerry's death, Joanne and her daughter, Laura Siegel Larson, served legal "termination notices" to DC Comics and its parent company TimeWarner, in an effort to recover a portion of the original copyright to Superman.[1] After two years, these notices became "effective," meaning that the Siegels owned (and were owed) 50 percent of the character since April 15, 1999.[2] One of the major repercussions of this ruling was that the Shuster estate could do the same in 2013. DC was now dealing with the possibility, if the courts upheld their claims, of the families someday owning 100 percent of the original character. Faced with myriad complicated legal questions, DC and the Siegels began negotiations. For all the surmised hostility between the two sides, there was also a symbiosis: Jerry and Joe had created the character, but DC Comics had strengthened and protected it; both sides knew this. But *Action Comics* came first.

Donenfeld, Liebowitz, and Weisinger were all gone. Lois Lane had outlasted them all. DC Comics was now run by a former writer, Paul

Levitz, who was a walking grin with glasses, jeans, and mustache, who still, when talking about comics, seemed ten years old. Like Jerry, Levitz broke into comics by self-publishing a fanzine; he went on to a long career of editing and writing at DC, most notably a must-read run on Jerry's old title *Legion of Super-Heroes*.[3] Both the Siegel and the Shuster families liked Levitz: he gave them tours and movie tickets, and most important, he knew his stuff. When the Shusters visited the DC offices, Levitz gestured at the huge mural of Superman panels on the wall and pointed to the lettering, which he identified as Frank's.[4] *Nobody knew that*.[5] Paul Levitz did; he knew the importance of history.

But Levitz also worked for a big corporation and acted accordingly. The rumors were that the Siegels were asking for $10 million up front or even a 50 percent outright interest in DC Comics revenue. Heads shook from side to side in the high offices. So in New York, Levitz did a presentation to the Siegels' lawyers, demonstrating that the family was asking too much, stressing that it was DC's "protectorship" of the character over the years that had resulted in much of Superman's value. Levitz used slides, props, and toys to explain the use of the brand, almost like a puppet show.[6] When questioned later, Laura would note that she and her mother understood DC's approach: "They wanted us to understand and appreciate the approach that DC Comics has had to exploiting Superman and the great job that they thought they had done."[7]

DC knew they had to take the Siegel proposal and pare it down.[8] DC eventually returned with an offer whereby the Siegels would surrender their portion of the copyright for a payday of $2 million, another million in advance, and a minimum annual sum of $500,000. In addition, the Siegels would get a 6 percent royalty of Superman and a 1 percent royalty of his publications.[9] Jerry and Joe would keep their credits, and the families would get full medical benefits. The Siegels accepted the offer on October 16, 2001, one day before what would have been Jerry's eighty-seventh birthday.

The work of the lawyers began, as both sides now had to hammer out the long-form agreement. The lawyer for the Siegels was Kevin Marks of the firm Gang, Tyre, Ramer & Brown, and he was excited—this was a major legal settlement that would successfully resolve a question that had tantalized Superman fans for years: *What if Superman left DC? What would happen? Could he go to Marvel? Could the Siegels produce their own comic? Would there be two Supermen? What about justice for the creators? Who deserves this most?* Web sites, the trades, and comics conventions had throbbed with these sorts of questions for years. So Marks wrote up what had been agreed to and sent it off. He even notes in a letter, "Many thanks for help and patience in reaching this monumental accord."[10] But as the contract took shape, back and forth, problems began to arise.

Marks saw several "trapdoors" in crediting and royalties, as well as new demands on the Siegels, including handing over "biographical material" to DC.[11] According to Marks, there were also problematic areas involving travel for the Siegels to promote the brand, profit "tails" on movies, and many other points.[12] Marks further believed that DC was limiting Superman royalties in team books such as *Justice League of America* down to 1 percent from a previously agreed 1.5 percent.[13] DC argued that these were all part of the original agreement. Marks was not really worried; these were just places to clarify.

DC sent a contract in early 2002 with little compromise; Marks still thought the issues could be dealt with in draft, but the Siegels did not agree.[14] Marks soon got a call that his client, Joanne Siegel, had written a strongly worded letter to DC about the most recent contract. She was not pleased. She wrote:

> *After more than half a century of DC Comics and its predecessors enjoying huge profits from my late husband's creations, while we lived in poverty for many of those years, the company is not satisfied. The beast hungers for more. Just like the Gestapo, your company wants to strip us naked of our legal rights.*[15]

She put it squarely on the lawyers: "Have you been aware that your representatives have gone too far? If not, you do now."[16] Laura would later testify that her mother stormed into her condo with this letter and asked her to type it up, shouting, "Don't change one word!"[17] Things were breaking down quickly.

On November 29, 2001, Marks had gotten a call from a fellow lawyer. His name was Marc Toberoff. According to Marks:

> He said he was a lawyer and that he represented individuals that had interests in rights to movie and other properties. . . . I also recall him saying that he had a separate company that was in the business of acquiring intellectual property rights . . . he

was interested in the Superman property and the Superboy property.[18]

Marks implied that the settlement process was just about over. Toberoff called him again in July 2002. Marks recalled that Toberoff asked him, "Can you tell me what DC Comics offered you?" Marks responded, "No, we have a confidentiality agreement."[19] Toberoff then boldly asked if he could present an offer to the Siegels along with his colleague, Ari Emanuel of the Endeavor Talent Agency. Marks stared ahead. Emanuel was a talent agent who was beginning to be known for his renegade style—he talked fast, wore great suits, and swore like a sailor in the middle of the Pacific. He had gotten busted for stealing client files after being fired from International Creative Management, but this had only added to his mystique in Hollywood, making his new agency, Endeavor, increasingly popular.[20] According to Marks, Toberoff said that the Siegel family had "perhaps the most valuable of properties" and he "wanted to make a proposal."[21] Marks responded: "I'm listening."

On a conference call in August 2002, according to Marks, Toberoff and Emanuel outlined what they would pay for the Superman property. They "made a proposal of $15 million and what was described as a meaningful back end, which I understood to be a contingent compensation position or a royalty position in the exploitation of the property."[22] Toberoff said in no uncertain terms, "This is the offer." Marks said he would take it to his clients.[23] He did.[24]

A month later, on September 21, 2002, Marks and his firm were terminated as counsel by the Siegels.[25] Soon after, Marc Toberoff took over as the Siegels' lawyer.[26]

By 2004, the Siegels filed to get an accounting of what they were owed from DC.[27] By 2008 the court ruled for apportionment, meaning a final number had to be calculated and agreed upon.[28] DC counterclaimed, and both sides agreed to have it decided in trial. In March 2008, Judge Stephen Larson upheld the initial decision: the Siegels did own their 50 percent and were entitled to profits since 1999.[29] Because Joe had no heirs, the 50 percent that would be his was owned by DC Comics until his family had a chance to reclaim it in 2013.

In 2006, an unknown person broke into Marc Toberoff's offices and stole a substantial amount of material related to the Siegel case. An anonymous package then mysteriously appeared on the doorsteps of DC's lawyers. A rambling page called the "Toberoff Timeline" was attached as a cover letter and outlined a chronological scenario alleging that Marc Toberoff had "devised a strategy whereas he has ultimately claimed as much ownership of the Superman copyright <u>personally</u> as he can."[30] The writer, anonymous, plots an elaborate scenario whereby Toberoff supposedly courted both the Siegel and the Shuster families independently (without telling them he was contacting the other), in order to eventually control the copyright himself through built-in contract points that would give him portions of the copyright. The writer states:

> As it stands right now, the single person who would stand to gain the MOST in a settlement with Time Warner regarding the ongoing SUPERMAN legal dispute would not be the heirs themselves, but Marc Toberoff.[31]

The anonymous writer tells the lawyers to "consider it an early holiday gift." Though the writer misspells Shuster as "Schuster" and sounds increasingly paranoid as the letter progresses, the damage was done.

DC then sued Toberoff for interfering with his clients' well-being. Toberoff was furious, especially because the documents were not immediately returned. By this time, DC had also fired their lawyers and had employed Daniel Petrocelli, the celebrity attorney who was famous for his successful representation of the family of Ron Goldman—and for his unsuccessful defense of Enron CEO Jeffrey Skilling.[32] Most important for DC and TimeWarner Petrocelli had successfully represented Disney against a rights chain for Winnie-the-Pooh by proving that his adversary had stolen documents.[33]

For this case against Toberoff, Petrocelli would depose nearly everyone in the story, giving them, some literally, their last word on Superman.

JEAN

Down south in Santa Fe, Jean Shuster Peavy, Joe's sister, is living in a house with her son, Warren, and her daughter, Dawn. Jean, who has not eaten red meat for fifty years, is a health advocate and enjoys the dry spiritual calm of New Mexico. She has hair red as fire and looks half her age. Her brother Frank died in New York on September 24, 1996. Jean, her husband, and Warren went to New York for a memorial service. When they came back, on October 3, 1996, Jean's husband tragically died in a car crash.[34] It was a terrible year.

Jean perseveres through her faith and optimism. She is still protective of her brother Joe, even though now only in memory. She has a Superman shelf in the house where she keeps all of the books that mention him. She has been in touch with a few of the authors, but not many. No one seemed willing to simply look her up in the phone book. She talks to Joanne every once in a while, on a lazy afternoon or on a birthday. But always about family, not about Superman.

After Joe died, his family found out he had more debts than assets.[35] Soon after, Frank and Jean signed a document with DC waiving their right to reclaim the copyright. In return, they got a pension and holiday bonuses. DC also paid all of Joe's expenses. "They took care of everything," Jean said. "Whatever had to be paid, they paid."[36] This was the old Depression way and also, in Jean's terms, "family stuff."[37] She still felt, very strongly, that Donenfeld had swindled her brother so long ago, but she separated that from the current leadership of the company, which was being very helpful to her.[38] Jean was being paid around $20,000 a year. In contrast, Joanne Siegel was supposedly getting "$126,148 and change" annually that was a combination of Jerry's pension and assurances for herself that she had personally negotiated with Time Warner CEO Steve Ross.[39] Joanne had also been collecting, according to DC's lawyers, over $1,200 a month from Joe to act as his agent when he was alive.[40]

WARREN

Mark Warren Peary goes by "Warren," the name of his father. He is Jean's son and Joe's nephew. He wrote a book with his dad, built houses, worked on screenplays in his spare time, was an actor (he changed his last name for the stage), and trades stocks from his home. He is quiet but has had big ideas his whole life, very much like his uncle Joe. He is the executor of the Shuster estate.[41] When the Warner Brothers lawyers fly him out to Los Angeles to take his deposition, he doesn't know what to expect.

In a warm Los Angeles office on January 29, 2011, the lawyers ask Warren about his lawyer, Marc Toberoff. Warren recalls how he contacted Toberoff after doing Internet research on copyright lawyers in 2001.[42] Once they talk on the phone, Warren enters into a joint venture agreement with Toberoff through one of his motion picture production companies called Pacific Pictures, on November 23, 2001. DC's lawyers later show Warren the agreement: "Why did you sign with Pacific Pictures?" Warren responds: "I—I don't know why he used that particular form."[43] The lawyers point out that "on this document is a signature there that appears to be Mr. Toberoff's signature, and underneath it says 'duly authorized agent of IP Worldwide/Estate of Joe Shuster.' . . . Do you see that?"[44] In this agreement, Toberoff is appointed agent of Joe's intellectual property. This first agreement is later voided.[45]

The lawyers press Warren about the so-called Toberoff Timeline. Warren tells the lawyers that "documents were stolen . . . from his office." The lawyers ask him: "How do you know that?" Warren responds that Toberoff "told me. . . . I'm aware that there were a number of factual errors and falsehoods . . . that are factually incorrect."[46] Warren notes that "in fact, that they [the Siegels] had cut off talks, fired their attorneys. . . . It was already—the relationship was already bad."[47]

But the lawyers are not done. They ask Warren if he knows that the Siegels have also claimed 100 percent ownership of Superboy, whose first adventure was drawn by Joe. One of the lawyers shuffles through his papers and produces a 1940 *Superboy* script that clearly lists Joe on the by-line.[48] Warren says, "I haven't seen this before."[49] There is a pause. Warren asks, "Can we get some air-conditioning in here?"[50]

The lawyers then sum things up to Warren: "Are you aware that the estate could lose this case? . . . You have entertained that as a possible outcome, correct?"[51] Warren answers, maybe for the first time, with complete calm and confidence: "I've only considered that like I would an asteroid hitting us and wiping out life on earth."[52] He reiterates that Toberoff is "very ethical, very knowledgeable, very intelligent."[53] Warren, like his uncle, has faith in what is right.

LAURA

Laura Siegel Larson, the daughter of Jerry Siegel, is questioned by DC on July 22, 2011. She matter-of-factly explains why they retained Toberoff back in 2002. Between him and Emanuel, Laura says that "we were kind of getting a two-for-one deal in a sense," to both try the case and explore their options with the property.[54] Joanne and Laura went out to dinner with Toberoff and Emanuel and saw their offices in Beverly Hills. The Siegels were, quite frankly, impressed. Toberoff was shorter but had a California tan and an easy, crinkly smile that spread across his face. And Ari was Ari: name-dropping and razor sharp, but with a strong political compass.[55] As they toured Toberoff's office, Laura met a guy who worked there, some lawyer who, in Laura's words, "was excited to be working on Superman."[56]

In late 2005, Laura got a call from this same man, asking her to meet. It seemed strange, she said, "but, you know, we were curious. We wanted to know what this guy had to say. He said he had information."[57] He was pushy that it be in person and not over the phone. When the man came to her condo: "He was talking all over the place and not very clear about what he was trying to express, so it was very hard to follow what he was saying," but it was information allegedly questioning Toberoff's motives in the case.[58] As the man left, he made the comment that he could represent them instead, as he had just been fired by Toberoff.[59] Laura shrugged and added, "It was a bold attempt on his part to steal my mom and I away from Mr. Toberoff as clients, and he wanted us to sign with him for him to be our attorney."[60]

During her deposition, Laura takes breaks; she is ill but has no problems answering in the strong voice she inherited from her mom. At one point, Petrocelli references the old Jack Benny gag "Your money or your life!" which ends with the classic line "I'm thinking! I'm thinking!" Petrocelli notes: "Marc, you're still smiling. You appreciate that, I know." Toberoff grins and says, "That's a good joke. That's a good joke."[61] But the core of the testimony is nothing of the kind as the two lawyers get combative over the daughter of Jerry Siegel. She is important, after all. When Petrocelli tries to push the importance of the stolen documents, Toberoff responds strongly: "This is something spun out of whole cloth in order to try and leverage a settlement, and we all know it."[62]

PETROCELLI: We'll get there.

TOBEROFF: You will not get there.

PETROCELLI: It may take time, but there's no quickness.

TOBEROFF: You don't have a prayer, and you know it.

PETROCELLI: I don't need prayers.

TOBEROFF: You don't have a—as—if—I could use an expression
from my father, but I probably shouldn't.

PETROCELLI: No, you shouldn't. You shouldn't invoke your dad.
Okay?[63]

In press materials, Marc Toberoff is sometimes pictured in an office, rich with wood, in front of a larger print of Superman. In an essay titled "Why I Sue Studios" for *The Hollywood Reporter,* Toberoff explains his philosophy:

> Because they give me no choice. I stand up for the rights of the very artists on whose talent their fortunes are built. At a time when studios must vigilantly prosecute piracy of their own intellectual property, there needs to be greater compunction about trampling on creators' rights. I enjoy making money like everyone else, but I also take on cases where I believe an injustice has occurred and something must be done about it. At the end of very long days (or years), that is what refuels me, and it's the only edge I've got.[64]

In some ways, Toberoff's methodology is similar to Donenfeld's back in the thirties: to use the legal system to secure valuable copyright properties. But Toberoff's mission is to return these rights to the creators, not the corporations. It is an important legal case for copyright and a dramatic reversal, in some ways, of what happened in 1938. Toberoff is referred to as the "legal Man of Steel" and a "superhero to rights holders" by *Variety* and a "brilliant crusader for the little guy" by *The New York Times. Forbes* lists him in 2010 as one of the "Seven Most Powerful People in Hollywood."[65] Like Petrocelli, he is a heavy hitter, and the conflict between the two soon becomes the drama:

PETROCELLI: I don't want to argue with you, and I regret the
few instances in which we have and apologize if I said anything in temper.

TOBEROFF: I accept your apology in this limited instance.

PETROCELLI: And I accept yours.

TOBEROFF: I didn't apologize.

PETROCELLI: Noted.

LAURA: You guys . . . [66]

Superman, at this moment, is somehow bigger than any Macy's Thanksgiving Day parade balloon drifting over a skyscraper. It is imaginatively worth millions of dollars, and just like the character's difficult publication in *Action* #1, it is being argued over by those who want to determine who controls it. They are trying to determine who gets to wear the costume. When Petrocelli asks Laura why she continues, she says confidently: "I believe I have very valuable rights and that at some point I will be able to profit from them"[67] "Why do you believe they're valuable?" the lawyer asks. "Because it's Superman," she says.[68]

LAST SON

Near the end of Laura's deposition, the questioning turns to Jerry's son with Bella. Laura describes him, sadly, as "the child of a very upsetting divorce, and he—you know, it hurts me to have to say this, but you know . . . a very kind of confused guy . . . very secretive. . . ."[69] This man, who had been unheard from in the story for decades, was now very important because just like Laura, he was entitled to 12.5 percent of the Superman property. But she is right: he was not very cooperative, had his own lawyer, was sometimes hard to get hold of, and, in Laura's words, was "kind of a loose cannon."[70] So Ari Emanuel and Marc Toberoff tried to buy his share outright. Negotiations with the son failed, and Emanuel the superstar, who promises fortune and treasure, was rebuffed by a solitary man who lived in Cleveland.[71] The lawyers give up; they would cross that bridge when it came up. It never did.

Jerry Siegel's son lived on the east side of Cleveland in a two-story brick house with a stone block drive. He lived alone on skinny 3605 Bendemeer Road, just down the street from a Jewish temple covered with curving, dotted characters. A kosher restaurant is around the corner. Kids in hats and curls laugh and run. He sat inside the house near a fan when it is hot outside. Sometimes, over the years, on the quiet street outside a car stopped for a minute and he held his breath and wondered. But the car eventually keeps going. Up and down the street, the black-garbed people walk to temple. Up and down. He was very active in the plumbers union and coached tae kwon do to kids at the community center. It made them feel stronger. He was strong, too, but his knee hurt all the time.[72] His doctor wanted to replace it. He missed his mother and his dog.

In a 1941 Superman story written by Jerry, Clark Kent opens his apartment door to find a baby left in a basket. The attached note reads: "I can tell from your article that you have a heart . . . please take good care of Bob . . . all my gratitude—A Mother." Clark completely panics and calls Lois, who is a lifesaver in helping care for the infant. But when she leaves, Clark is forced to deal with a screaming baby. So he starts doing super-feats all over the apartment, which make little Bob squeal with delight. Superman flies the baby all over the city. At the end of the story, baby Bob is reunited with his mother, and the exhausted Clark is relieved that he had to do this for only a day.[73]

I decide one day to write this man a letter. I turn on my computer on September 10, 2005, and see his response:

> *Subject: Jerry Siegel*
> *Hello Brad,*
> *Which grandfather did you get information on, and what is it? I can*
> *see no reason for the treatment my family and I received in print. . . .*
> *The real story is a lot different.*
> *Regards,*
> *Mike*[74]

He sends me a few actual letters and finally agrees to be interviewed. We make plans to have lunch. But on November 1, 2005, at two forty A.M., he writes: "Things have changed. I will not be available until early next year. I am sorry this happened." On November 22, he tells me that "we will meet sometime in the future."

Michael Siegel, Jerry's son, who was named after his father's father, who died in a clothing store in 1932, was born on January 27, 1944, and died on January 16, 2006, after complications from knee surgery. I drive by his house afterward and watch the snow fall slowly on his big pickup truck. I stay there for a while. He is buried in the last grave they have, next to his mother, in the Workman's Cemetery in Parma, Ohio.[75] Bella died earlier in 2002. Mike would visit his mother's resting place all the time, leaving small pebbles on her headstone.

After his death, Laura is asked about Mike Siegel by Petrocelli:

PETROCELLI: What did he do for a living?

LAURA: He was a plumber.

PETROCELLI: And so you didn't grow up close at all.

LAURA: I never met him. . . . The first time I ever saw what my brother looked like was after he died and I went to the home that he had shared with his mother.[76]

That they, half-siblings, never once met was a testament to the obvious mistrust and damage that had occurred decades before.[77] But though Mike Siegel never talked, not really, he did leave something behind: a letter, an artifact, written by him to Laura. He wrote to her on May 13, 2003, just as Toberoff and Emanuel were courting his percentage of the rights:

> *I really wish to discuss Marc Toberoff.*
>
> *I told you when he first contacted me; he wanted to buy my share of the copyright. Marc had a mysterious billionaire who wanted to invest in the Superman copyright, put 15 million dollars up front plus participation. When you signed with Marc the billionaire invested elsewhere.*[78]

Mike didn't trust these lawyers and their promised millions. When Laura is examined over his state of mind, she dismisses his claims. But still, this man who wouldn't send photographs of himself or even talk on the telephone had gone past all of that, for one moment, to seemingly warn his little half-sister. Laura admits that Mike's reference to the same $15 million figure—the same number that had initially lured her and her mother—was curious. "That was interesting, and that caught my eye," she says.[79]

In the end, most of the stories and rumors that people wanted to hear from Mike Siegel went mostly unsaid. Of Mike:

> "He was a wonderful guy," said a friend. "He was engaged but did not marry." She said when Siegel was 12 years old, his grandmother became ill. In what could have been a scene in a "Superboy" comic, the young Siegel picked up the woman and carried her through the house, across the yard and into the car to take her to the hospital.[80]

The father and son were clearly estranged. Mike would tell others that he remembered, as a kid, waiting at a Howard Johnson for his father to show up for a visit—only he never did.[81] Mike referred to his father as "Jerry Siegel." At the same time, he probably never knew that his father worried over him in the comics he wrote, about a boy with powers who had a monster for a father. For all that Mike said about the man who had abandoned him, there was a connection between them still, in both the lives they were later forced to lead and the source they looked to for comfort.[82] The stationery Mike used to type his letters to me had Superman printed on the background, faint but unmistakable, lifting that heavy car, now weightless, into the clear, open sky.

JOANNE

Joanne Siegel gives her deposition on August 2, 2006, in an office in Beverly Hills. They mostly ask her complicated questions about when Jerry first submitted *Superboy* and how much money DC was sending her. At one point, the lawyers have her look at the origin page of *Action* #1, pointing out the green rocket escaping the exploding planet. She chuckles and can't help noting that it looks "more like a cucumber."[83] She also talks about her dear husband, who would have loved such a joke, gone now almost ten years.[84] They ask her about the infamous "Gestapo" letter she wrote. She doesn't apologize. The last thing she says on the legal record for the case is, "That's what I thought you meant."[85]

Four years later, in December 2010, Joanne Siegel writes another letter, to Jeffrey L. Bewkes, the chairman and CEO of Time Warner, Inc., the owner of Warner Bros. and DC Comics. After outlining her family's long relationship with DC and Warner, she gets to the heart of the matter, assuring Bewkes that she and the Shusters "have done nothing more than exercise our rights. . . . Yet, your company has chosen to sue us and our long-time attorney for protecting our rights." Her next words are honest ones:

> *On December 1st I turned 93. I am old enough to be your mother. I have grown grandchildren. Unfortunately I am not in the best of health. . . . I suffer from a serious heart condition . . . forcing me to go through yet another stressful deposition could put me in danger of a heart attack or stroke. . . . Nonetheless your attorneys are forcing me to endure a second deposition . . . their intention is to harass me.*

Joanne writes that her daughter Laura is also being asked for multiple depositions. Joanne then asks a personal question that is, for many Superman fans following the case, a poignant one: "Do these mean spirited tactics meet with your approval? Do you really think the families of Superman's creators should be treated this way?"[86]

The purpose of Joanne's letter is to stop the "bad blood" of a "continued fight" and point out that only the attorneys will benefit from continued litigation. Joanne's answer to "saving time, trouble, and expense is a change of viewpoint." She hopes that "by paying the owed bill in full . . . it would be handled as a business matter, instead of a lawsuit going into its 5th year." She appeals to his sense of personal ethics, that "even though you will no doubt pass this letter on to your attorneys, the final decision is yours."

On February 12, 2011, two months later, Joanne, at age ninety-three, passed away. The enterprising, unlikely girl who became the model for the perfect match of brains and beauty for millions of girls and boys, women and men, was eulogized all over the world, appropriately, on Valentine's Day.[87]

Two years earlier, on July 11, 2009, Joanne had traveled back to Cleveland to dedicate a restoration of Jerry's old home on Kimberley Avenue in Glenville—now a neighborhood of foreclosures and crime, but made full of hope by a new red-and-blue fence made of steel, coats of paint, and a plaque reminding passersby of what had happened here.[88] The current owners of the house, Hattie and Jefferson Gray, sat on their porch and beamed.[89] And on the porch that Jerry used to almost leap over to run to Joe's, Joanne told an early Saturday morning crowd of kids, community leaders, and a man taking pictures that dreams can come true.[90] The restoration of the house, and the construction of another full-length fence where Joe's apartment used to stand (that depicted every page of the *Action* #1 story in full color), was made possible not by community grants, but by everyday fans. These ordinary people, from all over the world, bid on items donated by comics creators at the direction of novelist Brad Meltzer and a new local nonprofit organization, the Siegel and Shuster Society.[91] In addition to Joanne and her daughter, Laura, Jerry Fine was there, as were Joe's niece, Dawn, and his nephew, Warren. The skies downpoured all morning. There was still a big crowd.

When Joe's birthday was celebrated the night before with "the World's Biggest Superman Cake" in a downtown room full of fans, Laura raised her glass and her eyes filled at thoughts of "Uncle Joe," who was once small and dreamed of the impossible and who loved a girl he could never have.[92] For Cleveland and elsewhere, the efforts to remember the two men took on a solemn, mythic quality among all the capes and frosting. This would always be ongoing; this would always be family.

After her death, Joanne's strong letter to Time Warner was made public. Her heirs, as well as Joe Shuster's sister, Jean, and her children, continue to pursue legal action.[93] In late 2011, DC relaunched *Superman* with a brand-new *Action Comics* #1. In it, though Superman now wore jeans and was younger, the names and places were still the same: Krypton, Jor-El, Clark Kent. And on the title page, it read, like an inscription: "Created by Jerry Siegel and Joe Shuster."[94]

DAWN

The last to be questioned during the round of depositions was Dawn Peavy, Jean's daughter, on August 3, 2011, at the Santa Fe Hilton. Dawn is a single mother, divorced, and works for a food distributor—she has to skip work to be here. She has movie-star good looks, with long hair and her uncle's dark eyes. She knows very little of the lawsuit, simply because she doesn't have the time for it. When asked if she knows if a positive outcome to the case will change her life significantly, she says, "I don't know how to answer that. . . . No, I'd probably still work just as hard."[95] They question her about everything from Warren's status as executor ("I love my brother") to what the Siegels were doing. It is divide and conquer. "Are you a Superman fan?" they ask. "Yes," she answers.[96] They don't think she has any secrets, any knowledge (which is really what secrets are), so they just ask her about the people around her. When the lawyer asks her about what happens at home, Dawn answers, "When I come home, it's me and my mom . . . we make dinner, you know."[97] When they try to ask her more, her voice drops. "I don't want to talk about my mom."[98] Jean, who in 2009 was making plans to come to Cleveland for the house dedications, had fallen ill. There were more important things now. Before her stroke, one of the things Jean did was talk to Mike Siegel on the phone and, in her words, "tell him he was loved." And that she "understood." She told me about how Mike Siegel, who wouldn't talk to anyone else, then cried.[99] When the lawyers finally ask Dawn (hers is the briefest deposition) if the Siegels' termination of rights will affect the value of their own portion, she responds: "Just very simply, I think that a whole is always more valuable than part, than a part."[100]

(In October 2012, U.S. District Court Judge Otis Wright II ruled that the simple agreement that Jean and Frank made with Paul Levitz and DC after Joe's death had been the Shusters' last chance to reclaim their share of the Superman copyright. Their part in this battle was over. Toberoff, their lawyer, vowed to appeal.)

The central secret behind the creation of Superman is a true story about fathers and sons, and its cliff-hanger certainly involves family. Superman, as Clark and Kal-El, is part made into a greater whole. Just as its creation was meant to reunite a son with a father in an imagined reality, so too does the current state of Superman involve several identities—mothers, daughters, sons, guardians, and protectors—all working across deep fractures. Superman has been protected by very strong women, is tended to carefully by a large corporation, and remains enticingly attractive to outsiders who want to share in the story just as much as any of us do. Though split into invisible percentages, everyone wants to make a claim because everyone has, or dreams of, a connection to the Idea. There is even a strange exchange in Laura's deposition where the lawyers ask:

> DC: Did anybody ever tell you that there's a third person out
>   there claiming to own some part of Superman? Have you ever
>   heard that?
> LAURA: I have not heard that.
> DC: Thank you.[101]

From Donenfeld to Kenton to Anonymous, everyone wants to adopt the Man of Steel. There is a reason for that.

Jerry makes his own statement about family and what it might have to do with Superman in a story he wrote later in his career, during his anonymous years at National. In *Superman* #141, the cover shows Superman confronting his own lost parents. His mother, Lara, says, "He looks familiar!" as Jor-El wears a blazing sun on his chest. The three-part story, titled "Superman's Return to Krypton," is both epic and emotional, beginning with Superman accidentally crashing through the "time-barrier" into the past—and finding a living, flourishing Krypton. After running into a shoot for an "emotion movie" and seeing an actress named Lyla Lerrol, Kal-El finds that his parents—Jor-El and Lara—are about to be married that day. He observes their wedding wistfully and realizes that to be nearer to them, he has to "become their close friend without revealing my relationship to them."[102] Kal starts working as a lab assistant to Jor-El, and "before long, a strange kinship swiftly grows between the two. . . ." "Nicely done!" Jor-El says. "I hope you don't mind my giving you a little . . . *Ha, Ha . . . 'Fatherly'* advice from time to time!" Kal responds: "Please do!"[103]

Clark falls in love with Lyla Lerrol, and soon their "two hearts thrill as one."[104] But Kal finds that fate is unavoidable: Krypton starts to quake and other events move toward the conclusion that Clark cannot change the inevitable outcome on Krypton, where he is "just an ordinary mortal," so he resolves to meet his end with honor by Lyla's side—but he inadvertently ends up on a rocket, escapes, and goes through time again to end up floating in the exact place where Krypton used to be.[105] His home and family are gone, replaced by "deadly green kryptonite Meteors."[106] This scene is similar to the one in which Clark stands by his parents' graves, only here it is not his adopted parents, but his real ones. Here, in his second stint on Superman, Jerry has a more mature view. He no longer seeks revenge but finds acceptance.

In Superman mythology, the House of El dies catastrophically with Krypton, leaving only a single heir on a faraway world. But over time, miraculously, new people begin to come into Superman's life from unlikely places: Supergirl, Krypto, the city of Kandor, Jimmy, Lois, and Perry all become part of what would be called "the Superman Family." They are the parts of a whole. At the end of "Return to Krypton," Superman speeds toward Earth and admits to himself, "It's good to have . . . a second home."[107]

On Thursday, January 10, 2013, the Ninth Circuit Court of Appeals decided that the original 2001 agreement between the Siegels and DC was, in fact, a binding agreement. This surprise decision meant that the 2008 ruling whereby the Siegels had won a portion of the Superman copyright was now void. Time Warner/DC was once again the sole owner of Superman. They were ordered to pay the Siegels the original multimillion-dollar settlement they had agreed upon before the hiring of Toberoff. The Shusters were bound to their previous, much less lucrative settlement. Laura Siegel Larson's initial public response was about her father: "He and artist Joe Shuster created Superman, Clark Kent, Lois Lane . . . to give all of us hope and courage that good could triumph over evil, that justice could be achieved despite impossible odds and to inspire all of us to find strength and heroism in ourselves."[108]

Epilogue

THE SEARCH INTO SUPERMAN'S ORIGINS sometimes, admittedly, seems as never-ending as the character's battles against Brainiac, Luthor, and Darkseid. In a 1986 article for local newspaper *The Elyria Chronicle,* Arnold Miller writes about what it was like to grow up in Glenville a generation after Jerry and Joe. He remembers "a couple of other guys searching frantically through an empty apartment on Parkwood because someone said that it was the apartments that Joe Shuster—or was it Jerry Siegel—had lived in a couple years back. Surely he must have hidden behind some secret panel some original Superman drawings."[1] This story is repeated in many different incarnations as people make pilgrimages to various sites where the boys lived and worked, wondering about secret attics and spaces under floorboards.[2] People want things that may be worth money, but they also want answers: Why?

The story of the creation of Superman is about many things: it is just as much about the beginnings of corporate America and its relationship to popular culture as it is about artistic creation and familial relationships. It is a story about the haves and the have-nots—creators, a son, a father, the Depression, and companies and families trying to protect themselves and those who come after them. That a colorful pamphlet intended to be *thrown away after reading* has grown in value from ten cents to several million dollars in seventy-five years is not because old paper has suddenly become more valuable, but because we as a culture have determined that the character itself has. That such a high value is assigned to a fictional character speaks volumes about its readership.[3] Whether we want to admit it or not, we still like Superman. At the heart of this attraction is a fictional character whom most children know about by the time they are eight—by some sort of rocket ship osmosis to the brain—though we may not even know how or why. Superman's presence in our imagination is like that of Santa Claus, only not limited to a single holiday or season.

The story is also about a uniquely American friendship between two boys who grew up with overwhelmingly distant dreams of fame, riches, and girls in a time when such dreams, by virtue of their sheer impossibilities, somehow were easier to imagine. This is a friendship that was not made the instant they met as two teenagers, but was fully realized only decades later, when they lived just down the street from each other, at over seventy years old, with weakened knees and thinning hair. Theirs is not a story we can ever know for certain, which is why it will continue to be told and retold as half legend combined with new truth to form different kinds of answers as to how—and why—a man can fly. In many ways, the story of Jerry and Joe has become the Clark Kent portion of the larger cultural mythology of Superman. So we keep looking, still fascinated not by what they didn't achieve but by the sheer audacity of what they did. Much of Superman began as an economic venture—and the story must always be aware of this—but at heart, it was also a supreme act of will. An act made remarkable in the way it perfectly captured and commented on the time that it simultaneously leaped over.

But as much as the story is about collaboration, it is also about separation.[4] The iconic "S" on the T-shirts we wear is not only trademarked down to exact Pantone shades, but to the interior angles of the shield that surrounds it. So even if we buy a Superman shirt, the symbol is not ours, and thus somehow already lost. But imagination doesn't like being told what to do. Jerry and Joe wrote a lot about things like that. In *Dr. Occult* from *More Fun Comics* #9, the Vampire Master uses a strange machine to create a duplicate of Lois Amster, the girl Jerry liked: "With my invention, the Thought Materializer, I can create into actuality or destroy creatures of my imagination."[5] But the duplicate of Lois attacks him with a knife, screaming: "You will ***never*** destroy me!"

The symbol is as much about secret hopes and dreams as it is gaudy superhuman power swelling out against the five-sided shield hoping to contain it in a rational mathematical arrangement. For all the times we see the shield on shirts, on young and old alike, it also rests in secret under suits, uniforms, and camouflage. That is when the symbol is most powerful—as a secret waiting to be revealed.

In the forgotten corner of a dark bookstore, in a dusty box hidden on a shelf, another secret waits to be discovered. But this is not about Superman, though by now it is really all the same. With a tattered off-white cover, *Nights of Horror,* volume II, has a lurid cover drawn by Joe.[6] The second story in the book, with its blocky, offset type, is titled "See, Hear, Speak Evil!" and is written by a "Wood LaCrosse," an obvious sleight. The story itself is about a reporter who becomes embroiled in an investigation into a series of disappearances of local girls in Mound City.[7] His only clues are the skeletal figures that represent the traditional monkeys who cover their eyes, ears, and mouth, respectively, just as the title alludes to. As the story goes on, it turns into a murder case as the reporter is dragged deeper and deeper into a shadowy world of female slaves and killers who seem to return from the dead. Like most *Nights of Horror* stories, it is abysmal.

But it is not the story that is interesting. The main character is "Jerry Wood, police reporter for the Express."[8] The last name "Wood" is also the first name of the author. Since the author's name is obviously an alias, is the writer trying to tell us something by linking "Jerry" to the author's name? Once Jerry the reporter finds his first clue (the monkey figures), he meets another reporter who asks him, teasingly, "Playing with dolls?" This reporter, a friend, is "Kent Mitchell of the Courier."[9] This name is another clue: Kent, the famous last name of Clark, is here paired with the name of Mitchell, the first name of Jerry's father. The two reporters act like old pals, Mitchell leaning in his window, giving him paternal advice. Jerry responds: "That's what makes you a good police reporter, Mitch."[10] There is a moment's pause as they regard each other, finally.

A few pages in, we find that two of the girls who are missing are sisters, and their names are Norma and Rita, the names of Jerry Siegel's nieces, the same who appeared in *Federal Men.*[11] In every piece of work he did, Jerry always left clues. The robbers had left none, so maybe he felt he had to. Joe's were obvious: the squint and shoulder and his own trademark signature; the art is unmistakable. Jerry's were sometimes hidden a little deeper. There are other "clues" that Jerry might have written into this particular story—names of characters that line up with Long Island places like Redfern Avenue and Myrtle Place—but it is the names of the main characters that are the most suggestive.[12] If Jerry did secretly reteam with Joe in the 1950s to do a story for *Nights of Horror* with Joe drawing Superman look-alikes, you can imagine them laughing like high schoolers. If so, it would mean that they weren't always apart during the dark times. They weren't fighting; instead, they were working together, in secret, just like the old days. It didn't matter what they were working on, not really, just that they were working on it together. Jerry was telling a story and Joe was providing the pictures that made it all come alive, just as in a newspaper. The story in the magazine is a ridiculous one, but then again, sometimes *Superman* is, too. What matters here, with this secret, is that there is no cape, but just the reporter, still trying to make things right.

Notes

Prologue

1. Jean Shuster Peavy, interview by author, June 25, 2005. Partial transcript in "I Was Just the Kid Sister Peeking Around the Corner," *Alter Ego* 79, July 2008, 11–17.
2. Jerry Siegel, letter to *Science Wonder Stories,* November 1929, 570. To avoid repetition, I will list all primary sources and newspaper articles only in the notes. Cited, published books and articles that are generally available will be repeated in the bibliography.
3. Ibid.
4. The details of the death of Michel Siegel have been reconstructed from facts in *The Cleveland Press* and *The Plain Dealer* from May to July 1932, Sanborn fire insurance maps of his store, his death certificate, and official police reports.

1. The Eyes

1. Her maiden name varies in the historical record from Kottiarsky and Katharske to Coclosky. See "Julius Shusterowich," *Canada Marriages, 1801–1928* (Provo, UT: Ancestry.com Operations, 2010), http://www.ancestry.com. They were married on September 14, 1913. See "Chajka Katharske," *Border Crossings: From Canada to U.S., 1895–1956* (Provo, UT: Ancestry.com Operations, 2010), http://www.ancestry.com, for a possible candidate.
2. Spellings include Ogeeva, Oleksiivka, Orichovec, Oćwieka, and Alekseevka.
3. John Klier, *Russians, Jews, and the Pogroms of 1881–1882* (Cambridge, MA: Cambridge University Press, 2011).
4. "Russian City Burning, Jews Being Massacred," *The New York Times,* December 13, 1905.
5. Shlomo Lombrozo, "Jewish Responses to Pogroms in Late Imperial Russia," *Living with Antisemitism: Modern Jewish Responses* (Hanover, NH: University Press of New England, 1987), 256. Because I have not been able to pinpoint

Ida's location, I am using this event, which I believe took place nearby, as a representative example. See Peavy, interview. Jean says her mother "fled from a pogrom."

6. "Jack Shusterowitz," *Canada Marriages, 1801–1928*. They were married on June 30, 1912. She is here named "Bessia."

7. R. Douglas Francis and Chris Kitzan, eds., *The Prairie West as Promised Land* (Calgary: University of Calgary Press, 2007). Also see T. M. Devine and Jenny Wormald, eds., *The Oxford Handbook of Modern Scottish History* (New York: Oxford University Press, 2012), 164.

8. Jesse O. McKee, *Ethnicity in Contemporary America: A Geographical Appraisal* (Lanham, MD: Rowman & Littlefield, 2000), 22.

9. "An act to limit the migration of aliens into the United States . . ." *The Statutes at Large of the United States of America, from December 1923 to March 1925*, vol. XLII (Washington, DC: Government Printing Office, 1925), part 1, 153–69. Also see Cynthia S. Becker, *Immigration and Illegal Aliens: Burden or Blessing?* (Farmington Hills, MI: Gale Group Press, 2007).

10. Peavy, interview.

11. Ibid.

12. Ibid.

13. "Julius Schusterwitz," *Canadian Passenger Lists, 1865–1935* (Provo, UT: Ancestry.com Operations, 2010), http://www.ancestry.com.

14. Ibid. The *Uranium* was torpedoed and sunk on May 5, 1917.

15. Ibid.

16. Ibid. Records vary between September 2 and 3.

17. "Julius Shusterowich," *Canada Marriages, 1801–1928*. Jack and Bessie were married first, on June 30, 1912.

18. Ibid.

19. "Julius Schuster," birth certificate, July 14, 1914, Toronto, Ontario, Joe Shuster Collection, Special Collections Research Center, Kelvin Smith Library, Case Western Reserve University, Cleveland, Ohio. This is the first step in a larger collection that will be the first Siegel and Shuster repository in the world, fittingly located five minutes from where they both grew up. Special thanks to Susie Hanson, Nora Blackman, Andrew Kaplan, Joanne Eustis, Mel Higgins, and Mike Burkey. The collection itself was supported by a 2007 Library Opportunity Fund Award, completed with the help of Earnestine Adeyemon and a Freedman Fellowship. The Shuster Collection is supported by a strong comics list in the library, organized by William Claspy.

20. "Julius Schuster," *1930 United States Federal Census* (Provo, UT: Ancestry .com Operations, 2002), http://www.ancestry.com. Jeanetta was born on February 1, 1921.

21. *Toronto City Directory*, 1915. Thanks to Paul Sharkey.

22. Jerry Siegel and Joe Shuster, interview by Shel Dorf, "Remembering the 30's," *Siegel and Shuster Dateline 1930's* 1 (Guerneville, CA: Eclipse, 1984), 16.

23. Henry Mietkiwicz, "Man of Steel, Pen of Gold," *Comic Book Marketplace* 22, 1995, 27.

24. Doug Taylor, *There Never Was a Better Time: Toronto's Yesterdays* (Bloomington, IN: iUniverse, 2008), 229–31. Later on, costumed versions of Felix the Cat, Bugs Bunny, and Popeye would join the parade.

25. Joe Shuster, interview by Henry Mietkiwicz, *The Toronto Star,* April 26, 1992.

26. Peavy, interview.

27. Ibid.

28. "Ida Shuster," *Border Crossings: From Canada to U.S., 1895–1956* (Provo, UT: Ancestry.com Operations, 2010), http://www.ancestry.com. Also see Peavy, letter to author, May 9, 2009. Also see "Julius Schuster," *Detroit Border Crossings and Passenger and Crew Lists, 1905–1957* (Provo, UT: Ancestry.com Operations, 2006), http://www.ancestry.com.

29. D. Van Tassel and John J. Grabowski, eds., *The Encyclopedia of Cleveland History* (Bloomington: Indiana University Press, 1987).

30. "Cleveland—a Scientific Glimpse," *Science and Invention,* August 1930, 312.

31. Ibid.

32. *Cleveland City Directory,* Cleveland, Ohio, 1929.

33. Siegel and Shuster, "Remembering the 30's," 16.

34. Jerry Fine, interview by author, June 25, 2010.

2. The Dreamer

1. "Tsk! Tsk! Tsk!," *Glenville Torch,* October 27, 1932.

2. "Jerome Siegel," birth certificate, file no. 191416012, October 17, 1914, Ohio Department of Health, on file at Cuyahoga County Recorder's Office.

3. Victoria Fleming and George L. Rafter, "Superman: 40 and Still a Hero," *The Plain Dealer Sunday Magazine,* December 3, 1978.

4. *Cleveland City Directory,* Cleveland, Ohio, 1914.

5. *The Plain Dealer Sunday Magazine,* July 26, 1925.

6. Ibid., September 12, 1926.

7. Jerry's last mention on the Seck page is in *The Plain Dealer Sunday Magazine,* July 6, 1932.

8. *The Plain Dealer Sunday Magazine,* August 29, 1926.

9. *Cleveland City Directory,* Cleveland, Ohio, 1933. "Kimberley" changes to "Kimberly" at various points over the years. To avoid confusion, I will use "Kimberley" because it occurs the most in this context, except when it is used otherwise in primary sources.

10. Charles Redlick, "The Street," *Olympiad,* Glenville High School, 1930, 112–13.

11. Ibid.

12. Irv Fine, Rita Hubar, and Norma Wolkov, interview by author, February 3, 2010.

13. Benjamin Nugent, *American Nerd: The Story of My People* (New York: Scribner, 2009), 55. Also see David Anderegg, *Nerds: How Dorks, Dweebs, Techies,*

and Trekkies Can Save America (New York: Tarcher/Penguin, 2011). Also see "Jelly Tot, Square Bear-Man!," *Newsweek,* October 28, 1952, 28. "In Detroit, someone who once would be called a drip or a square is now, regrettably, a nerd, or in a less severe case, a scurve."

14. Peavy, letter to author, April 13, 2008.
15. Fine, Hubar, and Wolkov, interview.
16. Mike Ashley and Robert A. W. Lowndes, *The Gernsback Days* (Rockville, MD: Wildside Press, 2004).
17. Hugo Gernsback, "Fiction Versus Fact," *Amazing Stories,* July 1926, 291.
18. Harold Hersey, ed., *The New Pulpwood Editor* (Silver Spring, MD: Adventure House, 1965).
19. Ashley and Lowndes, *Gernsback Days,* 250.
20. Hugo Gernsback, "Ralph 124C 41+," *Amazing Stories Quarterly* (Winter 1929), first published 1911. *Ralph* was also available as a mail-order book from Experimenter Publications for $2.15. Also see Gary Westfahl, *Hugo Gernsback and the Century of Science Fiction* (Jefferson, NC: McFarland, 2007), 97–148.
21. Jerry Siegel, letter to *Amazing Stories,* August 1929. Since Jerry used so many different names during his life, I am citing his real name in the notes to make reference easier. If he is using an alias or a fuller form of his name, I will make note of it in the text itself.
22. Jerry Siegel, letter to *Science Wonder Stories,* November 1929.
23. Ibid.

3. The Education of Jerry Siegel

1. The mascot of the Glenville Tarblooders is a half-man, half-robot cyborg. The story behind the nickname and the chant "Tar-Blood! Whack-Thud!" comes from the local Glenville men, who, at the time the school was being built, spent their days ramming railroad stakes into the ground. This grueling work would often result in hot tar being spit back onto them, opening wounds, making them look as if they were sweating black blood. In Jerry and Joe's time, the mascot was a strange football man with gangly limbs and a head. At some point, this creature transformed into a complete Tin Man robot. I think that the popular visit of robot Herbie Televox as reported in *The Torch* on February 26, 1931, facilitated this transformation into a science fiction mascot. The template for the current mascot was designed by *Torch* cartoonist Martinez Garcias in 1973, when he was a sophomore.
2. Reuben Weltman, interview by Ed Wittenberg, "Superman Creator Flew High, Friend Says," *The Sun News,* July 13, 2006: "[Siegel] was a nice, mild person. He wouldn't hurt a fly. That was the kind of kid he was." Thanks to Kurt Koenigsberger.
3. Larry Tye, *Superman: The High-Flying History of America's Most Enduring Hero* (New York: Random House, 2012), 4. Though there are many hinted-at references to Jerry being bullied, the only primary account of it is in his autobiography, which was written in several different forms. And there is cer-

tainly no reason to doubt it, as there are numerous references to bullying in many of Jerry's works. Never published, the autobiography itself has been held by a few collectors and quoted from in some other works; it also appears (in fragments) in the public record of the various court cases. I will make some reference to it here, but mostly through anecdotes. Jerry was, first and foremost, a storyteller.

4. The Film Club also notes that "members of the 'Torch' staff too, will be immortalized by these movies—probably their only approach toward immortality." These films have not been found. See *The Plain Dealer,* January 14, 2012. Recently, an audio reel was discovered at Glenville of a speech given to the school on April 26, 1967, by Martin Luther King Jr. The recording was found by art teacher Jayne Sylvester and Glenville student L. A. Littlejohn in a pile of discarded material in the library that the class was given permission to make "art-robots" out of. The tape was subsequently transferred to a public digital format by Case Western Reserve University media officer Jared Bendis.

5. *The Plain Dealer,* January 9, 1930.

6. Dennis Dooley, "The Man of Tomorrow and the Boys of Yesterday," in *Superman at Fifty!* (New York: Collier, 1988), 19–34. I am greatly indebted to Dooley (and his coeditor, Gary Engle), especially for his fascinating investigation into the contents of *The Torch.* The early gift of this book from my father and Dooley's thesis—that Siegel and Shuster populated their work with their life experiences—greatly inspired this book.

7. Gordon B. Berryman and Frederic D. Aldrich, eds., *Style Book of The Glenville Torch* (Cleveland: Glenville High School, 1927).

8. Ibid.

9. Dooley, "Man of Tomorrow," 28.

10. Jerry Siegel, "In the Happy Days to Come," "The Reflector" (supp. *The Glenville Torch*), May 29, 1930.

11. Ibid.

12. Jerry's female subject cannot be named definitively because there are at least three Miriams at Glenville during this time. "Mysterious Occurrence Amazes Two Scientists," *The Torch,* March 26, 1931, does name "Miriam Mann." There is also "Miriam Leininger." Some of Jerry's other *Torch* writings name other women he is enamored with—not only at Glenville, but at other schools—including a Ruth and an Ethel.

13. Jerry Siegel, "Editor Receives Math Puzzle from Author," *The Torch,* October 12, 1930. Also see Jerry Siegel and Joe Shuster, interview with Thomas Andrae, "Of Supermen and Kids with Dreams," in *Creators of the Superheroes* (Neshannock, PA: Hermes Press, 2011), 23. "Fantastic Fiction" was another pseudocompany that Jerry apparently invented as a vehicle for some of his work as Hugh Langley, though no copies of this work seem to have survived.

14. Ashley and Lowndes, *Gernsback Days,* 217. Also see Jim Steranko, *The Steranko History of Comics,* vol. 1 (Reading, PA: Supergraphics, 1970), 39. Steranko's history is one of the first to link the creation of Superman to the pulp tradition.

15. Weltman, "Superman Creator Flew High." According to Weltman, "Jerry was always interested in the heavens. . . . When we were around 14, we met a kid who had a telescope, and we started a telescope club. We used to go over to this kid's house a couple nights a week and look at the stars. It was very interesting."

16. Jerry Siegel, "Professor Sights Stupefying Vision," *The Torch,* October 19, 1930.

17. "Four Students Win Mention in Contest," *The Torch,* December 18, 1930.

18. Jonathan Munby, *Public Enemies, Public Heroes* (Chicago: University of Chicago Press, 1999).

19. Dooley, "Man of Tomorrow," 25.

20. S. S. Van Dine, "Twenty Rules for Writing Detective Stories," in *The Art of the Mystery Story* (New York: Biblo and Tannen, 1976), 189, first published in *The American Magazine,* September 1928.

21. Ibid.

22. Jerry Siegel, "Stiletto Vance Solves Baffling Crime Not Yet Committed by Shooting to Kill," *The Torch,* December 11, 1930.

23. Jerry Siegel, "Vance Deserts Crime for Literary Contests," *The Torch,* March 5, 1931.

24. Ibid.

25. Ibid.

26. Jerry Siegel, "Vance's Breath-o-Scope Solves Mystery Puzzle," *The Torch,* March 12, 1931. Amazingly, the breathoscope was an actual invention of New York police around 1919, designed to test a person's breath for levels of alcoholic consumption.

27. Jerry Siegel, "Detective Tries Composing," *The Torch,* April 30, 1931.

28. Jerry Siegel, "Two Torch Sleuths Murdered but Only Dead from Neck Up," *The Torch,* November 19, 1931.

29. *The Torch,* February 19, 1931.

30. Ibid., February 26, 1931.

31. Ibid., May 12, 1931.

32. Jerry Siegel, letter to *Astounding Stories of Super-Science,* January 1931, 138.

33. Jerry Siegel, "Bulumni," *The Torch,* May 28, 1931.

34. Ibid.

35. Jerry Siegel, "Attention M," *The Torch,* March 5, 1931.

36. Dooley, "Man of Tomorrow," 21.

37. Milt Gross, interview with Jerome Schwartz, *The Torch,* November 26, 1930.

4. How to Meet Your Best Friend

1. Peavy, letter to author, May 9, 2009.

2. *Cleveland City Directory,* Cleveland, Ohio, 1931.

3. Peavy, letter to author, May 9, 2009. Also see *Cleveland City Directory,* Cleveland, Ohio, 1934.

4. Peavy, interview.

5. Peavy, letter to author, May 9, 2009. Her father "enjoyed the job and told us how nice the doctors and nurses were to him."

6. Fleming and Rafter, "Superman: 40." These authors claim that Joe was five feet two inches tall.

7. "Joe Shuster," *Canadiana* #44, In the Game Trading Cards, 2011.

8. Joe Shuster, interview by John Nunes, "Superman Creator Is Mild-Mannered," *The Times-Advocate,* August 14, 1977. Joe claims that "I didn't meet Jerry . . . until high school." See Tye, *Superman,* 14, who claims that Joe introduced himself to Jerry in the school library.

9. Siegel and Shuster, "Of Supermen and Kids with Dreams," 24. This is a more comprehensive version of the historic interview with both men (and Joanne Siegel) by Thomas Andrae, first published in *Nemo: The Classic Comics Library* 2, August 1983, with Geoffrey Blum and Gary Coddington. It was also reprinted in the eighteenth edition of *The Official Overstreet Comic Book Price Guide,* 1988–1989, (New York: The House of Collectibles, 1988).

10. *Olympiad,* 1932, 77, shows a photograph of the Art Club with a smiling kid in glasses who might be Joe. The walls of the room are hung with theatrical posters, including one for *The Bat,* with a portrait reminiscent of Lon Chaney in *The Phantom of the Opera* (1925).

11. Jerry Siegel, "Backstage," *The Torch,* January 12, 1933.

12. John P. Kasson, *Houdini, Tarzan, and the Perfect Man* (New York: Hill & Wang, 2001).

13. "Battle with the Apes," *Tarzan of the Apes Radio Serial,* American Gold Seal Productions, World Radio Network, September 14, 1932.

14. Hugo Gernsback, "Evolution on Mars," *Science and Invention,* August 1924. Articles such as this one "proved" how such superhuman feats could be possible on other planets.

15. Edgar Rice Burroughs's *A Fighting Man of Mars* and others were serialized in *The Cleveland Press.* The contrast of such bizarre alien fiction with actual news (which was on the same page) is a parallel to the Clark Kent/Superman dichotomy.

16. Siegel and Shuster, "Of Supermen and Kids with Dreams," 34.

17. "Edgar Rice Burroughs—Creator of 'Tarzan,'" *Tip-Top Comics,* November 1936.

18. Ibid.

19. Ibid.

20. Jerry Siegel, "Goober the Mighty Discovers Countless Foes in Wilderness," *The Torch,* May 7, 1931.

21. Ibid.

22. Jerry Siegel, "Goober, the Mighty, Returns to Page with Breath-Taking Story of Battle in Jungle," *The Torch,* October 1, 1931.

23. V. T. Hamlin, *The Man Who Walked with Dinosaurs* (Columbus: Ohio State University Press, 1996). Goober has many similarities to *Alley Oop,* the famous daily comic strip about a caveman. Though *Alley Oop* didn't start until

December 5, 1932, its original title was *Oop the Mighty* and the main love interest was also named "Oola." Alley Oop's creator, V. T. Hamlin, lived in the Cleveland suburb of Lakewood and drew the strip at the NEA Syndicate in downtown Cleveland at 1200 West Third Street.

24. "The Funny Papers," *Fortune*, April 1933, 45. A condensed version of this article also appears in *Reader's Digest*, May 1933.

25. Ibid., 47.

26. Ibid., 49.

27. "How Comic Cartoons Make Fortunes," *Modern Mechanix*, November 1933, 32.

28. Ibid., 36.

29. Beerbohm, Robert, "The Big Bang Theory of Comic Book History," *Comic Book Marketplace*, August 1997, 55. Beerbohm, who is among the first to frame the creation of Superman as a collective event, notes that *Interplanetary Police* was probably also inspired by Edmond Hamilton's *Interstellar Patrol* series of stories.

30. Frank Paul's famous *Buck Rogers* cover on *Amazing Stories*, August 1928, depicts Buck in a red suit, flying into the air with the aid of a technological harness.

31. Tye, *Superman*, 4.

32. Jack Williamson and Betty Williamson, e-mail to author, February 19, 2006. Jack remembers that Jerry wrote him a letter at this time about a story containing "all geometric characters—a cube, a sphere, etc." This was probably the "Death of a Parallelogram" story that Jerry entered in a *Torch* contest and was trying to get published in the pulps. Jack politely suggested that Jerry write about "flesh and blood" instead. Jerry also allegedly introduced Jack (through the mail) to science fiction writer Edmond Hamilton, with the result that Jack and Ed became lifelong friends. In the late seventies, Jack arranged for a special award to be given to Jerry and Joe by the Science Fiction Writers of America. Jerry and Joe could not attend, but DC editor Julius Schwartz accepted on their behalf. According to Jack, Julie so appreciated his having orchestrated the award that "he became [Jack's] friend for life."

33. Jerry Siegel, letter to *Astounding Stories*, August, 1931, 273–74. Mort Weisinger had a letter in the same magazine: "We Readers are frequently asked as to how we would run the magazine if we were Editors. Well, here is my conception of the ideal magazine: . . . I would only have such renowned Authors as Burroughs, Mac-Isaac, and a few others . . . there's a goal to aim for," 277.

34. "Ideal High School Faculty," *The Torch*, March 10, 1932.

35. Jerry Siegel, "Backstage," *The Torch*, May 26, 1932.

36. "Impossible to See," *The Torch*, April 21, 1932.

37. Ibid.

38. Jerry Siegel, "Five Men and a Corpse," *The Torch*, January 14, 1932.

39. Patricia Hassard, interview by author, July 8, 2006. In one contest sponsored by local radio juggernaut WHK, Bernie designed an album cover for organ-

ist Helen Wyant's "Sleepy Moon." He won seventeen copies of the record. Bernie also worked on TV game shows and helped design the timeless mod sets for television juggernauts *Jeopardy!* and *Concentration.* Bernie died in 2006, five months after his beloved wife, Ann. His last artistic project was painting a bedroom mural of Woodstock from Schulz's *Peanuts* for one of his grandchildren.

40. Jerry Siegel, "Five Men."
41. Ibid.
42. Bert Lexington, "Death by the Stars," *Superman Archives* 1 (New York: DC Comics, 1989), 179. In this story, the protagonist dies but "was really alive. He had put himself in a state of suspended animation." "Bert Lexington" could be an alias of Jerry's and is possibly an early version of "Lex." National's offices were also at 480 Lexington, opening the possibility that Luthor as evil mastermind might have been a swipe at Donenfeld.
43. Siegel and Shuster, "Remembering the 30's," 17.
44. Jerry Siegel, "Reader Sights," *The Torch,* March 10, 1932. Also see Dooley, "Man of Tomorrow," 23.

5. Cosmic

1. Forrest Ackerman, e-mail to author, March 3, 2006. Forry once had a complete set of the Siegel and Shuster *Science Fiction* fanzines.
2. Les Daniels, *Superman: The Complete History* (San Francisco: Chronicle Books, 1998), 12. Julie Schwartz notes that Jerry was one of their first subscribers. Also see Beerbohm, "Big Bang," 51–52.
3. Siegel and Shuster, "Of Supermen and Kids with Dreams," 23. Tye, *Superman,* 12, also lists another alias as "Charles McEvoy."
4. Clare Winger Harris, letter to *Wonder Stories,* August 1931.
5. *The Author and Journalist* 16–18, bound, 1931, 34.
6. Ibid.
7. Ibid., 94.
8. *Cleveland City Directory,* Cleveland, Ohio, 1930. The previous inhabitants of the Morantz house were a family named "Lane."
9. Hassard, interview.
10. Jerry Siegel (w) and Joe Shuster (a), *Science Fiction* 1, October 1932. The monthly dating for the individual issues is by no means certain, so I will identify them only by issue number and year. Since the fanzines are very rare, I was able to study only #3 in its entirety; the rest I have seen only in pieces. Thanks also to Melanie Maksin and Anne Garrison of the Swarthmore College Library. I was able to track down two people who had complete sets of the magazine. One of them, Jim Halperin of Heritage Auctions, kindly agreed to copy them for me. On June 14, 2006, I was on the phone with him as his assistant started scanning the first issue. I heard a ripping sound in the background and froze. Halperin laughed and said: "Let's both agree not to feel bad about that page that came loose in the process." A complete set sold on September 12, 2011, for $11,950.

11. This design was taken directly from *Amazing Stories Quarterly,* which had the same style of contents page. See the fall 1929 issue for a good example.

12. Jerry Siegel, "Serialette," *The Torch,* October 13, 1932.

13. *The Torch,* November 17, 1932.

14. Dooley, "Man of Tomorrow," 30.

15. Murray Greenberg, *Passing Game: Benny Friedman and the Transformation of Football* (New York: Public Affairs, 2008).

16. "Glenville Boy Is Winner on Poster," *The Plain Dealer,* November 8, 1932.

17. Ibid.

18. Ibid.

19. "Pupil Wins First Prize in Contest," *The Torch,* November 24, 1932.

20. Ibid.

6. Reign

1. Jerry Siegel, letter to *Detective Comics* 512, March 1982.

2. Siegel and Shuster, "Remembering the 30's," 17.

3. Jerry Siegel, letter to *Detective Comics.*

4. Nate Brightman, e-mail to author, December 2, 2011.

5. Siegel and Shuster, "Remembering the 30's," 17.

6. Jerry Siegel (w) and Joe Shuster (a), *Science Fiction* 3, January 1933.

7. Sax Roehmer's *Fu Manchu* series of stories, based around a villain, were very popular in the early thirties. Jerry references them in his letter to *Detective Comics* 512.

8. Siegel and Shuster, *Science Fiction* 3.

9. Steven Nickel, *Torso: The Story of Eliot Ness and the Search for a Psychopathic Killer* (Winston-Salem, NC: John F. Blair, 2001).

10. Siegel and Shuster, *Science Fiction* 3.

11. Ibid.

12. Miles J. Breuer, "The Fitzgerald Contraction," *Science Wonder Stories,* January 1930. This is an allusion to a scientific theory that tried to explain the negative results of the 1887 Michelson-Morley experiment that took place at modern-day Case Western Reserve University in Cleveland. Michelson and Morley were trying to detect the so-called aether, which was the theoretical medium through which light traveled. Their inability to detect "aether flow" opened the door to special relativity. The Lorentz-Fitzgerald theory hoped to prove that the findings of Michelson-Morley did not necessarily negate the existence of the aether.

13. Siegel and Shuster, *Science Fiction* 3.

14. Ibid.

15. Ibid.

16. Ibid.

17. Presumably after, and possibly to impress, Jack Williamson.

18. Siegel and Shuster, *Science Fiction* 3.

19. Ibid.

20. Ibid.

21. Beerbohm, "Big Bang," 56. They even compared him with Frank Paul.

22. Siegel and Shuster, *Science Fiction* 3.

23. Ibid.

24. Ibid.

25. Jerry's sloping Underwood typewriter was part of the exhibit *ZAP! POW! BAM! The Superhero: The Golden Age of Comic Books, 1938–1950* at the William Breman Jewish Heritage Museum in Atlanta, Georgia, which subsequently traveled to several other museums. Jerry used a portable Royal typewriter for train trips to and from New York.

26. Francis Flagg, "The Superman of Dr. Jukes," *Wonder Stories,* November 1931.

27. Ibid.

28. Ibid.

29. Ibid.

30. Ibid.

31. Ibid.

32. Ibid.

33. Ibid. Also see Glen Cadigan, *The Legion Companion* (Raleigh, NC: TwoMorrows, 2003), 20–25. Jerry admits, much later in life, that "writers, working in their lonely little room, are always interested in learning how other writers (and artists) manage to do their very best work."

34. Arthur A. Stuart, "Someday We'll Look Like This," *Popular Science,* July 1929, 47.

35. "Predicts New Organs of Thought in Man," *Popular Science,* May 1930, 32.

36. Siegel and Shuster, "Remembering the 30's," 17.

37. Beerbohm, "Big Bang," 57. Beerbohm notes that in the August 1933 issue of *Science Fiction Digest* there is an announcement that *Science Fiction* would be returning with a new issue #6, with Bernard J. Kenton as editor.

38. *Wonder Stories* had a whole set of science fiction novels that were advertised with an illustration of a filled bookshelf, the ultimate expression not only of education, but of economic capability. The picture included *A Fighting Man of Mars* by Edgar Rice Burroughs, *The Earth Tube* by Gawain Edwards, *Green Fire* by John Taine, and *Ralph 124C 41+* by Hugo Gernsback, among others.

39. H. P. Lovecraft, letter to Clark Ashton Smith, March 21, 1932. Lovecraft made visits to Cleveland in the twenties, most notably after his wife, Sonia, moved there for work.

40. Edmond Hamilton, *The Metal Giants* (Washborn, ND: Swanson, 1935). Thanks to Margaret Tenney of the University of Texas Library for locating an original copy. There are no illustrations.

41. Hugh Langley was a common character name in late-nineteenth-century fiction, especially in periodicals. It is most associated in underground circles as the name of an infamous author who "edited" *The Tides Ebb Out to the Night*, a pseudojournal that raised eyebrows when it was published in the 1890s. A reviewer for the December 5, 1896, issue of *The Academy* writes: "This is the imaginary journal of a modern, introspective, chloral-drinking,

thoroughly selfish young man. It may be taken seriously or otherwise." The book, because of its decadence and drug use, seems to have been an occult sensation in the 1920s. Even today, it is highly prized for its rarity and reputation.

42. For years, this film could be seen only at pulp conventions and at the end of an old *Tarzan and the Green Goddess* VHS release. It is now readily available online on YouTube.

43. Jerry Siegel (w) and Joe Shuster (a), *Science Fiction* 4, 1933.

44. Ibid.

45. Ibid.

46. Mollie Merrick, "Two Scientists Engaged to Make Prehistoric Monsters for New Fantastic Thrills," *The Plain Dealer,* January 22, 1933. Note Merrick's alliterative name.

7. Into the Air

1. "Clevelander Taught the Creator of Popeye," *The Plain Dealer,* October 15, 1938.

2. *Cleveland School of Art Catalog,* Cleveland, Ohio, 1934–1935. The evening coursework went from seven to nine P.M. on Mondays and Thursdays and cost $10 for fifteen lessons.

3. Joe Shuster Collection. Joe kept a lot of newspaper comics sections, some from as far back as 1923 and from places as distant as Seattle and San Francisco.

4. Murphy Anderson interview, in *The Krypton Companion* (Raleigh, NC: TwoMorrows, 2006), 126.

5. Siegel and Shuster, *Interplanetary Police,* in *Siegel and Shuster Dateline 1930's* 1 (Guerneville, CA: Eclipse, 1984), 11–15. The two comics in the *Dateline* series were published by Eclipse, now out of print, and are must-haves for readers interested in their juvenilia.

6. Siegel and Shuster, *Snoopy and Smiley,* in *Dateline* 2.

7. Ibid.

8. Thomas Andrae, "*Funnyman,* Jewish Masculinity, and the Decline of the Superhero," in Andrae and Gordon, *Siegel and Shuster's Funnyman: The First Jewish Superhero, from the Creators of Superman* (Port Townsend, WA: Feral House, 2010), 54.

9. Siegel and Shuster, *Goober the Mighty,* in *Dateline* 1, 21.

10. Ibid., *Jimmy Grant,* in *Dateline* 1, 23.

11. Ibid., *Jerry the Journalist,* in *Dateline* 1, 24.

12. Ibid., *The Pinkbaums,* in *Dateline* 1, 26.

13. Jerry Siegel, introduction, *Dateline* 1, inside front cover.

14. Ibid.

15. Ibid.

16. Mike Benton, *Masters of Imagination: The Comic Book Artists Hall of Fame* (Dallas: Taylor Publishing, 1994), 19. The comics tabloid is listed in *The Overstreet Comics Price Guide* under "Promotional Comics" as *Taylor's Christ-*

mas Tabloid. The owner of the tabloid has chosen to remain anonymous. Joe could have just contributed some cartoons to *The Cleveland Shopping News* itself; there is one particular Santa in a Christmas issue who looks a lot like Joe's work.

17. Tye, *Superman*, 12. Jerry also allegedly had an early short story published in *The Sunday Buffalo Times* called "Monsters of the Moon."

18. Siegel and Shuster, "Remembering the 30's," 16.

19. Siegel and Shuster, *Dateline* 1, 2. Of these strips, *Kaye* in particular is intriguing, as it begins when "a great scientist is hit by a car" as phantomlike shapes grin and leer over the Flatiron building at the intersection of Broadway and Fifth in New York. The strip promises that it will be "the strangest story ever told."

20. Beerbohm, "Big Bang," 59.

21. See Daniels, *Superman*, 17. Also see Beerbohm, "Siegel & Shuster Presents . . . The Superman," *Comic Book Marketplace*, June 1996, 45–50.

22. Ibid.

8. Morning

1. Steranko, *Steranko History of Comics*, 35. Almost every account of the creation of Superman—and certainly every book about its creators that I reference in these pages—bears witness to some version of this story. Steranko's assumed interviews with Jerry (presented as quotes) also offer a glimpse into the process that no previous work does. I do something similar in this book, but only for unimportant dialogue to drive the narrative—and as homage to Steranko.

2. Ibid. Also see Daniels, *Superman*, 18.

3. Fine, Hubar, and Wolkov, interview.

4. "Ten Dead as Ohio Is Heat Weary," *The Plain Dealer*, July 2, 1933.

5. *The Plain Dealer*, June 18, 1933.

6. Ibid.

7. Ibid.

8. Ibid.

9. Ibid.

10. Ibid.

11. Don Hutchinson, *The Great Pulp Heroes* (Las Vegas: Book Republic Press, 2007).

12. *The Plain Dealer*, June 18, 1933.

13. *The Plain Dealer*, July 29, 1932, and October 8, 1939. Readick is described as being five feet five inches tall and weighing 130 pounds.

14. Martin Grams Jr., "The Shadow: The NBC Season," *Radiogram* 35, October 2010, 9. Readick went on to play reporter Carl Phillips in Orson Welles's famous 1938 broadcast of *The War of the Worlds*. Welles had replaced Readick on *The Shadow* in 1937.

15. *The Plain Dealer*, June 18, 1933.

16. Ibid.

17. Ibid.

18. *The Plain Dealer,* July 2, 1933.

19. Ibid.

20. *The Plain Dealer,* June 18, 1933.

21. Ibid.

22. Ibid.

23. Beerbohm, "Siegel & Shuster Presents."

24. Daniels, *Superman,* 17.

25. Ibid. *Detective Dan* the comic book was canceled after one issue, but Marsh transformed the idea into a successful newspaper strip named *Dan Dunn,* which he produced until 1942.

26. Beerbohm, "Siegel & Shuster Presents," 49. Also see Siegel and Shuster, "Of Supermen and Kids with Dreams," 27.

27. Tye, *Superman,* 14.

28. Beerbohm, "Siegel & Shuster Presents," 46. Also see Jerry Siegel, letter to Alan Light, January 10, 1976. Jerry writes, "I have heard of *so-called* early Superman strips [and] art work supposedly produced by Joe and me which I believe to be fraudulent. Rumors are not necessarily true."

29. Peavy, letter to the author, April 13, 2008. Jean says they met in 1930 when Joe was sixteen and already at Glenville.

30. Beerbohm, "Siegel & Shuster Presents," 49, also notes this discrepancy. Daniels, *Superman,* 16, shows a version that looks exactly the same, but with a copyright date of 1933.

31. Tye, *Superman,* 17.

32. Gerard Jones, *Men of Tomorrow* (New York: Basic Books, 2005), 113. Jones (and Will Murray) suggests that Graff's Phantom Magician character in his *Patsy* strip might be an early Superman swipe—or possible inspiration. Also see Beerbohm, "Big Bang," 58.

33. Patricia Hassard, e-mail to author, August 10, 2006. Patricia (Bernie's daughter) confirms that these preliminary Superman drawings did exist, but they fell victim to a "furious purging" by Bernie's wife in 1993 when they moved from Los Angeles to Richmond, Virginia.

34. *The Torch,* April 14, 1934. Because Sam liked planes, several classmates purchased books on flight for the school library as a remembrance.

35. Ibid., May 17, 1934.

36. The actual 1934 yearbook is very hard to find, as existing library copies in Cleveland and Glenville have gone "lost."

37. Jerry Siegel, letter to *Action Comics* 544, June 1983.

38. Russell Keaton, *The Aviation Art of Russell Keaton* (Amherst, MA: Kitchen Sink Press, 1995).

39. Jerry Siegel, letter to Russell Keaton, June 12, 1934.

40. Deborah Brunt, introduction, in Keaton, *Aviation Art of Russell Keaton.*

9. Major

1. Nicky Heron Brown, "Major Malcolm Wheeler-Nicholson, Cartoon Character or Real Life Hero? Correcting Hadju's *The Ten-Cent Plague,*" *Interna-*

tional Journal of Comic Art (Fall 2008), 242. Also see Nicky Wheeler-Nicholson Brown, interview with Jim Amash, "He Was Going to Go for the Big Idea," *Alter Ego* 88, August 2009, 49. Also see Jones, *Men of Tomorrow,* 101–02.

2. Jones, *Men of Tomorrow,* 101–02.

3. *Wooley's History of the Comic Book 1899–1936* (Buena Vista, FL: self-published, 1986). Also see Douglas Gilbert, "No Laughing Matter!," *Comic Book Marketplace* 36, June 1996.

4. Tom DeHaven, *Our Hero: Superman on Earth* (New Haven: Yale University Press, 2010). Also see DeHaven, *It's Superman* (New York: Ballantine Books, 2006), for a literary take on Superman, set in the 1940s.

5. Daniels, *Superman,* 23. Also see Major Malcolm Wheeler-Nicholson, letter to Jerry Siegel, June 6, 1935.

6. Siegel, letter to *Detective Comics.* The various original letters to and from Jerry in the thirties were all saved by Jerry and have been reprinted in several places, including as evidence in the various court cases. The case documents offer scanned copies but are not always easily available to everyone. Many of the letters also appear for the first time in Jerry's long letter to *Detective* and in his 1975 press release (both easily found online), so I have opted to cite those by date in the text and as one source here in the notes. Other letters that appear elsewhere will simply be cited as is. I have fact-checked letters across multiple sources when possible. A compendium of these letters and related correspondence would be a valuable resource.

7. Ibid.

8. Peavy, interview. Jerry was "interested in the occult." The one book that appears again and again in pulp advertisements is L. W. de Laurence, *The Great Book of Magical Art: Hindu Magic and East Indian Occultism and the Book of Secret Hindu, Ceremonial, and Talismanic Magic* (Chicago: De Laurence Company, 1911). I do not know if Jerry actually had this book, but if he had an occult book, this would be the one he could have obtained most easily through the pulps. *The Great Book* is also very representative of these types of books as a corpus. There was also a copy at the Cleveland Public Library. Originally published in 1898, *The Great Book* has remained in print almost constantly. Carolyn Morrow Long, *Spiritual Merchants: Religion, Magic, and Commerce* (Knoxville: University of Tennessee Press, 2001), 192, quotes de Laurence himself as saying he didn't believe anything in it. The book itself is filled with weird symbols, claims to ancient Jewish magic, and promises of power. Also see L. W. de Laurence, *The Master Key* (Chicago: De Laurence Company, 1911), 410, 73. Jerry also may have purchased *The Great Book's* highly advertised companion tome, which claimed to be able to unlock "the Duality of your Being" through empowerment of the "super-conscious mind." This kind of hyperbole is mirrored in Siegel and Shuster, "For Chislers Only," *Dateline* 1, 6.

9. Peavy, interview.

10. Siegel, letter to *Weird Tales,* October 1933.

11. Jim Steinmeyer, *Hiding the Elephant: How Magicians Invented the Impossible and Learned to Disappear* (Cambridge, MA: Da Capo Press, 2004).

12. Ashley and Lowndes, *Gernsback Days*, 124. Also see "Wee Girl Gone," *The New York Times*, November 18, 1928. Gernsback's public bet may have been at least partly motivated by the sad circumstances of his three-year-old daughter, Bernette, who was struck and killed by a cab after running back onto the street to retrieve some pennies she had dropped.

13. Jerry Siegel (w) and Joe Shuster (a), *Dr. Mystic*, in *Comics Magazine* 1, Centaur Publications, May 1936, was a reprint and possibly unauthorized.

14. "The Image" previously aired on the horror anthology radio show *The Witch's Tale* on February 8, 1932.

15. Grams Jr., "The Shadow," 10.

16. Jerry Siegel (w) and Joe Shuster (a), *Dr. Occult*, in *More Fun Comics* 12, August 1936.

17. Daniels, *Superman*, 25. Also see *Wooley's History of the Comic Book*.

18. See Robert E. Howard, "The Scarlet Citadel," *Weird Tales*, January 1933. Also see Robert E. Howard, "The Black Colossus," *Weird Tales*, June 1933. The word *Koth* (as an ancient country) appears previously in these two tales by Robert E. Howard, famous for his Conan character. The word would also appear in two H. P. Lovecraft stories written in the late twenties but unpublished until the early forties. Also see Peavy, interview. Occult's partner, Rose, would be the name of Joe's cousin, who would go on to a career as a Hollywood producer.

19. Hugh Langley (Jerry Siegel), "Good Luck Charm," *Superman Archives* 1 (New York: DC Comics, 1989), 179. Siegel's story about an occult charm is accompanied by an illustration of a gold circle with a mystic eye.

20. Jeffrey J. Kripal, *Mutants and Mystics: Science Fiction, Superhero Comics, and the Paranormal* (Chicago: University of Chicago Press, 2011), 47; Philip Jenkins, *Mystics and Messiahs: Cults and New Religions in American History* (New York: Oxford University Press, 2000), 98. Also see Christopher Knowles, *Our Gods Wear Spandex* (San Francisco: Weiser Books, 2007), 38. See *Popular Science*, October 1936, 121, and *Popular Mechanics*, January 1936, 28A, for a representative AMORC ad. Teenagers such as Jerry were probably drawn to these ideas because of their occult mystery and not for any intrinsic spiritual teachings.

21. Jerry Siegel (w) and Joe Shuster (a), *Dr. Occult*, in *More Fun Comics* 10, May 1936.

22. Ibid., *More Fun Comics* 20–23, May–August 1937.

23. Ibid., *More Fun Comics* 24, September 1937. In this story, Henri Duval (now reconceived as a French surrealist artist) is murdered.

24. The 1932 Universal Pictures film *Radio Patrol* with Robert Armstrong was showing in Cleveland at the Palace in June of that year.

25. Martin Sheridan, *Classic Comics and Their Creators* (Arcadia, CA: Hyperion Press, 1971), 143.

26. "Fighting Traffic Deaths," *The Plain Dealer*, July 25, 1936.

27. Tye, *Superman*, 5.

28. The strip was first titled *Calling All Cars,* with the subtitle "Starring Sandy Kean and the Radio Squad."

29. The name "Sandy Kean" might be a nod to *Little Orphan Annie's* famous canine sidekick. "Larry Trent" was probably taken from a Secret Service character of the same name in the 1929 Mascot film serial *The King of the Kongo,* a half-sound jungle picture. Boris Karloff also appears in this film as the shadowy "Scarface Macklin."

30. Jerry Siegel (w) and Joe Shuster (a), *Calling All Cars,* in *More Fun Comics* 11, July 1936.

31. Ibid.

32. Jerry Siegel (w) and Joe Shuster (a), *Radio Squad,* in *More Fun Comics,* September 1937.

33. Jerry Siegel (w) and Joe Shuster (a), *Federal Men,* in *New Comics* 2, January 1936.

34. Ibid., in *New Comics* 4–10, March–November 1936. The cover of *New Comics* 10 of a giant robot terrorizing the Capitol looks a lot like the cover for Edmond Hamilton's "The Metal Giants" in *Weird Tales,* December 1926. The image also resembles a cover by Norman Saunders (a) for *The Technocrats' Magazine,* 1933, about a political movement led by Howard Scott, who spoke at Glenville during Jerry and Joe's time there. In *The Plain Dealer,* December 3, 1932, Scott espouses a fear of a future dominated by the "battle between man and machines." There was a local magazine about the technocracy called *Eighteen Forty One* that was mostly text but always sported the symbol of the technocracy on its cover: a circular, yin-yang emblem. Also see "Giant Robots, Controlled by Wireless, to Fight Our Battles," *The Fresno Bee,* April 29, 1934. Though certainly out of Joe's neighborhood, this article might have been reprinted elsewhere; its depiction of a claw-handed robot dominating a devastated urban skyline is very similar to the *Federal Men* story.

35. Siegel (w) and Shuster (a), *Federal Men,* in *New Adventure Comics* 12, January 1937. Jor-L in this story also fiddles with a modernistic "radio." See Siegel and Shuster, "Of Supermen and Kids with Dreams," 16.

36. Siegel (w) and Shuster (a), *Federal Men,* in *New Adventure Comics* 14, March 1937. Formerly *New Comics,* the title changed to *New Adventure Comics* for 12–29. From 30 to the title's cancellation (as vol. 1) in 1983, it was named *Adventure Comics.*

37. Fine, Hubar, and Wolkov, interview. Jerry Siegel was always a hit with his nieces and nephews. He would play a game with Irv called Garbage, where the goal was to turn a nonsensical scribble into an actual picture. Later on, Jerry would take Irv to see the East 105th Street studio, where they produced the actual *Superman* comics. Irv is now a successful Cleveland real estate developer and charity organizer, working on nonprofit projects in his cousin's name.

38. Siegel (w) and Shuster (a), *Federal Men,* in *New Adventure Comics* 23, January 1938. Also see Rita Hubar, interview with William Meeks, July 10, 2009.

Jerry taught her why the keys on his typewriter were not in alphabetical order. Rita went on to a long career as a memorable schoolteacher.

39. Bart and Sally are in many ways an alternate, more idealized version of Lois and Clark. Without Clark's powers as Superman, they become much more equal. They can go on hair-raising adventures while still enjoying married life.

40. "Who Backs Black Legion?," *The Plain Dealer,* July 25, 1936. The Black Legion was a Klan splinter group operating around Detroit. Also see Rick Bowers, *Superman Versus the Ku Klux Klan* (Washington, DC: National Geographic Society, 2012), for a look at the radio show's treatment of the Klan over the summer of 1946 in the sixteen-part series of episodes titled *The Clan of the Fiery Cross.*

41. William D. Jenkins, *Steel Valley Klan: The Ku Klux Klan in Ohio's Mahoning Valley* (Kent, OH: Kent State University Press, 1990).

42. Frank Gervasi, "Iron Man Barkley," *Collier's,* April 9, 1949, 24–25.

43. Jerry Siegel (w) and Joe Shuster (a), *Spy,* in *Detective Comics* 20, October 1938.

10. Next

1. Jerry Siegel, Exhibit EE, *Joanne Siegel and Laura Siegel Larson v. Time Warner, Inc., et al.,* U.S. District Court, Central District of California, Case No. 2:04-cv-08400-SGL-RZ, filed July 28, 2008. These records also show that expenses of $5 were contributed and later refunded from Arthur J. Lafave, a local newspaper publisher Jerry probably went to for investment funds for their comics tabloid.

2. Ibid.

3. Jerry Siegel, letter to *Detective Comics.*

4. Ibid.

5. Ibid.

6. Ibid.

7. Ibid.

8. Ibid.

9. Jerry Siegel (w) and Joe Shuster (a), *Slam Bradley,* in *Detective Comics* 1, March 1937. Slam literally takes on all of Chinatown in his first adventure. Jerry may be drawing on the bloody tong wars of Cleveland between the On Leong and Hip Sing groups; the On Leong leader was killed with a meat cleaver, a shocking act that caused the city to round up every Chinese man in Cleveland.

10. Ibid., *Detective Comics* 5, June 1937.

11. Ibid., *Detective Comics* 23–24, December 1938–January 1939.

12. *Great Lakes Exposition Official Souvenir Guide,* Cleveland, Ohio, 1936. Also see John Vacha, *Meet Me on Lake Erie, Dearie!: Cleveland's Great Lakes Exposition* (Kent, OH: Kent State University Press, 2011). The Expo also displayed death masks of some of the torso victims in hopes of generating leads.

13. Jerry Siegel, letter to *Detective Comics*.

14. Ibid.

15. Ibid.

16. Ibid.

17. Ibid.

18. Irwin Donenfeld, interview by Robert Beerbohm, Mark Evanier, and Julius Schwartz, "There's a Lot of Myth Out There!," *Alter Ego* 26, July 2003. Also see Whitney Ellsworth, letter to Jerry Siegel, April 23, 1937; Ellsworth assures Jerry of National: "We are poor people."

19. Jones, *Men of Tomorrow,* 1–22, 41–62, for the most comprehensive look at Harry Donenfeld's life and career.

20. "Obscenity Decision Awaits a Reading," *The New York Times,* March 8, 1934.

21. Donenfeld, interview, "There's a Lot of Myth Out There!," 25. Herbie often told Julie: "If you don't have your feet on your desk, you're not working."

11. Muscle and Power

1. David L. Chapman, *Sandow the Magnificent: Eugene Sandow and the Beginnings of Bodybuilding* (Champaign: University of Illinois Press, 2006), is a fairly representative look at how strongman culture emigrated from Europe.

2. Bernarr Macfadden, *Vitality Supreme* (New York: Physical Culture Publishing, 1915), xi.

3. Mark Adams, *Mr. America: How Muscular Millionaire Bernarr Macfadden Transformed the Nation Through Sex, Salad, and the Ultimate Starvation Diet* (New York: HarperCollins, 2009).

4. Ibid.

5. Robert Ernst, *Weakness Is a Crime: The Life of Bernarr Macfadden* (Syracuse, NY: Syracuse University Press, 1990).

6. Also see *True Detective Stories, Photoplay,* and *The New York Evening Graphic,* which is considered a precursor to daily tabloid journalism. Also see Jim Bennett, www.bernarrmacfadden.com.

7. Siegel and Shuster, "Of Supermen and Kids with Dreams," 23.

8. "Breitbart Is Coming," *The Plain Dealer,* October 13, 1923. One-line ads began and ran until the review of his show on October 24, 1923. Breitbart would extend his stay because of brisk ticket sales.

9. Thomas Andrae, "The Jewish Superhero," in *Siegel and Shuster's Funnyman,* 43, offers a good look at Breitbart and some great photos of him in Cleveland in 1923.

10. Chapman, *Sandow the Magnificent,* 184, questions this story as yet another legendary feat ascribed to the Great Sandow.

11. "Strongest Man Asks Police Aid," *The Plain Dealer,* October 29, 1932. Zebic is later pictured with a chest full of medals.

12. "Vindicates Mummy's Status as Bolivian and Collateral," *The Plain Dealer,* January 10, 1937.

13. "Police Aid? Ah. No, Says Strongest Man," *The Plain Dealer,* November 1, 1932. In his prime, Professor Zebic did exhibitions at church wrestling matches, then sold restorative tonics. After "retiring," he opened the Samson Tea & Tonic Co. at 1285 East Seventy-ninth Street. He died on June 16, 1947, at age seventy-one.

14. Kasson, *Houdini,* 19. These men "tell us about how modernity was understood in terms of the body and how the white male body became a powerful symbol by which to dramatize modernity's impact and how to resist it."

15. "Bullet Flattened Out Against His Forehead," *The Houston Daily Post,* October 13, 1914. Also see Ed Spielman, *The Mighty Atom: The Life and Times of Joseph L. Greenstein* (New York: Viking, 1979), 52–54.

16. Spielman, *Mighty Atom,* 125–26. Also see "Mighty Atom, Super-Strong Man," *The Buffalo Evening Times,* September 29, 1928.

17. David P. Willoughby, *The Super-Athletes: A Record of the Limits of Human Strength, Speed and Stamina* (New York: A. S. Barnes, 1970), 181.

18. Michael Sangiacomo, e-mail to author, August 31, 2008.

19. Greenstein is also thought of as the inspiration for another superhero, the Atom, a masked man named Al Pratt who debuted in Ben Flinton (w) and Bill O'Conner (a), *All-American Comics* 19, October 1940. The Atom was a founding member of the Justice Society of America.

20. Jerry Siegel (w) and Joe Shuster (a), "Superman Joins the Circus," *Action Comics* 7, December 1938, reprinted in *Superman Chronicles* 1 (New York: DC Comics, 2006), 89.

21. Siegmund Klein, *Super Physique* (London: Mitre Press, c. 1945). Also see "Strong Man Saves Woman," *The New York Times,* September 30, 1926. Klein actually takes the next step to becoming an actual superhero by saving a woman named Ann Burke who is trapped on an upper floor of her building. Klein dangerously scales an electric sign and rescues her.

22. "American's Trial Put Off," *The New York Times,* May 11, 1934. Lionel Strongfort, an American citizen, was detained in Germany following an accusation of not reporting funds back to his country of birth.

23. Bernarr Macfadden, *Strengthening the Eyes* (New York: Macfadden Publications, 1924), 122, 159. One exercise worked "with fingers placed one on each side of the eyeball [then] make a gentle upward and downward movement. Use no pressure. The gentlest movement will suffice." Readers are also urged to "involve shadow boxing. . . . Strike out forward vigorously first with one fist and then with the other, continuing to alternate until slightly tired."

24. Photographs of Joe without his glasses reveal his big eyes, which more than a few girls would later find irresistible. But those eyes, large and gleaming, are also a prime indication of Graves' disease, which is essentially an overactive thyroid; additional symptoms include weight loss, increased appetite, and muscle weakness. (This is obviously not a professional diagnosis.) See Tye, *Superman,* 15, for Jerry Fine's point that Joe took "sight-seeing" classes while at Hamilton.

12. Frankenstein's Monster

1. Ina Rae Hark, *American Cinema of the 1930s: Themes and Variations* (Piscataway, NJ: Rutgers University Press, 2007), 6.

2. "Akron Disaster," Universal Newsreel, April 4, 1933, http://www.archive.org.

3. "Help Needy Says First Lady," partial newsreel, Universal, November 1, 1933, http://www.archive.org.

4. "Campaign and Election," Fox Movietone Newsreel, 1932, http://www.archive.org.

5. "Hairdresser Wins Lottery," partial newsreel, November 15, 1933, http://www.archive.org.

6. "Torpedoes Launched from Air," partial newsreel, Universal, October 23, 1933, http://www.archive.org.

7. "Griffith Park Relief Workers Demonstration," partial newsreel, Workers Film and Photo League, 1933, http://www.archive.org.

8. "Lindberghs Fly North on Epic Ocean Trip to Blaze New Air Route," Universal Newsreels, July 10, 1933, http://www.archive.org.

9. "Hitlerites Parade in Rain to Demonstrate Great Nazi Strength," Universal Newsreels, March 16, 1933, http://www.archive.org.

10. Andrae, "Jewish Superhero," 38–41. Also see Yudl Rosenberg, "The Golem, or The Miraculous Deeds of Rabbi Liva," in *Yenne Velt: The Great Works of Jewish Fantasy & Occult* (New York: Pocket Books, 1976), 162. The most interesting aspect of this account might be its presentation in literature as a historicized event similar to Hawthorne's *The Scarlet Letter* and Burroughs's *A Princess of Mars*. See Michael Chabon, *The Amazing Adventures of Kavalier & Clay* (New York: Picador, 2001), chapter 4, for a fictionalized account of the cultural (and physical) weight of the true Golem.

11. Jerry Siegel, letter to *Action* 544.

12. Siegel and Shuster, "Remembering the 30's," back cover. Also see Siegel and Shuster, "Of Supermen and Kids with Dreams," 29: "Joe and I, we practically lived in movie theaters."

13. Michael Sangiacomo, "He's Not Ready for Cycle to End, Glenville Bike Shop Owner Continuing Family Tradition," *The Plain Dealer,* September 26, 2006. Jack Gordon ran a porch-front bike shop in Glenville for the better part of the century, often fixing poor kids' bikes for free. His nephew Louis now runs the store, on a much bigger lot, selling parts online and showing local teenagers how to fix bikes.

14. "Potato Soup," *The Plain Dealer,* October 2, 1938.

15. "Beef Stew Supreme," *The Plain Dealer,* October 30, 1934.

16. Kasson, *Houdini,* 58: "This is a scene of male exhibition—perhaps tinged with exhibitionism." See Jerry Siegel and Joe Shuster, interview with Mike Olszewski and Bertil Falk, "Sidebar on the Origins of Superman," *Alter Ego* 56, February 2007, 6, in which Joe reveals of the costume design: "Yes, yes, I did that."

17. Benton, *Masters of Imagination,* 19. Joe said, "I was inspired. I did the artwork very rapidly. We hit the proper costume for Superman immediately."

18. Abe Coleman, "Big Jewish Muscle Man Grapples Here," *The Plain Dealer,* January 31, 1932.

19. *The Plain Dealer,* June 13, 1935.

20. Michael Chabon, "Secret Skin," *The New Yorker,* March 10, 2008, 65–69. Chabon writes that "modern aesthetics, with their roots in fantasies of power, speed and flight . . . was an invitation to enter into the world of story . . . to begin to wear what we know to be hidden inside us."

21. Beerbohm, "Big Bang," 58. According to Jerry, Joe collected the early Hal Foster *Tarzan* newspaper strip.

22. "Schmeling Wins in Knockout," *The Plain Dealer,* July 4, 1931. Also see *The Plain Dealer,* June 12, 1936. Schmeling said of opponent Joe Louis: "I don't believe there has been any such thing as a Superman." Also see *The Plain Dealer,* June 20, 1936. After Schmeling knocked Louis out, he said: "The myth of the Superman has been exploded completely." Also see Roger Dicken, "Say '*Shazam!*'—or Maybe '*Schmeling!*'" *Alter Ego* 64, January 2007, 20. Dicken argues that Schmeling was the character model for Captain Marvel, who first appeared in Bill Parker (w) and C. C. Beck (a), *Whiz Comics* 2, February 1940.

23. George F. Jowett, *Molding a Mighty Chest* (Scranton, PA: Jowett Institute of Physical Culture, c. 1931). See *Popular Mechanics,* March 1929, 96, for an ad where Jowett promises, "I guarantee to make a Super-man out of you."

24. Siegel and Shuster, "Of Supermen and Kids with Dreams," 33. According to this interview, the S symbol came about as a happy coincidence of common last-name initials. Other rumors include it being based on the logo of nearby Shaw High School, which indeed had a red "S," though it was paired with a big shark, making it an unlikely choice. The shield border, which changes quickly, looks more like a heraldic crest or police badge. As an inverted triangle, it is also one half of the Jewish Star of David, which, when engraved on gold, acts as protection from evil. The inverted "S" with the inflated top cleft also looks like the modern Hebrew *lamed* character, which signifies authority as the leader of a flock of sheep. But it also suggests a tie or bind. Its meaning is simply "toward."

25. Adam Roberts, "Is Superman a Superman?," in *The Man from Krypton* (Dallas: Ben Bella, 2006).

26. Siegel (w) and Shuster (a), *Spy,* in *Detective Comics* 25, March 1939.

27. "The Longest Wind," *The Plain Dealer,* September 3, 1932.

28. The term *Superman* also appears in many articles about eugenics. See "Superman a Being of Nervous Force," *The New York Times,* January 11, 1914. Also see "Mrs. Sanger Says Superman Is the Aim of Birth Control," *The New York Times,* January 31, 1922. The track results in the Cleveland and New York newspapers also list plenty of horses named "Superman."

29. Warren G. Harris, *Clark Gable: A Biography* (New York: Crown Publishing Group, 2005).

30. Siegel and Shuster, "Of Supermen and Kids with Dreams," 34. Joe says of Jerry: "As for Clark Kent, he combined the names of Clark Gable and Kent

Taylor." There is also pulp writer Clark Ashton Smith, of whom Jerry was a fan. I put enormous stock in Andrae's important interview, the only one of its kind. However, I do not always trust Jerry and Joe, who had been living under a specter of lawsuits and copyright issues all of their adult lives. Part of the goal of this book is to separate this fact from fiction using as many primary sources as possible in an accessible manner.

31. Herbert Johnson, "Superman Not So New," *The Greenville News,* March 30, 1952. Also see Peter Coogan, *Superhero: The Secret Origin of a Genre* (Austin: Monkeybrain Press, 2006). Coogan makes skillful note of the many precursor characters of the superhero, including Spring-heeled Jack, Hugo Hercules, and Popeye, among many others. Also see Will Murray, "The Roots of the Superman!," *Comic Book Marketplace* 63, October 1998. Murray notes the Savage connection as well: Doc Savage had a Fortress of Solitude, and his first name was Clark. A 1934 pulp house ad, first reproduced in Steranko, *Steranko History of Comics,* 19, also refers to Doc Savage as a "Superman." The ad, in its splitting, layout, and ten-cent symbol, looks somewhat similar to the poster image seen in Beerbohm, "Siegel & Shuster Presents," 46. Also see Jerry Siegel and Joanne Siegel, interviewed by Murray Bishoff and Alan Light, "'Superman' Grew Out of Our Personal Feelings," *Alter Ego* 56, February 2007, 11. Siegel says: "Of course I read *Doc Savage.*"

32. Steranko, *Steranko History of Comics,* 15. Also see Will Murray, "Gladiator of Iron, Man of Steel," *Alter Ego* 37, June 2004. Murray wonders if Siegel made these denials to avoid legal action against him by Wylie. In Jerry Siegel, letter to Alan Light, January 16, 1976, Jerry specifically denies *Gladiator's* influence.

33. Steranko, *Steranko History of Comics,* 16–17.

34. C. A. Brandt, "Shades of the Nth Man," *Amazing Stories,* June 1930.

35. John Byrne, *Superman: The Man of Steel* (New York: DC/Ballantine Books, 1987). This eighties reboot of Superman dramatically recasts Clark as a high school football star who uses his powers to succeed on the field. Only when Jonathan Kent tells his adopted son of his origins does Clark turn toward responsibility.

36. Another source might be Jack Williamson and Dr. Miles J. Breuer, *The Girl from Mars* (Brooklyn: Gryphon Books, 1998), originally published in 1929. In this tale, as Mars explodes, a rocket finds its way to a farm on Earth. The polished green metal yields a human girl named "Pandorina." Beyond the science fiction elements of both stories, it is the inferiority complex of *Gladiator* that hearkens most to the heart of the Superman character and his dual identity of Clark Kent.

37. See Arie Kaplan, *From Krakow to Krypton: Jews and Comic Books* (Philadelphia: Jewish Publication Society, 2008). Also see Danny Fingeroth, *Disguised as Clark Kent: Jews, Comics, and the Creation of the Superhero* (New York: Continuum, 2007); and Simcha Weinstein, *Up, Up, and Oy Vey: How Jewish History, Culture, and Values Shaped the Comic Book Superhero* (Fort Lee, NJ: Barricade Books, 2009).

38. The pose of Christ, lifting the heavy cross with his legs, is very similar to the cover image of *Action Comics* 1.

39. "Millions All over World Preparing for Second Coming of Christ," *The Plain Dealer,* April 4, 1926.

40. Ibid.

41. Knowles, *Our Gods Wear Spandex,* 122: "At his core, Superman is a Messiah in the Biblical tradition who can also be seen as a metaphor for modern Jewish assimilation. The destruction of Krypton is an apt metaphor for the Diaspora, as well as for the assault on European Jewish communities that prompted their mass [im]migration to North America."

42. F. M. Messenger, *The Coming Superman* (Kansas City, MO: Nazarene Publishing, 1928), 7.

43. "New Exploding Star," *The New York Times,* December 12, 1937.

44. Siegel and Shuster, "Of Supermen and Kids with Dreams," 48.

45. *Joanne Siegel and Laura Siegel Larson v. Warner Bros. Entertainment Inc.,* U.S. District Court, Central District of California, Case No. CV-04-8400-SGL (RZx), August 12, 2009, 7.

46. Siegel, introduction, *Dateline* 1.

13. The Muse

1. John Sherwood, "Superman Still Makes Millions, but Not His Creators," *The Washington Star,* October 29, 1975.

2. Dooley, "Man of Tomorrow," 29. Also see Tye, *Superman,* 4, for a story of Jerry, like Charlie Brown, getting no valentines. According to Jerry, he wrote one to himself.

3. Jerry Siegel, *The Torch,* September 29, 1932.

4. Ibid. Also see Weltman, "Superman Creator Flew High." He says that "Lois was the name of a girl [Jerry] was crazy about in high school." Reuben lost touch with Jerry after leaving high school to join a harmonica band with his brother.

5. Lois Amster, interview with Thomas Andrae, in *Creators of the Superheroes,* 43–45. Also see Daniels, *Superman,* 19.

6. Paul H. Rothschild, e-mail to author, January 7, 2009. Also see Jerry Siegel, "Gorgeous Grads Grandstand as Galloping Goober Gathers Gossip," *The Torch,* January 18, 1934. Jerry may have interviewed Amster, though she never remembered it. He writes: "There comes a time in the careers of all high school students when they reach the point where everyone respects and appreciates them. Petite Lois Amster gave vent to the utterly unique words, 'I am sorry to leave Glenville High.' In being the only one to remark as to that fact, Lois was utterly utterly unique."

7. *The Torch,* December 8, 1932.

8. Amster, interview, 44.

9. Siegel (w) and Shuster (a), *Dr. Occult,* in *New Fun Comics* 1, October 1935. Also see *More Fun Comics* 7–9, January–April 1936.

10. Jerry Siegel, letter to *Time,* May 30, 1988, 6–7.

11. See Daniels, *Superman,* 20. Also see Amster, interview, 45. Jerry here states that "Lois Lane" was a direct modification of "Lola Lane."

12. Neil Moran, "The Tooth," *Astounding Stories,* April 1934. Also see Lois Lane, "The Purple Sedan," *Weird Tales,* August 1929. Thanks to Glenn Goggin for this reference of Lois as pulp writer. This same issue featured an Edmond Hamilton *Interstellar Patrol* story. Also see Everett Franklin Bleiler and Richard Bleiler, *Science-Fiction: The Gernsback Years* (Kent, OH: Kent State University Press, 1998). This is an indispensable resource for research into the pulps.

13. Jerry Siegel, "The Story Behind *Superman* #1," http://site.Superman-thrutheages.com.

14. "Helen Kovacs," *1930 United States Federal Census* (Provo, UT: Ancestry.com Operations, 2002), http://www.ancestry.com. Her name on her birth certificate is "Jalon."

15. Joanne Siegel, letter to author, January 28, 2007: "I believe it was my ad. I was so young. . . . No experience described me all right. It makes me laugh now." Though I have a few letters from Joanne, having met her once, she and her daughter, Laura, politely declined to be interviewed for this book owing to their ongoing legal situation. In deference to their privacy, I have used only information that is publicly available. The one exception is this letter from Joanne verifying that the ad was hers. Since her status as the model for Lois Lane is held in question by some, I thought it important to include this.

16. Jerry Siegel, "'Superman' Grew Out of Our Personal Feelings About Life," 7–8. Also see Joanne Siegel and Laura Siegel Larson, panel discussion, Hanna Theater, Cleveland, Ohio, July 9, 2009. Available online on www.youtube.com.

17. Ibid. Also see Siegel and Shuster, "Remembering the 30's," back cover. Joe Shuster, sketch of Lois Lane, *Infinity* 4, 1972, inside front cover. Joe says he especially liked copying the Vargas girls and Russell Patterson.

18. Siegel and Shuster, "Of Supermen and Kids with Dreams," 31. Joe admits, "I started dating her first."

19. Joanne Siegel, panel discussion.

20. Siegel, "'Superman' Grew," 6.

21. Syd Weizel, Weizel Family Bible, http://www.hahnlibrary.net. The facts of the Weizel Bible account (dates and locations) do match up with more objective sources. And a "Mike Kovacs" is listed a few times in *The Plain Dealer* for public intoxication. Still, these facts come down over several generations and cannot be verified. I include it only as family lore that is publicly available.

22. Ibid. They lived at 7204 Grand Avenue.

23. Ibid.

24. Ibid.

25. I found the ad in 2006 in Kelvin Smith Library at Case Western Reserve University, after years of staring at left-to-right spinning microfilm.

26. Siegel (w) and Shuster (a), "The Case of the Broadway Bandit," *Detective Comics* 16, June 1938.

27. Ibid.

28. Ibid.

29. Tye, *Superman,* 122.

30. Joanne was married during her time away from Cleveland to someone named Joseph "Kulek" or "Kulik." His name also appears in conjunction with an early photo of Joanne that he presumably took. There was a Joseph Kulik from Salem, Massachusetts, whose photographic work on the Polish community of Salem later became recognized for its historic and artistic significance. This Kulik also, at the beginning of his career, took fashion photographs of women much like the Joanne photo. Kulik's son Thad, however, says it is definitely not the same man.

31. Siegel and Shuster, "Remembering the 30's," back cover.

32. Siegel (w) and Shuster (a), "Case of the Broadway Bandit."

14. The Works

1. Beerbohm, "Big Bang," 58. Beerbohm writes about a strip that was shopped around in 1934 by Conrad Rupert and Clay Ferguson Jr. about a superpowered alien, though one very different from Superman.

2. Major Malcolm Wheeler-Nicholson, letter to Jerry Siegel, October 4, 1935.

3. United Feature Syndicate, letter to Jerry Siegel, February 18, 1937.

4. Trojan Publishing, letter to Jerry Siegel, October 29, 1937.

5. Jerry Siegel, letter to Jack Liebowitz, December 6, 1937. Thanks to Lauren Agostino for this letter.

6. Ibid.

7. "Bankruptcy Proceedings," *The New York Times,* December 30, 1937. Donny Press was joined in the lawsuit by Photochrome Inc. (suing for $10,686) and World Color Printing (for $22,270). The company was renamed National Periodical Publications.

8. Ibid.

9. Douglas Wheeler-Nicholson, interview by Jim Amash, "His Goal Was the Graphic Novel," *Alter Ego* 88, August 2009, 30–32. Douglas claims that the Major was being fed false sales figures by Donenfeld and Liebowitz and that the bankruptcy judge was a good friend of Harry's. Also see Nicky Wheeler-Nicholson Brown, interview with Jim Amash, "He Was Going to Go for the Big Idea," *Alter Ego* 88, 45. Nicky states some of the truest words about the inherent problems of this whole story, regardless of perspective or any amount of primary materials: "Everything was said, nothing was written."

10. Donenfeld, interview, "There's a Lot of Myth Out There!," 7–9. Most histories have referred to Gaines by his given name, "Max," but according to Irwin, Gaines "was never called Max." Julie Schwartz retorted: "I always called him Mr. Gaines." Irwin's version of the story is that Gaines urged Harry to do more comic books, but Harry said he needed content, so Sheldon Mayer dredged up the Superman proposal and Harry liked it, or at least could live with it. Irwin also claims that his father was friends with Frank Costello, the head of the Mafia.

11. Frank Jacobs, *The MAD World of William M. Gaines* (New York: Bantam, 1973), 54–55.

12. Siegel, "Story Behind *Superman* #1." Also see Exhibit X, *Joanne Siegel and Laura Siegel Larson v. Time Warner Inc., et al.,* U.S. District Court, Central District of California, Case No, 2:04-cv-08400-SGL-RZ, July 28, 2008.

13. Vin Sullivan, letter to Jerry Siegel, January 10, 1938.

14. Nelson Bridwell, "Siegel, Shuster and Superman," *Amazing World of DC Comics Special Edition* 1, DC Comics, February 1976, 27.

15. "M. C. Gaines," in *Fifty Who Made DC Great*, DC Comics, 1985, 4. In this very carefully worded set of corporate biographies, the Gaines entry has no real mention of his role in Superman.

16. Jerry Siegel and Joe Shuster, letter to Jack Liebowitz, March 3, 1938. There were actually a few versions of the contract, with different signees.

17. "$420 'Superman' Check Sells for $160,000," *The New York Times*, April 18, 2012. The actual check itself appeared in late 2011 and was auctioned to the public in early 2012, where it fetched an astounding $160,000. Everyone always imagined the check was for a pristine, infamous $130, but the inclusion of moneys for some of their other work in *Detective* and *New Adventure* just drives home the fact that by this time, Jerry and Joe were both comics professionals. Their names are misspelled by Jack Liebowitz on the check itself, causing them to sign it on the back with alternate spellings.

18. Vin Sullivan, letter to Jerry Siegel, February 4, 1938.

19. Siegel, "Story Behind *Superman* #1," 7. Also see Jones, *Men of Tomorrow*, 123–24.

20. David Saunders, "H. J. Ward (1909–1945)," *Illustration* 29 (Spring 2010): 52–54.

21. Avi Dan Santo, *Transmedia Brand Licensing Prior to Conglomeration: George Trendle and the Lone Ranger and Green Hornet Brands, 1933–1966*, dissertation (Austin: University of Texas, ProQuest, 2006), 219, 271–370.

22. "Mickey Mouse Is Banned by Censors in Yugoslavia," *The New York Times*, December 2, 1937. Also see "Mickey Makes Trouble," *The New York Times*, December 12, 1937.

23. "Mickey Mouse Row Clarified Further," *The New York Times*, December 10, 1937. Also see "Writer in Trouble over Mickey Mouse," *The New York Times*, December 6, 1937; and "Mickey Mouse Gets Schools Approval," *The New York Times*, July 16, 1937.

24. Herbert Russell, "L'Affaire Mickey Mouse," *The New York Times Magazine*, December 26, 1937.

25. Jones, *Men of Tomorrow*, 141.

26. Daniels, *Superman*, 35.

27. Tye, *Superman*, 37–38, repeats a great anecdote from Yankee pitcher Lefty Gomez, who tells how Joe DiMaggio would later have him secretly buy *Superman* comics for him.

28. Seymour A. Davidson, "Strong Man Tricks Which You Can Do," *Science and Invention*, April 1931, 1081. Davidson writes, "The Vaudeville Strong

Man Excites Imagination, Arouses Envy, Holds Our Interest, and Amazes Us by the Spectacular Exhibitions Which Make Up His Act."

29. Harry Titus, *Miracles in Muscles* (New York: Titus School of Physical Culture, 1929), was shown in pulp advertisements and could have easily been part of Joe's physical fitness library. The accompanying letter promises "Super-Health!" and "Super-Strength!" The frontispiece "photo" of Titus combines a photograph of his head on a painted, bulging torso; it was reality made better through artistic imagination.

30. The Hudson Super Six logo was an inverted triangle with "USA" spelled inside; the middle "S" was larger than the other letters.

31. Grant Morrison, *Supergods* (New York: Spiegel & Grau, 2011), 6–7. Morrison wonderfully describes the famous face in the front left corner of the cover: "his face a cartoon of gibbering existential terror, like a man driven to the city limits of sanity by what he has just witnessed." Morrison goes on to say the man's face is a direct parallel to Edvard Munch's famous painting *The Scream.* Also see H. W. Caslor, "When Broadway Went Up in the Air," *Science and Invention,* October 1930; on page 498, there is a small headline illustration of cars being blown up with scared men, one of them in the left foreground, running toward the reader. Also see Flagg, "Superman of Dr. Jukes," 744, where the introductory illustration depicts a shadowy man in the back right with the same round face and cap as the screaming man. In the actual story of *Action* #1, the gangster "Butch" adopts a similar pose and face in the original panel where Superman lifts the car.

32. See *Laura Siegel Larson v. Warner Bros. Entertainment Inc. and DC Comics,* United States Court of Appeals, Ninth Circuit, CV-04-8400 ODW (RZx), 2012. Warners made the claim that the *Action* #1 cover was not drawn by Joe, that house artists cobbled it together from interior images. This accusation raises many claims about collaboration, authorship, and copyright. But anyone who has looked at Joe's art for more than two issues will tell you this is ridiculous.

33. Peter Coogan, "The Definition of the Superhero," in *A Comics Studies Reader* (Jackson: University Press of Mississippi, 2009), 77–93, offers the most comprehensive definition of a superhero.

34. The planet is not named "Krypton" until Jerry's unpublished 1940 script "The K-Metal from Krypton."

35. The Cleveland Jewish Orphan Asylum is evoked visually in the expanded origin page of *Superman* 1 (1939) and was a present fear for young Clevelanders.

36. Jerry Siegel (w) and Joe Shuster (a), *Action Comics* 1, 1938; "Bullet-proof Vest Resists Fire of Three Pistols," *Popular Mechanics,* May 1924. The concept of being "bulletproof" was important in the 1930s and manifested itself as the vest used in gangland newspaper dramas both real and imagined. The vest was appreciated not just for its ability to save lives but also as a technological marvel. Being able to deflect bullets was also a strongman feat. Circus ads show "Captain Henry Smith" readying himself to take a giant bullet fired at

his chest. Smith wears trunks, gladiator boots, and a smile. Also see Harold Gray, *Little Orphan Annie,* in *The Plain Dealer,* June 24, 1935. The Mighty Punjab wears a bulletproof vest, which saves his life. "Uncle Ray's Column," *The Plain Dealer,* March 6, 1950, mentions a "Bulletproof Man" at the turn of the century who would allow himself to be shot at by anything. When he finally died of a wound, they found powdered glass lining his coat.

37. See Don Charles, "Ants Fight Like Humans," *Science and Invention,* March 1931, 982. Also see Hugo Gernsback, "Ant Civilization," *Science and Invention,* April 1929; and Frederic Barrett, "If You Were Knee High to a Fly," *Popular Science,* March 1934. *Gladiator* also makes mention of this analogy.

38. Clark's first paper, *The Daily Star,* is named after *The Toronto Daily Star,* now known as *The Star.*

39. This was also the address of *The Plain Dealer,* perhaps as sly revenge by Jerry for not covering his father's death or publishing his own stories.

40. Before kidnapping her, the thugs get to Lois through a "Robber's Dance," meaning they can steal her as a partner from the hapless Clark.

41. John Kobler, "Up, Up and Awa-a-y! The Rise of Superman, Inc.," *The Saturday Evening Post,* June 21, 1941, 73.

42. See Jones, *Men of Tomorrow,* 1–22, for much more on Harry Donenfeld. Admittedly, it is perhaps too easy to make Harry the bad man because there is so little material available that is written directly by him. But that was Harry's way: he was remembered by those who knew him as a force of nature who did business by handshakes, drinks, and favors—not letters and notes.

43. Jared Bond, "The Year DC Abandoned Superman . . . as Captain Marvel Looked On!," *Alter Ego* 98, December 2010, 78. On September 22, 1938, Detective Comics, Inc., licensed the newspaper strip to McClure. The deal was that the rights would transfer again on July 22, 1941. The judge "ruled that Detective Comics and the McClure Newspaper Syndicate were involved in a joint venture."

44. Jack Liebowitz, letter to Jerry Siegel, September 28, 1938.

45. Kobler, "Up, Up and Awa-a-y!," 73.

46. *Joanne Siegel and Laura Siegel Larson v. Warner Bros. Entertainment Inc.,* U.S. District Court, Central District of California, Case No. CV-04-8400-SGL (RZx), August 12, 2009, 20.

47. Jones, *Men of Tomorrow,* 146–47. There is a telling photo of Gaines at Superman Day at the World's Fair, blowing up a balloon, cigarette in hand, in plaid blazer with a sun hat. He was certainly part of the success of the character and was celebrating as such.

48. Bruce W. Farcau, *The Chaco War: Bolivia and Paraguay, 1932–1935* (Westport, CT: Praeger Publishers, 1996), 41–47. Also see David Hartzler Zook, *The Conduct of the Chaco War* (New York: Bookman Associates, 1961), 101.

49. "Find 20 Bodies in Gas-Filled Mine," *The Plain Dealer,* November 5, 1930.

50. Siegel (w) and Shuster (a), "Superman Plays Football," *Action Comics* 4, September 1938, reprinted in *Superman Chronicles* 1 (New York: DC Comics, 2006), 47.

51. Ibid., "Superman Declares War on Reckless Drivers," *Action Comics* 12, May 1939, reprinted in *Superman Chronicles* 1 (New York: DC Comics, 2006), 154–66.

52. Ibid., "Superman's Phony Manager," *Action Comics* 6, November 1938, reprinted in *Superman Chronicles* 1 (New York: DC Comics, 2006), 70–75.

53. Jerry Siegel, letter to Jack Liebowitz, September 26, 1938.

54. Siegel (w) and Shuster (a), "Superman in the Slums," *Action Comics* 8, January 1939, reprinted in *Superman Chronicles* 1 (New York: DC Comics, 2006), 110.

55. Ibid., "Wanted: Superman!," *Action Comics* 9, February 1939, reprinted in *Superman Chronicles* 1 (New York: DC Comics, 2006), 112.

56. Nickel, *Torso.*

57. Michael Sawyer, *In the Wake of the Butcher: Cleveland's Torso Murders* (Kent, OH: Kent State University Press, 2001). Also see "Hunt Torso Clew in Gullies Today," *The Plain Dealer,* September 14, 1936; "Calls Torso Killer New Insane Type," *The Plain Dealer,* September 16, 1936; "Maniac Is Hunted in Torso Deaths," *The Plain Dealer,* September 18, 1936; "Hunt Torso Suspect on Transient's Tip," *The Plain Dealer,* October 18, 1936; Thomas W. Wolfe, "Torso Killer Hunt Nets Queer Fish," *The Plain Dealer,* May 30, 1937. See also Brian Bendis (w) and Mark Andreyko (a), *Torso* (Berkeley, CA: Image Comics, 2001), for a fictionalized account in graphic novel form. The Cleveland Police Department Museum maintains a standing exhibit on the officially unsolved Torso Murders case.

58. Siegel (w) and Shuster (a), "Wanted: Superman!," *Action Comics* 9, February 1939, reprinted in *Superman Chronicles* 1 (New York: DC Comics, 2006), 113.

59. Ibid., "Superman and the Dam," *Action Comics* 5, October 1938, reprinted in *Superman Chronicles* 1 (New York: DC Comics, 2006), 68.

60. Ibid., "Wanted: Superman!," *Action Comics* 9, February 1939, reprinted in *Superman Chronicles* 1 (New York: DC Comics, 2006), 113.

61. JFK appeared in several later *Superman* comics, including the bittersweet *Superman* 170, July 1964.

62. Jerry Siegel (w) and Joe Shuster (a), *Superman* 1, DC Comics, July 1939, reprinted in *Superman Chronicles* 1 (New York: DC Comics, 2006), 204.

63. Ibid.

64. When they moved to New York, they lived at Electra Court, Apt. A-38, 40-15 Eighty-first Street, Jackson Heights, Long Island.

65. Metropolis was probably named after Fritz Lang's 1927 film. See Hugh Ferriss, *The Metropolis of Tomorrow* (Mineola, NY: Dover Architecture, 2005), reprint of 1929 edition, for an equally stark and science fiction take on a futurist urban skyline. Also see Edwin Schallert, "Movie Portrays City of the Future," *Science and Invention,* December 1930, which shows stills from a futurist film titled *Manhattan Fifty Years from Now.*

66. Because there was no need for mail during their time in New York, very little is known of their time there.

67. Brian Walker, *The Comics* (New York: Abrams, 2006), 23. These numbers have been reprinted in almost every discussion about the newspaper syndication, but all without citation, so we cannot be sure they are accurate; nonetheless, the strip was an enormous early hit. Also see Jared Bond, *The Speeding Bullet,* online at http://www.thespeedingbullet.com. The newspaper strip had lots of firsts for Superman continuity: the first appearance of Mr. Mxyzptlk, the first time Luthor appears bald, Lois and Clark's first "wedding," and others.

68. "Help Wanted—Male," *The Plain Dealer,* August 30, 1942. Also see "Artist," *The Plain Dealer,* February 27, 1942.

69. James Vance, "A Job for Superman," *Superman: The Dailies 1939–1942* (New York: Sterling, 2006), 6–11. The preface has a good overview of the general interaction among the different artists in the studio. My major regret in this book is not giving enough room for the *Superman* artists who helped Joe and thus saturated popular culture with Superman by the early forties. Without these artists, Superman would not be the cultural icon it is today. See Jerry Siegel, "Story Behind *Superman* #1." Jerry says: "Joe and I were very proud of these talented, capable men who, supervised by Joe, brought a lot of pleasure to the readers of *Superman.*"

70. Steranko, *Steranko History of Comics,* 39.

71. Rudi Franke, "The Saga of Jerry Siegel and Joe Shuster," *Voice of Comicdom* 4, April 1965. Thanks to Mitch Fraas.

72. "Superman Is Coming to Plain Dealer Sunday," *The Plain Dealer,* January 18, 1940.

73. Ibid.

74. Ibid.

75. "Siegel, Schuster Start Strip of Syndicated Superman," *The Torch,* February 29, 1940.

76. Jake Rossen, *Superman vs. Hollywood: How Fiendish Producers, Devious Directors, and Warring Writers Grounded an American Icon* (Chicago: Chicago Review Press, 2008), 49. The bodybuilder Mayo Kaan claimed to have been the original model for Superman, but this has been widely questioned.

77. Ibid.

15. New Frontiers

1. Fine, Hubar, and Wolkov, interview: "In high school, [Jerry] took one girl to a dance and that was about it."

2. "Not in the News," *The Middletown Times Herald,* August 22, 1936.

3. Jerry Siegel and Joe Shuster film footage, c. 1939–1944, Joe Shuster Collection, Special Collections Research Center, Kelvin Smith Library, Case Western Reserve University, Cleveland, Ohio. The visual details of Jerry and Bella's married life, including the hot dog, may be found in a series of 16mm home movies that surfaced on eBay in early 2006. The seller, a dealer in ephemera film, claimed to have bought them as part of an estate lot. After months of talking to the dealer and helping identify the subjects, I paid to

have him make digital copies of the films for me. Several months later, I finally received a portion of the films. The subjects are mostly Jerry and Bella, but Joe also appears, raising the possibility that they may have been filmed by Joe, who is known to have bought a camera once the money started coming in. I sent copies to both the Siegel and the Shuster families. The appearance of the films seemed to coincide with the death of Jerry's son in University Heights in Cleveland, so I contacted the lawyer for his estate, who was unconcerned. I tracked down the person who sold the original films to the dealer, and he admitted their pedigree, saying he had made a mistake and that "maybe there is a way to resolve this." I found out soon after that the dealer sold the original reels to Time Warner. Time Warner swiftly included most of the footage in their DVD documentary *Secret Origin: The Story of DC Comics* (2010). I screened some of this footage for the first time in public as part of my documentary film *Last Son* in Cleveland in the summer of 2008. I have since deposited them, available to the public, as part of the Joe Shuster Collection at Case Western Reserve University. Years later, I found out that in late 2006 the remainder of the movies had been sold on eBay, by the same dealer, in three separate auctions totaling over $5,000.

4. Fine, Hubar, and Wolkov, interview.
5. "Cleveland Jewish Ladies Auxiliary," *The Plain Dealer,* February 8, 1931. Also see *The Cleveland Foreign Language Newspaper Digest* 3 (Cleveland: Work Projects Administration in Ohio, 1937), 278. Mrs. Siegel and Mrs. Lifshitz are listed in the minutes: Siegel as "chairman" and Lifshitz as "toastmaster," who introduced several seminary members. The record states, "Thanks is given to Mrs. Lifshitz for her good work." This account is in stark contrast with others who portray Bella's mother as illiterate and uneducated.
6. Jerome Siegel and Bella Lifshitz, marriage license no. 61045, June 10, 1939, Cuyahoga County, Ohio.
7. Tye, *Superman,* 47.
8. This address appears on one of the film packages from Eastman Kodak in Rochester, New York.
9. *Cleveland City Directory,* Cleveland, Ohio, 1942.
10. One reel shows Jerry and Bella hosting a backyard summer party full of iced tea and smiles. Jerry plays croquet and collapses into a hammock with Bella; they are very affectionate with each other.
11. Peavy, interview.
12. *The New York Times,* August 29, 1958, reads, "$200 reward for the return of 22-pound package of film addressed to Jerry Siegel. 15 E 53 st NYC call HI 6-0603." Whether this is the same Jerry Siegel (and film) is unknown.
13. Peavy, interview.
14. Ibid.
15. Ibid.
16. Ibid.
17. Ibid.
18. *Cleveland City Directory*, Cleveland, Ohio, 1942.

19. Peavy, interview.

20. "Miss Earhart Legally Dead," *The New York Times,* January 6, 1939.

21. John W. Sullivan, "Uranium's Superpowered Particles and Elements," *The Plain Dealer,* April 6, 1939.

22. Charles Serry, "As Reporter Saw Terror of Quake," January 26, 1939.

23. Siegel (w) and Shuster (a), "Superman on the High Seas," *Action Comics* 15, August 1939, reprinted in *Superman Chronicles* 2 (New York: DC Comics, 2007), 17.

24. The same character name from *Spy.*

25. Jerry Siegel (as Hugh Langley), "Changer of Destiny," *Superman* 4, Spring 1940, reprinted in *Superman Archives* 1 (New York: DC Comics, 1989), 238–39.

26. With apologies to Matt Wagner (w) and Amy Reeder Hadley (a), *Madame Xanadu* 10, 2009.

27. Wayne Boring, interview by Richard Plachter, *Amazing Heroes* 41, February 15, 1984.

28. Thomson would later assume the superhero identities of Mister America and the Americommando. Baily also drew the first adventures of the superhero Hour-Man with writer Ken Fitch in *Adventure Comics* 48 (1940).

29. See *Fame and Fortune,* February 1929, for a cover by Frank S. Lawton that features a green-hooded figure, which was a fairly common pulp mystery image.

30. Eugene Baily, e-mails to author, June 15 and 25, 2010. In addition to illustrating public service announcements, Baily published a series of comics titled *Stories of the Opera,* about Carmen, Faust, Aida, and Rigoletto, from 1949 to 1950. Baily wrote and directed *Bobby Benson* on WOR Radio in New York City and was also, like many of his contemporaries, a contributor to *Cracked* from 1958 to 1959. He also worked with puppet entertainer Shari Lewis on an early television program. Baily retired with his wife to a lakeside house in Mahopac, New York, where he died on January 19, 1996, at the age of seventy-nine.

31. Jerry Siegel (w) and Bernard Baily (a), *More Fun Comics* 52, February 1940, reprinted in *The Golden Age Spectre Archives* 1 (New York: DC Comics, 2003), 15.

32. Ibid., 19.

33. Jerry Siegel (w) and Bernard Baily (a), *More Fun Comics* 53, March 1940, reprinted in *The Golden Age Spectre Archives* 1 (New York: DC Comics, 2003), 29.

34. Ibid., 30–31.

35. "Youth Is Shot Fleeing from Traffic Police," *The Plain Dealer,* February 3, 1929.

36. "Fights for Dog, Shot to Death," *The Plain Dealer,* June 23, 1930.

37. "Fourth Suspect in Murder of Meat Dealer Captured," *The Plain Dealer,* January 21, 1933.

38. "Admits Being with Slayer in Robbery," *The Plain Dealer,* December 1, 1937.

39. "William S. Corrigan," *The Plain Dealer,* May 27, 1938.

40. "William Corrigan," *The Cleveland Press,* May 28, 1938.

41. Craig Corrigan, interview with author, May 5, 2010. Corrigan, William's grandson, shared this information with his own son, who responded, "Those stories were very cool."

42. Jerry Siegel (w) and Joe Shuster (a), "Superman vs. the Cab Protective League," *Action Comics* 13, June 1939, reprinted in *Superman Chronicles* 1 (New York: DC Comics, 2006), 190.

43. Ibid., "The Return of the Ultra-Humanite," *Action Comics* 17, October 1939, reprinted in *Superman Chronicles* 2 (New York: DC Comics, 2007), 115.

44. Ibid., "Superman and the Purple Plague," *Action Comics* 19, December 1939, reprinted in *Superman Chronicles* 2 (New York: DC Comics, 2007), 134.

45. Ibid.

46. Jerry Siegel (w) and Joe Shuster (a), "Superman and the Screen Siren," *Action Comics* 20, January 1940, reprinted in *Superman Chronicles* 2 (New York: DC Comics, 2007), 191.

47. Siegel (w) and Shuster Studio (a), "Europe at War, Part 2," *Action Comics* 23, April 1940, reprinted in *Superman Chronicles* 3 (New York: DC Comics, 2007), 41.

48. Ibid., "Luthor's Undersea City," *Superman* 4, Spring 1940, reprinted in *Superman Chronicles* 3 (New York: DC Comics, 2007). Also see *Superman* 12, September–October 1941, for a better monster fight.

49. Jerry Siegel (w) and John Sikela (a), "Powerstone," *Action Comics* 47, April 1942, reprinted in *Superman Chronicles* 8 (New York: DC Comics, 2010).

50. See John H. Dryfhout, *The Work of Augustus Saint-Gaudens* (Hanover, NH: University Press of New England, 2008), 296. Completed in 1908, the statue is on a small island intersection between Euclid and Martin Luther King Boulevard.

51. William T. Horner, *Ohio's Kingmaker: Mark Hanna, Man & Myth* (Athens: Ohio University Press, 2010).

52. Frank Irving Cobb, *Cobb of the World: A Leader of Liberalism* (Hallendale, FL: New World Book, 1924), 169.

53. Yua-ling Chin, "American Politics: A Chinese View," *American Mercury,* May–August 1925, bound, 358.

54. Solon Lauer, *Mark Hanna: A Sketch from Life, and Other Essays* (Cleveland: Nike, 1901), 22.

55. Edwin Balmer and William MacHarg, *The Achievements of Luther Trant* (Boston: Small, Maynard, & Co., 1910).

56. Jack Liebowitz, letter to Jerry Siegel, March 1, 1940.

57. Jerry Siegel (w) and Hal Sherman (a), *Star Spangled Comics,* October 1941.

58. One of the first mechanical heroes was "the Huge Hunter; or, the Steam Man of the Prairies," a top-hat-wearing steam robot by Edward S. Ellis teamed with an electrical genius "teenaged boy named Johnny Brainerd."

Also see Tim DeForest, *Storytelling in the Pulps, Comics, and Radio* (Jefferson, NC: McFarland, 2004), 18.

59. Robotman is the final cog in the line of imaginative creation that began with Edmond Hamilton's *Metal Giants* through Televox and Elektro, the Westinghouse robot at the 1940 New York World's Fair.

60. Jones, *Men of Tomorrow,* 149.

61. Andrae, *Creators of the Superheroes,* 56–89. Kane did so with the help of his father.

62. Marc Tyler Nobleman (w) and Ty Templeton (a), *Bill the Boy Wonder: The Secret Co-Creator of Batman* (Watertown, MA: Charlesbridge, 2012).

63. See Don Cameron (w) and Bob Kane (a), *Batman* 13, October–November 1942, reprinted in *Batman: The Dark Knight Archives* 4 (New York: DC Comics, 2003). Jerry himself appears in a one-panel cameo in "The Batman Plays a Lone Hand" in *Detective* 13, where he is hounded for an autograph.

64. Jerry Siegel (w) and Leo Nowak (a), "The Archer," *Superman* 13, November–December 1941, reprinted in *Superman Chronicles* 7 (New York: DC Comics, 2009). This story begins a long tradition of Robin Hood archers in comics who are of sometimes questionable ethics, including Green Arrow and Hawkeye. Another supervillain, the Light, appears in the same issue in a separate story.

65. *Action Comics* 46, March 1942; *Action Comics* 44, January 1942; *Superman* 14, January–February 1942; *Superman* 15, March–April 1942; *Superman* 16, May–June 1942; *Action* 49, June 1942; *World's Finest* 6, Summer 1942; and *Superman* 14, January–February 1942, respectively.

66. Jerry Siegel (w) and John Sikela (a), "The Man Who Put Out the Sun," *Action Comics* 53, reprinted in *Superman Chronicles* 10 (New York: DC Comics, 2012).

67. Will Murray, "The Driving Force That Really Made DC Great: Whitney Ellsworth and the Rise of National/DC Comics," *Alter Ego* 98, December 2010, 9. The mischievous imp, first called "Mr. Mxyztplk," appears to cause chaos in Superman's life in the newspaper strip on February 21, 1944. Alvin Schwartz and Whitney Ellsworth were said to be the writers, but Jerry was insistent to others that he created it. Mxy not only looks but acts much like Slam Bradley's Shorty. Jerry Siegel (w) and Joe Shuster (a), *Superman* 30, September 1944, is the character's first appearance in the comic book.

68. Andrae, "*Funnyman,* Jewish Masculinity, and the Decline of the Superhero," 69. Andrae also notes the influence of "Al Capp's Joe Blyfstyk."

69. This is the first taste of the Silver Age.

70. Dwight R. Decker, "The Reich Strikes Back," *Alter Ego,* November 79, July 2008, 25–31. Also see Kobler, "Up, Up and Awa-a-y!," 15.

71. Decker," The Reich Strikes Back."

72. Ibid.

73. Ibid.

74. Jerry Siegel (w) and Wayne Boring (a), "The Dukalia Spy Ring," *Superman* 10, May–June 1941, reprinted in *Superman Chronicles* 6 (New York: DC Comics, 2009), 44.

16. Top of the World

1. All of the visual imagery of the fair is from the home movies.
2. Tye, *Superman,* 39.
3. James Mauro, *Twilight at the World of Tomorrow: Genius, Madness, Murder, and the 1939 World's Fair* (New York: Ballantine Books, 2010), 10. Thanks to NYPD lieutenant Bernard Whalen.
4. *DC Comics Rarities* (New York: DC Comics, 2004), 7–209.
5. "Program for Today at the World's Fair," *The New York Times,* July 3, 1940.
6. "World's Fair Daily," *The New York Times,* July 3, 1940. Thanks to Randy Duncan, who first uncovered some of this information about Superman Day.
7. There were still real-life stories for Superman. Lois and Clark help an Iowa baseball pitcher (reminiscent of Cleveland Indians great Bob Feller, who himself came from Van Meter, Iowa) find his calling in the big leagues. See John Sickels, *Bob Feller: Ace of the Greatest Generation* (Sterling, VA: Potomac Books, 2005). Hall of Famer Feller, known as "the Heater from Van Meter" and "Rapid Robert," left baseball in his prime to join the navy during World War II, was a national hero, and appeared in comics as a superstar. Also see Joyce Kaffel, "Digging Up Superman," *Alter Ego* 98, December 2010, 25. Feller is shown at a dinner with Mort Weisinger, Jack Schiff, and Herbie Siegel around 1948, the year the Cleveland Indians last won the World Series.
8. Milton Bracker, "Turnstiles at Fair Click Record Tune," *The New York Times,* July 4, 1940.
9. "Weissmuller to Be Expo's Water Star," *The Plain Dealer,* April 6, 1937.
10. Bracker, "Turnstiles."
11. "Police Die in Blast," *The New York Times,* July 5, 1940.
12. "3 Bomb Alarms Prove to Be False," *The New York Times,* August 15, 1940; "Nazi Flag is Found," *The New York Times,* August 8, 1940; "Bomb Nets an Alien," *The New York Times,* August 6, 1940; "Crowd Unaware of Bomb Tragedy," *The New York Times,* July 5, 1940.

17. How to Kill a Superman

1. "2 New Clues Found in Fatal Bombing," *The New York Times,* July 8, 1940. The bomb at the World's Fair was reported as containing "an unusual alloy" or element.
2. Kryptonite by name would not appear in the comics until *Superman* 61 in 1949. Its many colorful varieties, capable of many outrageous effects, would blossom in the Silver Age.
3. "See Flaming Light Race Across Sky," *The Plain Dealer,* November 20, 1939.
4. Jerry Siegel, letter to Jack Liebowitz, October 15, 1942.

5. Tor Kinlok, *Superman Through the Ages* (n.p.: Lodestone Press, 2006). The "Great Rao" was the first to coordinate a public, digital version of the K-metal story on his indispensable Web site, Superman thru the Ages (http://site.supermanthrutheages.com). Artist Angel Criado worked with Peter Jones, Charlie Roberts, and Thomas Andrae to re-create the story. Also see Mark Waid, "K-metal: The 'Lost' Superman Tale," *Alter Ego* 26, July 2003, 34–40. After seeing pages of the story at the 1988 Cleveland Superman Exposition, comics writer and Superman fan Waid actually found the original typewritten script. Alone at the DC offices on the Wednesday before Thanksgiving, Waid was shuffling through a file and "was stunned to come across a dusty, forgotten ream box filled with faded, blurred carbon copies of typewritten manuscripts. And not just *any* manuscripts." Jones, *Men of Tomorrow*, 181–86, marks the moment of the story's cancellation as when Jerry lost the character to editorial for good. Also see Alex Ross, *Alter Ego* 30, November 2003. Ross believes that "Jerry Siegel was taking steps to evolve the archetypal superhero story beyond the repetitive dramas . . . which kept the characters' relationships from maturing."

6. Will Murray, "The Kryptonite Crisis," *Alter Ego* 37, June 2004, 18–31. Murray theorizes that the story would have run in *Superman* 8 or *Action* 31, both in 1940. Also see Roy Thomas, "K Is for Krypton," *Alter Ego* 79, July 2008, 18–24.

7. Over the Mutual Broadcasting System, it was broadcast from August 31, 1942, to February 4, 1949, as a fifteen-minute serial, running three or five times a week. From February 7 to June 24, 1949, it ran as a thrice weekly half-hour show. The series shifted to ABC Saturday evenings on October 29, 1949, and then returned to afternoons twice a week on June 5, 1950, continuing on ABC until March 1, 1951.

8. Harold Gray's *Little Orphan Annie* newspaper strip introduced the miracle metal "Eonite" in 1935. It was a kind of shmoo-like everymetal, but evil developers craved it for personal profit. The material is certainly different from kryptonite, but the name is similar.

9. Donenfeld, interview, "There's a Lot of Myth Out There!," 4–5. Harry Donenfeld sued Fawcett because he thought that *Captain Marvel* was regularly swiping covers, themes, and images from *Superman* comics.

10. Jack Liebowitz, telegram to Jerry Siegel, Western Union, April 3, 1939. Also see Ken Quattro, "Superman vs. the Wonder Man 1939," *Alter Ego* 101, May 2011, 27–58.

11. Whitney Ellsworth, letter to Jerry Siegel, September 11, 1945. Also see Murray, "Driving Force That Really Made DC Great," 17.

12. Jerry Siegel, Fred Allen, and Harry Donenfeld, "Up in the Sky! Look!," *Alter Ego* 26, July 2003, 29–33. Michael Leach found the interview on a 78 rpm recording from 1948. A downloadable version in mp3 format is available at http://www.Supermanhomepage.com, a resource and daily news site run by Steve Younis.

13. Ibid. The broadcast is filled with plenty of half-baked Superman jokes by Allen: "Well, if he wears woolen underwear all the year round he sure gets action [laughter]."

14. Bud had a great way of dropping his voice a bit for Superman and keeping it a bit higher for Clark Kent; this became the standard for those actors who followed him.

15. Macy's took out full-page ads featuring Superman leading kids directly into the Superman Store.

16. "Superman to Strut over Macy Parade," *The New York Times,* November 19, 1940. The float was made at the Goodyear company in Akron and arrived in a three-foot-square box.

17. When rubber got scarce during World War II, the mayor ordered the floats melted down.

18. "Two Papas No Superfluity for Superman," *The Plain Dealer,* November 17, 1940.

19. Christopher Evans, *The Plain Dealer Sunday,* December 17, 2001. There are many stories like this, not all of them true.

20. Program, "The Temple Father-Son Banquet," The Temple at Hotel Statler, February 9, 1941, Cleveland, Ohio.

21. Jerry Siegel, letter to Jack Liebowitz, May 26, 1941.

22. J. A. Wadovick, "Superman 'Dads' Learn Hard Way," *The Plain Dealer,* June 18, 1941.

23. Ibid.

24. Ibid.

25. Kobler, "Up, Up and Awa-a-y!," 14.

26. Ibid., 70.

27. Ibid., 76.

28. Peter Schork IV, interview with author, March 19, 2012.

29. Kobler, "Up, Up and Awa-a-y!" 78. Also see Siegel, "'Superman' Grew," where Jerry claims that the Kobler article had mistruths.

30. Fine, Hubar, and Wolkov, interview. Also see Cynthia Sykes, "When It Comes to Volunteering, the Sky's the Limit for Norma Wolkov, 87," www .cleveland.com, September 12, 2011. Norma Wolkov, Jerry's niece, has worked and volunteered at Rainbow Babies and Children's Hospital in Cleveland for nearly forty years. She wears a bright red jacket decorated with pins as she helps young patients with heartbreaking disease. "This is my second family," Norma says. "It's all about working together and helping." In the entire interview she does not once mention her connection to Superman.

31. Ibid.

32. *The Plain Dealer,* August 18, 1941.

33. The voice of Superman for the series was initially provided by Bud Collyer, who also provided the lead character's voice for the *Superman* radio series. Joan Alexander was the voice of Lois Lane, a role she also portrayed on radio alongside Collyer. Sammy Timberg composed the dramatic musical score.

34. Joe Shuster, interview by Mietkiwicz. In his last known interview, Joe revealed that the original Toronto Star building at 80 King Street West in Toronto was the inspiration for the Daily Star building. But the Star building was not completed until 1929; Joe left Toronto in 1924. Clevelanders have long believed that the former Ohio Bell building (now the AT&T building) at 750 Huron Road was the inspiration, though no written record of this exists. The Daily Planet building first appears in the Fleischer cartoon *The Arctic Giant,* released in February 1942. This version, complete with a rotating globe at its apex, seems to be based on the old Paramount Building in New York City (now called the 1501 Building). Also see Vince Fago, interview by Jim Amash, "I Let People Do Their Jobs!," *Alter Ego* 1, November 2001. The original studios were located across from the Flatiron Building. See Jerry Siegel (w), Joe Shuster (a), and John Sikela (a), "Superman, Matinee Idol," *Superman* 19, November 1942, for the first appearance of the Planet building with a globe on it.

35. "Superman's Creators to Star at State," *The Plain Dealer,* October 10, 1941. They also appeared on *The Horace Heidt Show* on WTAM Radio on August 11, 1942.

36. The first nine cartoons were produced by the Fleischer Studios. In 1942, Fleischer Studios was renamed Famous Studios. The first film, released on September 26, 1941, was nominated for an Oscar. See Richard Fleischer, *Out of the Inkwell: Max Fleischer and the Animation Revolution* (Lexington: University of Kentucky Press, 2005).

37. Jerry Siegel (w), Joe Schuster (a), and John Sikela (a), "Superman, Matinee Idol," *Superman* 19, November 1942, reprinted in *Superman Chronicles* 10 (New York: DC Comics, 2012).

38. Ibid.

39. Earl Blondheim, letter to *The Washington Times,* December 20, 1941.

40. John Sikela was a very valuable contributor to the Superman enterprise. His daughter Joan has written a book about him titled *The Illustrator.*

41. Jerry Siegel (w) and Ed Dobrotka (a), "Case of the Funny Paper Crimes," *Superman* 19, November 1942, reprinted in *Superman Chronicles* 10 (New York: DC Comics, 2012).

42. Russell Maloney, "Li'l Abner's Capp," *Life,* June 24, 1946, 58–76. This article also reproduces part of a short comics autobiography by Capp himself for returning World War II vets, which describes his own struggles after losing a leg; like *Li'l Abner,* the comic is sweet and funny. Maloney, in "Li'l Abner's Capp," 58, notes that "*Li'l Abner* is syndicated to upward of 500 newspapers, whose combined circulation is at least 27,000,000." Capp, unlike Jerry, had an extensive FBI file with actual strips used as evidence of possible Communist ties. Capp was eventually cleared of any patriotic doubt, though he had ongoing controversy over his personal life.

43. Jerry Siegel (w) and John Sikela (a), "A Goof Named Tiny Rufe," *Action Comics* 55, December 1942, reprinted in *Superman Chronicles* 10 (New York: DC Comics, 2012). Also see *Newsweek,* July 12, 1943, 70. This article discusses

Capp's famous parodies of other cartoons, including the popular *Fearless Fosdick,* his version of *Dick Tracy.*

44. Siegel (w) and Sikela (a), "A Goof Named Tiny Rufe."

45. Ibid.

46. Ibid.

47. Al Capp, *Li'l Abner,* Sundays, October 12–26, 1947. Capp also spoofed Superman in "The Flying Avenger" in 1941 and "Melvin the Flying Martian" in 1953. Thanks to Mike Olszewski.

48. See Alexander Theroux, *Enigma of Al Capp* (Seattle: Fantagraphics Books, 1999).

49. Dominique Mainon and James Ursini, *Modern Amazons: Warrior Women on Screen* (Pompton Plains, NJ: Limelight, 2006), 120.

50. Ibid. They have a memorable exchange in "Scat, Darn Catwoman" (1967). Batman: "I'll do anything to rehabilitate you." Catwoman: "Marry me." Batman: "Anything but that. . . ."

51. Roger Stern, introduction, in George Lowther, *The Adventures of Superman* (Bedford, MA: Applewood Books, 1995; originally published 1942), xiii–xiv.

52. Lowther, *Adventures of Superman.* Also see *Steel Drivin' Man: John Henry, the Untold Story of an American Legend* (New York: Oxford University Press, 2008), for more comparisons to John Henry.

53. See Lowther, *Adventures of Superman.* These names would extend to the movie serials and the *Adventures of Superman* TV show with George Reeves. See Nelson Bridwell, introduction, in *Superman from the 1930s to the Seventies* (New York: Crown Publishers, 1971). Bridwell observes that "it was partly the multiplicity of media in which Superman appeared that dictated the changes in him."

54. Beerbohm, "Big Bang," 50, 54.

55. Jerry Siegel (w) and Joe Shuster (a), *Superman* daily strip, McClure syndication, February 16–18, 1942.

56. Jerry Siegel, letter to Jack Liebowitz, October 15, 1942.

57. Ibid.

58. Paul Kupperberg, *Superman* script samples. They are indeed marked in red pen.

59. Whitney Ellsworth, letter to Jerry Siegel, February 19, 1941. Also see Siegel and Shuster, "Of Supermen and Kids with Dreams," 49.

60. Lauretta Bender and Reginald S. Lourie, "The Effect of Comic Books on the Ideology of Children," *The American Journal of Orthopsychiatry* vol. 11, issue 3 (July 1941): 540–50. See John A. Lent, "Introduction: The Comics Debates Internationally: Their Genesis, Issues, and Commonalities," in Lent, ed., *Pulp Demons: International Dimensions of the Postwar Comics Campaign* (Cranbury, NJ: Associated University Press, 1999), 13. Also see Bart Beaty, *Frederic Wertham and the Critique of Mass Culture* (Jackson: University Press of Mississippi, 2005), 112.

61. Margaret Kessler Walraven and Alfred Lawrence Hall-Quest, *Teaching Through the Elementary School Library* (New York: H. W. Wilson, 1948), 80.

62. Catherine Mackenzie, "Children and the Comics," *The New York Times,* July 11, 1943. Also see Sheridan, *Classic Comics,* 234. The Enoch Pratt Library in Baltimore also put "Superman Recommends" signs by certain books—which would then be swiftly snatched up.

63. *The Plain Dealer,* March 14, 1943.

64. Ibid., April 4, 1943.

65. James Barron, "The Mystery of the Missing Man of Steel," *The New York Times,* April 18, 2010. The painting was finally found in 2010, hanging in the library of Lehman College in the Bronx. See Saunders, "H. J. Ward," 64, for a full history of the painting's remarkable creation. In Kobler, "Up, Up and Awa-a-y!," 15, the painting is pictured behind a grinning Donenfeld and his staff, almost like a painted religious icon.

66. Michael T. Gilbert, "Wayne Boring: Superman and Beyond," *Alter Ego* 9, July 2001. This cartoon might have been made for workplace humor purposes only. It is dated c. 1973 and shows, from left to right, Jack Schiff, Jack Liebowitz with Jerry Siegel and Joe Shuster, Herbie Siegel, Mort Weisinger, and someone unknown.

67. Jerry Siegel (w) and Leo Nowak (a), "The Invention Thief," *Superman* 14, January–February 1942, reprinted in *Superman Chronicles* 8 (New York: DC Comics, 2010).

18. Private

1. "Stadium and Avenue Jammed for Festival and Parade," *The Plain Dealer,* July 6, 1943.

2. Murray, "Driving Force That Really Made DC Great," 9. Murray describes the story of the U.S. government censoring a *Superman* daily story line involving a cyclotron, which was deemed an atomic secret. See Brian Cronin, *Was Superman a Spy? And Other Comic Book Legends Revealed* (New York: Plume, 2009). Also see Daniels, *Superman,* 69.

3. "Half of Superman Drafted; Partner Awaits Army Call," *The Plain Dealer,* June 6, 1943.

4. Jerome Siegel, U.S. Army Personnel Record, Service Number 35067731, served June 28, 1943, to January 21, 1946. Jerry's long army records were most likely destroyed in a St. Louis fire at the National Personnel Records Center on July 12, 1973.

5. Mackinnon Simpson, *Hawaii Homefront: Life in the Islands During World War II* (Honolulu: Bess Press, 2008).

6. *The Story of the Stars & Stripes,* Department of Defense film, 1960, available at http://www.archive.org.

7. Jerry Siegel, "Take a Break," *Stars and Stripes,* Pacific edition, August 8, 1945.

8. Clyde Lewis was the artist of *Fatso, Private Buck,* and *Herky* and assisted on *Alley Oop.* Later in life, he did strips for *The Sacramento Union.* There was another artist, later in the tenure of "Take a Break," who signed his work "HR."

9. "Slight Atomic Bomb Improvement Could Threaten Universe," *Stars and Stripes,* August 13, 1945.

10. Jerry Siegel, "Take a Break," *Stars and Stripes,* Pacific edition, August 9, 1945.

11. Ibid.

12. Ibid., August 10, 1945.

13. Ibid.

14. Ibid., August 14, 1945.

15. Ibid., August 15, 1945.

16. Ibid., December 7, 1945.

17. Ibid., August 14, 1945.

18. Ibid., August 18, 1945.

19. Ibid., August 16, 1945.

20. Ibid., July 6, 1945.

21. Ibid., July 7, 1945.

22. Ibid., July 9, 1945.

23. Ibid., July 17, 1945.

24. Ibid., July 16, 1945.

25. Ibid., July 18, 1945.

26. Ibid.

27. Ibid., July 20, 1945.

28. Ibid., July 26, 1945.

29. Ibid., December 14, 1945.

30. Ibid., June 27, 1945.

31. Ibid., December 26, 1945.

32. Leonard Lyons, "Broadway Gazette," *The Washington Post,* December 19, 1944.

33. "Kilroy Was Here; Mystery Message Traced to Source," *The Nevada State Journal,* December 2, 1945. Almost every article about Kilroy makes similar claims about "solving" the mystery, yet most of them disagree.

34. Clyde Ward, "Kilroy, Was He There?" *The American Legion Magazine* 62–63, bound, 1957, 37.

35. Siegel, "Take a Break," May 1, 1945.

36. Murray Korngold, "Who the Hell Is Kilroy?" *Stars and Stripes,* Pacific edition, August 18, 1945.

37. Siegel, "Take a Break," August 25, 1945.

38. Ibid., September 4, 1945.

39. Ibid., November 23, 1945.

40. Ibid., January 12, 1945.

41. Ibid., September 18, 1945.

42. Michael T. Gilbert, "Editorial," *Alter Ego* 11, November 2001, FCA section, 22–23. Jerry is careful about copyright: "Up in the sky! It's a bird—It's a bird—It's— . . . no, it isn't . . . oh, yes it is . . . oh, no it isn't . . . oh, yes it is . . . oh, no it isn't . . . oh, to heck with it! . . ." Also see Jerry Siegel (w) and

Gerald Green (a), "Super G.I.," *Midpacifican,* December 30, 1944. See "Yonkers Man Draws Super GI, Army Version of Comic Strip," *The Herald Statesman,* January 6, 1945. Thanks to Jamie Reigle.

43. Corporal John Duke, "Fathers of Superman, Tarzan, Renfrew Meet," *Midpacifican,* September 2, 1944. The article notes that "not present at the Superman-Tarzan-Renfrew conference in Waikiki was . . . Norman Marsh," the creator of *Detective Dan Dunn.*

44. *The Washington Post,* September 20, 1944.

45. Siegel, *Stars and Stripes,* Pacific edition, January 2, 1946.

19. Superboy

1. "A Son Is Born to Superman Author," *The Plain Dealer,* January 29, 1944.

2. "Milestones," *Time,* February 14, 1944.

3. Siegel, "Take a Break," *Stars and Stripes,* Pacific edition, September 4, 1945.

4. Lauren Agostino, "Jerry Siegel and Superboy," The (Strange) State of Siegel and Shuster Scholarship, Comic Arts Conference, San Diego Comic-Con International, July 25, 2009. Jerry's initial *Superboy* proposal is dated November 30, 1938, and reads: "Though the strip would feature super-strength it would be very different from the Superman strip inasmuch as Superboy would be a child and [his] type of adventures very much different. There'd be tons of humor, action and the characters would be mainly children of about 12 yrs. rather than adults." In December 1940, Jerry sent a full thirteen-page script; National asked for more time to decide. Agostino's discoveries, presented for the first time on this panel, were met with audible surprise because these documents substantially alter the timeline for previous notions of when *Superboy* was first proposed. Her physical evidence is a copy of the dated script itself as well as the entire file of the 1947 court case, making her version the new historical authority.

5. Also see Joe Sergi, "Man Versus Superman," *Comics Now!* 3, Summer 2008, 26. There are many other resources for information on the legal cases, but none are as comprehensive, and many are written for a legal audience.

6. Robert W. Kelly, *The 30th Log* (New York: Robert W. Kelly Publishing, c. 1944–1945), 346. Joe also did a sketch (and self-caricature) for *The Golden Gate Guardian.* Also see Charlie Roberts, "Superman and Joe Shuster in World War II," *Alter Ego* 56, February 2007, 10.

7. Joe Shuster, letter to Jerry Siegel, October 1, 1944, courtesy of Lauren Agostino. Lauren also suggests that Jerry tried out another non–Shuster Shop artist for the early *Superboy* proposal.

8. Benton, *Masters of Imagination,* 25. Editor Jack Schiff said that Joe sat down for two to three hours and designed *Superboy* for them in 1944.

9. Jerry Siegel (w) and Joe Shuster (a), *More Fun Comics* 10, May 1936.

10. Greg Travis, *Galen Gough: The World's Miracle Strong Man* (Benton, KY: Greg Travis Pub., 1996).

11. Roy Thomas, "Super-Postscript," *Alter Ego* 37, June 2004, 31. Jerry was also furious, as he revealed in a quiet subway ride to Roy Thomas in the late sixties, that the mention of his Superboy idea in the Kobler *Post* article may have led to the first appearance of Captain Marvel, Jr., a few months later in *Whiz Comics* 25, December 1941. Marvel, Jr., is the only member of the Marvel family to wear blue tights.

12. Daniels, *Superman,* 70. Also see Fred G. Beers, "From the Northwest Corner," column in *The Perry Daily Journal,* February 8, 1996, Cherokee Strip Museum, http://www.cherokee-strip-museum.org. There is anecdotal evidence that Siegel was working on a lawsuit while in the army. Beers writes: "When I worked with Jerry on *Stars & Stripes* in 1944–45, he spent every off-duty hour writing letters to lawyers and others in a futile attempt to establish his share of ownership in the Superman bonanza. It was a sad spectacle for those of us who had come to know him as a colleague."

13. Jerry Siegel, press release, 1975. Phil Yeh was the first person to recognize the importance of the release. Later on, Mike Catron, Superman historian and comics publisher, published the entire letter, along with an introduction, for *The Comics Journal* and on his personal Web site, thus giving anyone with online access the ability to see it—which is the kind of saturation that Jerry originally hoped for. It is worth noting that all of Jerry's quotes in his various releases and letters, which can be cross-checked with original sources, do match up perfectly. The junior journalist hinges everything on the evidence. The judge also included a ruling against *Lois Lane, Girl Reporter,* a weird newspaper strip that ran without their permission (or help), but with the byline "By Jerry and Joe." Also see *Jerome Siegel and Joseph Shuster v. National Periodical Publications,* United States Court of Appeals, Second Circuit, 508 F.2d 909, 1974.

14. Leo Dorfman (w) and Curt Swan (a), *Superman* 162, July 1963, reprinted in *Showcase Presents: Superman* 4 (New York: DC Comics, 2008), 268. In this story, Superman splits into two separate beings: Superman-Red and Superman-Blue.

15. According to Agostino, the 1947 court case documents this.

16. Peavy, interview. Also see Bill Geerhart, e-mail to author, June 11, 2010. According to Zugsmith's son Michael, his father never graduated high school, making any description of him as an accredited lawyer rather dubious. He most likely functioned as the negotiator between Jerry and Joe and National. A Shuster sketch of Superman with Zugsmith in a double-breasted suit with slicked-back hair reads: "To Zuggy—In grateful admiration and appreciation to a Super-Swell guy." Also see C. Jerry Kutner, *Bright Lights Film Journal* 20 (November 1997). Kutner writes about Zugsmith's infamous exploitation movie career but also notes that "any fair assessment of Albert Zugsmith should begin with the fact that once upon a time in Hollywood . . . this man produced at least four genre masterpieces: Jack Arnold's *The Incredible Shrinking Man,* Douglas Sirk's *Written on the Wind* and *The Tarnished Angels,* and Orson Welles's *Touch of Evil.*"

17. "The Press: Superman Adopted," *Time,* May 31, 1948. Also see Sergi, "Man Versus Superman," 28.

18. According to Lauren Agostino, they basically sold the Superboy character back to National for around $100,000.

19. "Newspaper Comics Council Comic Strip Ball," April 1, 1948, Toni Mendez Collection, the Ohio State University Billy Ireland Cartoon Library & Museum, Columbus, Ohio.

20. Tye, *Superman,* 116.

21. Vin Sullivan, interview with Joe Latino, Rich Morrissey, Ken Gale, and Tom Fagan, "Vin Sullivan: The ME Decades," *Alter Ego* 10, September 2001, 9.

22. Benton, *Masters of Imagination,* 26. Joe's style is very apparent in the newspaper strip, which started after the book folded in 1948. The comic book was drawn primarily by a combination of John Sikela, Dick Ayers, Marvin Stein, and Ernie Bache.

23. Andrae, "*Funnyman,* Jewish Masculinity, and the Decline of the Superhero," 77.

24. The 1950 sequel was titled *Atom Man vs. Superman.*

25. Daniels, *Superman,* 72–73.

26. Daniel Best, ed., *The Trials of Superman* II (Australia: Blaq Books, 2012), 204, available for free online at http://ohdannyboy.blogspot.com. Best compiles the available depositions and transcripts into three volumes. I have chosen to quote this compilation because it is much easier to reference than the original documents—and it is available for anyone to download. Best has done a great service to readers in presenting this material as is.

27. Daniels, *Superman,* 72–73.

28. *The Plain Dealer,* July 15, 1948.

29. Bella Siegel and Jerry Siegel, divorce, no. 592351, July 26, 1948, Cuyahoga Common Pleas Court, Cleveland, Ohio.

30. "Superman Creator Wed," *The Plain Dealer,* October 15, 1948.

31. Jerome Siegel and Joanne Kovacs, application for marriage license, no. 187448, November 3, 1948, Cuyahoga County, Ohio. They were granted a waiting period waiver by probate judge Nelson Brewer.

32. Sophie Kovacs, death certificate, March 3, 1948, Ohio Department of Health. She was in a Cleveland state hospital for nearly fifteen years for dementia, possibly linked to breast cancer. Her death certificate lists "Schizophrenia, type not stated."

33. Bella Siegel and Jerry Siegel, divorce.

34. Daniels, *Superman,* 73

35. Fine, Hubar, and Wolkov, interview.

36. Nikki Bruno, "Clevelander in New York," *The New York Times,* October 11, 1945: "Miss Jean Adele, formerly known as Jeanetta Shuster . . . has been cast in a leading role in the Theater Workshop's production of 'Blind Alley.' The young actress is rapidly gaining the attention of New York's leading agents and producers." Also see *The Plain Dealer,* October 11, 1942. Jeanetta was

married on November 1, 1942, to Harry Edelman, and they lived at 92–120 Queens Blvd., in Forest Hills, New York. Harry served in the army until 1945 while she lived in Toronto with her uncle Jack. They were divorced soon afterward.

37. Peavy, interview.

38. Ibid.

20. Fifties

1. Jerry Siegel, letter to FBI, received November 28, 1951.

2. John Edgar Hoover, letter to Jerry Siegel, c. November–December 1951.

3. William McDermott, "McDermott on Pocket Books," *The Plain Dealer,* September 12, 1952. Also see David Hadju, *The Ten-Cent Plague: The Great Comic-Book Scare and How It Changed America* (New York: Picador, 2009), 235. Superman was mostly immune to the comics scare of the fifties, but not completely. See Daniels, *Superman,* 131. Wertham thought Superman provided an unfavorable example of a "super-race."

4. *The Plain Dealer,* March 19, 1952.

5. "Police Readers Trail Crime in Pulpwoods," *The Plain Dealer,* May 14, 1949.

6. Ibid.

7. Jerry Siegel, letter to Watson Davis, director of science services, received November 26, 1951.

8. Ira Yarbrough Jr., e-mail to author, March 14, 2012. *Tallulah* was drawn by "Yar," short for artist Ira Yarbrough, who worked in the Shuster Shop inking *Superman* in the 1940s. His son, a painter, says that his father helped create the look for Mr. Mxyzptlk.

9. *The Oakland Tribune,* May 9, 1950.

10. Anderson interview, in *The Krypton Companion,* 120–21. *Jon Juan,* in a red short cape, is the Latin lover stereotype with a Jerry twist: "Can I help it if their neglected women cast lovelorn glances in my direction? <pant>: Can I be blamed if my nimble tongue sought out the proper words to solace thwarted femininity?" *Lars of Mars* is more Buck Rogers and was later transformed into a 3-D comic. *G.I. Joe* began with issue 10 in 1950 (a common trick) and focused on the Korean War.

11. Jim Simon and Joe Simon, *The Comic Book Makers* (Lakewood, NJ: Vanguard Productions, 2003), 104. This book also recounts the infamous story of Joe Shuster, allegedly showing up at National as a delivery boy in the sixties and told to never come back.

12. Hassard, interview.

13. *Adventures of Superman,* TV series, 1952–1958. Phyllis Coates played Lois Lane in the first season. See Michael J. Hayde, *Flights of Fantasy: The Unauthorized but True Story of Radio & TV's Adventures of Superman* (Duncan, OK: BearManor Media, 2009). Also see Michael J. Bifulco, *The Original Superman on Television* (n.p.: CreateSpace, 2011).

14. "Ellsworth to Head Prod. of Superman," *Billboard,* May 23, 1953.

15. *The Sarasota Journal,* December 16, 1975. Much of the hunger strike story is hard to pin down to facts.

16. *Lantern Copy* clippings, Special Collections and University Archives, Jean and Alexander Heard Library, Vanderbilt University, Nashville, Tennessee. Thanks to Teresa Gray.

17. "$1,000,000 Damage Suit," *Editor and Publisher,* August 23, 1952. Thanks to Allan Holtz.

18. In the promotional poster for her act, she is described as "Vivacious and Versatile, Comedienne of Songs and Comedy Characterizations!"

19. *The New York Times,* November 23, 1954.

20. Ibid., December 20, 1954.

21. Craig Yoe, *Secret Identity: The Fetish Art of Superman's Co-Creator Joe Shuster* (New York: Abrams ComicArts, 2009). Joe never publicly acknowledged *Nights of Horror,* much less the Brooklyn killings, so it cannot be said for sure that he knew about their connection. But the prolific coverage of the case in New York newspapers has to suggest otherwise.

22. Ibid., 17, 27–33. Yoe claims that co-publisher Clancy wrote the stories. According to Jim Linderman, "Justin Kent" was the alias of writer Kenneth Johnson. Writers and artists, including Kent, were detained and testified, but Joe's name appears nowhere in the available court records.

23. James Jackson Kilpatrick, *The Smut Peddlers* (New York: Doubleday, 1960). This book includes some of Mishkin's testimony as well as that of his publisher, Maletta. Also see Whitney Strub, *Perversion for Profit: The Politics of Pornography and the Rise of the New Right* (New York: Columbia University Press, 2010).

24. Dick Ayers, interview with Roy Thomas, "A Life in the Gowanus," *Alter Ego* 10, September 2001, FCA section, 19.

25. Stefano Piselli and Riccardo Morrocchi, eds., *The Art of Stanton: Master of Bizarre* (Florence, Italy: Glittering Images, 1993). Also see Eric Kroll and Eric Stanton, *The Art of Eric Stanton: For the Man Who Knows His Place* (Berlin: Taschen, 1997).

26. Joe Shuster (a), *It's Continental* 1, c. 1955.

27. Peavy, letter to author, May 10, 2009: "I know it was a dark time in Joe's life and he would have been embarrassed to know that his secret desperation in finding a job was so public."

28. Shuster, *It's Continental.*

29. Ibid.

30. Peavy, letter to author, May 10, 2009.

31. "School Marks 30th Birthday," *The Plain Dealer,* February 6, 1958.

32. Yoe, *Secret Identity,* 23–27.

33. Ibid. His name was Jack Koslow.

34. Ibid.

35. Victoria Graham, "Superman's Creators Are Living on Pennies," *Stars and Stripes,* Pacific edition, December 6, 1975.

36. Ibid.

21. Invisible Kid

1. Jerry Siegel (w) and Bill Fraccio (a), *Mr. Muscles* 22–23, Charlton Comics, March–August 1956.

2. Jerry Siegel (w) and John Buscema (a), *Nature Boy* 3, Charlton Comics, March 1956. After issue 5, the title changed to *Li'l Rascal Twins*.

3. Jerry Siegel (w) and Ogden Whitney (a), *Ken Winston,* 1954–1955.

4. His last address was 8311 Parmenter Drive, Parma, Ohio.

5. Daniels, *Superman,* 107.

6. Donenfeld, interview, "There's a Lot of Myth Out There!," 23–25. Irwin says he hired Jerry after Jack Liebowitz sent him over. Irwin also claimed that they paid for an eye operation for Joe at this time and that Mort in fact wrote most of Jerry's Silver Age stories. My examination of biographical elements in these stories somewhat refutes this claim.

7. Michael Eury, "Jerry Siegel's Return to Krypton," in *The Krypton Companion,* 48–49.

8. Jerry did not create these characters. Their first appearances are as follows: "Supergirl," Otto Binder (w) and Curt Swan (a), *Action Comics* 252, May 1959; "Brainiac," Otto Binder (w) and Al Plastino (a), *Action Comics* 242, July 1958; "Krypto," Otto Binder (w) and Curt Swan (a), *Adventure Comics* 210, March 1955; "the Legion," Otto Binder (w) and Al Plastino (a), *Adventure Comics* 247, April, 1958; "Bizarro," Otto Binder (w) and George Papp (a), *Superboy* 68, 1958. See Alvin Schwartz, interview by Jim Amash, "I've Always Been a Writer," *Alter Ego* 98, December 2010, 41; Alvin claims he created Bizarro for the newspaper daily strip.

9. They lived in a small white house at 3575 Manhasset Court in Seaford, Long Island.

10. Lana first appears in *Superboy* 10, September–October 1950. She was a retroactive addition created by Bill Finger and John Sikela.

11. "Metropolis Mailbag," *Action Comics* 267, August 1960.

12. Jerry Siegel (w) and George Papp (a), "The Unwanted Superbaby," *Adventure Comics* 299, August 1962, reprinted in *Showcase Presents: Legion of Super-Heroes* (New York: DC Comics, 2007).

13. Jerry Siegel (w) and Jim Mooney (a), "The Bride of Mr. Mxyzptlk!," *Action Comics* 291, August 1962, reprinted in *Showcase Presents: Supergirl* 2 (New York: DC Comics, 2008), 124–27.

14. Ibid., "The World's Greatest Heroine!," *Action Comics* 285, February 1962, reprinted in *Showcase Presents: Supergirl* 2 (New York: DC Comics, 2008), 34.

15. Ibid., 40.

16. Ibid., 41.

17. Jerry Siegel (w) and George Papp (a), "The Ghost of Jor-El," *Superboy* 78, January 1960.

18. Ibid.

19. Cadigan, *Legion Companion,* 20–25.

20. Jerry Siegel (w) and Jim Mooney (a), "Supergirl's Three Super Girl-Friends!," *Action Comics* 276, May 1961, reprinted in *Showcase Presents: Supergirl* 1 (New York: DC Comics, 2007), 437.

21. Jerry Siegel (w) and John Forte (a), "The Secret Origin of Bouncing Boy!," *Adventure Comics* 301, October 1962, reprinted in *Showcase Presents: Legion of Super-Heroes* 1 (New York: DC Comics, 2007), 201.

22. Abraham Aamidor, *Chuck Taylor, All Star* (Bloomington: Indiana University Press, 2006).

23. Jerry Siegel (w) and John Forte (a), "The Fantastic Spy!," *Adventure Comics* 303, December 1962, reprinted in *Showcase Presents: Legion of Super-Heroes* 1 (New York: DC Comics, 2007), 222.

24. Jerry Siegel (w) and Jim Mooney (a), "Supergirl's Three Super Girl-Friends!," 437.

25. Jerry Siegel (w) and John Forte (a), "The Stolen Super Powers!," *Adventure Comics* 304, January 1963, reprinted in *Showcase Presents: Legion of Super-Heroes* 1 (New York: DC Comics, 2007), 243.

26. Caroline Dove, letter to "The Legion Outpost," *Adventure Comics* 311, August 1963.

27. Jerry Siegel (w) and John Forte (a), "The Secret of the Mystery Legionnaire!," *Adventure Comics* 305, February 1963, reprinted in *Showcase Presents: Legion of Super-Heroes* 1 (New York: DC, 2007), 251.

28. This is in direct contrast with the Clark Kent identity, which is revealed to the reader in the first pages of *Action Comics* 1.

29. Ben Conner, letter to "Smallville Mailsack," *Adventure Comics* 308, May 1963.

30. Otto Binder (w) and Curt Swan (a), "The Old Man of Metropolis," *Action Comics* 270, reprinted in *Showcase Presents: Superman* 2 (New York: DC Comics, 2006), 391.

31. Ibid., 393.

32. Ibid., 395.

33. Ibid., 396.

34. Kobler, "Up, Up and Awa-a-y!," 76.

35. Binder (w) and Swan (a), "The Old Man of Metropolis," 396.

36. Paul Kupperberg, e-mail to author, June 19, 2010.

37. Binder (w) and Swan (a), "The Old Man of Metropolis," 396.

38. Jerry Siegel (w) and Curt Swan (a), *Superman* 149, November 1961, reprinted in *Showcase Presents: Superman* 3 (New York: DC Comics, 2007), 177.

39. "Big TB Hospital Turns to Cancer," *The New York Times,* May 1, 1955.

40. Donenfeld, interview, "There's a Lot of Myth Out There!," 24–25. Also see *The New York Times,* February 28, 1965. His obituary states, "He was a true humanitarian."

41. "National Periodical Secondary of $4,515,00 Stock Sold Out," *The Wall Street Journal,* March 5, 1965. Once Harry died, Jack Liebowitz and Mort Weisinger reduced their own shares considerably.

42. Jerry Siegel, letter to *Detective Comics.*

22. Bizarro No. 1

1. G. Bernard Kantor, letter to *Amazing Stories,* August 1965.
2. Al Ries, e-mail to author, March 16, 2011.
3. "The Shake of Things to Come," *Famous Monsters,* June 1960.
4. Bernard J. Kenton, letter to *Amazing Stories,* April 1932, 91.
5. Kenton also had a letter published in the October 1933 *Weird Tales,* famous for its Margaret Brundage Batwoman cover. With a similar style, Kenton mentions that "it is my prediction . . . that the men of exceptional intellect will turn to crime when legitimate channels of amassing wealth are unnavigable; compared to them, Al Capone will look like a kid stealing milk bottles." Thanks to Stephen Lipson.
6. Sam Moskowitz, *The Immortal Storm: A History of Science Fiction Fandom* (Atlanta: Science Fiction Organization Press, 1954), 15: "Siegel himself wrote fiction under the nom de plume of Bernard J. Kenton."
7. Arnold Drake, "Sidewalk Photographer Develops Visions of 'Success Simplified,'" *The Plain Dealer,* February 18, 1952.
8. Ibid.
9. Ibid.
10. Ibid.
11. *Eighteenth Annual Report of the Securities and Exchange Commission Fiscal Year Ended June 30, 1952* (Washington, DC: U.S. Government Printing Office, 1953): "The complaint alleged violations of sections 5 (a) and 17 (a) (2) and (3) of the Securities Act of 1933, section 15 (a) of the Securities Exchange Act, and section 203 (a) of the Investment Advisers Act of 1940. . . . National Evaluators had been retained to locate missing stockholders of a corporation who were entitled to $30,000 in dividends; that the proceeds from the sale of the stock would be paid into the company when, in fact, Kantor appropriated such proceeds to his own use; that a 'satisfactory refund' of monies paid by the public to National Evaluators for investigating the value of securities would be made when, in fact, the refund was made in shares of the company, which were worthless. The complaint further alleged that the defendants had engaged in the business of being a broker dealer and investment adviser without registering with the Commission."
12. Drake, "Sidewalk Photographer Develops Visions."
13. *Billboard,* September 9, 1957.
14. Ibid., November 4, 1957.
15. Ibid., February 24, 1958.
16. I have chased "Bernard J. Kenton" for years. I assumed that his letters to the pulps were just Jerry in disguise, but their differences in style were so great that I began to entertain the idea that they might be two different people. Why did Jerry then populate his entire body of work with variations on Kenton's name? Was it a thank-you or a private joke? See Bernard Kantor, death certificate, January 13, 1967, Ohio Department of Health. The death certificate notes that Bernard's parents were Max and Sophie Kanter; a look at the 1920 census reveals a Bernard Kenton with the same parents living in Brooklyn,

New York. In the next census, Bernard is gone from the family. At the same time, a "Bernard Kenton" shows up in Cleveland as a boarder, in a house a few blocks from Glenville High School. After his terrible diagnosis in October 1965, he was in the home from December 5, 1966, to January 13, 1967. His gravestone at Chesed Shel Emeth Cemetery in Cleveland is simple, listing only the year of his death and his last name as "B. Kantore." Even in death, Kantor is elusive.

17. Beerbohm, "Big Bang," 58. After years hunting for facts about Kantor, I came across this small paragraph in a trade magazine. Though there is no mention of this letter in the Moskowitz archives, it seems that he experienced a change in thinking as well. I have never seen this letter, but I trust Beerbohm on its authenticity. According to Lauren Agostino, Jerry may indeed have bought plots when things got heavy.

18. Ibid.

19. Ibid.

20. Bruce Minzer, letter to "Metropolis Mailbag," *Superman* 140, October 1960.

21. Kantor remains a lesson to all scholars that history is not static; it changes over time. Like *Superman* comics, the history of Siegel and Shuster has a shifting continuity that may never fully fit together.

22. Bridwell, "Siegel, Shuster and Superman," 29: "Could the Name of Kenton have suggested Clark Kent?" Bridwell's question, first asked in 1976, was never answered.

23. 'Nuff Said

1. Donenfeld, interview, "There's a Lot of Myth Out There!," 26.

2. Ibid.

3. Will Murray, "Superman's Editor Mort Weisinger," in *The Krypton Companion*. Also see Hank Weisinger interview, "A Fond Remembrance of Mort Weisinger by His Son," in *The Krypton Companion*, 16–17. Also see Mort Weisinger, "I Flew with Superman," *Parade*, October 23, 1977. Mort claims that "it was my job to plot his adventures, create new villains, manipulate his romantic life . . . [but] . . . the incessant deadline pressures sent me to a shrink, gave me an ulcer, hypertension and insomnia. . . . I resented basking in reflected glory." For an illustrated version in the context of auteur theory, see Hank Weisinger, interview with Arlen Schumer (a), "I Sustain the Wings," *Alter Ego* 112, August 2012. Also see Al Plastino interview by Michael Eury, in *The Krypton Companion*, 40. Plastino recalls, "What used to turn me off was when Shuster and Siegel used to come in and Mort would talk to them like they were dirt. I could never understand that." Kaffel, "Digging Up Superman," is the best, perhaps final, word on the paradox that is Mort Weisinger.

4. Will Murray, "Superman's Editor," *The Krypton Companion*, 13.

5. Jones, *Men of Tomorrow*, 308.

6. Sergi, "Man Versus Superman," 28.

7. Ibid.

8. Thomas, "Super-Postscript," 31. In 1966–1967, Jerry worked as a proof-reader at Marvel under Thomas. Also see John Romita, interview by Tom Spurgeon, *The Comics Journal* 252, May 15, 2003. As a young bullpenner at Marvel, the now legendary Romita sat next to Bill Everett (creator of the Sub-Mariner character) and Jerry Siegel. Romita remembers that "it was like sitting next to George Washington and Abraham Lincoln. . . . I used to say to myself, 'I'm sitting next to Jerry Siegel. I'm sitting next to the guy who created this whole industry' [Laughter]."

9. The unforgettable opening with Pierce as Captain America can, amazingly, be found on www.youtube.com.

10. Will Murray, "Those Mighty, Mighty Crusaders," *Alter Ego* 96, August 2010, 15. A fan named Paul Seydor sent in a picture that was printed in *Adventures of the Jaguar* 8, September 1962, of all the Archie heroes as a single supergroup; he titled it "The Anti-Crime Squad." The name "Crusaders" might have been picked by Jerry, possibly after a proactive unit of men who organized in Depression-era Cleveland for temperance and marched around the city.

11. Jon B. Cooke, *The T.H.U.N.D.E.R. Agents Companion* (Raleigh, NC: TwoMorrows Publishing, 205), 85.

12. In Jerry Siegel (w) and Paul Reinman (a), *Fly Man* 31, Archie Comics, May 1965, Fly Man stops the Spider from destroying the 1964 New York World's Fair. When the stories were collected in *The Mighty Crusaders: Origin of a Super-Team* (Toronto: Canada Archive Comics/Red Circle Productions, 2003), there was no dress mention of Siegel, only in the foreword by Michael Uslan and Robert Klein: "It would be several issues before the world at large was told who the writer was . . . it was Jerry Siegel, the creator of Superman!" Also see *High Camp Super-Heroes* (New York: Belmont, 1966). This mass-market digest reprinted some of these stories with "By Jerry Siegel, Originator-Writer of Superman" emblazoned on the cover. Jerry also provides a brief, high-energy preface.

13. Jerry Siegel (w) and Paul Reinman (a), *Fly Man* 32, July 1965.

14. Ibid., *The Mighty Crusaders* 3, March 1966.

15. Ibid., *Fly Man* 39, September 1966.

16. Ibid.

17. Ibid., *The Mighty Crusaders* 7, November 1965. See Murray, "Those Mighty, Mighty Crusaders," 28. Moore originally wanted to begin *Watchmen* "with the body of the original Shield being fished out of the water." Also see Jerry Siegel (w) and Paul Reinman (a), *Fly Man* 34, November 1965. The Shield addresses the stone form of his father: "I promise you this, Dad! You'll become restored to life again, if it's humanly possible! But you'll be restored in an **honorable** way, suitable to your great tradition."

18. Jerry Siegel (w) and Paul Reinman (a), *The Mighty Crusaders* 7, October 1966.

19. Ibid., *The Mighty Crusaders* 5, June 1966.

20. Ibid., *Fly Man* 37, May 1966.

21. Jerry Siegel (w) and Tom Gill (a), *The Owl* 1 and 2, Gold Key Comics, January 1967, January 1968.

22. Jerry Siegel (w) and Reg Bunn (a), *The Spider: King of Crooks* (London: Titan Books, 2005).

23. Alberto Becattini, "Jerry Siegel's European Comics!!," *Alter Ego* 59, June 2006. Jerry did an amazing seven years of stories about Mickey, Goofy, and Uncle Scrooge for the Italian comic *Almanacco Topolino* from September 1972 to December 1979. Also see Jerry Siegel (w) and Paul Reinman (a), *The Shadow* 8, Archie Comics, September 1965. Jerry transformed the fedora-wearing avenger into a green-costumed superhero. Also see Siegel, *The Spider*. The Spider was a weekly British strip in *Lion* from 1965 to 1969; Jerry did not create him but included elements from Spider-Man's menagerie, including a "Dr. Mysterioso" and a "Sinister Seven."

24. George W. Woolery, "Frankenstein, Jr.," in *Children's Television: The First Thirty-Five Years, 1946–1981* (Lanham, MD: Scarecrow Press, 1991), 110–11; *Frankenstein, Jr. and The Impossibles*, Warner DVD, 2011. I have not found any official credit of Jerry as writer on the show.

25. Woolery, "Frankenstein, Jr.," 265.

26. Jack Mendelsohn, interview with Jim Amash, "Life's Not Over Yet," *Alter Ego* 102, June 2011, 32.

27. Jerry Siegel (w) and Ralph Reese (a), "Let the Dreamer Beware," *Psycho* 5, 1971, reprinted in *Reese's Pieces* 2, October 1985.

28. Ibid.

24. Fortress of Solitude

1. Dick Giordano (a), Ray Osrin (a), and Joe Shuster (a), *Hot Rods and Racing Cars*, Motor Magazines/Charlton, 1951. Osrin was the editorial cartoonist at *The Plain Dealer* from 1966 to 1993. Other comics that Joe supposedly contributed partial art to include *Space Adventures* 11; *Strange Suspense Stories* 19, 21, 22; *This Magazine Is Haunted* 18; *The Thing* 16; *Crime and Justice* 19–21. See Kevin Harrison, "Siegel and Shuster Bibliography," http://www.enjolrasworld.com, 2002, for the fullest available bibliography of their work.

2. *It's a Bird . . . It's a Plane . . . It's Superman,* book by David Newman and Robert Benton, music by Charles Strouse, lyrics by Lee Adams, New York, Alvin Theatre, March 29, 1966, to July 17, 1966.

3. Mary Breasted, "Superman's Creators, Nearly Destitute, Invoke His Spirit," *The New York Times,* November 22, 1975.

4. Peavy, interview.

5. Laura Stevenson, "Superman's Creators Signed Away Their Baby 41 Years Ago, and Therein Lies a Sad, Sad Tale," *People,* February 12, 1979.

6. Breasted, "Superman's Creators, Nearly Destitute."

7. Ibid. Also see Joanne Siegel, panel discussion.

8. The chronology of the names of the company that would eventually become DC Comics is complicated. The Major's company, Nicholson Publishing,

began publishing comics as National Allied Publications. The Major and Donenfeld then partnered to form Detective Comics, Inc. When Donenfeld took over National Allied Publications, the new merger became National Comics Publications. Superman, Inc., was later formed to handle the licensing and merchandising of the Superman brand. All-American Comics began as a separate publishing arm but was then absorbed, and all of the disparate companies were organized as National Periodical Publications. National went public in 1961. The old name Detective Comics stuck around as a nickname in the form of DC Comics and also appeared in the trade dress logo. In 1967, Warner Communications bought National. In 1977, publisher Jenette Kahn officially changed the name of the company to DC Comics, Inc. For ease of reference, I am using "National" for all pre-1977 references and "DC Comics" for afterward. Though personnel come and go and the nomenclature is sometimes awkward, it is essentially the same publisher.

9. Stevenson, "Superman's Creators Signed Away." Jerry received $100 a week, and Joe got $50 "here and there."

10. Ira Berkow, "Superman Haunts Creator Jerry Siegel," *The Sarasota Journal,* December 16, 1975. Berkow reports that "during some of this time, Siegel and Shuster lost contact."

11. Murray Bishoff, *The Comics Buyers Guide,* April 1, 1975.

12. Bishoff and Light went on to impressive careers: Bishoff became managing editor of *The Monett Times* in Missouri, where he uncovered and wrote about racial violence in Pierce City at the turn of the twenty-first century. Alan Light continues to write and is an accomplished photographer; he generously provides his personal photos of comics and Hollywood celebrities under a Creative Commons license.

13. David Laurence Wilson, "The Comic Confab: I'm an Artist for the People," *The Los Angeles Free Press,* August 22, 1975.

14. Inkpot awards were given that day to Barry Alfonso, Brad Anderson, Edgar Rice Burroughs, Daws Butler, Richard Butner, Robert Bloch, Vaughn Bode, Shel Dorf, Will Eisner, Mark Evanier, Gil Kane, Alan Light, Dick Moores, George Pal, Rod Serling, Joe Shuster, Jerry Siegel, Jim Starlin, Jim Steranko, Ted Sturgeon, Larry ("Seymour") Vincent, and Barry Windsor-Smith.

15. Murray Bishoff, "The Siegel & Shuster Deal at 30," *Alter Ego* 65, February 2007, 36.

25. Motion

1. Breasted, "Superman's Creators, Nearly Destitute."

2. Rossen, *Superman vs. Hollywood.*

3. Holy Bible, revised standard version (Iowa Falls, IA: World Bible Publishers, 1952).

4. Jerry Siegel, press release. Catron makes the great point that this letter was "the second most important thing [Jerry] wrote in his life."

5. Ibid.

6. Yeh and Kosht, "Supersham!," *Cobblestone,* November 1, 1975.

7. Ibid.

8. Bob Greene, "Able to Leap Tall Buildings, Superman Can't Aid His Creator," *The Pittsburgh Press,* November 19, 1975.

9. Ibid.

10. Ibid. There are many urban legends about Jerry and Joe: a common one insists that Jerry once threatened to jump off a skyscraper in New York City dressed as Superman in order to protest National's treatment of him. See "Artist of 'Super Duper Men' Copies Stunts; Climbs 3 Stories up Building as Crowd Gasps," *The Plain Dealer,* September 21, 1941, for the possible origin of this story. The news reports that a comic book artist named Robert LaMont was "perched on a third-floor ledge of 131 East Forty-seventh Street." Close to "1,000 spectators" gathered to see him jump, but the truth was he had just forgotten his key and was trying to get into his apartment.

11. Robert Lipsyte, *An Accidental Sportswriter: A Memoir* (New York: Ecco, 2012).

12. Ibid.

13. Neal Adams, interview by Michael Eury, *The Krypton Companion* (Raleigh; NC: Two Morrows, 2006), 106.

14. Ibid., 108. Also Neal Adams, e-mail to author, October 7, 2012.

15. Adams interview, *The Krypton Companion,* 104.

16. AP Newswire, "Superman's Creators Need His Help," November 25, 1975.

17. Adams interview, *The Krypton Companion,* 106.

18. Elliot S. Maggin, "How a Real Hero Saved the Mild-Mannered Creators of Superman," *The Village Voice,* January 19, 1976, 14. According to Maggin, "When Emmett suffered a heart attack in his thirties, a psychologist told him to stop working for his uncle."

19. Adams, e-mail to author.

20. Adams interview, *The Krypton Companion,* 104. Also see Tye, *Superman,* 217. Emmett has a different version, calling the decision strictly a business one for a sum tantamount to "chicken feed."

21. *The Washington Star,* December 10, 1975. Also see Bishoff, "Siegel & Shuster Deal," 37. Even though their media coverage grew to the highest possible levels, Jerry never forgot Alan Light's ongoing coverage and support in the *Guide* and wrote in several times to thank not only Alan but all readers of the *Guide.*

22. Adams, e-mail to author.

23. Sam Chu Lin, "Superman Creators," *CBS Evening News with Walter Cronkite,* December 23, 1975. Also see Sergi, "Man Versus Superman," 26. The actual numbers remain elusive because they were supposedly adjusted over time.

24. Maggin, "How a Real Hero Saved," 15. Maggin also tells a different version where Adams left for Florida with no address and told everyone involved to pester Emmett to include the byline as part of the deal.

25. "About the Production . . . ," *Superman: The Movie,* promotional booklet, Warner Bros., c. 1978: "Superman, a genuine American folk hero, was born in Cleveland, Ohio, the brainchild of writer Jerry Siegel and cartoonist Joe Shuster."

26. David Vidal, "Superman's Creators Get Lifetime Pay," *The New York Times,* December 24, 1975.

27. Ibid.

28. Maggin, "How a Real Hero Saved," 15.

29. Bob MacKenzie, "Did Superman Sell Out?," *The Oakland Tribune,* January 12, 1976.

30. Maggin, "How a Real Hero Saved," 14.

31. Ibid., 15.

32. Ibid. See "Jack Liebowitz, Comics Publisher, Dies at 100," *The New York Times,* December 13, 2000. Jack, Emmett's uncle, did live to be one hundred and would be eulogized as "the comic-book publisher whose business acumen helped turn Superman, the creation of two teenage cartoonists, into the most recognizable superhero in the world." Elliot S! Maggin has twice run for the House of Representatives, in 1984 and 2008. His famous middle initial "S!" was perpetuated by Julius Schwartz when he was his editor. Maggin wrote two very popular Superman novels: *Last Son of Krypton* (1978) and *Miracle Monday* (1981). See Elliot S! Maggin (w) and Curt Swan (a), *DC Comics Presents* 87, November 1985; he also created Superboy-Prime, the only hero on a parallel dimension Earth. Superboy-Prime later turned into a psychotic killer in the series *Infinite Crisis* (2005), around the same time the Siegels initiated legal moves to reclaim the Superboy copyright. See Kurt Busiek (w) and Stuart Immonen (a), *Superman: Secret Identity* (New York: DC Comics, 2005), for a great story inspired by Maggin's original Superboy-Prime.

33. Digby Diehl and David Kaestle, *Tales from the Crypt: The Official Archives* (New York: St. Martin's Press, 1996), 19. Also see "Two Men Are Killed in Crash of Motorboats on Lake Placid," *The New York Times,* August 21, 1947. Charlie Gaines was killed in 1947 saving a ten-year-old boy named Billy Irwin from an oncoming boat. See William M. Gaines, interview by Gary Groth, "An Interview with William M. Gaines," *The Comics Journal* 81, May 1983, for an account of his father's business by Charlie's son, Bill, who would go on to run (and lose) EC Comics. Charlie and Bill had a very difficult father-son relationship. Also see Jacobs, *MAD World,* 129.

34. Larry Siegel, "Superduperman," *MAD* 208, July 1979, reprinted in *MAD About Super Heroes* (New York: Barnes & Noble, 2006).

26. Bachelor No. 2

1. Joe Shuster, interview by Nunes.

2. Peavy interview.

3. Joe Shuster, greeting card for Judy Calpini, Joe Shuster Collection.

4. Judith R. Calpini was born Judith Ray Herring on March 1917 and died December 1, 2003. She was previously married to Sylvio Calpini and divorced in February 1967.

5. L.V.X. is Latin ("LVX") for *lux,* meaning "light."

6. Though many of the New Age California religions embraced the existence of alien beings, Mother Elizabeth Clare Prophet saw such creatures as malevolent.

7. J. Gordon Melton, *Encyclopedia of American Religions* (Farmington Hills, MI: Gale, 2003), 894.

8. Joshua David Stone, *The Ascended Masters Light the Way: Beacons of Ascension* (Flagstaff, AZ: Light Technology, 1995), 239.

9. Maria Carlson, "Fashionable Occultism: Spiritualism, Theosophy, Freemasonry, and Hermeticism in Fin-de-Siècle Russia," in Bernice Glatzer Rosenthal, ed., *The Occult in Russian and Soviet Culture* (Ithaca, NY: Cornell University Press, 1997), 140.

10. Mother Elizabeth Clare Prophet, *The Age of the Divine* (Gardiner, MT: Summit University Press, 2006), viii.

11. Judy Calpini, letter to Mother Elizabeth, Joe Shuster Collection.

12. Calpini marks the letter as confidential. I share it only because 1) someone in her family most likely sold the collection, thus indicating a desire to no longer keep this confidentiality; and 2) so little is known about Joe's personal life (especially in comparison with Jerry's) that this letter (and indeed this collection) fills a void in our understanding of him.

13. R. Swinburne Clymer, *Books of Rosicruciæ* 2 (Quakertown, PA: Beverley Hall, 1947), 65.

14. Joe and Judy lived at 1319 Hornblend #5, San Diego, California 92109, at an apartment complex, newly built in 1969.

15. Joe Shuster, Christmas card to Judy Calpini, Joe Shuster Collection.

16. Jean Peavy, letter to Joe Shuster, May 24, 1977, Joe Shuster Collection. Jean at this time was living at 4713 Tumbleweed in El Paso, Texas.

17. Mrs. J. Shuster to Ted Nathan, Western Union telegram, May 27, 1977, Joe Shuster Collection. Judy calls it a stroke, but Jean later refers to it as a "nervous breakdown."

18. Joe Shuster, letter to Judy Calpini, Joe Shuster Collection.

19. Ibid. Also see Frank Shuster, letter to Judy Calpini, December 18, 1977: "It was wonderful to hear from you with the news that all is well again between you and Joe. Joe spoke with me on the phone and his whole attitude is different now. . . . I feel it would be the best thing in the world for Joe to be married to you rather than to live apart and remain single." While she and Joe were separated, Judy also talked with Frank Shuster over the phone. He was still living in the apartment in Queens and was suffering from a mysterious ailment. Judy seems to have encouraged Frank to try psychic healing, which he seemed open to. See Frank Shuster, letter to Judy Calpini, August 28, 1977: "As Joe will tell you, I do not talk much about myself with people as it is. Thank you for your help and concern."

20. Jean Shuster Peavy, letter to Judy Calpini, Joe Shuster Collection.

21. Stevenson, "Superman's Creators Signed Away." Joanne's T-shirt reads "Lois Lane" in iron-on transfer lettering.

22. "Space Shuttle," *CBS Evening News with Dan Rather,* February 3, 1984. Similarly, William Shatner delivered the final wake-up call for *Discovery* on the last manned space shuttle flight.

23. Otto Friedrich, "Up, Up and Awaaay!!!," *Time,* March 14, 1988: "The only Superman enthusiasts not taking part in the current festivities are Siegel and Shuster, both 73, living three blocks from each other in retirement in Los Angeles." Also see Tye, *Superman,* 272, who quotes Mark Evanier as saying that Jerry and Mort Weisinger actually became friends in old age.

24. Joe Shuster, letter to *Action Comics* 544, June 1983.

25. Joe Shuster, interview by Mietkiwicz.

26. Mietkiwicz, "Man of Steel," 27.

27. Joe Shuster, interview by Mietkiwicz.

28. Burt A. Folkart, "Joe Shuster, Co-Creator of Superman, Dead at 78," *The Los Angeles Times,* August 3, 1992. On the copy housed in the Joe Shuster Archive, Judy writes in the margin in unsteady blue pen: "July 30, 1992."

29. "The Bell Tolls for Superman," *The New York Times,* September 5, 1992.

30. Sid Couchey, letters to author, 2009–2011. Sid was born in Cleveland, Ohio, on May 24, 1919. He moved to New York, graduated from what would become the School of Visual Arts, and was eventually hired by Harvey Comics, where he worked on *Little Lotta, Little Dot,* and *Richie Rich* for over a decade, usually uncredited, adding his own style to the Harvey line. In his later years, Sid moved to Essex, New York, and became locally famous for drawing Champy, the mythical sea creature of Lake Champlain. His mural of the creature, done tongue-in-cheek in "the style of the Old Masters," stretches across the wall of the Ticonderoga Cartoon Museum. A lifelong fan of the Cleveland Indians, Sid, in his later years, threw out the pitch at an Indians–Expos game and promptly started a tongue-in-cheek Hall of Fame for Celebrity First Pitchers. They met at a local bookstore; he even drew up his own baseball card. He died at age ninety-two on March 11, 2012, in South Carolina, where he spent the winters with Ruth, his wife of fifty-two years. He proposed to her in a comic book.

31. Shuster, *Kosmo the Whiz Kid,* unpublished script, Joe Shuster Collection. Kosmo is initially named "Golly Galloo," but this is scratched out and renamed in the script itself. In the early Couchey pictures, Golly Galloo is a boy, not a robot. The name is suggestive of "the Great Gazoo," the mischievous short alien who first appeared on *The Flintstones* on October 29, 1965, and was voiced by Harvey Korman.

32. Ibid.

33. Ibid.

34. When Alexander Hamilton Junior High finally closed a few years ago, my dad (who attended Hamilton from 1946 to 1948) and I went to the school to see if this painting had survived. After some creative negotiations between

my dad and the security guard, we were allowed in and sprinted up to the art room. In that quiet room in a massive, beautiful school, there was nothing left but a few chairs. My dad pointed to a wall and there was a faint outline of a large piece of paper. We stared at it together. There was nothing there, so we went to get some pizza instead.

35. Jerry Siegel (w) and Scott M. F. Johnson (a), *Sgt. Space Cop,* Fandom House, Summer 1987.

36. Steve Gerber, interview by John Morrow, "The Other Duck Man," in *The Collected Jack Kirby Collector* 2 (Raleigh, NC: TwoMorrows, 2004), 72.

37. Jerry Siegel (w) and Val Mayerik (a), "The Starling," *Destroyer Duck* 2–7, Eclipse Comics, January 1983–May 1984.

38. Steve Gerber, response to Mike Sopp, letter to *Destroyer Duck* 4, October 1983. Gerber tells readers that "the Starling is definitely not Superman reconstituted. Jerry has something far more provocative in mind for this strip."

39. Siegel and Mayerik, "The Starling."

40. The titles are provocative: *Redd Death and Life Queen I, II* (1980), *Doomsday-y-y Komics* (1982), *The Fabulous Misfits* (1983), *Monster Boy* (1983), *It's a Crime, Comics!* (1985), *Battling for Britain* or *John Bull, Freedom-fighter* (1986). There are also scripts for a relaunch of *Funnyman* with Joe listed as the artist, including "The Return of Funnyman" (1979) and "The Case of the Obnoxious Vice-President" (1978). If found, this *Funnyman* material could be their last collaboration. Jerry was also at work on an autobiography; some pages survive in personal collections, as court evidence, and presumably with the family. See Siegel, "Superman Grew," 12. Jerry notes of his manuscript: "There are so many fantastic, unbelievable things that happened that I think, if it is ever published, it will be an extremely unusual book."

41. Laura Siegel has had a long career in show business and in news on both sides of the camera. After being a child actor in *Sons and Daughters* (1974) and on various TV specials, she moved to broadcast news and production in local TV and on CNN. See "Laura Siegel," http://www.imdb.com, for a full list. One of her most interesting contributions to popular culture is her early appearance in "Who's Sorry Now?" *Happy Days,* September 2, 1974, where she played Rita DeFazio, the first DeFazio on *Happy Days,* a year before Penny Marshall began playing Laverne.

42. John McNamara (w) and Michael Lange (d), "Swear to God, This Time We're Not Kidding," *Lois & Clark: The New Adventures of Superman,* season 4, episode 3, Warner Brothers Television, aired October 6, 1996.

43. Dan Jurgens, Karl Kesel, et al. (w), and Murphy Anderson, John Bogdanove, et al. (a), *Superman: The Wedding Album,* December 1996.

44. Ibid.

45. Julius Schwartz, *Man of Two Worlds: My Life in Science Fiction and Comics* (New York: Harper Entertainment, 2000).

46. Jerry Siegel, *Zongolla the Ultroid,* unpublished script, c. 1982. A copy of the original script of *Zongolla* was given to me in October 2010 by longtime DC writer/staffer and Archie Comics writer Paul Kupperberg, who said it "most

likely" was given to him by his mentor, Julie Schwartz. Paul has kept it safe for years; I am very thankful for his generosity in giving me a copy for this book and to Marc Tyler Nobleman for putting us in contact.

47. Ibid.

48. Ibid.

49. Robert McG. Thomas Jr., "Jerry Siegel, Superman's Creator, Dies at 81," *The New York Times,* January 31, 1996. Also see Cadigan, *Legion Companion,* 25.

27. Both Sides

1. Mikhel Yankel Segalovich, son of Nokhum and Leya (Feygelevich), "Lithuania Births," July 25, 1872, ALD Database, http://www.jewishgen.org. They were described as a "family from Krakes"; Michel's mother was a widow from a previous marriage.

2. Mikhel Iankel Segaliovich, marriage to Sora Meita Khaikels, "Lithuania Marriages and Divorces," October 15, 1898, ALD Database, http://www.jewishgen.org.

3. The written history on the treatment of Jews conscripted into the Russian army is mostly literary. A story about kneeling on the peas comes from Rabbi Yitzchak Zilber, *To Remain a Jew: The Life of Rav Yitzchak Zilber* (Nanuet, NY: Feldheim, 2010). A wider history may be found in Iokhanan Petrovskiĭ-Shtern, *Jews in the Russian Army, 1827–1917: Drafted into Modernity* (Cambridge, MA: Cambridge University Press, 2009).

4. Jones is the first author to look at the immigration of Michel Siegel to America in detail and how it connects to the creation of Superman. See Brad Meltzer, *The Book of Lies* (New York: Grand Central, 2008). Meltzer, a novelist and comics writer, picks up this idea in a thriller based around Michel Siegel and occult biblical lore. Meltzer is the only person I know to have actually seen a photo of Michel Siegel in full Russian uniform.

5. See Richard Rhodes, *Masters of Death: The SS-Einsatzgruppen and the Invention of the Holocaust* (New York: Vintage, 2002), 215.

6. Michel Siegel, U.S. Department of Labor, naturalization form, February 16, 1922.

7. Ezra S. Brudno, *The Fugitive* (New York: Doubleday, 1904). Michel Siegel's story is very common. Brudno offers a fictionalized version of getting out of Russia and assimilating culturally into America; Brudno also provides one of the first fictional accounts of living through a pogrom.

8. Movsha Iankel, "Lithuania Deaths," October 21, 1904, ALD database, http://www.jewishgen.org.

9. *Cleveland City Directory,* Cleveland, Ohio, 1904–1932.

10. Ibid., 1932.

11. Tye, *Superman,* 6.

12. Michael Siegel, obituary, *The Plain Dealer,* June 4, 1932.

13. Louis B. Seltzer, *The Years Were Good* (Cleveland: World Publishing Company, 1956), 189.

14. "Dies After Robbery," *The Cleveland Press,* June 3, 1932. A casualty report is also filled out on June 3, 1932, in Form D that lists "Sudden Death."
15. "Michel Siegel," death certificate, October 17, 1914, File No. 191416012, Ohio Department of Health. I first learned the truth about the crime in 2005 after finding the June 3, 1932, *Cleveland Press* article about his death. With help from Pat Sanney at the Cleveland Police Department and with the written permission of Police Chief Michael McGrath, I was granted access to the records department and, eventually, the Siegel death certificate. I presented this information publicly in a paper titled "Superman's Fathers" at a meeting of the Popular Culture Association in Atlanta, Georgia, on April 14, 2006. This information was also part of my documentary film *Last Son,* which first screened on July 26, 2008, in Cleveland, Ohio, at the Ingenuity Festival. Marc Tyler Nobleman discovered that there was more paperwork attached to the case; I made a request for these records that was granted on March 1, 2007. See Marc Tyler Nobleman (w) and Ross Macdonald (a), *Boys of Steel: The Creators of Superman* (New York: Alfred A. Knopf, July 2008). Marc's moving story is the first published account of the heart attack story. Also see David Colton, "Superman's Story: Did a Fatal Robbery Forge the Man of Steel?," *USA Today,* August 25, 2008. See David J. Kracijek, "Truth, Justice and a Stickup," *The New York Daily News,* August 30, 2008.
16. Criminal complaint, Form B, City of Cleveland Police Department, June 2, 1932.
17. Detective Kurt Gloeckner, letter to Chief Cornelius Cody, Departmental Information, June 2, 1932.
18. Ibid.
19. Ibid. This aspect of the crime scene remains unexplained. A physical blow could indeed have been struck.
20. Ibid.
21. Criminal complaint.
22. John Ewing, death certificate, January 6, 1941, State of Ohio, Department of Health. Also see *Cleveland City Directory,* Cleveland, Ohio, 1940.
23. Pat Sanney, conversations with author, 2005. Most of the police records from the 1930s were lost to fire.
24. Gloeckner, letter.
25. Meltzer, *Book of Lies,* 433–34: "I am convinced that the only reason young Jerry Siegel dreamed of a bulletproof man is because of the robbery that took his father." Meltzer sums it up nicely that "there are parts of this story that cannot be argued away . . . it's vital that we know where these myths come from, even if it means admitting our own vulnerabilities." The Cleveland police have no surviving records of the Siegel robbery, so whether or not there was an ongoing investigation or any official suspects is unknown. Under the legal system today, such a crime would probably be prosecuted as "involuntary manslaughter," according to Cleveland attorney Dean Valore, who notes that these types of quick clothing thefts remain commonplace.

26. Paul W. Walter, "Kurt Gloeckner Was a Cop You Remembered," *The Plain Dealer,* April 16, 1963.

27. "Charge Union Auto Drivers Boss Police," *The Plain Dealer,* June 27, 1934. Both Gloeckner and Corrigan were later accused of using strong-arm tactics on the part of a local drivers union.

28. Michael Siegel, Application for Letters of Administration, Cuyahoga County Probate Court, State of Ohio, Doc. 246, No. 209622, August 29, 1932. Also see Michel Siegel, Account Statement, Berkowitz Funeral Home, June 5, 1932, on file at Cuyahoga County Probate Court.

29. "Fail to Find Slayer Who Shot Grocer," *The Plain Dealer,* June 10, 1932.

30. Ibid.

31. "Crime Club Figure Cited for Murder," *The Plain Dealer,* August 11, 1932.

32. Ibid.

33. Berryman and Aldrich, *Style Book of The Glenville Torch,* 16–17.

34. Jerry Siegel (w) and Joe Shuster (a), "Superman and the Skyscrapers," *Superman* 2, Fall 1939, reprinted in *Superman Chronicles* 2 (New York: DC Comics, 2007), 91. This episode has local parallels to the long process of building Cleveland's Terminal Tower. See Erick Trickey, "Iconic Cleveland," *Cleveland Magazine,* August 2009. Also see "Buried Alive in Concrete," *The Plain Dealer,* October 17, 1928; two workers, Patrick Toolis and Patrick Cleary, both died when a 103-foot shaft they were in filled with concrete and collapsed. Their bodies were recovered, contrary to urban legend. Also see Richard Tibbs, "Terminal Tower Complex," *Builder's Exchange Magazine,* December 2003. Workers placed a pair of overalls filled with concrete in a joist bay between floors, surprising some unsuspecting building inspectors.

35. Jerry Siegel (w) and Joe Shuster (a), "Superman, Champion of the Oppressed!," *Action Comics* 1, June 1938, reprinted in *Superman Chronicles* 1 (New York: DC Comics, 2006), 8.

36. Ibid., "Superman and the Jewel Smugglers," *Superman* 3, Winter 1939, reprinted in *Superman Chronicles* 2 (New York: DC Comics, 2007), 178.

37. See Neil Chethik, *FatherLoss: How Sons of All Ages Come to Terms with the Deaths of Their Dads* (New York: Hyperion, 2001). Chethik argues that this kind of imaginative fiction can be a common response to a father's death. Chethik writes of a boy named Mitchell who, after his father dies of leukemia, imagines that the doctors really took him to prison, and "he managed to convince himself that his dad was really alive" (24). Jerry Siegel is doing something similar: creating a world where his father can live an invulnerable, fantastic life. This is also prefigured in Dr. Occult, whose "mortal remains" die, only to be reborn by the "Lord of Life." This is the Frankenstein story given more heroic underpinnings. Like Horace and Shakespeare, Siegel seemed to believe in poetic transformation as a useful metaphor for immortality.

38. The hat might be a nod to his father, who sold them at his store. Jerry himself could (supposedly) write *Superman* only when wearing an old brown fedora, which traveled as part of the *ZAP! POW! BAM!* exhibit that originated

at the Breman Museum. Clark's hat, like the glasses, is a disguise meant to fool us by lowering our collective expectations. Clark is not a normal person, but he wants us to think he is. Everyday clothing—not just the colorful costume—is vitally important to the Superman conceit.

39. Sigmund Freud, *The Standard Edition of the Complete Psychological Works of Sigmund Freud* 23 (London: Hogarth Press, 1976), 86.

40. Jerry Siegel (w) and Joe Shuster (a), "Superman Declares War on Reckless Drivers," *Action Comics* 12, May 1939, reprinted in *Superman Chronicles* 2 (New York: DC Comics, 2006), 160.

41. William Shakespeare, *Hamlet* (New York: Simon & Schuster, 2003). Horatio, Bernardo, and Marcellus also see the ghost in act I, scene 1, and again in act I, scene 4, and they hear the ghost at the end of act I, scene 5—but they never see and hear him at the same time (as Hamlet and the audience do).

42. Jerry Siegel (w) and Joe Shuster (a), "Origin of Superman," *Superman* 2, Fall 1939, reprinted in *Superman Chronicles* 2 (New York: DC Comics, 2007), 195. The idea of Superman as ghost also echoes Hugo Gernsback's contest to prove that spirits exist in the material world.

43. "Jor-L" as Superman's father does not appear until the *Superman* newspaper comic debuts in 1939. His name changed to "Jor-el" in the George Lowther novel *The Adventures of Superman* (1942). It later became "Jor-El."

44. Jerry Siegel (w) and Joe Shuster (a), "Speeding Towards Earth," *Superman* newspaper strip, reprinted in *Superman: The Dailies 1939–1942* (New York: Sterling, 2006), 17.

45. Ibid., 13. There are advertisements in *The Plain Dealer* and the Glenville yearbook for "Kalal Optometrists Since 1906." Located at 5747 Broadway, they advertised in the paper with a pair of big, round eyeglasses.

46. Ibid. Jor-L is not Mich-L, but the dash might be a response to Michel changing his name. Or it could be indicative of the traditional dash used to write the name of the Jewish God (G-d), whose other name, "El," is also evoked here.

47. Siegel (w) and Shuster (a), *Dailies,* 14–15.

48. Ibid, 17.

49. Chethik, *FatherLoss,* 34, echoes that this is another common response to a father's death as felt by their sons: many missed their dads desperately but also felt relief that their fathers were no longer looming over them. Of course, those who experienced relief usually felt guilty about it [and] were able to turn the tragedy into an opportunity. Still, Chethik's use of "many" seems subjective.

50. Tony Goodstone, *The Pulps* (New York: Chelsea House, 1970), xv. Goodstone posits that "the rise of the superhero occurred simultaneously with the downfall of real life idols during the Depression, as public figures and heads of households lost power to unnameable forces."

51. Jerry Siegel (w) and Joe Shuster (a), "Superman Joins the Circus," *Action Comics* 7, December 1938, reprinted in *Superman Chronicles* 1 (New York: DC Comics, 2006), 96. Another criminal shoots at Superman and then

"faint[s] away from sheer fright!" This specific sequence of shooting, Superman being immune, and then fainting is repeated again and again throughout Siegel's Superman stories. Having Superman actually punch a criminal might make more visual sense for the graphic narrative, making this particular order of events more interesting. Though no gun appears in the police report, clearly there was some mention of one connected with the Siegel robbery for it to travel through not only family history but now the Superman continuity as well. Then again, it might be an idealization of the event: without a gun, the man simply faints.

52. Jerry Siegel (w) and Joe Shuster (a), "Origin of Superman," *Superman* 1, July 1939, reprinted in *Superman Chronicles* 1 (New York: DC Comics, 2006), 196.
53. Michael Siegel, Application for Letters of Administration, Cuyahoga County Probate Court, State of Ohio.

28. The House of El

1. Sergi, "Man Versus Superman," 30.
2. The financial breakdown was Joanne, 25 percent; her daughter and Jerry's son, 12.5 percent each.
3. David Teather, "After the 30-Year Struggle, a Heroic Victory," *The Guardian,* November 8, 2003. Levitz has long been considered a creator's ally.
4. Peavy, interview.
5. Ibid.
6. DC also showed the 1998 American Express TV commercial featuring Jerry Seinfeld and Superman. Seinfeld himself wanted Superman to be drawn in the Curt Swan style.
7. Best, ed., *Trials of Superman,* 138. Laura argues that "they let the character sort of dwindle while other minor characters were being licensed and marketed and sold to movies." The lawyer asks: "Do you recall any of the minor characters you had in mind?" Laura answers: "Well, I'm talking about things like Spider-Man, made into movies and things of that sort."
8. Ibid., 239. Marks says that DC was introducing "factors designed to whittle down the proposal we made." Also see ibid., 242. Laura remembers that DC Comics executives got very excited over Superman's abilities in *Action Comics* #1 as differing from his current power set in subtle but legally important ways: "He's not flying. He's leaping."
9. Ibid., 280–82. At one point, DC allegedly insists that when Superman does enter the public domain, the Siegels "would be prohibited" from exploiting it. Because of this "unflinching position," Marks notes that "this negotiation has ended on a very bitter note . . . and the DC position was very difficult, problematic, and emotional for my clients." DC later supposedly pulled back on this point.
10. Ibid., 289.
11. Scott Warren Fitzgerald, *Corporations and Cultural Industries: Time Warner, Bertelsmann, and News Corporation* (Lanham, MD: Lexington Books, 2012).

Warner Communications, itself a remnant of the Kinney National Company, was known as Warner Bros. (its popular motion picture subsidiary) until it merged with Time Inc. in 1989 to create Time Warner. AOL bought Time Warner in 2000 to form AOL Time Warner. AOL was spun off in 2009, leaving only Time Warner. This corporation owns DC Comics, but since the copyrights to Superman are technically first owned by DC (then National)—and for ease in understanding—I am referring to the party, mostly, as DC Comics. The parties involved also frequently use "DC" in their statements.

12. These new issues supposedly centered most on royalties, especially in so-called team books, where Superman was not the star. There were issues if credit would appear just on screen projects and not in page advertisements. All of this information is speculative.

13. Best, ed., *Trials of Superman,* 294.

14. Ibid., 307.

15. Joanne Siegel, letter to DC Comics, May 9, 2002. She also writes: "There was no concern for the suffering it would cause Jerry Siegel's widow and his ailing, impoverished daughter."

16. Best, ed., *Trials of Superman,* 943.

17. Ibid., 942–44. Laura says of her mother: "She was constantly writing and drafting things, she wrote a children's book. She wrote, you know, just things that moved her, memories that she had from her youth."

18. Ibid., 291.

19. Ibid., 299.

20. Erika Lenkert, "Hotline to Hollywood," *Los Angeles Magazine,* March 1998, 109. Raised in suburban Chicago, Emanuel worked at ICM, where he was caught stealing client files when he left. His new agency, Endeavor, became so successful that it merged with the powerful William Morris Agency in 2009. He is the brother of Chicago mayor (and former White House chief of staff) Rahm Emanuel.

21. Best, ed., *Trials of Superman,* 300.

22. Ibid., 300.

23. Ibid., 302.

24. Ibid., 506. Marks also allegedly tells the Siegels that he will testify against them if they back out of the agreement.

25. Ibid., 944.

26. The Siegels and Shusters contend that Warren, Joe's nephew, found Toberoff on his own. Jean suggested him to Joanne, and the Siegels sought him out when they didn't like the way their agreement was shaping up. According to DC, Toberoff lured the Siegel estate away from the negotiation table for his own gain and possibly used the Shusters as his way in.

27. Sergi, "Man Versus Superman," 30–33.

28. *Joanne Siegel and Laura Siegel Larson v. Time Warner Inc., et al.,* U.S. District Court, Central District of California, Case No. 2:04-cv-08400-SGL-RZ, March 26, 2008.

29. Best, ed., *Trials of Superman,* 272. This also included the Spectre. Also see *Joanne Siegel and Laura Siegel Larson v. Time Warner Inc., et al.,* U.S. District Court, Central District of California, Case No. 2:04-cv-08776-SGL-RZ, March 31, 2008.

30. Best, ed., *Trials of Superman,* 272.

31. Ibid., 992.

32. Amy Wallace (w) and Ross MacDonald (a), "Lawyers, Tiggers & Bears Oh My!," *Los Angeles Magazine,* August 2002, 80. Petrocelli won the Goldmans $8.5 million in damages.

33. Claudia Eller, "Warner Bros. Alleges Scheme," *The Los Angeles Times,* May 14, 2010.

34. Best, ed., *Trials of Superman,* 671.

35. Ibid., 667, 670. Warren recalls that Joe, at the time of his death, "had a lady friend, who admitted . . . to me how generous he had been to her and her son. Her son is a psychology professor" (684). According to his family, Joe was essentially broke when he died.

36. Ibid., 332.

37. Ibid., 337.

38. Ibid., 688. Warren states: "I don't think she understood exactly what she signed . . . that's my impression."

39. Ibid., 184.

40. Ibid., 668.

41. Ibid., 640. Warren also says: "She wants us to—to be provided for and secure and she's 90 years old and she's had a stroke so she knows she's not going to be around forever and she doesn't really have any need for—for money."

42. Ibid., 354.

43. Ibid., 700.

44. Ibid., 376.

45. Ibid., 730.

46. Ibid., 745.

47. Ibid., 746.

48. At the same time, the Siegels served termination on the Superboy copyright in 2008. The court also ruled that Joe had actually given the go-ahead for Superboy. Superboy had not been too popular in the comics, but a derivative work, the television show *Smallville,* was very successful financially.

49. Best, ed., *Trials of Superman,* 771.

50. Ibid., 778.

51. Ibid., 798.

52. Ibid., 801. Petrocelli asks: "Are you aware of Mr. Toberoff having contacted third parties on behalf of the estate?" Toberoff jumps: "I instruct you not to answer. It implicates our communications." Also see ibid., 794. DC shows Warren an e-mail from Toberoff to individuals at Paramount dated April 29, 2010, and a vehicle pass that reads, "Pitched Superman," dated November 19, 2010, indicating that Toberoff was shopping the Superman property to rival movie studios.

53. Ibid., 339.
54. Ibid., 884. Laura calls this combination "a dynamic duo." Petrocelli adds: "Or we could go Clark Kent." Also see ibid., 899. Laura is very matter-of-fact: "He offered to put a substantial amount of money up front and, you know, if he was able to negotiate, you know, a good deal for us, that we would have meaningful participation, and it sounded interesting."
55. The HBO series *Entourage* character "Ari Gold" is based on him.
56. Best, ed., *Trials of Superman,* 910.
57. Ibid., 911.
58. Ibid., 922.
59. This is all Laura's testimony.
60. Best, ed., *Trials of Superman,* 916.
61. Ibid., 828.
62. Ibid., 914.
63. Ibid.
64. Marc Toberoff, "Power Lawyers," *The Hollywood Reporter,* July 13, 2011.
65. Toberoff & Associates, P.C., Web site, www.marctoberoff.com. Toberoff has produced several movies such as *Sons, I Spy,* and *Piranha 3DD.*
66. Best, ed., *Trials of Superman,* 961.
67. Ibid., 997.
68. Ibid.
69. Ibid., 950.
70. Ibid., 965.
71. Ibid., 510. Mike was allegedly asking for $200,000 annually.
72. Michael Sangiacomo, "Superman Creator's Son Lived and Died in Father's Shadow," *The Plain Dealer,* June 25, 2006.
73. Jerry Siegel (w) and Leo Nowak (a), *Superman* 13, November–December 1941.
74. Mike Siegel, e-mail to author, September 10, 2005.
75. Sangiacomo, "Superman Creator's Son."
76. Best, ed., *Trials of Superman,* 950.
77. Ibid., 841. Laura notes that Jerry and Bella had another child who, sadly, died at birth. See Tye, *Superman,* 116; the baby, born in 1946, lived for only eight hours.
78. Best, ed., *Trials of Superman,* 981.
79. Ibid., 982.
80. Sangiacomo, "Superman Creator's Son."
81. Tye, *Superman,* 293.
82. Michael Dougherty and Dan Harris, *Superman Returns: The Complete Shooting Script* (London: Titan, 2006), scene 324. At the end of *Superman Returns* (2006), Superman stands over his newly discovered son, about whom he has never been told. He repeats: "You will be different. You will sometimes feel like an outcast. But you will not be alone. You will never be alone. You will make my strength your own, see my life through your eyes, as your life will be seen through mine. The son becomes the father, and the father . . . becomes the son."

83. Best, ed., *Trials of Superman*, 199.

84. Ibid., 166.

85. Ibid., 206.

86. Joanne Siegel, letter to Jeffrey L. Bewkes, December 10, 2010, first reprinted by Nikki Finke, Deadline.com, March 27, 2011.

87. Jerry and Joanne are placed together at the famed "Hollywood Forever" cemetery in Los Angeles.

88. Michael Sangiacomo, "Super-Signs Installed in Superman's Old Glenville Neighborhood," *The Plain Dealer,* February 14, 2011. As an extension of the 2009 renovations, there are now commemorative street signs on Kimberley and Amor where Jerry's house and Joe's apartment building stood. Kimberley is "Jerry Siegel Lane," Amor is "Joe Shuster Lane," and Parkwood, the connecting street where Jerry ran to Joe's house, is "Lois Lane." Sangiacomo has been the tireless supporter of Superman appreciation in Cleveland for decades.

89. Olin S. Ellington, letter to *The Plain Dealer,* January 13, 1976. Ellington, who lived at 16022 Kimberley Avenue, wrote to the editor about city government: "But in America the beautiful definitive of altruism has become an antique relic of the past."

90. Jay Hoffman, "Great Caesar's Ghost! Superman Memorial Advised," *The Lima News,* July 24, 1977.

91. Douglas Belkin, "Superman Birthplace Is Restored," *The Wall Street Journal,* July 11, 2009.

92. The 2009 Cleveland celebration was not the first. See "Super-Hero's History Is Great Cleveland Story," *The Plain Dealer,* June 16, 1988. The Superman Exposition was very ambitious; Jerry and Joe did not attend, but numerous Superman writers, editors, and associated celebrities and fans descended on Cleveland for dinners, movie marathons, panel discussions, and a downtown parade. The organizers, among them Tim Gorman and Tony Isabella, produced a once-in-a-lifetime event, though financial issues made it difficult to sustain any long-term plans.

93. The Superman case is unpredictable and ongoing. On October 10, 2012, Warners filed a motion to the Court arguing that Toberoff's alleged indiscretions were enough to consider termination of the case. Three days later, Laura Siegel Larson responded in a public letter that appeared on various comics Web sites. She claimed that Warners indeed leaked the anonymous timeline and was involved in malicious stalling tactics. Laura vows: "Now the torch is in my hands and I won't be silent any longer about Warner Bros.' tactics. I refuse to be bullied or deterred from enforcing my family's rights, and fully support my attorney who has tirelessly defended them." The days after the initial motion was filed in California, Laura and her son James helped dedicate a new permanent Superman display at Cleveland Hopkins Airport, honoring her mother, father, and Joe Shuster. By the time this book is published, there will no doubt be more news about this case. I will update as needed at www.brad-ricca.com.

94. Grant Morrison (w) and Frank Quitely (a), *All-Star Superman* 12, October 2008. At the end of Morrison's yearlong story, the action shifts to within a "baby Universe," where a hand is shown penciling the Shuster Superman. The dialogue reads: "I really think this is it . . . third time lucky. This is the one. . . . This is going to change everything." Morrison seems to suggest that every universe has a Superman, but the allusion to the "third time lucky" might be to Shuster's version (1), the John Byrne reboot (2), and now Morrison's multidimensional, "never-ending" Superman (3). It could also be a reference to the *Action* #1 Superman being the third stage of a process that included the two earlier attempts of "Reign of the Super-man" and the *Detective Dan* proposal.

95. See also Best, ed., *Trials of Superman*, 1025–26. The DC lawyer, Mr. Kline, asks her: "And it would be a significant change in your life, would it not, if their efforts were successful and millions of dollars were obtained for your family; correct?" Dawn eventually responds: "I don't know how to answer that question. . . . No, I'd probably still work just as hard."

96. Ibid., 1023.

97. Ibid., 1028.

98. Ibid., 1035.

99. Peavy, letter to author, February 12, 2006.

100. Best, ed., *Trials of Superman*, 998.

101. Ibid., 104.

102. Ibid., 367.

103. Ibid., 368.

104. Ibid., 373.

105. Ibid., 379.

106. Ibid., 386.

107. Ibid.

108. Michael Sangiacomo, "Superman Belongs to Warner Bros.," *The Plain Dealer*, January 11, 2013.

Epilogue

1. Arnold Miller, "Don't Turn Man of Steel into Man of Quiche," *The Elyria Chronicle*, June 22, 1986. Miller writes, "I identify with Clark Kent."

2. Michael Sangiacomo, "Hopes for a Secret Stash at Legend's Home Dashed," *The Plain Dealer*, April 3, 2008. Sangiacomo and Brad Meltzer go to the Siegel house and find out that the attic has never been explored by the current inhabitants and get excited—but find out from the owners that it contains only insulation. This idea of rare artifacts—of monetary and historical value—has become the driving methodology behind Superman comics collecting and scholarship, much like Clark searching for relics of his alien heritage.

3. George Gene Gustines, "Look! Up in the Sky! It's an Astronomical Price for a Comic Book!," *The New York Times*, December 1, 2011. A copy of *Action Comics* #1 sold for $2.16 million in December 2011.

4. Jules Feiffer, *The Great Comic Book Heroes* (Seattle: Fantagraphics, 2003).

5. Jerry Siegel (w) and Joe Shuster (a), *Dr. Occult,* in *More Fun Comics* 9, March 1936.

6. Wood LaCrosse (w) and Joe Shuster (anonymous) (a), "See, Hear, Speak Evil!" *Nights of Horror* 2, Malcla Publishing, c. 1953, 44–80.

7. Mound City, Ohio, is the site of ancient burial mounds near the city of Chillicothe.

8. Later in the story he is referred to as "Jerry Quinn," but for the first three quarters of the story he is "Jerry Wood."

9. LaCrosse and Shuster, "See, Hear, Speak Evil!" 46.

10. Ibid., 47.

11. Ibid., 47, 60. In the story, Rita is Norma's younger sister, just as in real life. Also see Yoe, *Secret Identity,* 44. Yoe asked me years ago if I thought Jerry Siegel might have written any of these stories; I said no. Only in putting away the materials of this book did I open this particular *Nights of Horror* and catch the name "Mitchell."

12. LaCrosse and Shuster, "See, Hear, Speak Evil!" 47–55.

Bibliography

Adams, Neal. Interview by Michael Eury. In *The Krypton Companion*. Edited by Michael Eury. Raleigh, NC: TwoMorrows, 2006.

Andrae, Thomas. *Creators of the Superheroes*. Neshannock, PA: Hermes Press, 2011.

———, and Mel Gordon. *Siegel and Shuster's Funnyman*. Port Townsend, WA: Feral House, 2010.

Ashley, Mike, and Robert A. W. Lowndes. *The Gernsback Days*. Rockville, MD: Wildside Press, 2004.

Ayers, Dick. Interview with Roy Thomas. "A Life in the Gowanus." *Alter Ego* 10 (2001).

Barron, James. "The Mystery of the Missing Man of Steel." *The New York Times,* April 18, 2010.

Beerbohm, Robert. "Siegel & Shuster Presents . . . The Superman." *Comic Book Marketplace* (June 1996).

———. "The Big Bang Theory of Comic Book History." *Comic Book Marketplace* (August 1997).

Bender, Lauretta, and Reginald S. Lourie. "The Effect of Comic Books on the Ideology of Children." *The American Journal of Orthopsychiatry*, vol. 11, issue 3 (July 1941).

Benton, Mike. *Masters of Imagination: The Comic Book Artists Hall of Fame*. Dallas: Taylor Publishing, 1994.

Berryman, Gordon B., and Frederic D Aldrich, eds. *Style Book of The Glenville Torch*. Cleveland: Glenville High School, 1927.

Best, Daniel, ed. *The Trials of Superman*. Vols. 1–2. Australia: Blaq Books, 2012. http://ohdannyboy.blogspot.com.

Bleiler, Everett Franklin, and Richard Bleiler. *Science-Fiction: The Gernsback Years*. Kent, OH: Kent State University Press, 1998.

Brown, Nicky Heron. "Major Malcolm Wheeler-Nicholson: Cartoon Character or Real Life Hero? Correcting Hadju's *The Ten-Cent Plague*." *International Journal of Comic Art* (Fall 2008).

Brown, Nicky Wheeler-Nicholson. Interview by Jim Amash. "He Was Going to Go for the Big Idea." *Alter Ego* 88 (2009).

Cadigan, Glen. *The Legion Companion.* Raleigh, NC: TwoMorrows, 2003.

Chabon, Michael. "Secret Skin." *The New Yorker,* March 10, 2008.

Chethik, Neil. *FatherLoss: How Sons of All Ages Come to Terms with the Deaths of Their Dads.* New York: Hyperion, 2001.

Coogan, Peter. "The Definition of the Superhero." In *A Comics Studies Reader.* Jackson: University Press of Mississippi, 2009.

Cooke, Jon B. *The T.H.U.N.D.E.R. Agents Companion.* Raleigh, NC: TwoMorrows, 2005.

Daniels, Les. *Superman: The Complete History.* San Francisco: Chronicle Books, 1998.

Decker, Dwight. "The Reich Strikes Back." *Alter Ego* 79 (July 2008).

DeHaven, Tom. *Our Hero: Superman on Earth.* New Haven: Yale University Press, 2010.

Donenfeld, Irwin. Interview by Robert Beerbohm, Mark Evanier, and Julius Schwartz. "There's a Lot of Myth Out There!" *Alter Ego* 26 (July 2003).

Dooley, Dennis. "The Man of Tomorrow and the Boys of Yesterday." In *Superman at Fifty!* Edited by Dennis Dooley and Gary Engle. New York: Collier, 1988.

Eury, Michael, ed. *The Krypton Companion.* Raleigh, NC: TwoMorrows, 2006.

Feiffer, Jules. *The Great Comic Book Heroes.* Seattle: Fantagraphics, 2003.

Freud, Sigmund. *The Standard Edition of the Complete Psychological Works of Sigmund Freud.* Vol. 23. London: Hogarth Press, 1976.

Friedrich, Otto. "Up, Up and Awaaay!!!" *Time,* March 14, 1988.

Gilbert, Michael T. "Editorial." *Alter Ego* 11 (2001).

———. "Wayne Boring: Superman and Beyond." *Alter Ego* 9 (2001).

Goodstone, Tony. *The Pulps.* New York: Chelsea, 1970.

Hadju, David. *The Ten-Cent Plague: The Great Comic-Book Scare and How It Changed America.* New York: Picador, 2009.

Hersey, Harold, ed. *The New Pulpwood Editor.* Silver Spring, MD: Adventure House, 1965.

Holy Bible, revised standard version. Iowa Falls: World Bible Publishers, 1952.

Horner, William T. *Ohio's Kingmaker: Mark Hanna, Man & Myth.* Athens: Ohio University Press, 2010.

Jacobs, Frank. *The MAD World of William M. Gaines.* New York: Bantam, 1973.

Jones, Gerard. *Men of Tomorrow: Geeks, Gangsters, and the Birth of the Comic Book.* New York: Basic Books, 2005.

Kinlok, Tor. *Superman Through the Ages.* N.P.: Lodestone Press, 2006.

Kobler, John. "Up, Up and Awa-a-y! The Rise of Superman, Inc." *The Saturday Evening Post,* June 21, 1941.

Kracijek, David J. "Truth, Justice and a Stickup." New York *Daily News,* August 30, 2008.

Lipsyte, Robert. *An Accidental Sportswriter: A Memoir.* New York: Ecco, 2012.

Lowther, George. *The Adventures of Superman*. Bedford, MA: Applewood Books, 1995.

Meltzer, Brad. *The Book of Lies*. New York: Grand Central, 2008.

Messenger, F. M. *The Coming Superman*. Kansas City, MO: Nazarene Publishing, 1928.

Mietkiwicz, Henry. "Man of Steel, Pen of Gold." *Comic Buyer's Monthly* (1995).

Morrison, Grant. *Supergods*. New York: Spiegel & Grau, 2011.

Moskowitz, Sam. *The Immortal Storm: A History of Science Fiction Fandom*. Atlanta: Science Fiction Organization Press, 1954.

Murray, Will. "The Driving Force That Really Made DC Great: Whitney Ellsworth and the Rise of National/DC Comics." *Alter Ego* 98 (2010).

———. "Gladiator of Iron, Man of Steel." *Alter Ego* 37 (2004).

———. "The Roots of the Superman!" *Comic Book Marketplace* 63 (1998).

———. "Superman Editor Mort Weisinger." In *The Krypton Companion*. Edited by Michael Eury. Raleigh, NC: TwoMorrows, 2006.

———. "The Kryptonite Crisis." *Alter Ego* 37 (2004).

———. "Those Mighty, Mighty Crusaders." *Alter Ego* 96 (2010).

Nobleman, Marc Tyler (w), and Ross Macdonald (a). *Boys of Steel: The Creators of Superman*. New York: Alfred A. Knopf, 2008.

Rosenberg, Yudl. "The Golem, or The Miraculous Deeds of Rabbi Liva." In *Yenne Velt: The Great Works of Jewish Fantasy & Occult*. New York: Pocket Books, 1976.

Rossen, Jake. *Superman vs. Hollywood: How Fiendish Producers, Devious Directors, and Warring Writers Grounded an American Icon*. Chicago: Chicago Review Press, 2008.

Santo, Avi Dan. *Transmedia Brand Licensing Prior to Conglomeration: George Trendle and the Lone Ranger and Green Hornet Brands, 1933–1966*. Dissertation. Austin: University of Texas, ProQuest, 2006.

Saunders, David. "H. J. Ward (1909–1945)." *Illustration* 29 (2010).

Sawyer, Michael. *In the Wake of the Butcher: Cleveland's Torso Murders*. Kent, OH: Kent State University Press, 2001.

Seltzer, Louis B. *The Years Were Good*. Cleveland: World Publishing Company, 1956.

Sergi, Joe. "Man Versus Superman." *Comics Now!* 3 (Summer 2008).

Shakespeare, William. *Hamlet*. New York: Simon & Schuster, 2003.

Sheridan, Martin. *Classic Comics and Their Creators*. Arcadia, CA: Hyperion, 1971.

Shuster, Joe. Collection. Special Collections, Kelvin Smith Library, Case Western Reserve University, Cleveland, OH.

———. Interview by Henry Mietkiwicz. *The Toronto Star,* April 26, 1992.

Siegel, Jerry (w), and Bernard Baily (a). *The Golden Age Spectre Archives*. Vol. 1. New York: DC Comics, 2003.

Siegel, Jerry, Fred Allen, and Harry Donenfeld. "Up in the Sky! Look!" *Alter Ego* 26 (2003).

Siegel, Jerry, and Joanne Siegel. "'Superman' Grew Out of Our Personal Feelings." *Alter Ego* 56 (2007).

Siegel, Jerry, and Joe Shuster. Interview by Shel Dorf. *Siegel and Shuster Dateline 1930's* 1 (1984).

Siegel, Jerry (w), and Joe Shuster (a). *Superman Chronicles.* Vols. 1–10. New York: DC Comics, 2009.

———. *DC Comics Rarities.* New York: DC Comics, 2004.

———. *Showcase Presents: Legion of Super-Heroes.* Vols. 1–2. New York: DC Comics, 2007–2008.

———. *Showcase Presents: Superman.* Vols. 1–4. New York: DC Comics, 2005–2009.

———. *Showcase Presents: Supergirl.* Vols. 1–2. New York: DC Comics, 2007–2008.

———. *Superman Archives.* Vol. 1. New York: DC Comics, 1989.

———. *Superman: The Dailies 1939–1942.* New York: Sterling, 2006.

———. *The Adventures of Superboy.* New York: DC Comics, 2010.

Steranko, Jim. *The Steranko History of Comics.* Vol. 1. Reading, PA: Supergraphics, 1970.

Thomas, Roy. "K Is for Krypton." *Alter Ego* 79 (2008).

———. "Super-Postscript." *Alter Ego* 37 (2004).

Toberoff, Marc. "Power Lawyers." *The Hollywood Reporter,* July 13, 2011.

Tye, Larry. *Superman: The High-Flying History of America's Most Enduring Hero.* New York: Random House, 2012.

Waid, Mark. "K-metal: The 'Lost' Superman Tale." *Alter Ego* 26 (2003).

Walker, Brian. *The Comics.* New York: Abrams, 2006.

Walraven, Margaret Kessler, and Alfred Lawrence Hall-Quest. *Teaching Through the Elementary School Library.* New York: H. W. Wilson, 1948.

Weisinger, Hank. Interviewed by Eddy Zeno. "A Fond Remembrance." In *The Krypton Companion.* Edited by Michael Eury. Raleigh, NC: TwoMorrows, 2006.

Williamson, Jack, and Dr. Miles J. Breuer. *The Girl from Mars.* Brooklyn: Gryphon Books, 1998.

Willoughby, David P. *The Super-Athletes: A Record of the Limits of Human Strength, Speed and Stamina.* New York: A. S. Barnes, 1970.

Woolery, George W. "Frankenstein, Jr." *Children's Television: The First Thirty-five Years, 1946–1981.* Lanham, MD: Scarecrow Press, 1991.

Yoe, Craig. *Secret Identity: The Fetish Art of Superman's Co-Creator Joe Shuster.* New York: Abrams ComicArts, 2009.

Index

NOTE: Jerry stands for Jerry Siegel; Joe stands for Joe Shuster. Comic book characters are listed under their first names, e.g. Clark Kent in the C's. Women are listed under their married names, with cross-references from other names of theirs (e.g. Siegel, Joanne Carter). Names of foreign extraction are listed under their final Americanized spelling (e.g. Shuster).